Plundered Nations?

Plundered Nations?

Successes and Failures in Natural Resource Extraction

Edited by

Paul Collier
Centre for the Study of African Economies

and

Anthony J. Venables
Oxford Centre for the Analysis of Resource Rich Economies

First published 2011 by
PALGRAVE MACMILLAN

Palgrave Macmillan in the UK is an imprint of Macmillan Publishers Limited, registered in England, company number 785998, of Houndmills, Basingstoke, Hampshire RG21 6XS.

Palgrave Macmillan in the US is a division of St Martin's Press LLC, 175 Fifth Avenue, New York, NY 10010.

Palgrave Macmillan is the global academic imprint of the above companies and has companies and representatives throughout the world.

Palgrave® and Macmillan® are registered trademarks in the United States, the United Kingdom, Europe and other countries

ISBN 978–0–230–29022–8   paperback

This book is printed on paper suitable for recycling and made from fully managed and sustained forest sources. Logging, pulping and manufacturing processes are expected to conform to the environmental regulations of the country of origin.

A catalogue record for this book is available from the British Library.

A catalog record for this book is available from the Library of Congress.

10 9 8 7 6 5 4 3 2 1
20 19 18 17 16 15 14 13 12 11

Printed and bound in Great Britain by
CPI Antony Rowe, Chippenham and Eastbourne

*We would like to dedicate this volume to our
esteemed colleague
Dr. Zainal Aznam Yusof, 1944–2011*

Contents

Illustrations

Tables

Contributors

Editors

Paul Collier is the Director of the Centre for the Study of African Economies, University of Oxford, UK

Anthony J. Venables is the Director of the Centre for the Analysis of Resource-Rich Economies, University of Oxford, UK

Contributors

Christopher Adam is Research Associate at the Centre for the Study of African Economies, and Reader in Development Economics at the University of Oxford, UK

Olu Ajakaiye is Director of Research, African Economic Research Consortium (AERC), Nairobi, Kenya

Akpan H. Ekpo is the Director General of the West African Institute for Financial and Economic Management (WAIFEM), Lagos, and Professor of Economics, University of Uyo, Nigeria

Akram Esanov is a Senior Economist at Revenue Watch Institute, New York, USA

J. Rodrigo Fuentes is Associate Professor at the Institute of Economics, Pontificia Universidad Católica de Chile, Santiago, Chile

Bernard Gauthier is Professor at the Institute of Applied Economics, HEC, Montreal, Canada

Massoud Karshenas is Professor of Economics at the Department of Economics at the School of Oriental and African Studies, London, UK

Valery Kryukov is the Deputy Director of the Institute of Economics and Industrial Engineering, Siberian Branch of the Russian Academy of Sciences, Novosibirsk, Russia

Karlygash Kuralbayeva is a Research Fellow at the Centre for the Analysis of Resource-Rich Economies, University of Oxford, UK

Adeel Malik is a Globe Fellow in the Economies of Muslim Societies at the Oxford Centre for Islamic Studies, and a Lecturer in Development Economics at the University of Oxford, UK

Anthony M. Simpasa is a Manager in Market Studies, Financial Markets Department, Bank of Zambia, Lusaka, Zambia

Anatoly Tokarev is the Leading Research Fellow, Institute of Economics and Industrial Engineering, Siberian Branch of the Russian Academy of Sciences, Novosibirsk, Russia

Shamil Yenikeyeff is a Research Fellow, Oxford Institute for Energy Studies, and a Senior Associate Member, Russian and Eurasian Studies Centre, St Antony's College, University of Oxford, UK

Zainal Aznam Yusof is a Council Member of the National Economic Advisory Council (NEAC), Malaysia

Albert G. Zeufack is Director of Khazanah Research and Investment Strategy, Khazanah Nasional Berhad, Malaysia

Acknowledgements

This volume was sponsored by the Revenue Watch Institute thanks to the generous contribution of the Bill and Melinda Gates Foundation. Revenue Watch's partnership with leading academics is part of its programme of applied research to help transform resource wealth into well-being.

Revenue Watch promotes the effective, transparent and accountable management of oil, gas and mineral resources for the public good. Through capacity building, technical assistance, research, funding and advocacy, we help countries to realize the development benefits of their natural resource wealth.

The research was conducted under the auspices of the Centre for the Study of African Economies and the Oxford Centre for the Analysis of Resource Rich Economies at the University of Oxford.

1
Key Decisions for Resource Management
Principles and practice

Paul Collier and Anthony J. Venables

1.1 Introduction

The discovery and extraction of natural resources has the potential to finance rapid, sustained and broad-based development. However, harnessing this potential is difficult: the opportunity is often missed, and sometimes turns into a nightmare of corruption and violence. This study is based on the experience of eight countries that all had resource riches but were otherwise very different: Russia, Iran, Malaysia, Chile, Cameroon, Nigeria, Kazakhstan and Zambia. In retrospect, two of these stand out as resounding successes, achieving rapid growth with social peace. But *ex ante*, this could not have been predicted: they are Malaysia and Chile, countries utterly different from each other. One of the countries, Cameroon, has been an utter failure, with the main legacy of oil revenues being a diversion of politics from the well-being of citizens. As the consequences of different choices cumulate, the divergence between success and failure becomes astonishingly wide: Malaysia reduced poverty from 50 per cent of the population in 1970 to less than 4 per cent by 2007, whereas in Cameroon, all social indicators have deteriorated. The other five countries have had varying degrees of success and failure, although none has sustained rapid and widely diffused growth.

That six of these eight countries have failed to harness the full potential of natural resources illustrates that the process is difficult. For the depletion of natural assets to be converted into sustained development, a series of decisions has to be got sufficiently right. It is useful to think of these decisions as forming a chain made up of four links. The analogy of a chain is helpful because all of these links need to hold in order to achieve sustained growth: growth through the depletion of natural assets poses a 'weakest link' problem. The first link in the chain is that natural resources must be discovered and developed. Discovery is the production of information, a public good typically not aligned with private incentives. Development requires a sufficiently secure institutional environment that investors are willing to make the capital investments required. The second link is that a substantial proportion of the value of the resources extracted should be captured by the government through taxation. This involves the design and implementation of an appropriate contractual and fiscal system. It fails if revenue is siphoned off into corruption, if revenue is dissipated in rent-seeking behaviour or, at worst, in violent conflict. Third, enough of this value should go into asset formation so that the depletion of extractable assets is fully offset. Finally, the asset formation should be by means of domestic investment. This investment should diversify the economy, requiring that the investment process be sufficiently efficient to generate a return on investment at least as high as that available elsewhere in the world.

We now take each of these decisions in turn, drawing on the country evidence to illustrate the problems encountered.

1.2 Discovery and development of natural assets

The discovery of natural assets is about generating information through investment in prospecting. Economists now know that the market in information abounds in asymmetries, externalities and commitment problems. Resource extraction companies can be presumed to know more than governments about the chances of finding valuable resources: this is an information asymmetry. As a result, bilateral negotiations between a government and a prospecting company are liable to favour the company: competition between equally well-informed companies is the best way for the government to get value. Each discovery generates information on the chances of neighbouring discoveries: an externality. The preferred strategy for prospectors is to buy the rights to discoveries and then wait for others to make a strike; however, this privately optimal strategy is socially inefficient. Once a discovery has been made, the knowledge can potentially be expropriated by government: a commitment problem. This inability of many governments to make credible commitments not to expropriate discoveries reduces the incentive for companies to prospect.

The ideal sequence to address these problems would be to start with the government investing in as much public geological information as is practicable and then sharing this information with all potential companies. Directly, public information reduces the asymmetry of information between companies and government. But it also reduces the other two problems: there is less need to wait for others to prospect and, by reducing the risk that prospecting will not find anything, the commitment problem is also reduced.

Information provision has to be accompanied by an investment environment in which there are incentives for prospecting and for the development of discoveries. In the early 1970s, the governments of both Nigeria and Chile confiscated natural assets from resource extraction companies. In Chile, the Pinochet regime sought to live down this past government behaviour, introducing strong incentives for private investment and various arrangements purporting to guarantee investor rights. The government of Zambia also nationalized a private copper company in the 1970s, albeit with compensation, and subsequently it also tried to live down this history by guaranteeing terms for private investors. However, in Chile, the changes introduced by the Pinochet regime generated little investor response until after the transition to democracy. Investors were waiting to see whether the new 'guarantees' would be robust to regime change. Only once the new democratic government decided not to change the terms did investors arrive. In Zambia, where the government was already democratic, the investment response was more immediate. This suggests that the credibility of government is not just a matter of formal legislation, but of the wider context of governance in which it is set.

Having invested in public geological information and created a sufficiently secure environment for investors, the government should *auction* off plots for prospecting *gradually*. The use of an auction further reduces the problem of asymmetric information as well-informed companies compete against each other and thereby inadvertently reveal the true value of the prospect. The reason for selling auction rights gradually in geographic blocs is that it enables the government to benefit from the externalities of prospecting in the first round of blocs before selling further contiguous blocs.

Finally, it is important to require prospectors to invest in search within a relatively brief time period, such as 3 years. Otherwise, as noted, they have an incentive to wait for others to prospect. Yet, such a requirement is only as effective as the ability to monitor performance on the ground and enforce adherence to the contract in the courts. Hence, the government needs to build both of these capacities.

None of our eight countries came close to this ideal approach. By design, all of them had some valuable resource discoveries. However, there is clear evidence that underinvestment is a problem. In several countries, the volume of resource extraction has trended downwards, despite reasonable expectations that more resources are available for discovery. In Nigeria and Cameroon, oil production is lower now that it was 30 years ago, and in Zambia, copper production declined to only 40 per cent of its peak volume, until a change in incentives rapidly led to vast new deposits being discovered. At the opposite end of the spectrum, Chile has had a huge expansion in its copper output, driven by private investment, although as we discuss below, this was achieved at the cost of sub-optimal taxation. The difference between a path of volume expansion, such as that of Chile, and of volume contraction, in Zambia, Cameroon and Nigeria, has correspondingly large and important consequences for the path of revenues. Although a lack of prospecting shifts resource discovery (and hence revenues) into the future, this may be disadvantageous. Partly, in a developing economy, the return on investment should be higher than that elsewhere in the world, so that it should pay to get resources out of the ground sooner rather than later. Further, it is much easier to manage a steadily rising revenue stream than one that rises rapidly for a few years because of an initial discovery but then gradually contracts because the incentives for further prospecting are inadequate.

The phenomenon of underinvestment in prospecting observed in several of the eight countries is more general. Among the poorest countries, the average square mile of their territory has only one quarter of the known subsoil assets of the Organization for Economic Co-operation and Development (OECD) countries. This is unlikely to be because they actually have fewer natural assets; rather, it is that they have had weaker incentives for prospecting and so less investment in it.

1.3 Revenue capture

1.3.1 The taxation of resource extraction

The design of a tax system for resource extraction is complicated and politically sensitive. At the technical level, the appropriate tax regime depends on the geology. For example, among the countries considered here, both Zambia and Chile are copper producers. However, thanks to favourable geology, Chile is a low-cost producer, whereas Zambia is a high-cost producer. This implies that the rents on copper production in Zambia are smaller for any given world price, but also much more highly geared to the world price: the rents from a tonne of Zambian copper will be similar to those in Chile when world prices are very high, but fall to zero at prices at which rents are still present in Chile.

Hence, the Zambian tax regime should be much more strongly geared to the world price than that in Chile. Until the geology is known, such design issues cannot be ascertained. Once the tax regime is appropriate to the geology, there are advantages for the government if it can commit to it. However, as we will see from the history of commitments in Chile, in some political contexts, credible commitment is not really feasible. Tax regimes for natural resources have often changed repeatedly, usually because the design has not adequately envisaged changing circumstances. The credibility of the tax regime is, therefore, more dependent upon its being designed to anticipate changes in circumstances than it is to the niceties of the legal process. A well-designed tax regime remains reasonable to both parties in response to changing circumstances, such as new discoveries and changes in world prices. If the tax regime is badly designed, an effective commitment technology might well be detrimental to government, locking it in to a design that becomes inappropriate.

Typically, there is considerable 'resource nationalism'. One way in which this is addressed is by taking national ownership through a national resource extraction company. This is potentially complementary with a well-designed tax system: the national company is subject to the same tax regime as private companies, but its existence builds national capacity and so enables the tax regime to be better designed. However, the experience with national companies has been very mixed. Malaysia used a national company as part of a much wider strategy of resource nationalism. As we will see, revenues from natural resources were, in part, used to buy out the equity in foreign-owned resource extraction companies. Zambia also bought out the foreign copper company, but using borrowed money rather than revenues.

However, the key difference between the Malaysian and the Zambian experience was in the performance of the nationally owned firms. In Malaysia, the company was staffed with technocrats who were protected politically by the prime minister from populist pressures. Further, the staff appear to have internalized a mission to improve Bumiputera interests in society rather than use their positions to enrich themselves or their families. The company volunteered to retain a smaller share of profits for internal use than the world norm for oil companies. In contrast, the Zambian national company, ZCCM, gradually increased its internal retentions. Not only did it come to absorb all profits internally in the form of rising unit costs but, by the time it was dissolved, it was running a loss equivalent to 10 per cent of gross domestic product (GDP). Once privatized, unit costs rapidly and substantially fell, suggesting that what was happening was rent-seeking by public sector managers in various forms. In Chile, post-1990, the national company had to compete against several private companies that grew to account for around 80 per cent of output. For most of this period, the private companies paid virtually no tax, whereas the public company paid dividends and tax to the government, and so generated a disproportionate share of copper revenue.

A tax regime can be too favourable to private companies because tax rates are too low, because they can be avoided by allowable deductions from profits or because they are not properly enforced. All three features were common in the eight countries studied. During the 1990s in Russia, the federal government was weak and was out-bargained by the regions and the companies. The outcome was that both the companies and the regions were left with excessive shares of revenues. During the following decade, Vladimir Putin strengthened the federal government and sharply increased federal revenue, predominantly at the expense of the regions, but also of the companies. Despite the low taxation, there was little investment by companies because there was too much political uncertainty, analogous to Chile in the 1980s. Further, the regional governments, perhaps sensing that their advantage was likely to be temporary, sold off extraction rights by maximizing the initial payment at the expense of future revenues. In this situation of political flux, companies were well placed to play off the federal and regional governments against each other. In Chile, until 2006, the tax regime targeted profits but allowed many generous offsets for investment. The result was that, despite booming output and a world copper boom, tax receipts were negligible. In 2006, the government therefore switched the tax regime from a profits tax to a royalty system, which did not permit offsets but paid a proportion of revenues per tonne, immediately generating large revenues. Nigeria illustrates the third type of problem: under-reporting by companies. For many years, Nigeria lacked the capacity to audit oil companies, but did not bring in international audit companies. As a result, tax payments by oil companies were, in effect, voluntary. Finally, in 2004, a new finance minister brought in international auditors who discovered that payments had been insufficient to the order of several hundred million dollars.

There are some periods that are too politically uncertain to attempt something as fundamental as a long-term tax regime for natural resources. In Russia, Zambia and Chile, the initial attempt of attracting private investors was in unpropitious circumstances: a highly uncertain transition in Russia; a military regime that lacked long-term credibility in Chile; and a period of rock-bottom world prices in Zambia. In all three cases, the result was that private companies captured an excessive share of the resource rents. It would have been more appropriate to wait until there was greater certainty before attempting to attract private capital. Zambia is somewhat distinctive in that the uncertainty there concerned the market rather than the political system. The government was not the only player to be wrong-footed by the market: Anglo-American, a highly experienced resource extraction company, pulled out of Zambia at what was, in retrospect, precisely the wrong time, forgoing the benefits of future price increases and creating acute problems for the government.

The taxation of resource extraction evidently affects the incentives for investment in prospecting. Chile and Zambia have both succeeded in inducing foreign investment in prospecting by committing to long periods of tax exemption. Conversely, in Malaysia, taxation achieved particularly high rates of rent capture, and there is some evidence that this discouraged investment in prospecting. However, the appropriate trade-off between revenue and exploration is likely to be country specific, and indeed to change over time. From the public perspective, the objective is not to maximize discoveries or extraction. Malaysia had sufficient investment in prospecting that, given its tax regime, it was able to generate high and rising resource revenues. Development expenditures were not generally constrained by a lack of finance, nor was there a looming exhaustion of natural resources. Hence, there was no need to sacrifice revenues to induce further prospecting. Zambia is at the other extreme: development became acutely revenue-constrained and, by the late 1990s, the exhaustion of known copper reserves was an imminent prospect. Hence, there was little option but to make a short-term sacrifice of revenues in order to induce further prospecting. The policy error was to have conceded too much potential revenue too far into the future.

1.3.2 Avoiding political violence

Resource extraction can generate pressures for violence. However, it also generates revenues that can be used to address existing pressures for violence. Both of these effects are now reasonably well established, and both are evident from experience in the eight countries. Global statistical evidence finds that the risk of civil war (and other forms of internal violence) is reduced by economic growth and a higher level of income, but, controlling for the rate of growth, it is increased by revenues from resource extraction (Collier and Hoeffler, 2004; Miguel *et al.*,

2004; Besley and Persson, 2009). Among the eight countries, Nigeria, Russia, Malaysia, Iran and Chile have all experienced political violence, some related to resource extraction, some unrelated.

Violence was most clearly resource-related in Nigeria. In the late 1960s, the oil-producing region violently seceded, leading to a 3-year civil war. The predominant response to this was quasi-military. The three regions of Nigeria were gradually split up into a total of 36 small states, each incapable militarily of seceding from the other 35. Although this avoided violence organized by state administrations, by the 1990s, oil-related violence had re-emerged as an informal, quasi-criminal phenomenon targeting the local operations of the oil companies. It proved to be highly persistent and very costly. The informal violence was, in part, provoked by the combination of local environmental damage and manifest federal-level corruption, but was also increasingly opportunistic, kidnapping oil workers for ransom and stealing oil by tapping into pipelines. In response to the violence, the oil-producing states were allocated disproportionate shares of national oil revenues, but this failed to redress the problem. The large revenues provided to these states were usually captured by local politicians (sometimes in collaboration with gangs), leaving the well-being of residents unaffected. The disproportionate allocations may even have compounded the problem: not only did they fuel local political corruption but, by conceding the principle that these localities were entitled to more than other states, they implicitly granted co-ownership of the natural resource to the local population.

In Russia, following the break up of the Soviet Union, there was a credible fear that the resource-rich regions would secede. Various other regions of the USSR had seceded peacefully and, within Russia, Chechnya was attempting to secede violently. The response by the federal state was initially to accommodate economic demands by assigning revenue rights to the regions. In a confused legal situation, the principle of regional ownership of natural resources was largely conceded. As in Nigeria, the resource-rich regions were a small minority of the country, and so this principle conflicted with the objective of using the resources for national development. Post-2000, the approach was reversed. Ownership by the regions was revoked and instead concentrated at the federal level. The change in ownership was supported by a display of military might: part of the rationale for the heavy government military response to the Chechnyan secession may have been to discourage other such attempts. In effect, Russia had the same two approaches as Nigeria – inflicting military defeat on secessionists and conceding regional ownership of resources – but in Russia, the accommodation strategy was replaced by military force, whereas in Nigeria, the sequence was reversed. Both approaches proved to be very costly.

Iran had two phases of resource-related violence. During the 1970s, the Shah's attempt to spend exploding resource revenues as rapidly as possible led to social disruption. He personally ordered an already ambitious 5-year development plan to be quadrupled, over-ruling the advice of his technocrats. The resulting highly visible transformation of the society, with the rapid emergence of an affluent elite, presumably helped to provoke the religious fundamentalist backlash against modernization that toppled the regime. The second bout of oil-related violence was during the 1990s, when the oil revenues were used by a narrow, ideologically driven elite to prolong an international war with Iraq. Although Iran did not start the war, and it was ended by a settlement, it went on far longer than most international wars, for which the average is six months. Arguably, the narrow elite found the war a convenient justification for social control: the use of oil revenues for the war was thus a choice, rather than an unavoidable necessity.

In these three countries, resource extraction has thus contributed to secessionist violence, criminal violence and international war.

Two countries started from violence unrelated to resource extraction. In 1969, Malaysia experienced race riots, with the ethnic majority objecting to the privileged economic position of the ethnic minority Chinese. Although these riots were not induced by natural resources, the subsequent concern of the government to defuse racial tensions undoubtedly influenced policies towards the management of resources. Whereas in Nigeria and Russia, the responses were to accommodate by granting rights to revenues and to intimidate by military force, in Malaysia, the responses were economic. The revenues from natural resources were entirely concentrated at federal level: no regional ownership rights were conceded. The revenues were then used to finance a gradual accumulation of assets in the hands of the ethnic majority, while maintaining a rate of growth that was sufficiently rapid that this redistribution of assets did not require absolute reductions in the incomes of the initially advantaged racial groups. Essentially, the Malaysian strategy was peace through redistributed economic growth. The strategy was explicit, high-profile and relentlessly pursued for decades: members of the disadvantaged majority could be in no doubt that, through a variety of implementing approaches, this was the government's overarching policy. Purely as a peace strategy, this proved to be far more successful than either the Nigerian or the Russian approaches.

Somewhat analogous to Malaysia, Chile experienced a military coup followed by severe political violence in the early years of the Pinochet regime that was unrelated to resource extraction. Subsequently, however, there was a remarkably peaceful transition to social democracy in which the economic gains of the Pinochet era were preserved and extended. As in Malaysia, the politically disadvantaged appear to have drawn the conclusion from their experiences of a phase of social disturbance and a phase of rapid growth that they could benefit more from continued growth than from a return to confrontation.

What are the lessons to be learned from these very different experiences? One is that resource extraction carries downside risks: both political groups and organized criminals can use local grievance to mount resource grabs; and national elites can become cavalier about international warfare. The other is that, properly managed, the revenues from resource extraction can be a potent force for national social peace.

To reduce the risks of political secessionist and criminal responses, an effective military deterrent may be necessary to face down opportunistic criminal predation, but it is unlikely to be sufficient. Local claims for disproportionate shares of revenues need to be made to look greedy. This depends upon the chosen national use transparently benefiting ordinary citizens equitably. As, for sustainability, the depletion of natural assets should be offset by the accumulation of other assets, national use must also benefit the future. One politically realistic way in which the imperative of transparent equitable benefits to citizens can be reconciled with accumulating assets is to target children as the primary beneficiaries of resource revenues. The government of Malaysia expanded education and combined this with building long-term opportunities for employment, such as developing electronics in the impoverished district of Penang.

Meanwhile, environmental damage should be kept to a reasonable minimum by forcing resource extraction companies to face the full social costs of damage. This requires either an effective legal system or some government-provided substitute that assesses compensation for environmental damage. The resource extraction companies have learnt from the bitter experience of violence in the vicinity of their operations that there is good reason to avoid violence, but there is, nevertheless, a tension between their interest and the national interest. Resource extraction companies would prefer to buy peace by giving the local population a privileged share of revenues, but this would come at the expense of citizens elsewhere in the nation. Hence, there is a need for a government-generated approach based on compensating for actual

environmental damage, rather than the company-preferred one of enti-
tlements to shares of revenues.

1.4 Saving vs. consuming revenues

There are three distinct rationales for saving out of resource revenues.
The predominant one is that they are generated by depleting an asset
and so are unsustainable unless depletion is offset by accumulation.
Most countries do not save enough out of natural resource revenues.
Indeed, they often do not even know what the savings rate is because
there is no distinctive decision procedure. Although the appropriate
rate of savings out of resource revenues is likely to be much higher than
that out of other forms of tax revenue, it is usually likely to be considerably less than 100 per cent. A savings rate in the range 30–70 per cent
may be appropriate depending upon both objective economic conditions and the ethical framework adopted. Most economists use the
Utilitarian ethical framework to value the future relative to the present.
On this framework, in an economy that is poor but converging on the
OECD, the rationale for saving out of current revenues from depletion
is not to raise the long-run level of consumption. The society is currently much poorer than it will be once it has converged on the OECD,
and so there is a good case for spending some of the revenues on consumption until convergence has been achieved (Collier *et al.*, 2010).
The case for saving is partly to accelerate progress to convergence, and
partly, if resources are likely to be depleted before convergence is
achieved, to stretch the additional consumption financed by natural
resources beyond the time of their exhaustion or anticipated obsoles-
cence. Even on the simpler ethical framework that natural assets belong
to all future generations not just the present, there is a good case for
consuming some of the revenues. If natural assets can be converted
into other assets that are more productive, future generations can be
fully compensated for the depletion of natural assets even if only a proportion of the revenues are invested. Potentially, in a capital-scarce
economy, opportunities for high-return investment should abound.

The secondary reason for saving out of resource revenues is that they
are highly volatile due to the vagaries of discoveries and price movements. Hence, a spend-as-you-go policy would imply fluctuations in
public spending that would be disruptive. Whereas the former aims to
accumulate long-term assets, the latter aims to build up sufficient
liquidity to enable the society to stay on a path of spending that does
not inflict accelerations and reductions that are inefficient. If the

society were confident of its ability either to borrow through periods in which spending should exceed revenue or to insure against revenue fluctuations, then it would not need to build up assets for this purpose. However, in practice, as the 2008 global crisis demonstrated, many countries face borrowing constraints in world financial markets just when they need finance most, whereas insurance arrangements are often expensive and limited. Hence, building up liquidity is a sensible defensive strategy.

As we discuss below, only Chile and Kazakhstan have formally distinguished between the two rationales for saving out of resource revenues. Even this is relatively recent. Rates of asset accumulation have varied enormously between countries and between time periods. Malaysia has had an average savings rate of 37 per cent, and Kazakhstan initially had a savings rate of 78 per cent for over a decade, followed by one of 42 per cent until the global crisis of 2008. In contrast, most countries have accumulated liquid assets for relatively short periods and drawn them down in order to sustain spending once revenues faltered. This does not, however, imply that spending has been stabilized. As we discuss, a more common pattern has been that spending reductions have merely been postponed.

Institutional designs for savings out of resource revenues have also varied enormously. The analytical ideal would involve both data presentation and decision processes. In resource-rich economies, most tariff revenues are actually an indirect way of taxing natural resource extraction (Collier and Venables, 2011). Hence, they should be accounted as such in government budgets. Statements of revenue should be broken down so as to distinguish between those revenues that are sustainable and those that derive directly or indirectly from resource depletion, and so are unsustainable. The data on unsustainable revenues should then feed into a political decision process that sets the savings rate out of these unsustainable revenues. Further, as there are two distinct rationales for saving out of resource revenues, the combined savings rate should vary from year to year. The underlying rate of asset accumulation to offset depletion should be constant, but the rate appropriate for smoothing spending should swing from positive to negative depending upon judgements about market conditions.

Among the eight countries, the one that embarked on resource extraction with the most praised savings strategy ultimately completely failed to harness its natural assets for development. This was Cameroon, where the President established a dedicated overseas fund into which most of the nation's oil revenues were paid. The size of the fund was kept secret from the population and, indeed, from the government, being solely in the power of the President. At the time, this design was praised by the World Bank as a prudent approach: saving abroad was considered the right approach to avoid Dutch disease, whereas the secrecy surrounding the fund was considered appropriate to avoid populist political pressure for domestic spending. In the end the approach proved to be disastrous. The accumulation of liquid assets abroad enabled money to be brought back quickly following the revenue collapse of 1986. However, this merely deferred difficult spending choices: the repatriated money was largely dissipated in an ultimately unsustainable level of low-quality recurrent spending commitments built up during the boom years. Meanwhile, the secrecy surrounding the fund prevented any checks and balances on corruption. The money not repatriated is unaccounted for and presumed to be lost without trace. Cameroon has become, according to the various international ratings, the most corrupt country on earth.

Nevertheless, the need to accumulate assets abroad while providing political defences from populist pressure has been common to the two most successful countries, Malaysia and Chile. In Malaysia, the accumulation of foreign assets was done through two distinct strategies. The first was to use revenues to buy out the equity of foreign resource extraction companies operating in the country. This was managed by a committee and cleverly hitched the populist objective of resource nationalism to the prudent objective of asset accumulation. Initially, 67 per cent of the equity of firms operating in Malaysia was foreign-owned. By 1990, despite a large increase in the overall value of firms, through buy-outs, the foreign-owned proportion had been reduced to 25 per cent. The second strategy for the accumulation of foreign assets was carried out through the national oil company, which was encouraged by the prime minister to invest abroad, predominantly within the region of East Asia. The oil company reported directly to the prime minister, not to parliament, so as to guard against populist pressure. The company was not highly transparent, but it was subject to commercial discipline.

Chile created two international funds, one for long-term assets and the other for stabilizing expenditure given likely fluctuations in revenue. Its approach to ring-fencing these foreign assets was quite different from that of Malaysia. The government set up an independent committee of experts to determine the long-term price of copper, which was used to determine revenue flows into the fund, with the committee reporting directly to parliament. Hence, in Chile, parliament was seen as a safeguard against government abuse, whereas in Malaysia, government (in the office of prime minister) was seen as the safeguard against abuse by parliament. Chile has achieved an impressive accumulation of foreign assets from this strategy, although much of the effect of seemingly highly sophisticated rules has, in practice, been to lag increases in spending 1 year behind increases in revenues. Further, the rules have been changed almost every year. The changes have been technocratic, but the fact that they can so readily be made suggests that the rule structure does not currently amount to an inviolable institution. Arguably, what underpinned good fiscal choices in Chile was a deep popular understanding of these choices coming out of searing previous experience, rather than a set of technocratic constitutional rules.

Nigeria first established a foreign savings fund in the early 1990s. However, it was essentially decorative: analogous to a national airline with no planes, it fulfilled form but not function. By the onset of the reform period, 2003–07, there was virtually no money in it. In 2003, the reformers established a rule a little like that of Chile but without the independent committee of experts and without a clear distinction between stabilization and long-term accumulation. Indeed, given the context – an initial fiscal deficit and an incipient oil boom – the urgent matter was to slow the increase in spending. The 'long-term price' was set each year by the finance minister, with excess revenues going into a fund. As in Malaysia, the executive branch of government was seen as more prudent than the legislature. The vigorous opposition in Congress and the Senate to the Fiscal Responsibility Act tended to support this judgement. The fund was used in part to finance domestic investment, but also accumulated foreign financial assets. As Nigeria started the oil boom with a debt overhang, a further use of revenues was to pay off debt. In Nigeria, half the oil revenues accrue directly to the states rather than to the federal government. A major constitutional battle developed as to whether the federal government even had the right to undertake the macroeconomic management of these state-owned revenues. Currently, only a few states have passed Fiscal Responsibility Acts.

Like Nigeria, following the financial crisis of 1998, Russia prioritized its oil revenues for paying down debt and accumulating foreign assets. Like Nigeria, by the end of the oil boom, it had accumulated an impressive level of reserves. However, in both countries, the reserves were quickly run down during the global crisis of 2008. Currently, it is too early to judge whether this use of accumulated funds was wise. In favour of the decision, clearly the global crisis of 2008 was a highly exceptional event that warranted exceptional responses. However, against the decision, the outcome may well have replicated the Cameroonian experience post-1986 of burning up hard-accumulated financial assets in sustaining low-priority, recurrent spending decisions taken at the peak of the boom. By 2010, although Nigerian oil revenues had substantially recovered, they barely met public recurrent spending. The stabilization function may well have been given excessive priority relative to the function of accumulating assets for the long term.

Through a different route, Kazakhstan experienced a similar outcome. The government appeared to be highly prudent, establishing a foreign asset fund into which all oil revenues were paid and virtually eliminating foreign indebtedness. High savings rates were institutionalized by rules governing maximum withdrawals from the fund. However, this apparent prudency proved to have two points of weakness. The main one was that the private sector, via the local banks, used this government accumulation as implicit collateral for foreign borrowing. The banks then on-lent this borrowed money for property investment. This resulted in an asset bubble, which crashed at the time of the 2008 crisis. The government then had to repatriate a considerable part of its accumulated fund in order to bail out the banks. In effect, the apparently prudent behaviour by government permitted imprudent behaviour by the private sector and so was not, overall, as prudent as it looked. The second route for undermining the oil fund was that, in response to the 2008 crisis, the rules were changed to permit the fund to hold domestic assets. Very swiftly, one-third of the entire fund was reallocated into salvaging the banks, acquiring low-quality assets in the process.

Post-revolutionary Iran also created a foreign savings fund for oil revenues. However, it was repeatedly raided and so, as a long-term accumulation strategy, was more form than substance.

Hence, in Cameroon, Nigeria, Russia, Kazakhstan and Iran, for one reason or another, foreign asset funds that were intended to be long term were used to prop up what were probably rather low-quality forms of spending.

What are the lessons from this experience? Partly, it shows that, because foreign financial assets are liquid, they are intrinsically a hostage to fortune. Politically, it appears to be much more difficult to maintain these assets in the face of downturns in revenue than to accumulate them in the first place. Essentially, recurrent expenditures are politically extremely difficult to cut, and the financial sector cannot be allowed to collapse. If these are the political realities, then three related approaches not followed by any of these countries may be helpful. First, buffers can be placed on the rate of increase in recurrent public spending. Rapid increases in recurrent spending are liable to lead to a reduction in standards of scrutiny, and so low-quality spending, which then becomes locked in, drains funds intended for asset accumulation. Because resource discoveries and price spikes both give rise to brief periods in which public revenues rise at extraordinary rates, it is important to detach the rate of increase in spending from them. Second, in view of the experience in Kazakhstan, buffers also need to be placed by government on the rate of increase in private lending. The moral hazard associated with the accumulation of public foreign assets creates a bias towards risk in private lending that needs to be restrained. Third, withdrawals from a stabilization fund should not aspire to smooth the *level* of public spending, but rather its *rate of decrease*. The uncertainty around both depletion and commodity prices is such that stabilizing the level of spending is not feasible and attempts to do so risk merely postponing large and abrupt cuts in spending, rather than avoiding them. Hence, an orderly rate of decrease should be determined in advance. It may also be more politically feasible to maintain this rule, which inflicts limited pain at the onset of downturns, than to aspire to prevent any withdrawals for purposes of stabilization.

A second lesson is that rules may be less important than social understanding. The Chilean rule structure of a stabilization fund and a long-term asset fund correctly identifies the two core functions of foreign asset accumulation, but mostly elsewhere foreign asset funds are not sufficiently elaborate to make this distinction. Simple rules are thus liable to be inadequate in serving one or other of these functions, whereas elaborate rules that are not understood may not be robust. Related to the need for social understanding, potentially the president, government ministers, parliament and the popular media can each constitute 'the problem' against which rules try to guard. Perhaps, upon the discovery of valuable natural resources, a judgement needs to be made as to where the best defences lie, and initial institutional rules designed around this judgement. As a result, such initial institutions may look very different society by society. Yet over time, regardless of this initial judgement, the right approach may be to build a common understanding across society. As this happens, the initial design becomes increasingly redundant and may indeed become dysfunctional. The example of diamonds in Botswana illustrates this evolution. Although Botswana has always been a functioning democracy, when the government first received diamonds revenues, it decided that its decision to save much of these revenues would be virtually hidden from public scrutiny. Savings were merely reported as a single line item buried in the budget. Yet the government followed this up with a sustained education campaign to inculcate prudence into the population. Successive governments have been able to preserve highly prudent behaviour for several decades, accumulating massive foreign exchange reserves, without either dedicated foreign funds or complex rule structures. Public prudence has been underpinned by popular understanding. Even in Botswana, the accumulation of liquidity may, however, eventually have given rise to the problem of excessive protection of public spending during downturns. In 2009, a severe downturn in the global diamonds market coincided with a new president with ambitious spending plans facing an election. As a result, the fiscal deficit rose to 15 per cent of GDP.

In the absence of a critical mass of informed citizens, rule structures can easily become a sham, defusing pressure for change without altering real decisions. Cameroon is the clearest instance of rules as a smokescreen for inaction. The government has repeatedly created institutions that are superficially appropriate for the management of resource revenues, but for many years, none of them has proved effective.

A third lesson is that the liquidity of foreign financial assets may make them unsuited for the task of long-term asset accumulation. Debt reduction, as in Nigeria, or public investment abroad, as in Malaysia through its national oil company, may be better suited because they are much less reversible. However, the accumulation of real domestic assets may be the best defended form of accumulation. It is to this that we now turn.

1.5 Domestic investment

Domestic investment out of the savings from resource revenues is desirable for three distinct reasons, but there are potentially two important offsetting arguments for the accumulation of foreign assets.

1.5.1 Domestic vs. foreign asset accumulation

The first reason for domestic investment, noted above, is that, being illiquid, such assets are less prone to being dissipated in misguided attempts to sustain recurrent spending at excessive levels. The second reason, also noted above, is that, in a capital-scarce economy, returns should be higher than on foreign financial assets. The third is that properly chosen, domestic investment can transform the economy away from resource dependence, to a structure in which it is easier for ordinary citizens to generate productive livelihoods.

One potentially offsetting reason for the accumulation of foreign assets is indeed their liquidity. If the society can ensure that the depletion of foreign assets is never excessive, their greater liquidity is an advantage. For example, the Russian government may be thankful that, during the period 2000–08, it accumulated foreign assets so that it could cushion the global crisis without resorting to international borrowing.

The other potentially offsetting reason for accumulating foreign assets is the avoidance of Dutch disease. Foreign asset accumulation reduces pressures for the appreciation of the exchange rate. Although this is one way of helping non-resource exports, other ways that are less costly in terms of domestic investment forgone are likely to be more effective. Malaysia had long experience of export diversification, initially mounting a highly successful diversification from rubber to oil palm through public investment in new varieties, extension and subsidized smallholder replanting programmes through the Federal Land Development Authority (FELDA). Throughout, more than half of public investment was targeted on agriculture, on which the majority of the indigenous population were initially dependent, but increasingly, the government also promoted export diversification into manufacturing through targeted economic and social infrastructure. By 1987, manufactured exports overtook natural resource exports and are now many times larger. From the 1990s, an increasing proportion of public investment was for social infrastructure. Thus, over the decades, the composition of public investment changed, the sequence being first agriculture, then industry, and finally the social sectors. In the process, absolute poverty came down from 50 per cent of the population in 1970 to under 4 per cent by 2007.

Whereas attempts to change the real exchange rate over the long term are likely to be costly, there may be more scope for exchange rate management to assist diversification by avoiding temporary surges during commodity booms. In Zambia, an unfortunate conjunction of a copper boom, debt relief and monetary targeting led to a sudden real appreciation of around 80 per cent, which inevitably damaged non-resource exports. In contrast, Chile was able to go through the copper boom without any exchange rate appreciation thanks to its policy of using the boom to accumulate foreign assets. Although the Zambian authorities mismanaged the exchange rate, wrong-footing exporters, survey evidence on Zambian exporters finds that they are usually far more concerned about inadequate infrastructure than about the exchange rate.

Resource revenues spent effectively on improving the infrastructure for the export sector are likely to improve the competitiveness of exports more than are the same revenues accumulated abroad.

1.5.2 Managing domestic investment

If asset accumulation from resource revenues is to be domestic, the next question is whether this should be managed by the public or private sectors. Nigeria and Iran, on the one hand, and Kazakhstan, on the other, offer contrasting stories of investment disasters, one by the public sector, the other by the private sector. During the oil boom of the 1970s, the Nigerian government determined to use much of the revenues to accumulate public infrastructure which was, indeed, badly needed. Unfortunately, the management of this process went disastrously wrong. An uncoordinated programme of purchasing cement abroad in order to break a potential bottleneck in cement supplies led to the infamous 'cement Armada', in which massively excessive purchases clogged up Lagos harbour incurring demurrage. Rampant corruption in construction projects generated 'ghost' construction firms, which entered into contracts without either the capacity or the intention of delivering on them. One estimate suggests that 80 per cent of construction spending during this period was wasted. There was also a sharp increase in the unit cost of construction, so that much of the extra expenditure on public investment was dissipated. Meanwhile, private investment in Nigeria actually declined as private wealth was sent abroad, partly to benefit from an overvalued exchange rate, and partly because much of it was corruptly generated and so was more safely held in overseas banks. In Iran, the same oil boom was seized upon by the Shah as an opportunity to accelerate an economic transformation that was already astonishingly rapid. Prior to the boom, oil revenues had been well used to finance land reform, expand education and stimulate industrialization. However, the boom fed the Shah's delusions of grandeur. His insistence on quadrupling the development plan overnight was analogous to the grandiose plans of the Nigerian government. The implied annual growth rates for public investment expenditure were simply unmanageable, reducing established procedures to chaos and thereby enabling corrupt practices to thrive. Post-revolutionary Iran also adopted high rates of domestic investment but, for different reasons, failed to get good returns on it. Management of the investment process was largely delegated to quasi-charitable organizations, which lacked both scrutiny and expertise, resulting in poor selection and implementation of projects.

Whereas in Nigeria and Iran, it was public investment that went wrong, in Kazakhstan, it was private investment. As discussed above, the government saved abroad, but this provided collateral for local banks to borrow and lend for domestic private investment. Being land-locked, Kazakhstan has relatively few opportunities for export diversification. The main investment opportunities to which the private sector was attracted were in property. The resulting boom in property prices induced expansion in the construction sector, which consequently became the fastest growing sector of the economy. In 2008, the property bubble burst, leading to a banking crisis.

Neither of these strategies delivered appropriate domestic investment. Public and private investments are naturally complements, an example being roads and trucks: the return on each depends upon investment in the other. In Nigeria, public spending did not result in decent infrastructure, whereas in Kazakhstan, the government forwent needed investment in infrastructure in a misguided prudence, leading to wasteful private investment in residential and commercial property. The government cannot abrogate its role in providing infrastructure: resource revenues are an opportunity to finance this investment but, as Nigeria demonstrated, the government also needs to build the capacity to manage the process efficiently. Until 2004, Nigeria lacked basic procedures necessary for public investment, such as competitive and transparent tendering. Once these were belatedly introduced, the unit cost of projects fell by an estimated 40 per cent.

The government's role in stimulating complementary private investment need not be primarily via the provision of finance. Increasingly, where private returns are high, finance can be attracted, whether through raising the private domestic savings rate or through foreign borrowing and foreign direct investment (FDI). For example, Malaysia has been able to attract more FDI per capita than any other developing country. In part, by providing good infrastructure, the government will automatically be raising the return on private investment. However, it can supplement this effect by reforming regulatory practices so as to improve the private investment climate. There are now several global investment ratings, such as the World Bank's *Doing Business* annual assessments. Resource-rich countries tend to do atypically badly on these ratings. This may be systematic: resource revenues may reduce the need for the government to promote private investment. Iran is an extreme case in which, following the overthrow of the Shah, policy changes affordable because of the continuing oil boom sharply reduced private investment. Russia post-2000 is somewhat similar. Changes in government policies have led private investors to fear for the security of their assets, inducing massive private capital flight, estimated at up to US$300bn. In contrast, by implementing credible policy reforms, Chile post-1990 was able to attract considerable private investment without specific mechanisms for lending resource revenues to the private sector. Similarly, Zambia achieved a high investment rate out of the recent copper boom of around 60 per cent, entirely through inducing private investment in the copper sector by tax concessions: in effect, foreign copper companies captured boom rents but then invested much of them. Potentially, this is a good use of the boom rents as long as the government is able to capture the rents from the extraction generated by this investment. Overall, however, the poor performance of most resource-rich countries on the investment ratings suggests that there is considerable scope for relatively straightforward improvement.

Building the capacity for public investment and improving the environment for private investment are two pillars of the strategy of 'investing-in-investing' that is a critical policy response for the successful harnessing of natural resources. The remaining pillar is to lower the unit costs of construction. All fixed investment can be decomposed into equipment and structures. Equipment can be imported at world prices, but structures have to be produced domestically by the construction sector. As Nigerian experience illustrates, rising unit costs of construction can dissipate increased investment spending, and this problem of high costs is common to both the public and the private sectors. Yet there is considerable scope for public policy to address this problem, depending upon where the bottleneck is in the construction process. For example, in Nigeria, the bottleneck has long been cement: the richest Nigerian billionaire is a cement producer. Continuing deficiencies in port infrastructure have permitted the domestic price of cement to be far above world levels. In Zambia, a lack of basic construction skills contributes to high costs: the government had to recruit welders from East Asia, whereas prior investment in training facilities could have generated skilled local workers more cheaply.

1.6 Coping with adverse shocks

Most of the eight countries have been shock prone. Sometimes, these shocks have been generated by natural resource extraction; sometimes, the causes have been unrelated, but they have made the management of resource extraction more difficult.

1.6.1 Resource-generated adverse shocks

Revenues from resource extraction change abruptly, due to either step increases or volatility. A common policy error is to build systems of social protection during periods of peak revenue which then become unsustainable during downturns, as declining revenues collide with escalating needs. Zambia during the 1970s is a classic instance of this error: by the peak of the copper boom, the government had constructed an extensive welfare state, with guaranteed pan-territorial purchase prices for crops regardless of transport costs, and pan-territorial subsidies on food consumption. As world copper prices went into prolonged decline, this system initially continued to be financed by slashing investment spending, and finally had to be dismantled.

During a downturn, the primary shock to revenue reduces aggregate demand, and thereby reduces output in various sectors of the economy. This transmission from resource revenues on to the contraction of aggregate output amplifies the shock. However, the extent to which output contracts varies considerably depending upon the policy response. In Zambia, the shock to output was large, given the contraction in revenue, because of the maintenance of a fixed exchange rate and price controls. Both policies limited the extent to which factors of production were given incentives to move between sectors. A contrasting experience is the massive collapse in revenues from oil in Nigeria in 1986. Indeed, the loss of revenue was compounded by a sudden switch from foreign borrowing to debt repayment. During the boom, the government had geared up oil revenues by large foreign borrowing. The crash in the oil price induced international banks to downgrade Nigeria's creditworthiness so that it was not able to borrow further but still needed to service its accumulated debt. Yet despite this combined massive adverse shock, the policy response of a large devaluation enabled the economy to avoid output contraction. Indeed, aggregate output grew more rapidly in the 1986–89 period than it had during the boom years. The growth of output was, however, nowhere near sufficient to offset the decline in aggregate expenditure, and so living standards collapsed. The reduction in living standards would, however, have been even more severe without the devaluation and accompanying reallocation of production. This pattern appears to be general: exchange rate flexibility and policies that enable firms to expand and contract rapidly both reduce the shock to output from any given decline in resource revenues (Collier and Goderis, 2009).

The appropriate management of revenue volatility is predicated on the larger issue of how revenues from resource extraction should be used overall. We have noted above a tendency for excessive protection of public consumption during downturns by repatriating foreign financial assets. However, where a government is already saving and investing a substantial proportion of resource revenues domestically, the task of smoothing consumption in the face of a decline in revenue is less daunting. In resource-rich countries with high gross investment, it is easier to cope with revenue volatility while protecting both the level of consumption and the rate of return on investment. Volatility in revenues can be absorbed by changing investment because the implied swings in investment are proportionately smaller and so more manageable. A well-run resource-rich country would thus have a high average level of investment, but considerable investment volatility around this high average.

The cost of protecting consumption (both public and private) in this way – and hence, the extent to which it is appropriate – depends upon the degree to which volatility in investment reduces the average return on investment. Hence, policies that reduce the cost of investment volatility permit enhanced social protection. Which policies are appropriate?

One policy is the preparation of projects. In the public sector, periods of low investment would be used to prepare a stock of ready-to-implement projects that met agreed criteria. In periods of high investment, these projects, rather than momentary political priorities, would be implemented. Private sector investment in resource-rich countries seems to be particularly prone to property bubbles, a recent example being that in Kazakhstan. Social protection during periods of low commodity prices is, in part, dependent upon caution during periods of boom.

A second set of policies would aim to flatten the supply curve in the construction sector, so that periods of boom and bust did not map into large changes in unit costs. However, stabilizing aggregate consumption by learning to live with volatility in investment inflicts volatility on one relatively small sector of the economy, namely the construction sector. In turn, volatility in this sector creates social distress in those households dependent upon workers in the sector. Hence, addressing this problem could be a distinctive feature of targeted social programmes in resource-rich economies. The key transmission on to the incomes of ordinary households is via fluctuations in employment in construction, so that ideal social protection would provide counter-cyclical employment in the sector. If investment is to be volatile, the remaining degree of freedom in the system is the labour intensity of investment projects. During revenue booms, what is abundant is foreign exchange, and so the ideal projects are intensive in imported capital goods. Conversely, during revenue slumps, employment can be cushioned relative to the overall decline in investment if labour-intensive projects are prioritized.

This suggests that an important criterion for project preparation and selection should be the ratio of imported capital to employment. In effect, trucks should be imported during booms and roads built during slumps. Because neither the exchange rate nor the wage rate are fully flexible markets, price signals alone cannot be relied upon to effect these changes in composition. There is little else that can be used to affect private investment, but public investment, although notoriously unresponsive to price signals, can navigate by decision rules that exaggerate the swing between the two types of project and so compensate for the inadequate swing in the composition of private investment. In the countries we have studied, public investment projects are prepared by each ministry without consideration for the overall macroeconomic context. Ministries of finance ration the number of projects so as to fit available revenues, but the actual composition of projects is not done with reference to the macroeconomic cycle. Schemes such as food-for-work are *ad hoc* responses triggered by social need. In technical terms, the ideal would be for public projects to be prepared using two sets of shadow prices, one for boom conditions and one for slumps. Hence, the ranking of available projects would change over the course of the cycle. This was not the practice in any of the countries in our sample, but it suggests that even 'best practice' may fall considerably short of policies that would be most effective.

1.6.2 Shocks from other causes that influenced resource management

Russia following the fall of the Soviet Union is a classic instance of a shock whose cause was unrelated to resource extraction but was critical in shaping its management. As the Soviet Union disintegrated, ownership of its hugely valuable natural resources became the focus of power struggles between the regions and the federal government, and the object of opportunistic plunder by officials in strategic positions. By 1998, the legacy of these two phenomena was a seriously weakened central government, humiliated by the financial crisis in emerging markets, and new billionaires who were acquiring political power. The overarching objective of the policies instigated by the new leader, Putin, was to restore the power of the centre by confronting the regions and the oligarchs and, by using the revenues diverted from these initial beneficiaries, to repay debt and accumulate foreign exchange reserves, thus also escaping dependence on the international community. By 2008, Putin had succeeded in these objectives, choosing very high rates of saving from oil revenues. However, the motivation for high savings was probably not so much a custodial approach to the value generated by natural resources for future generations, as a concern to regain full *de facto* sovereignty as quickly as possible. When the global financial crisis plunged Russia into a new economic crisis, the accumulated reserves were rapidly drawn down to avoid politically more difficult adjustments. Unsurprisingly, in the context of this political earthquake, the key economic decisions concerning resource extraction were not significantly influenced by considerations of long-term economic advantage. There was not sufficient political stability to build credible institutions that could administer a set of rules. Nor, given the fundamental economic disputes raging in the society, could a critical mass of informed opinion be built that could agree on an appropriate set of rules for resource management. These key tasks remain for Russian society once conditions are sufficiently stable to permit them.

Iran following the fall of the Shah was a somewhat analogous situation of political earthquake. Although mismanagement of the resource boom triggered the Shah's downfall, the incoming regime was not primarily concerned with resource management. On the contrary, continuing revenues from the oil boom merely enabled it to pursue an economic strategy that would otherwise quickly have been ruinous, as happened in many other societies. The closest analogy is, perhaps, current governance in oil-rich Venezuela.

Chile following the coup against the socialist regime of President Allende is another example of a political earthquake essentially unrelated to resource extraction. Searching for vestiges of legitimacy, the Pinochet regime adopted pro-market economic policies that proved highly successful overall, but the specific policies concerning resource extraction were, to an extent, stymied by the lack of the long-term credibility of the regime. In retrospect, the two great successes of the Pinochet regime were to demonstrate to a majority of the population that pro-market economic policies were more beneficial to them than socialism and to design a successful transition back to democracy. The democratic government came to power free of either political or economic crisis and hence had the space to design good institutions for resource management. It used this space very well, presumably underpinned by popular understanding of the issues. It created or took over institutions which (in our judgement) are much closer to what would be ideal given the economic circumstances of the country than the other societies we have discussed.

1.7 Conclusions

The preceding remarks preview some of what has been got right, and some of what has gone wrong. Evidently, the story is much richer than can be identified by broad-brush statistical analysis, and the following chapters fill in more of the detail.

References

Besley, T. and T. Persson (2009) 'The Origins of State Capacity: Property Rights, Taxation, and Politics', *American Economic Review*, 99, 1218–44.

Collier, P. and B. Goderis (2009) 'Structural Policies for Shock-prone Developing Countries', *Oxford Economic Papers*, 61, 703–26.

Collier, P. and A. Hoeffler (2004) 'Greed and Grievance in Civil War', *Oxford Economic Papers*, 56, 563–95.

Collier, P. and A.J. Venables (2011) 'Illusory Revenues: Import Tariffs in Resource-rich and Aid-rich Economies', *Journal of Development Economics*, 94, 202–6.

Collier, P., R. van der Ploeg, M. Spence and A.J. Venables (2010) 'Managing Resource Revenues in Developing Economies', *IMF Staff Papers*, 57, 84–118.

Miguel, E., S. Satyanath and E. Sergenti (2004) 'Economic Shocks and Civil Conflict: An Instrumental Variables Approach', *Journal of Political Economy*, 112, 725–53.

2
Governance and Oil Revenues in Cameroon

Bernard Gauthier and Albert Zeufack

2.1 Overview

Using recently available datasets on oil production, the World Bank's Adjusted Savings data and building on recent literature, this chapter estimates the oil rent effectively captured by Cameroon since 1977 and analyses factors explaining the aggregate savings and spending decisions from the oil rent that led to very poor development outcomes. The chapter finds that Cameroon may have captured a sizeable portion of its oil rent – around 67 per cent. However, only about 46 per cent of total oil revenues accruing to the government between 1977 and 2006 may have been transferred to the budget. The remaining 54 per cent is not properly accounted for. Poor governance explains this disastrous outcome. The lack of a transparent and accountable framework to manage oil revenues has translated into a failure to engage in medium- to long-term development planning for the country, predatory behaviour and widespread corruption. International organizations' push for improved governance and transparency in the oil sector has not yielded any significant success. The Extractive Industry Transparency Initiative (EITI), although a noble idea, is also at great risk of capture. The chapter suggests changes in the incentives structure to reduce collusion and improve governance.

2.2 Introduction

Cameroon, with its abundant natural resource base, varied climate and diversified population, is one of the potentially richest countries in sub-Saharan Africa. It is a coastal economy with an important port, large and dynamic cities, a very strong agricultural base and abundant natural resources. However, Cameroon's growth performance since Independence has been very mixed, and the country has become one of the best examples of the resources curse.

Despite all its riches, Cameroon's growth performance has been dismal and volatile. The annual average growth rate was around 3.5 per cent over the past four decades, which is less than half the average of lower–middle-income countries. Gross domestic product (GDP) growth averaged 5.7 per cent between 1972 and 1979, driven by the cocoa and coffee boom. Oil discovery and production starting in 1977 (just before the second oil choc of 1979) led to a shift in growth trajectory with the country growing at around 9.4 per cent between 1977 and 1986. However, this high-growth episode was short-lived. A combined drop in the prices of commodities and oil, coupled with mismanagement, plunged the country into a severe economic crisis. Between 1986 and 1993, GDP contracted by 5 per cent on average, a combined 27 per cent over the 8-year period, reducing per capita income in 1993 to half its 1986 level (Figure 2.1). This growth collapse happened despite the country's reluctant engagement with the International Monetary Fund (IMF) in September 1988 for a series of structural adjustment programmes later supported by the World Bank.

The spell of negative growth culminated in a 50 per cent devaluation of the Central African franc (CFAF) in 1994. A set of accompanying measures was implemented, aimed at reforming public finances and the macroeconomic environment, including tax and commercial policies. Since 1995, the country has resumed with positive growth rates,

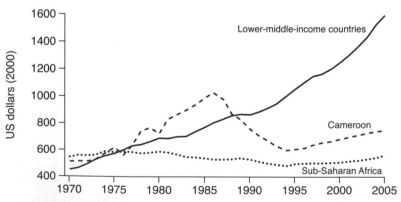

Figure 2.1 GDP per capita: Cameroon vs. sub-Saharan Africa and lower–middle income countries 1970–2005

Source: IMF (2007a).

but has been struggling to grow above 5 per cent. This slight rebound observed after the devaluation, mostly driven by a surge in timber exports and forestry depletion, has not lived up to expectations. Growth between 2001 and 2007 was one percentage point lower than the 4.5 per cent achieved between 1995 and 2000, and Cameroon was poorer in 2007 than it was in 1985.

Most importantly, analysis of development outcomes reveals a very bleak picture, and suggests that Cameroon did not harness its oil resources for sustained growth and development. Since the mid-1980s, the already poor physical, social and human capital indicators have deteriorated dramatically. Development outcomes have continued to free fall. Life expectancy has decreased from 56 to 50 years between 1996 and 2005. Over the same period, infant mortality increased from 61 to 78 per 1000, and child malnutrition increased from 14 to 22 per cent. The education system, once one of the best in Africa, has collapsed. Primary school gross enrolment decreased from 101 per cent to 91 per cent between 1996 and 2005. Secondary education gross enrolment rates declined to 25 per cent in 2000 from 28 per cent in 1990, and poverty has increased. The question, therefore, is not whether oil has contributed to growth or not, but what factors explain aggregate savings and spending decisions from the oil rent that led to such poor development outcomes.

Using recently available datasets on oil production, the World Bank's Adjusted Savings data and building on recent literature (Cossé, 2006), this chapter estimates the oil rent effectively captured by Cameroon since 1977, analyses aggregate investment and savings decisions from the oil rent and factors explaining the country's poor development outcomes. Using production-sharing rules and production data from independent sources, the chapter estimates the net revenue that should have accrued to the country yearly since 1977 and assesses the revenue gaps. We argue that the government behaved as if the boom was permanent, more so after 1982, and misjudged the severity of the 1986 crisis. The lack of transparency and accountability, fuelled by internal political pressures from a bumpy presidential transition, led to suboptimal spending policies.

We find that contracting arrangements between Cameroon and the international oil companies are relatively favourable to the country. As a consequence, Cameroon might have captured a sizeable portion of its oil rent – around 67 per cent. However, only about 46 per cent of total oil revenues accruing to the government between 1977 and 2006 might have been transferred to the budget. The remaining 54 per cent are not properly accounted for and may have been looted. The chapter argues that poor governance is the culprit. The lack of transparency and accountability in oil revenues management has translated into a failure to engage in medium- to long-term development planning for the country. The initial boom in investment between 1982 and 1984 quickly gave place to lavish consumption.

The decision to 'save' Cameroon's oil revenues abroad proves to have been sub-optimal given the lack of a transparent and accountable framework to manage them and the poor governance record of the country. Furthermore, because developing countries are capital scarce, their natural resources revenues should be used to accumulate assets within the country rather than in foreign assets that, on average, will yield lower returns (see Collier *et al.*, 2009).

Donors, who should share the blame for inconsistent advice and weak monitoring, have been pushing for improved governance and transparency in the oil sector for the past 20 years without significant success. Efforts to increase transparency in the sector seemed to have stalled, if not backtracked. The Extractive Industries Transparency Initiative (EITI), although a good initiative, is also at risk of losing credibility. The chapter suggests ways to change the incentives and reduce collusion, including the creation of an energy regulatory agency, the strengthening of donors' monitoring capacity and willingness to push hard reforms in the oil sector and overall governance structure.

The remainder of the chapter is organized as follows. Section 2.3 describes the oil sector in Cameroon and institutional arrangements governing the sector. Section 2.4 presents a measure of the potential oil rent that has accrued to Cameroon in the last three decades, as well as the gap between the rent and what has been officially recorded in the government budget. Section 2.5 examines savings and spending decisions to uncover the extent to which the rent was used to promote sustained growth. Section 2.6 examines the level of corruption, overall governance and transparency in the oil sector and suggests measures to improve transparency and oil revenue management in Cameroon. Section 2.7 concludes.

2.3 The oil sector in Cameroon

This section describes the oil sector in Cameroon in terms of size, scope and the institutional arrangements that characterize the sector. The first part describes the oil sector and its importance in the economy. The second part presents the institutional and fiscal arrangements governing the sector. As we will see, the institutional arrangements are quite unique and complex. An Oil Code has been adopted in the last decade, but oil extracting companies continue to operate within a hybrid fiscal system. At the core of the sector is a public corporation directly controlled by the presidency: the National Hydrocarbons Company (*Société Nationale des Hydrocarbures*, SNH). The public corporation is the main joint venture associate in oil production, the transit of the overall government oil take, as well as the sector regulator.

2.3.1 The oil sector

Cameroon is characterized by a rich geographic, ethnic and cultural diversity. Its population, predominantly rural, is estimated at 18.5 million (2007) and is composed of more than 250 ethnic groups and 200 languages. The primary sector accounts for about 21 per cent of GDP, with about 70 per cent of the population depending on agriculture, livestock rearing and fishing for their livelihood (World Bank, 2006a). The secondary sector represents about 32 per cent of GDP and the service sector 46.4 per cent (EIU, 2008).

The country is endowed with important natural resources including various mineral and forest resources, with dense forest covering about 40 per cent of the land area, as well as oil and gas resources.

Oil exploration in Cameroon, which began in 1947 during the colonial period, led to the discovery of the first commercial deposits in 1972. Commercial production started in 1977 in the Rio del Rey basin on the west coast of Cameroon, run by the French oil company Elf-Aquitaine.

Cameroon is a small oil producer on the world scene. Its daily crude oil production is about 87,000 barrels (2007), down from its peak of 186,000 barrels a day in 1985. It is the smallest producer in Africa, far behind Nigeria, Africa's largest oil producer, with about 4 per cent of its northern neighbour's oil output.

Cameroon's proven oil reserves are also relatively small, estimated at about 540 million barrels, with an additional 960 million barrels of probable oil reserves (IMF, 2007a: 16). However, with the retrocession of the potentially oil- and gas-rich peninsula of Bakassi by Nigeria in August 2008, new explorations have been registered and discoveries are expected to boost the country's reserves considerably (EIU, 2008).

Despite being a small player by world standards, the oil sector plays a major role in production, exports and government revenues in Cameroon. In 2007, oil share of total GDP was 9 per cent, down from close to 30 per cent at the peak of the oil boom in 1985 (see Figure 2.2).

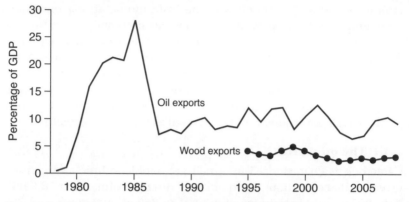

Figure 2.2 Oil and wood in Cameroon as a percentage of GDP

The significance of the oil sector is even more visible with regard to its contribution to the country's foreign exchange earnings and government revenues. Crude oil products are the country's main export, representing more than 55 per cent of export revenues in 2007 (down from close to 80 per cent in 1985), far beyond timber and wooden constructions, at about 15 per cent of revenues, and cocoa beans, at 0.2 per cent.[1]

The government's revenue base is dominated by oil, which represented 33 per cent of government revenues in 2007, down from almost 48 per cent in 1985. As a percentage of GDP, oil revenues represented about 6 per cent of total GDP in 2007, against nearly 14 per cent in 1985.

2.3.2 Main actors

Oil exploration and production in Cameroon are carried out by international oil companies (IOCs), in a joint venture agreement (*Accord d'association*) with the state, represented by SNH.

Created in 1980 as an autonomous public corporation, SNH acts as the government's holding company for participation in joint ventures. It has overall responsibility for management of the sector. Its mandate includes: (1) the management of state interests in the oil sector; (2) the promotion, development and monitoring of oil activities throughout the national territory; and (3) the commercialization of Cameroon's share of crude oil production (SNH, 2008). Direct control over SNH is exercised by the President of the Republic, who appoints the director of the public corporation, while the Secretary General of the presidency acts as the president of the SNH executive board.

The main IOCs currently active in oil production in Cameroon include Total E&P Cameroon (a subsidiary of French Total), Pecten Cameroon (a subsidiary of Royal Dutch Shell) and Perenco Cameroon (a subsidiary of French Perenco), with the first two representing over 90 per cent of oil production.[2] In addition, 11 companies are involved in exploration activities.[3] Oil production is mainly offshore and most of the country's oil is exported.

In addition to SNH joint ventures' equity stakes in Total, Pecten and Perenco, the public corporation holds shares in other companies involved in downstream oil sector activities, notably the country's refinery SONARA (*Société Nationale de Raffinage*). The SNH portfolio also includes shares in 12 other domestic companies (World Bank, 2006a).

Although SNH plays a vital role in the oil sector, as regulator and joint venture associate in all oil activities, two line ministries share some responsibilities over the sector: the Ministry of Energy and Water (MINEE) and the Ministry of Industry, Mines and Technological Development (MINIMIDT), which is responsible for the issuance of mining titles for the extraction of oil. There are overlapping responsibilities and conflicts of attribution among the different line ministries and public agencies in the oil sector (World Bank, 2006a: 68).[4]

2.3.3 Institutional arrangements

Prior to the adoption of the Oil Code in 1999, there was no specific legislation regulating the sector. Instead, activities in the sector were governed by the 1964 Mining Law (Loi 64-LF-3) supplemented by the 1978 Law (Loi 78-14).

Under that regime, oil taxation in Cameroon was based on a complex system, in many respects unique in the world. Whereas most countries use one of the two main forms of petroleum taxation prevalent today, either production-sharing agreements or tax and royalties, Cameroon uses a hybrid system combining production sharing and taxation, as well as a guaranteed mining rent (World Bank, 1990: 92). Under this system, state involvement in the oil sector takes the form of a compulsory 20 per cent SNH equity participation in the operating IOCs and a 50 per cent share in a joint venture arrangement with the same operators. This results in a 60 per cent SNH equity share in all oil activities.[5]

The IOCs and SNH sell their respective shares of crude oil production on the international markets. A joint commission comprising SNH and oil companies determines the official sale prices of oil, which are then used to establish tax obligations.[6]

In addition to the obligation to conclude production-sharing arrangements (PSAs) in accordance with the 1978 Law, each IOC must conclude a Convention of Establishment (*convention d'établissement*), part of the Investment Code, in accordance with the 1964 Mining Law. The agreement covers the company's country-wide interests, although conditions specific to each permit are set in a separate decree. The agreement defines the rights and obligations of the two parties, including fiscal provisions.

The main elements of the special fiscal regime applying to the oil sector include: (1) a higher corporate income tax (IS) rate of 57.5 per cent on net profits;[7] (2) production royalties levied at a rate of 12.5 per cent, coupled with a minimum mining rent of 13 per cent guaranteed to the operator;[8] and (3) other corporate taxes including land royalties and flat fees.

The adoption of an Oil Code in 1999 (Loi 99-013) sought to simplify the legislative and fiscal environment for IOCs, improving the incentive environment for exploration and extraction and attracting new investments in the sector (EITI, 2007). The code defines two types of contracts, from among which firms are free to choose: the concession contract and the production-sharing contract (Cameroon National Assembly, 1999).[9] Although in the former system, IOCs were required to sign both a Convention of Establishment and a Contract of Association, under the new Oil Code, only one oil contract is signed between the state and IOCs.[10]

Despite the fact that several contracts have been signed under the new Oil Code, the two systems still coexist. Currently, only exploration activities are carried out under the new regime, and all extraction activities are still governed by the former system[11] (EITI, 2007). The new code includes various incentives for IOCs.

In addition to the share of physical production, IOCs transfer dividends to the SNH as well as a series of taxes including taxes on profits, the proportional mining royalties, flat fees, land royalties and royalties proportionate to production (EITI, 2007: 26). In turn, SNH is expected to remit these payments to the treasury as well as its benefits from oil sales and its own required fiscal contributions.[12]

Figure 2.3 presents financial flows between the IOCs, SNH, the state and the Central Bank.

The level of government revenue from oil production depends on the specific conditions agreed between the SNH and the private IOCs, as defined in the PSAs. The oil take also depends on production and transport costs. In Cameroon, a large share of the fixed cost is now

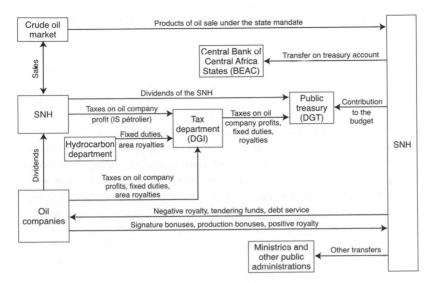

Figure 2.3 Financial flows between the IOCs, SNH and the state
Sources: EITI (2007); SNH (2007).

amortized, whereas transportation costs from offshore platforms are low. As mentioned above, under the PSAs, SNH is entitled to a share of IOC physical production. The share varies depending on the level of cumulative production from a given exploration permit. It was initially set at 60 per cent when the production level falls below 15 million tons, 65 per cent between 15 and 30 million tons, and 70 per cent once it exceeds 30 million tons (World Bank, 1990: 93). Production has gradually been increased and is now reported to be 70 per cent (EITI Cameroon, 2007: 15). The oil revenues accruing to the government are hence quite high relative to other oil-producing countries and amount to between 67 per cent and 70 per cent of the value of oil exports (World Bank, 2006a: 69; EITI Cameroon, 2007).

2.4 Estimations of the oil rent

Section 2.3 described the oil sector in Cameroon, namely its size, scope and the institutional arrangements that characterize the sector. This section assesses the oil revenues that accrued to the country as a result of concession agreements with oil companies. In particular, we try to establish the extent of the revenues related to oil extraction that have not been used for public purposes. That is, we assess how much rent that accrued to Cameroon as a nation has not been disclosed or transferred to the budget.

This section is made up of two parts. The first describes the data sources and the strategy for measuring the oil rent. We then measure the rent using official oil production figures released recently, government budgetary data as well as independent estimates of oil production in the country. We show that the oil rent in Cameroon during the last three decades was substantial. We also measure the gaps between the rent measured using independent estimates and official government figures. We show that the gap is substantial. Furthermore, we measure the gap between the government oil revenues measured using independent estimates and what is appearing in the budget. We show that the gap between the estimated government oil revenues and what is appearing in the government budget is significant and tends to increase over the period. Accordingly, a large part of government oil revenues in Cameroon is unaccounted for and seems to have been expropriated.

2.4.1 Data sources and strategy to estimate the oil rent

The oil sector in Cameroon has been surrounded by official secrecy for most of the last 30 years. During that period, the level of transparency in oil revenues has improved slightly under the influence of donors, as we will see in Section 2.6. Still, very little is known about the level of revenues accruing to the country and the use of these resources.

To estimate the oil revenues accruing to the country since the beginning of oil production, we make use of production data released recently by SNH as part of the recent EITI exercise in Cameroon (see Section 2.6 for details). These data comprise yearly physical production levels for the last three decades (Tamfu, 2008). The official data also comprise the country's official budgetary data, part of the finance laws that present official oil revenues for most years during the period.

In addition to these official data, we make use of independent oil production figures produced recently as part of a World Bank project that has estimated the rents of various mineral resources over time including oil. The World Bank's Adjusted Saving Project (WBASP) has estimated rent for a number of countries, including Cameroon. The dataset includes production data, prices and costs over time. WBASP production data are obtained from different sources, in particular the International Energy Agency (IEA); British Petroleum (BP); Statistical Review of World Energy (2007, 2008); International Petroleum Encyclopaedia; and the United Nations Monthly Bulletin of Statistics. This relatively recent dataset has been used in recent empirical studies on the estimation of wealth arising from natural resources (e.g. World Bank, 2006b) and on the effects of natural resources revenues (e.g. Collier and Hoeffler, 2005).

Our strategy is to estimate the oil revenues and oil rent (oil revenues minus costs) accruing to the country over the last 30 years using these various data sources. In particular, we assess the difference between the estimated government oil revenues accruing to the country and the oil revenues appearing in the budget. We measure first the oil revenues and oil rent and then the discrepancy between the estimated rent and official figures.

2.4.2 Estimations of the oil rent and oil revenue gap

Figure 2.4 presents oil production in Cameroon in millions of barrels per year (left axis) according to the WBASP and SNH data from the beginning of oil production in 1977. The evolution of oil prices during the period is also presented using WBASP and BP price data (right axis).

We observe that oil production in Cameroon peaks at about 65 million barrels per year around 1985–86 and then declines until about 1995, when another increase in production is observed. For the entire period, we note that the independent production estimates of WBASP are almost consistently above SNH official production figures.

The beginning of oil production in Cameroon coincides with the three-fold increase in oil prices following the first Organization of Petroleum Exporting Countries (OPEC) oil embargo in 1979. Oil prices peaked at

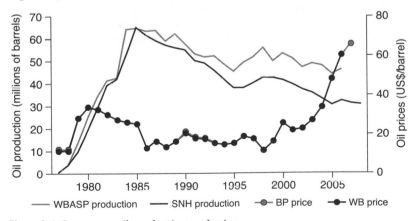

Figure 2.4 Cameroon oil production and price

Note: As Cameroonian crude oil is of significantly lower quality than the standard Brent, a discount is applied on Cameroon oil exports of about 3 per cent. World Bank prices already account for this discount, whereas BP prices have been adjusted to the average selling price of Cameroon oil.

about US$34 in 1980, then dropped by half between 1985 and 1986. Between 1988 and 1990, prices soared again. Since 1999, oil prices have risen tremendously, especially since 2002.

There are two periods of high-level oil revenues in Cameroon. The first is observed during the 1979–85 price hike period, which corresponds with the oil boom in Cameroon. The second is observed since 2002 with the tremendous increase in oil price, which corresponds with a second oil boom.

Indeed, Cameroon's gross oil revenues grew exponentially during the first few years of oil production. Cameroon tapped into the oil bonanza created by the oil embargo, and gross revenues jumped to about US$1.7 billion in 1985.

With the subsequent drop in oil prices, which reached a low of US$13.6 in 1988, the decrease in gross oil revenues was substantial between 1985 and 1988. The decrease in oil production combined with the important decline in prices and in the US dollar brought a steep decline in revenues. Afterwards, the increase in oil prices led to a second peak in oil revenues of about US$1.2 billion in 1990. Oil revenues then fell by half until 1998. With the important price increase since 1999, revenues have grown almost exponentially, reaching close to US$3 billion in 2006.

From these figures, we deduce the yearly production costs to obtain the oil rent. Appendix Table A.2.1 presents estimates of unitary production costs in Cameroon during the period.

Figure 2.5 shows the oil rent during the period using World Bank and SNH oil production estimates. We observe that, similar to the oil revenues, the evolution of oil rent shows two peaks, one during the oil boom of 1979–85 and the second during the current oil price boom. Over the 30-year period, the cumulative net oil rent that has accrued to Cameroon is about US$27 billion (not shown).

We then measure the gap between the oil rent as measured using independent estimates and official government figures. Figure 2.6 presents the yearly and cumulative oil rent gap. We observe in particular that, over the period, the cumulative net oil rent gap has been more than US$5 billion.

Finally, we estimate the government oil revenues during the period. We do so by measuring the share of the oil rent accruing to the state. There are two main categories of transfers made to the state by IOCs in Cameroon, as discussed in Section 2.3: production-sharing agreements and taxes and royalties. On average, the 'oil take' or share accruing to the country is about 65 per cent (EITI, 2007). In addition, we also con-

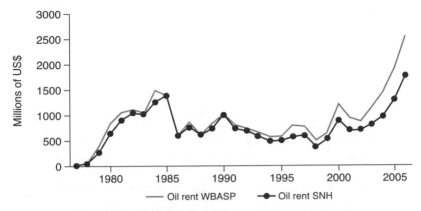

Figure 2.5 Oil rent (in US$ million)

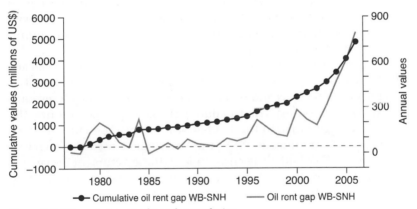

Figure 2.6 Oil rent gap: yearly and cumulative

sider the costs supported by SNH in its management role in the oil sector. These costs represent about 3.5 per cent of SNH oil sales or oil revenues as estimated based on the average of SNH reported costs for the last 5 years. These administrative costs are then subtracted from the SNH share of net rent.

Using this information, we estimate the net revenues that should have accrued to the state yearly during the period using the independent production estimates. We then measure the difference between these estimates and the oil revenues reported in the country's budget. The yearly and cumulative gaps in government oil revenues are presented in Figure 2.7.

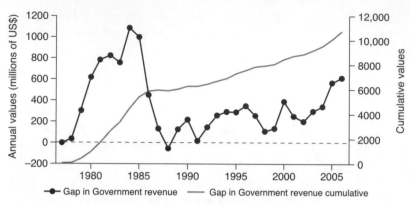

Figure 2.7 Government oil revenue gap: yearly and cumulative

We observe that the gap is substantial. For instance, the yearly gap between the estimated revenues and those appearing in the budget laws amount to US$400 million in 1980 as well as in 1984, far above the estimated 'secret accounts' estimated by the World Bank during that period. The gap reached about US$600 million in 2006.

Interestingly, the gap in government oil revenues for 1985, 1986 and 1988 is negative. For those 3 years, the estimated yearly government oil revenues from oil PSAs and oil tax revenues are below the oil revenues reported in the country's budget during the same period. This negative gap could suggest that, in the first few years of the economic crisis that hit Cameroon starting in 1985, the government used the secret oil accounts to try to buffer the crisis. Indeed, the government declared in 1987 that Cameroon would manage through the crisis without borrowing from the IMF. We estimate that, during the period 1985–88, about US$900 million of the extra budgetary account accumulated during the period 1977–85 was injected into the budget.[13] It is therefore plausible that the government first used resources from the secret accounts and only changed course to sign a stand-by agreement with the IMF in September 1988 when it realized the solution might not be sustainable.

Finally, examining the cumulative difference between the estimated government oil revenues and the official budgetary figures, we observe that the gap is very substantial. Since 1988, the first year when oil revenues started appearing in the budget, the Cameroonian government has reported oil revenues amounting to US$9.1 billion (as of 2006). Given that the estimated total oil revenues accruing to the government between 1977 and 2006 are around US$19.8 billion, this would imply that around US$10.7 billion or 54 per cent of oil revenues has not been disclosed or transferred to the budget.[14] This amount may have been privately appropriated, although it is not clear which part was appropriated by oil companies and government officials.[15]

2.5 Oil revenues savings revisited

Section 2.4 of this paper has established that, although Cameroon captured a sizeable portion of the oil rent between 1977 and 2007, only a third was included in the budget, and the remaining portion was not properly accounted for, as it was 'saved' abroad. In this section, we investigate why this decision to 'save', first hailed by most experts, including those in the Bretton Woods institutions, as an example of good management of oil resources, turned out to be disastrous for the country.

2.5.1 Oil and development outcomes

Until the mid-1980s, Cameroon was portrayed as an example of good management of oil resources and a likely candidate to escape Dutch disease. Benjamin and Devarajan (1986), for instance, write: 'The track record of some of the other oil exporters has not been exemplary. But the distinctive feature of Cameroon oil sector and the cautious approach of its policy makers give one cause for optimism' (p. 188). The 1988 *World Development Report*, in a background paper on Cameroon, noted that: 'Largely through prudent fiscal policy, it avoided many of the adverse consequences of boom experienced by other commodity-exporting countries' (World Bank, 1988: 33).[16]

By 1989, however, it had become clear that Cameroon was facing the symptoms of Dutch disease. Devarajan and de Melo (1987) and Benjamin *et al.* (1989) found, using a computable general equilibrium (CGE) model, that the oil boom has been followed by a contraction in other commodities' exports. Indeed, when oil revenue jumped from 0 to 46 per cent of export revenue between 1978 and 1982, representing 13 per cent of GDP, large inflows of foreign exchange led to soaring domestic absorption. Public spending increased from 17 per cent of GDP in 1978 to 26 per cent in 1986. The spending spree led to inflationary pressures, real exchange rate appreciation and rapidly increasing wages, hindering the competitiveness of the non-commodity traded sectors (export as well as import substitutes). This resulted in a sharp decline in non-oil exports (agriculture and manufactured goods). Interestingly, in 2006, the World Bank Development Policy Review on Cameroon reads: 'It is important to note that Cameroonian officials were warned at the time of the problems of sustainability of such pro-cyclical budget policy and the potential onset of Dutch disease. Unfortunately they chose to ignore this warning and failed to make the necessary adjustments' (World Bank, 2006a). It is important to recognize, beyond the blame game, that policy blunders were made at a time when neither the World Bank nor the government could claim they knew exactly what the right policy was for managing natural resources revenues.

The policy failure and the subsequent growth collapse have led to disastrous development outcomes. Between 1996 and 2005, life expectancy decreased from 56 to 50 years, reflecting the decrease in access to health services, the dramatic increase in malnutrition and the spread of HIV/AIDS, the prevalence rate of which rose from 2 per cent in 1991 to 7.2 per cent in 1998. The mortality rate for children under 5 years rose from 144 to 155 per 1000 live births between 1991 and 1998 and has only returned to its 1991 level in 2004. The infant mortality rate increased steadily from 65 per 1000 live births in 1991 to 77 in 1998, and to 74 in 2004 (Table 2.1).

During the same period, the chronic child malnutrition rate increased from 23 per cent to 30 per cent. Chronic malnutrition was evidenced by drastic changes in the three indicators of *stunting* (a measure of inadequate food intake over time), *wasting* (a measure of acute malnutrition due to short-term food deprivation or infection) and *underweight* (a composite indicator of stunting and wasting). The relatively high maternal mortality rate (669 per 100,000 live births) also carries a rural/ poor bias. In 1998, less than one-third of women from the poorest quintile (29 per cent) had deliveries attended by a medically trained person, compared with 90 per cent of women from the richest quintile.

Table 2.1 Public health indicators

Health indicators	1991	1998	2004
Infant mortality rate (per 1000)	65	77	74
Chronic malnutrition rate (%)	23	29	30
Rate of low birth weight (%)	16	22	–
Maternal mortality rate (per 1,000 000 live births)	430	430	669
Assisted childbirth rate (%)	63.8	58.2	61.8
Vaccination rate (DTP3 in %)	34	48	48.2
Utilization rate of public health facilities (%)	30	–	–
HIV/AIDS prevalence rate (%)	2	7.2	5.5

Source: World Bank (2006a).

Also, roughly 60 per cent of women from the poorest 20 per cent of the population received antenatal care from a trained person compared with close to 100 per cent of women from the richest 20 per cent.

The education system, once one of the best in Africa, has also collapsed. Primary school gross enrolment decreased from 101 per cent to 91 per cent between 1996 and 2005, and secondary education gross enrolment rates declined to 25 per cent in 2000 from 28 per cent in 1990. Although real government spending per student has increased over time and is comparable to countries at a similar level of development, the outcomes are much lower. There is a low primary school completion rate, a very low transition rate from primary school to secondary school, of around 60 per cent, and a low retention rate within the secondary school system.

Most importantly, access to public services in Cameroon has become more unequal. There are growing disparities among regions, as well as between the poor and non-poor. The primary school enrolment rate is significantly lower for the poor compared with the non-poor (74 per cent vs. 82 per cent in 2001), as well as for rural relative to urban areas (73.5 per cent vs. 90.5 per cent in 2001). Between 1996 and 2001, although enrolment rates increased for non-poor (from 75 per cent to 83 per cent) and for urban areas (from 81 per cent to 90.5 per cent), they decreased significantly for the poor (from 77.2 per cent to 74.1 per cent), while remaining stagnant for the rural areas (from 74.5 per cent to 73.5 per cent) (World Bank, 2006a). These trends are indicative of widening, rather than narrowing, gaps between social groups, as well as regions (World Bank, 2006a: 21).

2.5.2 Explaining the poor outcomes: a story of consumption smoothing gone wrong

2.5.2.1 To save or not to save?

At the start of oil production in 1977, the President of Cameroon decided to create an extra-budgetary account (*Compte Hors-Budget*, CHB) abroad to manage oil revenues. Cameroon's decision to 'save' its oil reserves abroad, it was argued, was sound for at least two reasons. First, it would help to avoid oil dependency and Dutch disease and, second, the boom was allegedly temporary, as the rate of depletion of oil was believed to be very high. Benjamin and Devarajan (1986) wrote: 'Cameroon is traditionally not an oil producer, nor will it be one in about ten years or so' (p. 186). A World Bank report stated: '. . . the authorities rightly considered oil revenues as temporary resources' (World Bank, 1987: 26).

Until the end of the 1980s, Cameroon was still seen as a good example of oil resources management (see Devarajan and de Melo, 1987; World Bank, 1988). The 1988 *World Development Report*, in a background paper on Cameroon's case, noted that: 'Largely through prudent fiscal policy, it avoided many of the adverse consequences of boom experienced by other commodity-exporting countries' (p. 33). Looking back at how erratic oil gross oil rents turned out to be (see Figure 2.8 in Section 2.4) due to fluctuations in prices, production and the value of the US dollar, saving oil revenues '. . . to smooth out intertemporal consumption and investment would have been a wise decision' (see van der Ploeg and Venables, 2008).

However, judging by the development outcomes seen above, and learning from the recent literature, 'saving' Cameroon's oil revenues abroad was not an optimal decision. However, understanding Cameroon's fast transition from 'best in class' to one of the worst cases of resources curse requires looking beyond the pure economic analysis of savings behaviour to address political economy considerations.

2.5.2.2 The political economy of oil revenues management in Cameroon

The political economy dimension is crucial in explaining oil revenue spending decisions in Cameroon. The first issue to consider is the decision to establish the CHB. Given the autocratic nature of the political regime at the time of oil discovery, it is useful to question the president's incentives for creating the CHB. Was this the fact of a benevolent and enlightened dictator following Hartwick's rule,[17] or was this just a trick to divert the public's attention away from oil revenues with the clear intention of misappropriating the rent? Jua (1993) and Zeufack (2001) argue that the creation of the CHB was clearly ill-intended. In support of this thesis is the secrecy that surrounded the CHB. There was no attempt to assess or publish the size of the 'extra-budgetary account'. Until now, there was virtually no information whatsoever on the transactions on the account between 1977 and 1980, and information on the contribution of this account to the budget between 1980 and 1985 has only been approximated by the World Bank. Basic information such as the currency in which the resources were placed is a state secret. Discussion of its management is taboo and could lead to imprisonment, if not worse.[18] Therefore, the Cameroonian CHB was not comparable to a sovereign wealth fund (SWF) or an oil fund. The same lack of transparency[19] continued even after Mr Biya took over from Mr Ahidjo as president.

The bumpy transition between President Ahidjo and President Biya in 1982 is, indeed, the second issue that deserves consideration, as it had a lasting impact on savings and spending policies. On 6 November

1982, Ahmadou Ahidjo, the first president of Cameroon, after 25 years of autocratic rule, resigned in a surprise move and peacefully handed over power to Paul Biya, his then prime minister. However, he stayed in control behind the scenes, retaining the presidency of the Cameroonian National Union (*Union Nationale Camerounaise*, CNU), the single political party. Very soon, the dualism at the top of the state resulted in clashes. In August 1983, the fall out between Ahidjo and Biya was officialized, and Ahidjo was accused of attempting to overthrow the new president. Ahidjo, who called it a 'truly false *coup d'état'*, was forced into exile, and most of his partisans, mainly from his ethnic group (Fulbe) who formed the presidential guard and kept key cabinet positions, were purged, creating some ethnic tensions.

On 6 April 1984, there was a missed *coup d'état*, claimed by Ahidjo from his exile. The coup reinforced ethnic tensions, especially between the north and the south. The youth, very loyal to the incoming president, opposed the coup and fought the junta on the streets of Yaoundé, the capital city. After the 1984 missed coup, the presidency seemed to be under siege. The president engaged in populist policies to consolidate his power with the youth and reward the ethnic-based pressure groups that had supported him during the coup. Generous programmes for university scholarships and the construction of student dormitories and auditoria were launched. In parallel, the lack of transparency was reinforced in a context characterized by increasing cronyism and military and security spending. These political pressures may have led to sub-optimal savings and spending policies, for example in prolonging the government's consumption spree well beyond the start of the 1986 crisis.

2.5.2.3 Un-smooth consumption

There was an increase in investment in the early years of the oil boom (see Figure 2.8). For example, the government's capital expenditures tripled in 1 year, from CFAF 73.2 billion in 1980 to CFAF 226.2 billion in 1981. However, from 1982, and even more so after 1984, the government behaved as if the boom was permanent. Consumption and transfers increased significantly and, as the country misjudged the severity of the 1986 crisis, the consumption spree continued until the signing of stand-by agreements with the IMF in September 1988. Typically, the country followed a variant of the permanent income hypothesis, as described by van der Ploeg and Venables (2008).

Investment collapse Starting in 1988, structural adjustment policies implemented by the IMF and the World Bank led to an abrupt end to

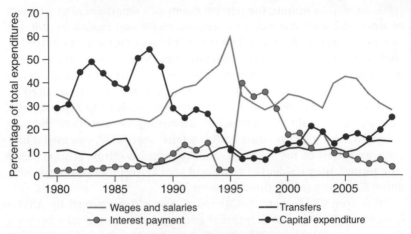

Figure 2.8 Composition of public expenditures

consumption and transfer stopping policies, but also to investment. Capital expenditures were cut dramatically, falling sharply from 12.4 per cent of GDP in 1986 to 3.5 per cent by 1993. This coupled with the decline in income and thus private savings led to a collapse in the overall investment rate from 25 per cent in the early 1980s to 14 per cent by 1993. The drop in capital investment is more dramatic when we consider only capital expenditures financed from domestic sources (Figure 2.9).

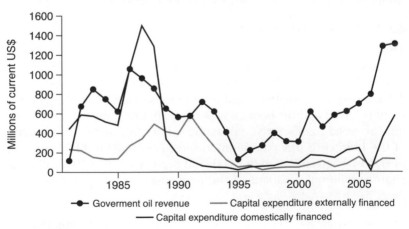

Figure 2.9 Oil revenue and capital expenditure

From 1988 onwards, there is virtually no correlation between capital expenditures and oil revenues. The lack of transparency and accountability in oil revenues management in Cameroon has translated into a failure to engage in medium- to long-term development planning for the country. Cameroon's oil revenues were not invested in physical, social or human infrastructure, but lavishly consumed. Indeed, disbursements from the CHB to the budget and to finance any infrastructure in the country were at the sole discretion of the President, and even relevant ministers did not know in advance how much the amount would be.

Permanent rise in public spending　Recurrent expenditures grew by nearly 15 per cent a year between 1981 and 1985 in real terms, some six percentage points higher than in the pre-oil era. Of this, wages and salaries and materials and supplies grew by little over 11 per cent a year, whereas subsidies and other current transfers grew by nearly 25 per cent a year in real terms. As shown in Figure 2.8, total spending (especially wages and transfers) increased dramatically between 1984 and 1986. Civil servants received consistent pay rises, university students received increases in their scholarships and programme coverage was expanded.

The consumption spree continued after 1986 as the government may have misjudged the severity of the crisis and thought it was a temporary blip. The president declared that 'the crisis was just passing through Cameroon and the country was not in crisis'. Just as in the permanent income hypothesis, he thought, at the end of the windfall in 1986, that he had sufficient foreign reserves to finance the permanent increase in public spending without having to apply for IMF funding. This decision was most convenient, given the IMF record of interference and requirements for transparency. By 1993, the country was running a fiscal deficit of 8 per cent of GDP.

2.6 Governance, corruption and transparency in the oil sector

Section 2.5 of this study has shown that oil revenues in Cameroon were not used to ensure sustained growth. Policy choices were dismal, and public investments were not sufficient to maintain public capital stock. Experience has shown that, especially in countries that did not develop a sufficient governance quality level before the natural resources windfall, natural resource rent leads to rent-seeking and corruption (Sala-i-Martin and Subramanian, 2003; Karl, 2007). Cameroon, as we will see, is no exception. This section analyses the environment of poor governance and corruption in which policy choices were made during the last three decades, in particular the lack of transparency in the management of oil revenues. It examines the role played by donors such as the World Bank and the IMF in trying to reform institutional arrangements in the country over the last few decades, notably in the oil sector.

The first part of this section examines the poor level of governance and high corruption level in Cameroon. The second part reviews the evolution of oil sector transparency and juxtaposes it with donors' activities in the country. The context is one of weak monitoring and incomplete reform implementation. Although donors have been the main advocates for greater transparency, the fundamental institutional reforms that could have led to improvements in accountability and transparency – notably the creation of a regulatory agency in charge of the oil sector – were not pushed to the forefront and wait to be implemented.

2.6.1 Governance and corruption

Cameroon is one of the most corrupt and poorly governed countries in the world. In the last 10 years, Cameroon was ranked the most corrupt country in the world twice according to the Transparency International (TI) corruption perception index (CPI).[20]

The overall state of governance in the country is considered poor according to most indexes of governance quality. Various measures of governance have been devised in the last decade to assess governance quality, that is the institutional structure and decision-making environment at the political and economic level. Most of these measures emphasize three main characteristics: (1) an efficient and capable state; (2) accountable to its citizens; which (3) operates under the rule of law (Kaufmann *et al.*, 2008). One of the main sets of governance indicators is the World Bank World Governance Indicators (WGI). The index presents the views of a large number of enterprises, citizens and experts on the quality of governance relating to six dimensions of governance: (1) control of corruption; (2) rule of law; (3) voice and accountability; (4) government effectiveness; (5) regulatory quality; and (6) political stability. The percentile rank of Cameroon on each of these six governance indicators is presented in Table 2.2 along with the average values for African and middle-income countries. As shown, the quality of governance in Cameroon is very low. Cameroon ranks in the bottom quintile of countries overall for all dimensions of governance, except political stability, where it is in the bottom third, and is below that of other middle-income and other African countries on all dimensions.

Table 2.2 Governance indicators: Cameroon, African and middle-income countries (World Governance Indicators 2007)

	Percentile rank (0–100)		
Governance indicators	Cameroon	Sub-Saharan African countries	Middle-income countries
Control of corruption	15.9	30.7	37.4
Rule of law	12.9	28.3	37.7
Voice and accountability	21.2	33.2	38.4
Government effectiveness	17.1	26.8	37.2
Regulatory quality	24.3	27.8	36.9
Political stability	31.3	34.2	39.4

Percentile rank indicates the percentage of countries worldwide that rate below Cameroon, African countries and middle-income countries. Higher values indicate better governance ratings.

Source: Kaufmann *et al.* (2008). According to various other measures of governance, institutional quality, in particular the level of corruption, is very problematic in the country. According to the TI Global Corruption Barometer 2007, 79 per cent of citizens in Cameroon report having paid bribes to government officials during the past 12 months – the highest rate of bribe payments among African countries surveyed. Businesses operating in the country also cite corruption as one of their main problems, being reported as the second most important constraint for doing business according to the World Economic Forum's Global Competitiveness Index, just after access to financing (World Economic Forum, 2007).

Various other governance quality indicators also point to a very low governance level in the country. For instance, according to the World Economic Forum's 2007 Global Competitiveness Index, Cameroon is the third worst country overall in the international index in terms of diversion of public funds (126th out of 128 countries). The country also ranks very near the bottom with regard to strength of auditing and accounting standards and public trust of politicians (122nd and 120th respectively). Overall, it ranks 120th out of 128 countries for its institutional environment, as measured by the independence of its judiciary, the efficacy of government and the level of corruption (World Economic Forum, 2007).

Civil liberties and political rights, two fundamental components of democratic life and good governance, are also perceived as severely deficient in the country. According to the Freedom House index, which has evaluated the state of civil liberties and political rights around the world since 1973, Cameroon ranks very near the bottom. The overall ranking of countries along this index classifies countries as 'free,' 'partly free' and 'non-free'. Whereas before 1977, Cameroon was classified as 'partly free,' the first year of oil production is characterized as having been marked by a worsening of civil liberties and political rights. Since that year, the country has been classified as 'non-free,' an unenviable status it has kept for the last 30 years (Freedom House, 2008).

Another index of democracy, the Polity IV index of civil liberties and democratic governments (Marshall and Jaggers, 2006), also emphasizes the very poor level of governance in Cameroon. According to this index, Cameroon has been classified as an 'autocratic regime' since Independence in 1960. Although the late 1980s and early 1990s marked the beginning of a democratic era for several African countries, this process did not take place in Cameroon. The change in regime associated with the withdrawal of President Ahidjo in 1982 did not provide much improvement in the level of democracy: from 1977 to 1992, Cameroon continuously registered a score of 0 in the democracy index, the lowest score in the index.[21]

An often emphasized explanation for the persistence of autocratic regimes in oil states is associated with the mechanisms of a *'rentier* state' created by oil revenues and the associated coercion and/or corruption (Jensen and Wantchekon, 2004). Indeed, at the core of the autocratic regime in place in Cameroon is the existence of an oil revenue rent and, more significantly, the secrecy surrounding its size and usage. We saw in Section 2.3 that a very important share of the country's oil take was unaccounted for. We now turn to this specific question of lack of accountability and transparency in the petroleum sector in Cameroon and, in particular, the role played by donors in influencing oil revenue transparency.[22]

2.6.2 Oil revenue transparency and donors' role and relationships

Secrecy has been the norm in the oil sector in Cameroon since the beginning of oil production. Although the government of Cameroon has agreed to gradually provide more transparency over the period, mainly in response to donor pressure, the situation, as we will see, is still very far from full transparency and accountability.

2.6.2.1 *Periods of transparency in oil revenues*

The level of transparency in the oil sector during the last three decades could be divided into five main periods.

First period: 1977–79 'opaque'   At the time of the discovery of oil off the west coast of Cameroon and its subsequent commercial production in 1977, there was no specific state structure in existence to regulate the sector or the relations with IOCs. Responsibilities regarding the management of the sector, relationships with oil companies and the use of oil revenues were directly assumed by the country's president. Full secrecy surrounded contractual arrangements with IOCs, and public oil revenues were deposited in secret accounts (Delancey, 1989). Various authors have speculated about the destination of the oil revenues. Benjamin and Devarajan (1986) support the view that they were deposited outside the Cameroonian banking system. In particular, despite Cameroon's obligation through membership of the Central African Currency Union (*Banque des Etats de l'Afrique Centrale*) to keep its official reserves in the Bank of France, the government of Cameroon was reportedly accumulating sizeable foreign exchange outside the Bank of France, probably in US banks. This secrecy surrounding oil revenues during this initial period has not been lifted since then. Hence, this period could be seen as one of total opacity in the management of oil resources, the negotiation of oil contacts and the management of oil revenues by the president. How much revenues accrued to these secret foreign accounts, and their use, has never been established.

Second period: 1980–86 'secret accounts'　In 1980, the SNH was created to assume responsibility for the oil sector, in particular to oversee the relationships with oil companies and manage oil revenues. Despite the creation of the public corporation, the president of the Republic did not abandon control over the oil sector. The SNH was placed under his direct authority with the SNH administrative board's president headed by the Secretary General of the presidency and the SNH president appointed by the country's president. To date, these fundamental institutional arrangements defining presidential control over SNH have not been modified. Furthermore, the creation of the SNH did not modify the level of secrecy surrounding oil revenues. As during the first period, oil revenues transferred by IOCs or derived from SNH direct oil sales were deposited in secret bank accounts.

Citizens had virtually no information on the level or usage of oil revenues. Indeed, during the economic boom period that accompanied the oil boom, very little information circulated openly in the country about oil sector activities. Oil revenues were not an openly discussed issue, and citizens had very little means of getting information about the sector. The government of Cameroon is highly centralized and secretive. At this time, in particular, no dissidence was tolerated, a policy enforced at times by violent measures (French National Assembly, 1999).

With no official information about oil revenues available, the population had to rely on vague statements made by high-level officials during this period.

The population was also repeatedly told that the country's oil reserves were very limited and would, at best, last a decade. These beliefs that oil revenues were modest and transitory helped to reduce expectations relating to the importance of the oil manna, along with the need for public scrutiny.

Third period: 1987–90 'off-budget' When the external shocks hit the country, starting in 1985, the government had just adopted its sixth 5-year plan (1986–90). The authorities first chose to push ahead with their state-led development strategy, and eventually tried to reduce spending as discussed in Section 2.4. However, investments and wage bills in the boom period were hard to roll back, and large deficits and domestic arrears appeared. Discussions were initiated with the IMF and the World Bank in 1987, leading to the signing of an IMF stand-by-agreement in 1988. It would be the first in a series of eight IMF agreements to date and an equal number with the World Bank.

A year after the first IMF agreement, a first structural adjustment loan (SAL) was completed with the World Bank with the support of various bilateral and multilateral donors such as the African Development Bank. The SAL sought to reduce the role of the state in the economy and liberalize and reform several sectors, especially banking, insurance and labour laws.

Two breakthroughs with regard to oil revenue transparency are directly associated with these first agreements with Bretton Woods (BW) organizations. The first was immediately visible during the negotiations of the stand-by-agreement, as oil revenues appeared in the state's finance law for the first time. Indeed, oil revenue transfers under the heading *Redevance pétrolières* were reported as an off-budget account in the budget for the first time in 1987.[23]

The second breakthrough in revenue transparency during that period was the first World Bank and IMF scrutiny of Cameroonian oil revenues. In a confidential 1987 Country Economic Memorandum, the World Bank presents, for the first time, estimates of oil revenues transferred from the secret accounts to the budget for the period 1980–85. These estimates were, however, speculative given the Cameroonian authorities' refusal to provide official oil revenue figures to the BW organizations. Estimates were thus constructed by the World Bank using various independent data sources (for example, major commercial banks, Bank of Central African States (BEAC) accounts).

Although estimating revenues was an important first step towards increasing transparency in the sector, the BW organizations did not sanction the authorities regarding the secret contractual arrangements with the IOCs, nor the use of secret bank accounts or the overall 'secrecy surrounding critical oil-sector data' (World Bank, 1987: ii).

Indeed, transparency in the management of oil resources was not seen as paramount during that period. Although the World Bank perceived the lack of transparency as presenting shortcomings,[24] it simultaneously considered the practice to favour good public resources management, in particular by preventing undue expectations from the public.

The first doubts about the potential negative effect on accountability of secrecy in the sector were raised in a 1988 World Bank report. However, the report again sides with the Cameroonian authorities' approach, emphasizing the advantages that secrecy presents for reducing public expectations:

> While this secrecy has potentially dubious effects on the responsibility and accountability for public revenues, it does presumably have the benefit of reducing various pressures to increase government spending, which emerge once it becomes clear that the government is flush with funds.
>
> World Bank (1988: 36)

Overall, BW organizations' reports during that period lauded the government of Cameroon for the management of the budget and the secrecy surrounding oil revenues: 'The policy of using discreetly the revenues from oil-production sharing to finance additional investments and various expenditures through the extra-budgetary accounts . . . permitted the Government to avoid excessive public expectations and was probably the key to its prudent management of oil resources and external borrowing' (World Bank, 1987: 26).

However, around 1989, when it was becoming clear that Cameroon was facing Dutch disease symptoms, the opinions of analysts and the BW organizations about the 'prudent management' of the Cameroonian authorities started to change (for example, Benjamin *et al.*, 1989).

Furthermore, authors such as Jua (1993) believed that the secrecy was a scam by the authorities to hide misappropriation of funds. Also, despite the official appearance of oil revenue transfers in the finance laws starting in 1988, van de Walle (1994: 141) posited the existence of important secret oil accounts controlled by the President.

Fourth period: 1991–99 'partial SNH audits'   Another milestone in terms of oil revenue transparency was reached in 1991, the year of the second adjustment programme with the IMF. For the first time that year, some components of SNH activities were partially audited. That same year, the first warnings about the lack of transparency in government of Cameroon activities were issued by the World Bank.

A year later, the World Bank issued its most severe criticisms (probably to date) about the Cameroonian authorities' mismanagement of funds and lack of accountability. In the confidential 1992 *Country Strategy Paper*, which would never even be officially released internally, for the first time, the World Bank specifically raises the problems of corruption in Cameroon. It calls for deep governance reforms and forecasts problems in future lending operations if no remedies are found.

> In a tribalized and often corrupt administration, public policy is subverted to serve private interests and resources are wasted or diverted to private use. The administration is overly centralized and decision making authority too highly concentrated. [. . .] There is widespread lack of transparency and accountability. [. . .] further lending operations are unlikely to achieve their objectives in the absence of reforms in governance and institutional capacity.
>
> World Bank (1992: 9–10)

Although the 1992 *Country Strategy Paper* clearly identified governance problems and called for explicit institutional reforms regarding transparency and the role of the SNH, most of these reforms have yet to be implemented. As we will see, these issues haunt the World Bank and IMF to this day.

Still, despite the non-implementation of these fundamental governance reforms and the slow pace of other less fundamental reforms, BW organizations and bilateral donors' lending activities went forward (for details, see Gauthier and Zeufack, 2010). Indeed, following the CFAF devaluation in 1994, given Cameroon's loss of creditworthiness for International Bank for Reconstruction and Development (IBRD) lending, a second structural adjustment credit was developed by the International Development Association (IDA), the World Bank concessional window (for details, see Gauthier and Zeufack, 2010). The World Bank 1994 adjustment programme once again underlined the need to improve accountability and transparency in the oil sector.

As part of the aid package, a series of reforms were to be implemented by the government of Cameroon, including audits of SNH operations, consolidated statements of its operations and partial privatization.[25]

Various other World Bank reports during the period also emphasized the weak level of governance in the country. For instance, a 1996 report underlines the high level of corruption affecting all components of society, and questions the legitimacy of the government.

> The legitimacy of the present administration is broadly challenged among civil society, not just among fringe secessionist elements. Falling living standards and collapsing social services, since the oil boom started to wane, have sapped taxpayer discipline, just as flagrant corruption and rent-seeking activities feeding on the declining State have undermined social solidarity . . . [. . .] . . . and led to a governance gap.
>
> World Bank (1996: 2)

Despite these bleak diagnoses and various recommendations for reforms included in the World Bank and IMF aid packages, very little progress on the governance and oil transparency front were made during this period. Nevertheless, in August 1997, a new 3-year Economic and Financial Programme supported by the IMF's Poverty and Growth Alleviation Facility (PAGF), as well as the third structural adjustment credit (SAC III) of the World Bank, were signed.

Hence, a decade after the first adjustment programme was launched, a new generation of reforms was put forward. Both BW organizations programmes included a reform agenda dealing with governance and corruption issues, in particular: (1) improvement in public finances and expenditure management; (2) greater transparency in the management of public affairs; and (3) anti-corruption efforts.

In June 2000, the IMF considered that the government of Cameroon was achieving sufficient progress in its reform agenda and declared that the 1997–2000 programme had reached a satisfactory conclusion. According to the IMF, the reform programme had led to a series of economic and structural reforms that have contributed to improving governance in the country, in particular in the oil sector.

Interestingly enough, during that period, while the Cameroonian authorities were receiving praise from donors, the country also received, two years in a row, the dubious distinction of being declared the most corrupt country in the world according to the TI corruption index.

Fifth period: 2000–present 'partial verification HIPC/EITI'   The year 2000 could be seen as the beginning of a new stage in oil revenue transparency. The satisfactory completion of the 1997–2000 IMF lending programme led to a potentially huge reward for the government of Cameroon, the establishment of an IMF- and World Bank-supported Heavily Indebted Poor Countries (HIPC) facility, which would ultimately erase most of Cameroon's external public debt.[26]

The debt reduction package put forward as part of the HIPC initiative was substantial. Including the 'traditional' reduction given by the Paris and London Clubs, the debt reduction was about US$4.9 billion (in 1999 net present value (NPV) terms) (World Bank, 2006a).

In theory, the HIPC *ex ante* conditionality approach would constitute an increase in incentive for the country to reform. This was indeed the hope of HIPC designers.

The HIPC programme was designed with a series of specific policy targets attached to conventional IMF operations in the country during the period. In exchange for debt alleviation, the country was asked to commit to a new round of reforms and implement a series of specific measures. The IMF recognized the high level of corruption and poor governance in the country and again called for new reforms:

> The quality of public services is poor, and corruption widespread. This reflects the very poor state of governance with respect to public resource mobilization and management, service delivery, and oversight functions.
>
> IMF (2000: 23)

Again, as was the case in previous reform programmes initiated by the BW organizations, specific emphasis was placed on improving accountability in public management and transparency, particularly in the oil sector.

However, instead of carrying out fundamental institutional reforms in the oil sector called for in the decision point documents, the government of Cameroon chose to demonstrate its commitment by adopting a 5-year National Governance Programme (*Programme National de Gouvernance*, PNG I) in 2000. The programme aimed at fighting corruption, strengthening public financial management, transparency, accountability and participation in public affairs, and improving justice and human rights. In itself, the adoption of the PNG was seen as a milestone for the government of Cameroon by the BW organizations. The HIPC's completion point was to be reached in 2004. However, the deadline was missed because of various delays and difficulties in implementing reforms. To prove its commitment anew, the government of Cameroon adopted a second PNG in 2005. Furthermore, in March 2005, it announced its intention to join the Extractive Industries Transparency Initiative (EITI) to signal its determination to improve governance in the oil sector. We will discuss this initiative in detail below.

Following these last minute commitments, the HIPC completion point was declared in 2006, which represented a windfall of about US$5 billion for the government of Cameroon. The HIPC completion point documents proudly report that the action plan for improving governance and combating corruption has been satisfactorily implemented by the government of Cameroon.[27] The report was highly optimistic about the progress accomplished during the HIPC period.

However, another World Bank document released in the same year presents an opposite view on the pace of reforms in Cameroon.

> . . . after Cameroon reached HIPC completion point in April 2006, the drive seems to have lost momentum and is now stalled [. . .] Obviously, a rekindled effort is needed from the GoC if its well-publicized anticorruption campaign is to remain credible to the populations, gain steam and help improve governance, the business climate and the effectiveness of the administration.
>
> World Bank (2006a: 163)

2.6.2.2 Extractive Industries Transparency Initiative (EITI)

As mentioned above, another step put forward by the Cameroonian authorities before the HIPC completion point was adherence to the EITI initiative. The initiative put forward by EITI international, a non-governmental organization (NGO) based in Oslo, seeks to strengthen governance in developing countries by improving transparency and accountability in the resource sectors. It is based on a voluntary approach whereby developing country governments and companies involved in the extractive sectors are encouraged to disclose the amounts paid to or received by them. The information is then presented to an independent third party for verification and subsequently disclosed to the population.

The World Bank perceived important benefits from the initiative:

Cameroon's recent decision to adhere to the Extractive Industries Transparency Initiative (EITI) and swift actions by the GoC to comply with EITI guidance constitute important signals to improve governance in oil and is likely to boost transparency and credibility, and hence effectiveness.

World Bank (2006a: 69)

In September 2008, 21 countries were listed as candidates, including 14 African countries. None has yet achieved the 'compliant' status, which requires going through a validation process within 2 years of becoming a candidate.

In Cameroon, two EITI committees were established, which comprise representatives of the state, parastatals, private oil companies and civil society.[28] To implement the disclosure process part of the initiative, starting in 2006, an independent conciliator collected and reconciled data on petroleum production, payments made by the oil companies to the government and the corresponding receipts by the government for the period 2001–05. Two EITI reconciliation reports for Cameroon have been published,[29] which have been praised by the IMF and World Bank (IMF, 2007b: 69, Article IV). However, the EITI reports and process in Cameroon could be criticized on a number of fronts, in particular the following:

(1) Compensation and financing of EITI committees   There are important problems linked to the source of financing of EITI committees and potential conflict of interest associated with abnormal levels of compensation for committee members (van Hulten, 2008b). Although the World Bank had established a trust fund in collaboration with the EITI partners to support EITI implementation, in Cameroon, the Ministry of Economy and Finance (MEF) became partly responsible for financially supporting the committees, and the Minister of Finance has discretion over the compensation of committee members. Members' compensation, initially set at CFAF 100,000 per meeting, reaches CFAF 500,000 (about US$1000) (which is more than twice the regular monthly salary of a university professor and more than the country's annual GDP per capita) if the agenda of the meeting involves a lengthy paper. Presence at a meeting is not required to receive the compensation (van Hulten, 2008b).

In addition, there has been a multiplication of subcommittees which meet several times a month. Every committee member sits on more than one subcommittee, raising their compensation by a multiple. The

EITI process has hence become a very lucrative business, especially in relative terms for NGOs and other civil society members.[30] This raises the problem of conflict of interest as committee members become, in practice, paid employees of the MEF and see their incentives to support decisions that go against government interest weakened considerably.

(2) Reconciliation vs. audit   Another shortcoming in the EITI process is associated with the initiative's rules themselves. Despite a unique labelling system, the EITI process allows countries to use discretion in the application of its so-called 'international standard'. In particular, countries could choose whether to use a simple reconciliation process of declared payments and revenues of government and firms, or whether to go further and allow payment and revenue data to be audited under accepted international auditing standards (World Bank, 2008: 23–4). Countries could thus adapt the process and make key decisions on the scope of the EITI divulgation process, which lead to very different types of EITI programmes.

In Cameroon, the government decided not to allow audits of oil revenues and only to implement a reconciliation process. The EITI process is hence weakened considerably by the use of unaudited revenue and payment data. Indeed, the consultant report states:

> The audit and certification of data are not included in our scope of work. . . . It is not our task to review the completeness of the sources of the considered incomes and of the oil companies . . . our intervention does not aim at discovering errors, illegal acts or other irregularities, nor at verifying whether the sources of the oil companies' incomes and the state and its organs are actually comprehensive.
>
> EITI Cameroon (2006: 13)[31]

(3) Inadequacy of the reconciliation reports   Another shortcoming lies in the poor quality of the information provided in the official public documents published as part of the EITI process in Cameroon, because fundamental information is missing. In particular, only aggregated figures for the country's total oil production are presented, with no details provided on each of the companies' production and payments to SNH and the Treasury.[32] These aggregated figures lose even more relevance given that the list of IOCs having provided financial statements is incomplete.[33] Furthermore, only a limited number of financial transfers between IOCs and SNH were examined, and some categories of taxes and royalties were excluded.

Further, while the process should have included the analysis of the declared transfers by oil companies to the tax authorities, the Treasury and SNH, in practice, only a subset of oil companies operating in Cameroon were analysed by the consultant.[34]

(4) Technical capacity of committee members   Another important problem associated with the EITI process is related to the lack of technical capacity of the EITI follow-up committee in Cameroon, especially among NGO representatives. As reported by the *Declare What You Pay Coalition* in Cameroon, very few NGO committee members had the necessary training to understand the content of EITI reports, which greatly weakens the capacity of the committee to act as a watchdog of the transparency process.

(5) Validation process   Finally, as mentioned above, Cameroon hopes to become an EITI 'compliant' member before 2010. A 2-day pre-validation seminar was held in Yaoundé in September 2008, which was attended by key players in the oil sector. Although the World Bank and the EITI international representative expressed support for a positive review of the Cameroon candidacy at that meeting, the pre-validation exercise and the overall EITI process in Cameroon seems very weak and flawed. Indeed, the participants at this pre-validation process were mainly interested in how to publicise and develop a positive image of the oil sector, rather than in the content of the transparency initiative process. Furthermore, as discussed above, the reconciliation exercise in Cameroon has very limited scope and fundamental information is missing.

The EITI validation process does not provide sufficient rigour to the exercise to ensure real transparency of the sector and the release and verification of the production and financial information provided by IOCs and the government. These information and reconciliation processes should be compulsory, and be done through formal audits of the sector. They should also be inclusive of all activities and players.

Given its overall lack of rigour in Cameroon, the EITI process risks becoming just another rubber-stamping mechanism to ensure additional funding for the country with no guarantee of proper usage. Hastily validating this process could prove harmful to Cameroon as it will relieve the pressure on the country to implement much needed reforms to improve accountability and transparency in managing public resources. It would also certainly damage the reputation of the EITI as a transparency certification process on the international scene.

2.6.3 Cameroon's commitments vs. actual governance reforms

The bottom line is that the government has been very keen to make commitments to donors to carry out governance reforms over the last 20 years, with few results. In practice, very few institutional reforms have been truly implemented. When institutional reforms have taken place, they have been very slowly enacted and, when put in practice, were mainly symbolic and inefficient in promoting better governance.

For instance, the creation of an audit chamber (*Cour des Comptes*) was announced in January 1996 (Law no. 96-06; 18 January 1996) to oversee external audits of government activities. The law creating the chamber, however, was only passed 7 years later in 2003 (World Bank, 2006a: 154), and the chamber became partly operational only in 2006 with some hiring of staff. As of 2008, it is not yet operational. Furthermore, the office has not yet completed a review of government accounts and it is not expected to do so before 2012.[35]

Moreover, a government plan to fight corruption was put forward in 1999 with the creation of a National Observatory. It later became the National Anti-Corruption Commission (*Commission Nationale Anti-Corruption*, CONAC) in 2006. Although donors labelled the commission as independent and praised its establishment, CONAC is not yet operational (as of November 2008) and is not independent. Indeed, currently, CONAC's president and members, budget, work plan and the follow-up of its reports are all determined by the country's president (van Hulten, 2008b: 17).

Another example of hollow institutions: in 2006, a law was adopted prescribing that all high-level government officials, from the president down to the director level, must declare their possessions at the beginning and end of terms of office. However, the commission that was expected to enforce the law has never been created.

The inefficiency of institutional reforms in Cameroon could probably be best exemplified by SNH's oil accounts and cash transfers. As seen above, since its creation, SNH has engaged in transferring oil revenues towards discretionary activities under the guidance of the country's president. During what we called the second transparency period (1980–88), the revenues were directed towards secret accounts. These revenues were partly officially transferred to the budget starting in 1988 and later transparency periods. Over the years, however, SNH retained a fraction of the revenues for discretionary activities outside the budget process. Table 2.3 presents an estimation of these transfers for the period 2003–07.

Table 2.3 Cameroon cash advance by SNH (%)

	2003	2004	2005*	2006	2007
Presidency	21.7	37.5	24.8	NA	NA
Defence	34.1	32.8	63.5	NA	NA
Cameroon Airlines	32.0	15.0	5.7	NA	NA
Other	12.2	14.6	6.0	NA	NA
Total	100.0	100.0	100.0	NA	NA
				NA	NA
As a percentage of SNH's revenue	24.6	23.0	19.3	2.9	5.1
As a percentage of total government revenue	5.1	4. 9	5.0	1.1	1.9
As a percentage of budget expenditures	13.1	10.8	14.4	1.4	2.3
As a percentage of GDP	1.1	1.1	1. 0	0. 2	0.4
Memo					
As a percentage of budgetary allocation					
Presidency	44.5	71.1	70.2	84.7	40.0
Defence	59.7	54.0	92.6	26.8	13.9

NA, not available.

*Jan–July estimation.

Sources: Cossé (2006: 15, Table 2) for 2003–05; IMF (2007b: 40, article IV) for 2006; SNH's data for 2007 and discussion with World Bank Cameroon representative; presidency and defence data in Dynamique Citoyenne (2008: 23) for the years 2006–07.

Donors' documents frequently mention these problems of direct SNH transfers, and calls for the closing of this tap have become a recurring theme over the years. From as early as 1991, this objective is put forward in World Bank and IMF documents as a required reform in the oil sector. Nearly 10 years later, the HIPC Decision Point document announced that these transfers have basically stopped due to the efficiency of the reforms put in place.

There have been major advances in transparency in the use of oil revenues: SNH is subject since 1997 to annual audits by an international reputed firm . . . (and) . . . *Virtually all the oil revenues are now transferred from the National Oil company (SNH) to the budget.*

IMF (2000: 16) (our emphasis)

However, during the following years, SNH transfers continued, whereas subsequent donor reports again claim that the transfers have been discontinued (World Bank, 2006a: 52–3).

The latest step in the attempt by the IMF to stop the discretionary transfers has been to create a compulsory performance criterion in the IMF programme.[36] The objective was to 'convert the quantitative benchmark on cash spending by SNH to a performance criterion, reflecting the authorities' commitment to refrain from extra-budgetary spending' (IMF, 2007b: 27). The future will tell whether the IMF will be able to hold the country to its commitment in this regard.

2.6.3.1 Gap in revenues and stages of transparency

An even clearer demonstration of the symbolic nature of the country's commitment to reform is to look at the evolution of oil revenues not transferred to the budget during the last two decades of donor-supported adjustment programmes.

In Section 2.3, we estimated the oil revenues accruing to the nation over the period using independent estimates of oil production and compared them with the official figures transferred to the budget. It is interesting to examine the evolution of the oil revenue gaps during the five periods of oil revenue transparency identified to see whether the reforms put forward over the years have been more symbolic than effective in reducing unaccounted oil revenues.

Table 2.4 presents the breakdown of the gap in oil revenues measured in Section 2.4 according to the five periods of transparency.

We observe in Table 2.4 that, during the opaque period 1977–79, the level of unaccounted oil revenue amounts to about US$334 million.

Table 2.4 Breakdown of cumulative gap in government oil revenues (in US$ million)

Period	Opaque	Secret accounts	Off-budget	Partial SNH audit	Partial audit/ HIPC, EITI	Cumulative gap
Years	1977–79	1980–86	1987–90	1991–99	2000–06	1977–2006
Period cumulative gap	333.5	5516.0	414.0	1794.3	2602.7	10,660.4
Yearly average of the period	111.2	788.0	103.5	199.4	371.8	
Total CHB amount (1980–86)		4726.0				

CHB, Extra Budgetary Account (*Compte Hors Budget*); HIPC, Heavily Indebted Poor Countries; EITI, Extractive Industries Transparency Initiative.

This is a relatively small amount compared with subsequent years, but these were the initial years of oil production in Cameroon and the production levels were quite limited during these first 3 years.[37]

During the oil boom period of 1980–87, oil revenues were still being placed in secret accounts and were not included in reporting procedures. Our estimate of the unaccounted oil revenues is about US$5.5 billion.

During the years after the collapse of the economy, the government tried to maintain the same state-led development strategy as discussed in Section 2.4. Interestingly enough, the official oil revenues appearing in the budget during that period are almost equivalent to the estimated oil revenues. The estimated unaccounted revenues for the period are only about US$76 million (period 1987–88). As mentioned previously (see Section 2.4), it appears that, during the crisis years, before the establishment of donor-supported assistance programmes, the government adequately transferred oil revenues to the budget and the oil gap was minimal.

In 1991, as part of donor negotiations, the first audit of the SNH was officially realized, and the management of oil revenues should have improved. However, the reverse situation is observed. With the donor-supported economy, the level of unaccounted oil revenues increased to US$1.8 billion during the period 1991–99.

The same paradoxical situation is observed for the subsequent period. With the introduction of the HIPC programme with its various performance criteria and the launching of the EITI initiative in 2005, the situation was expected to improve. Unfortunately, the opposite situation is observed. The estimated level of unaccounted revenues has never been higher: an estimated US$2.6 billion for the period 2000–06.

It therefore appears that, despite all their good intentions and all the commitments they were able to obtain from the country, donors were not able to bring about effective governance reforms in the country. The situation of oil revenue management does not seem to have improved; on the contrary, the SNH discretionary transfers have continued, but even more importantly, the level of unaccounted oil revenues actually appears to have increased over the years.

2.6.3.2 CHOC (Change Habits Oppose Corruption) programme

The obvious very slow pace of anti-corruption and governance reform progress in the country has been noted by some donors. A group of six bilateral donors supported by the United Nations Development Programme (UNDP) therefore decided to put together a special anti-corruption programme, CHOC, to investigate the situation on the ground, including the inefficiency of the official anti-corruption commission, CONAC, and propose improvements.

In its first main report in June 2008, CHOC, headed by a former deputy from the Netherlands, presented very negative conclusions. Essentially, it argues that the assumptions on which all the programmes put forward by donors are based – that the Cameroonian authorities had the intention to reform, to pursue the good of the population and reduce corruption – were wrong. The commission report states:

> The most important basic assumption of the donors funding project CHOC and this is not different in other documents, strategies, plans, reviews, etc. regarding Cameroon, is that those in economic and political power in Cameroon want to end corruption [. . .]. Should we not ask the question whether it is reasonable to expect that those in power stop the rich flow of means that they enjoy at the moment?
>
> van Hulten (2008a: 1)

The CHOC commission also declined to collaborate with the anti-corruption agency, CONAC, which was considered unfit to pursue its mission as long as it had not gained independence from the presidency.

> . . . such collaboration, given the present state of CONAC, is impossible as CONAC is unfit for the fight against corruption in Cameroon. [. . .] Essential is that CONAC becomes independent and operational.
>
> van Hulten (2008b: 9)

The report sees the direct link between the presidency and CONAC, perceiving the official anti-corruption activities in a political perspective: 'the official fight against corruption is used for political purposes by the President' (van Hulten, 2008b: 17).[38]

Furthermore, the report attributes a direct role to oil and forestry companies in exacerbating corruption, and further mentions that '. . . national and expatriate companies fuel the corruption to maintain their position in the world markets (petrol, wood) . . .' (van Hulten, 2008b: 1). The report concludes that 'methodology and tactics of the fight against corruption have to be re-invented acknowledging that the political will does not exist' (van Hulten, 2008b: 2).

2.6.4 Conclusion

Cameroon has a long history of poor governance and corruption, and a similarly lengthy donor history. The country has been evolving under donor-supported adjustment programmes for the last 20 years. During that period, the level of transparency in oil revenues has improved slightly, yet the impact on the level of estimated corruption has been slight. Donors have been actively trying to move the country along the path to reforms, including those related to governance issues. In several official donor documents, institutional reform objectives specify anti-corruption and governance initiatives.

Ultimately, however, weak monitoring and incomplete reform implementation have prevailed. Most institutional reforms carried out during the period were more symbolic than effective. The fundamental institutional reforms that could have led to improvements in accountability and transparency – notably the creation of an independent energy regulatory agency – were not pushed to the forefront and have yet to be implemented. The Audit Court and Anti-corruption Commission are still not functional, nor are they independent from the presidency's direct influence. The SNH, under the control of the president, retains its multiple roles of joint venture associate of all oil activities, manager of the country's oil revenues and regulator of the oil sector. Furthermore, despite theoretical progress in transparency, the gap in oil revenues paradoxically appears to have increased over time, notably during the last stages of the implementation of HIPC and EITI.

Hence, after 20 years of adjustments and reforms, the oil sector remains at the centre of rent extraction, regime maintenance and corruption. Although they have been the main advocate of governance reforms, donors have played a determining role in maintaining the autocratic regime in place over the years. They have provided the country with multi-billion dollar financial support since 1988 in the form of loans and grants. This funding has led to the accumulation of a huge external debt, which, ultimately, has been forgiven by the same donors through multilateral and bilateral debt relief, rewarding the authorities for good macroeconomic performance and policies. However, governance has clearly suffered despite being officially on the agenda since the early 1990s.

Cameroon's case is interesting as it is symptomatic of much larger problems in donor–recipient country relationships and, in particular, of the difficulties in dealing with autocratic regimes. Donors largely assumed they were dealing with a well-intentioned government, as most of the programmes put forward rested on the assumption that the authorities truly intended to reform and act for the good of the population. Compounding this false assumption is the lack of institutional memory and misaligned incentives. Donor agencies' officers tend to have weak incentives to focus on governance and corruption issues and to monitor recipient governments. The incentive structure is designed to uphold a good working relationship with client countries rather than alienating them by pushing for difficult choices often required in governance reforms. Indeed, promotion and remuneration structures depend on the satisfaction of clients' objectives and staff capacity to implement projects and programmes. Furthermore, there are currently no adequate microlevel indicators of governance, corruption and public service delivery, allowing proper recipient country monitoring and comparison over time and across countries.

The last step in this donor–recipient game is the EITI initiative, which, in itself, is a good potential first step towards opening up the sector to more scrutiny. However, the implementation of the initiative in Cameroon is deeply flawed. The oil data verification and reconciliation process is badly mishandled. Furthermore, EITI international seems itself to have an incentive to turn a blind eye to these shortcomings in the implementation process in Cameroon. Nonetheless, giving a 'compliant' status to Cameroon without the proper level of data quality and verification would clearly jeopardize the initiative itself and the seal of quality it represents.

2.7 Summary

Oil has been a curse for Cameroon, one of the potentially richest countries in sub-Saharan Africa. Although the discovery of oil in 1977 and initial prudent management accentuated hopes, Cameroon has become an example of growth collapse. GDP contracted by 5 per cent on average per year, a combined 27 per cent over the 8-year period, dropping per capita income in 1993 to half its 1986 level. In 2007, Cameroon was still poorer than in 1985. In this chapter, we have analysed the oil sector in Cameroon and, in particular, the level and use of the oil rent. We argue that, despite advantageous contracting arrangements and an 'oil take' of about 67 per cent, the autocratic nature of the political regime and the political dynamics in Cameroon have led to very poor institutional arrangements for oil revenue management.

Although Cameroon may have captured a sizeable portion of its oil rent – around 67 per cent – only about 46 per cent of total oil revenues accruing to the government between 1977 and 2006 may have been transferred to the budget. The remaining 54 per cent is not properly accounted for and may have been looted. Oil revenues were not invested domestically in physical, social or human capital as a priority, but 'saved' abroad and ultimately dilapidated. In the mid-1980s, the government behaved as if the oil boom was permanent and the 1986 crisis temporary, increasing borrowing and consumption compounded by reduced investment leading to disastrous development outcomes.

This chapter argues that poor governance is the culprit. The lack of a transparent and accountable framework to manage Cameroon's oil revenues facilitated the plundering of resources. This lack of transparency and accountability translated into a failure to engage in medium- to long-term development planning for the country. The lack of a medium- to long-term framework for infrastructure development or of a long-term vision for the country has led to predatory behaviour and widespread corruption. Corruption and weak governance are at the heart of the problem, a problem self-reinforced by oil revenues, lengthy political tenure and lack of political freedom.

Donors have been pushing for improved governance and transparency in the oil sector for the past 20 years without significant success. The EITI, although a good initiative, is also at high risk of capture. There is a need for reforms to reduce incentives for collusion, for example creating an independent energy regulatory agency. Also, donors should develop and make use of better microlevel indicators of governance and corruption and of quality of service delivery to avoid capture. A case in point is the EITI process, which needs more tightening and more serious validation if it is to improve transparency in the oil industry and make a genuine difference.

Acknowledgements

This chapter was written as part of a project funded by the Revenue Watch Institute, which acknowledges the support of the Bill and Melinda Gates Foundation. We thank participants at seminars and conferences at the Oxford Centre for Analysis of Resources Rich Economies (Oxford, December 2008), the Global Development Network (Kuwait City, February 2009), the Centre d'économie de la Sorbonne (Paris, April 2009) and CERDI (Clermont-Ferrand, France, April 2009) for their comments. We are particularly grateful to Paul Collier, Rick van der Ploeg and Anthony Venables from Oxford University for valuable comments. We thank Luc Désiré Omgba for research assistance and numerous staff from the World Bank for helpful discussions. We are indebted to the numerous people from the civil society for sharing their invaluable insights during field visits in Cameroon. All errors remain ours.

Notes

1 Cameroonian exports are made up of around ten products, including primary aluminium, cotton, coffee and bananas (World Bank, 2006a: 6).

2 The respective shares of oil production in Cameroon in 2006 of Total, Pecten and Perenco are 68 per cent, 23 per cent and 9 per cent.

3 As of 30 June 2008, 11 permits and exploration authorizations for areas of 14,522,28 km^2 and 14 concessions and authorization of extraction for areas of 2,248,84 km^2 were active (Tamfu, 2008).

4 Notably, there is an insignificant delimitation between the SNH as a regulatory agency and as the party to an oil contract (World Bank, 2006a).

5 SNH equity shares include participation in the operating committee of joint ventures and on the board of directors of the IOCs (World Bank, 1990).

6 A differential is established for the different types of crude oil and takes into account the selling price of each operator. These official prices are then promulgated by the president of the Republic.

7 This rate is specified in the 1978 Law, but IOCs could also be subjected to a more advantageous rate of 48.6475 per cent, which is the dividend tax inclusive rate of the general tax code. Compared with the general tax code, rules regarding the determination of taxable income are more advantageous for IOCs as the limits placed on certain deductions (interest, technical assistance) are eliminated and accelerated depreciation is allowed. Also, IOCs' revenues are calculated on the basis of official prices posted by the government instead of the actual market selling prices (World Bank, 1990: 92–3).

8 IOCs are, indeed, entitled to a fixed net rent of 13 per cent of the gross rent after taxes and all other fiscal obligations. This means that the production royalties are variable and could be negative if necessary (that is, transfer to the IOC) to ensure the minimum mining rent. The minimum rent is calculated for each exploration permit (for examples of calculation, see EITI Cameroon, 2007: 15).

9 The concession contract gives IOCs the right to dispose of hydrocarbons extracted from a specified perimeter. The contract establishes the rights and obligations of the state and the holder during the period of validity of research permits and, in the case of discovery of commercially developable oil deposits, during the period of validity of the operating concession. The holder of the concession contract finances oil operations and collects hydrocarbons during the period of validity of the contract, subject to the rights of the state to collect royalty in 'kind'. The production-sharing contract offers an exclusive operating licence to its holder, for a specified area. Production is shared between the owner and the state in accordance with the terms of the contract. Permission duration is 30 years for liquid hydrocarbons (25 years for solid), and is renewable once for a period of 10 years (Cameroon National Assembly, 1999).

10 Contracts are relatively inclusive and comprise various elements expected in such contracts such as environmental protection, decommissioning and site restoration.

11 Since the adoption of the Oil Code in 1999, ten oil contracts have been signed and four were in negotiation at the end of 2008. Some oil companies are offering to abandon the old regime and operate within the framework of the Petroleum Code (Tamfu, 2008).

12   Before revenue transfers to the public treasury, SNH is entitled to cover two categories of expenditures: (1) Expenditures under the mandate. These expenses consist of expenses incurred for the commercialization of oil on behalf of the state; (2) Association spending: SNH's share of production costs and debt service. These are charged by operators. Exploration expenses are divided equally between SNH and the foreign partners, as are new investment costs (EITI, 2006).

13   It should be noted that the extra-budgetary account is estimated to have represented about US$5.24 billion in 1985. If we subtract the oil revenues traced by the World Bank during the period, the net gap of unaccounted revenues during that period was about US$1.5 billion.

14   Even if we assume that the World Bank estimates of the non-budgetary oil account for the 1980–85 period and the Tables of financial and economic operations (*Tableau des Opérations Financières et Économiques*, TOFE) figures for 1986 were somewhat transferred to the budget, but not reported, which is unlikely, the amount of net oil revenues unaccounted for would still be around US$5.9 billion, equivalent to one-third of the total rent (see Table 2.8).

15   Our calculations are based on oil production data published on the World Bank Adjusted Saving Project website, 2008 edition. However, since the publication of our working paper (Gauthier and Zeufack, 2009), a completely revised version of the oil production data for Cameroon has been published on the WBASP website. Information obtained from WBASP managers indicates that the source of the change is the International Energy Agency (IEA), which obtained the data directly from the Cameroonian government. Although it is not clear what prompted the revision, which affected the last two decades of data, it only adds to the confusion. The new production figures are now even lower than SNH's own numbers. Using the new series, the oil revenue gap would be reduced to about US$5.9 billion during the 1977–2006 period. Using SNH's own production data as a threshold, the difference between Cameroon estimated oil revenues and reported oil revenues during the period is still an impressive US$7 billion or 35.2 per cent of the estimated total oil revenues accruing to the government.

16   DeLancey (1989) and other experts also spoke favourably of Cameroon's good management of the oil revenues.

17   Hartwick's rule suggests that the marginal 'Hotelling rents' on natural resources should be fully saved and re-invested in physical capital, infrastructure or education (see Hartwick, 1977).

18   A Cameroonian journalist, Puis Njawe, was imprisoned in 1976 for daring to ask the question: what should the country do with the upcoming oil revenues?

19   Section 2.5 will elaborate more on transparency issues and highlight the role of international institutions.

20   Cameroon ranked 85 out of 85 countries in the CPI index in 1998, and 98 out of 98 countries in 1999. It currently ranks 141 out of 180 countries in the CPI 2008 (www.transparency.org).

21   See Marshall and Jaggers (2006) database of political indicators.

22   By donors, we mean international financial institutions such as the IMF, the World Bank and the African Development Bank (ADB), together with bilat-

eral donors. The most important bilateral donors in Cameroon are France, Germany and the European Community.

23 Jua (1993: 141) also believes that the IMF placed pressure on Cameroon to include oil revenues in the budget.

24 'Detailed public finance accounts are not available, nor are data on the execution of the extra-budgetary accounts' (World Bank, 1987: 2). 'Official information on oil reserves, production and revenues is not available' (idem: 6). The report states further: 'Overseas earnings from (oil) production are generally held in overseas accounts [. . .] Overseas holdings are generally a closely-held secret' (World Bank, 1987: 32).

25 The IMF reports that audits of SNH activities were performed during the period 1997–2000 by independent accounting firms, and the SNH accounting and data systems were modified to bring them in line with international standards (IMF, 2000, Annex 51). However, these reports do not provide information about the specific nature of these reforms, and audit reports were never made public.

26 During the oil boom and subsequent years, Cameroon had accumulated very important public external debt, which amounted in 1999 to US$7.8 billion (85 per cent of GDP), and absorbed 23 per cent of government revenues (see Section 2.4). Cameroon's large public external debt led the country to face five rescheduling agreements with the Paris Club between 1989 and 1997, and the debt stock was considered unsustainable (World Bank, 2006a: 71). Most of the debt was owed to bilateral donors (69 per cent, including France 25 per cent and Germany 18 per cent) and international organizations.

27 Indeed, in addition to close to US$2 billion in debt alleviation provided by HIPC, the completion point decision was associated with additional relief under the Multilateral Debt Relief Initiative (MDRI) of almost US$3 billion. Overall, the result has been a decrease in the stock of external debt and debt service, reducing the external debt over export and GDP ratio from 153 per cent at end-2005 to 13 per cent at end-2006, and from 33 per cent to 3 per cent in 2006 (World Bank, 2006a: 71).

28 The EITI Follow-up Committee created in June 2005 by the Ministry of Economy and Finance (MEF) is the body in charge of decisions and management of the initiative in Cameroon. The Technical Secretariat is the coordination body of the Follow-up Committee and is also attached to the MEF. The Follow-up Committee was initially supposed to be composed of 15 members, but later grew to 25 (17 from NGOs, three from oil companies and five ministry representatives); it is presided over by the MEF.

29 The first report covers the period 2001–04 and the second the year 2005. The EITI reports on Cameroon are available at www.eitransparency.org.

30 van Hulten (2008b) calls it 'silence money'. Furthermore, the CHOC director expressed disbelief at the request and submitted a formal complaint to the World Bank and IMF representatives, to no avail.

31 In its reconciliation exercise, the EITI consultant (selected by the Follow-up Committee) used data transmitted by oil companies on a requested template instead of making use of audited financial statements by oil companies and SNH. The consultant therefore did not perform an audit or even a limited examination of oil or financial transfers or physical flows from the oil sector as well as flows to and from the government.

32   Although the consultant officially produced two reports, one with detailed figures of disaggregated forms for each of the companies' declared payments and income flows received by the state, and the other with only aggregate figures, only the latter report was made public.

33   Oil companies officially covered in the 2001–04 reconciliation exercise include: Total (E&P) Cameroon, Pecten Cameroon, Perenco Cameroon and Exxon Mobil Cameroon. Oil companies operating in Cameroon excluded from the reconciliation exercise are Euroil Ltd, Amerada Hess, Addax Petroleum, Noble, Grynberg, Philips Petroleum and Turnberry. Furthermore, Exxon Mobil did not transmit financial information (EITI Cameroon, 2007).

34   See footnote 33.

35   EITI pre-validation process discussions, Yaoundé, September 2008.

36   See Gauthier and Zeufack (2010) for further discussions.

37   It is interesting to note that our estimates constructed using independent production figures are very similar to those put forward by the World Bank. Indeed, a 1994 report arrived at the same amount of about US$350 million of undisclosed funds for the period. See Gauthier and Zeufack (2010) for details.

38   The report states: 'The arrest of ministers is best understood as a realignment of political friends and foes by the President, not as a bold move forward in the fight against corruption. It is a handy tool to raise overseas expectations of desirable changes in Cameroon while, at home, they keep friends in line and enemies quiet' (van Hulten, 2008b: 17).

References

Benjamin, N.C. and S. Devarajan (1986) 'Oil Revenues and the Cameroonian Economy' in M.G. Schatzberg and W.I. Zartman (eds) *The Political Economy of Cameroon*. New York: Praeger, pp. 161–88.

Benjamin, N., S. Devarajan and R. Weiner (1989) 'The "Dutch Disease" in a Developing Country: Oil Revenues in Cameroon', *Journal of Development Economics*, 30, 71–89.

BP (2007) *Statistical Review of World Energy 2007*. British Petroleum. Available at www.bp.com.

BP (2008) *Statistical Review of World Energy 2008*. British Petroleum. Available at www.bp.com.

Cameroon National Assembly (1999) *Code Pétrolier Loi no. 99-013*. December 1999. Yaoundé, Cameroon: Cameroon National Assembly.

Collier, P. and A. Hoeffler (2005) 'Resource Rents, Governance, and Conflict', *Journal of Conflict Resolution*, 49, 625–33.

Collier, P., F. van der Ploeg and A. Venables (2009) *Managing Resource Revenues in Developing Economies*. OxCarre Research Paper no. 2009-14. Oxford University.

Cossé, S. (2006) *Strengthening Transparency in the Oil Sector in Cameroon: Why Does it Matter?* IMF policy discussion paper 06/02. Washington, DC: IMF.

DeLancey, M. (1989) *Cameroon: Dependence and independence*. Boulder, CO, and London: Westview Press.

Devarajan, S. and J. de Melo (1987) 'Adjustment with a Fixed Exchange Rate: Cameroon, Cote d'Ivoire and Senegal', *World Bank Economic Review*, May.

Dynamique Citoyenne (2008) 'Budget 2008: L'espérance du point d'achèvement 'est-elle qu'un mirage?'. Yaoundé, Cameroon: Dynamique Citoyenne.

EITI (2005) *Extractive Industries Transparency Initiative: Source Book*, March.

EITI (2006) *Extractive Industries Transparency Initiative: Report of the International Advisory Group.*

EITI Cameroon (2006) 'Reconciliation of the Financial and Physical Flows as regards the Cameroon EITI for the Years 2001–2004'. Committee for the follow up of Cameroon Extractive Industries Transparency Initiative (EITI), Republic of Cameroon, Ministry of Economy and Finance, Mazars and Hart Group.

EITI Cameroon (2007) 'Reconciliation of the Financial and Physical Flows as regards the Cameroon EITI for the Year 2005'. Committee for the follow-up of Cameroon Extractive Industries Transparency Initiative (EITI), Republic of Cameroon, Ministry of Economy and Finance, Mazars and Hart Group, March. Available at http://eitransparency.org/UserFiles/File/cameroon/2nd_cameroon_audit_report_french.pdf, retrieved in March 2008.

EIU (2008) *Cameroon Country Report.* London, UK: Economist Intelligence Unit.

Freedom House (2008) *Freedom in the World 2008: The Annual Survey of Political Rights and Civil Liberties.* Washington, DC: Freedom House.

French National Assembly (1999) *Rapport dRinformation sur le rôle des compagnies pétrolières dans la politique internationale et son impact social et environnemental.* Rapport no 1859-01, Commission des Affaires étrangères, Paris, France. Available at http://www.assemblee-nationale.fr/rap-info/i1859-01.asp, retrieved in July 2008.

Gauthier B. and A.G. Zeufack (2009) 'Governance and Oil Revenues in Cameroon'. Paper presented at the Global Development Network 10th Anniversary Conference, Kuwait City, February 2009.

Gauthier B. and A.G. Zeufack (2010) *Governance and Oil Revenues in Cameroon.* OxCarre Research Paper no. 38, February 2010. Oxford Centre for the Analysis of Resource Rich Economies, Oxford University.

Hartwick, J.M. (1977) 'Intergenerational Equity and the Investing of Rents from Exhaustible Resources', *American Economic Review*, 67, 972–4.

IMF (2000) *Cameroon Article IV Statistical Appendix.* IMF Country Report No. 00/80. Washington, DC: International Monetary Fund.

IMF (2007a) *Cameroon Selected Issues.* IMF Country Report No. 07/287. Washington, DC: International Monetary Fund.

IMF (2007b) *Cameroon Article IV Statistical Appendix.* IMF Country Report No. 07/286. Washington, DC: International Monetary Fund.

Jensen, N. and L. Wantchekon (2004) 'Resource Wealth and Political Regimes in Africa', *Comparative Political Studies*, 37, 816–41.

Jua, N. (1993) 'State, Oil and Accumulation' in P. Geschiere and P. Konings (eds) *Itinéraires d'accumulation au Cameroun/Pathways to Accumulation in Cameroon.* Paris: ASC-Karthala.

Karl, T.L. (2007) 'Ensuring Fairness: The Case for a Transparent Fiscal Social Contract' in Humphreys, Sachs and Stiglitz (eds) *Escaping the Resource Curse.* New York: Columbia University Press, pp. 256–85.

Kaufmann D., M. Mastruzzi and A. Kraay (2008) *Governance Matters VII: Aggregate and Individual Governance Indicators, 1996–2007.* World Bank Policy Research Working Paper No. 4654. Washington, DC: The World Bank.

Marshall M. and K. Jaggers (2006) 'Polity IV Project: Political Regime Characteristics and Transitions, 1800–2006'. Available at http://www.systemicpeace.org/polity/polity4.htm, retrieved in September 2010.

Ngodi, E. (2005) *Gestion des ressources pétrolières et développement en Afrique*. Présentation à la 11ème Assemblée générale du CODESRIA, 6–10 décembre 2005, Maputo, Mozambique.

Sala-i-martin, X. and Subramanian A. (2003) *Addressing the Natural Resource Curse: An Illustration from Nigeria*. NBER Working Paper Series w9804. Cambridge, MA: NBER.

SNH (2007) *The Hydrocarbons Sectors in Cameroon*. APPA Bulletin no. 10. Yaoundé, Cameroon: Societé Nationale des Hydrocarbures.

SNH (2008) 'Presentation of the SNH', Societé Nationale des Hydrocarbures. Available at http://www.snh.cm/, consulted in September 2008.

Tamfu, S. (2008) 'Perspectives for the Petroleum Extraction and Production Sector in Cameroon'. Exploration Manager, SNH. Presented at the Cameroon EITI Workshop, 22–23 September 2008, Yaoundé, Cameroon.

van der Ploeg, F. and A. Venables (2008) *Harnessing Windfall Revenues: Optimal Policies for Resource-Rich Developing Economies*. OxCarre Research Paper no. 2008-09, Oxford Center for the Analysis of Resource Rich Economies, Oxford University.

van de Walle, N. (1994) 'Neopatrimonialism and Democracy in Africa, with an Illustration from Cameroon' in J.A. Widner (ed.) *Economic Change and Political Liberalization in Sub-Saharan Africa*. Baltimore, MD: Johns Hopkins University.

van Hulten, M. (2008a) *Three Months Cameroon: 1st Quarterly Report of the CHOC Project based on the Annual Work Plan 2008*. Yaoundé, Cameroon: UNDP.

van Hulten, M. (2008b), Perception as a cause of corruption, the Cameroon case, Inaugural Lecture at SAXION Academy of Governance & Law, November 7, 2008, ISBN 978-90-811048-3-8.

World Bank (1987) *Cameroon: Recent Performance and Adjustment to Declining Oil Revenues*. Country Economic Memorandum, 6395-CM. Washington, DC: World Bank.

World Bank (1988) *World Development Report 1988: Background Paper*. Washington, DC: World Bank.

World Bank (1990) *Republic of Cameroon Social Dimensions of Adjustment Project*. Report no. 8451-CM. Washington, DC: World Bank.

World Bank (1992) *Country Strategy Paper*. June. Washington, DC: World Bank.

World Bank (1994) *Republic of Cameroon: Economic Recovery Credit*. Country Economic Memorandum, P-6359-M. Washington, DC: World Bank.

World Bank (1996) *Republic of Cameroon Country Assistance Strategy*. Country Economic Memorandum, 15275-CM. Washington, DC: World Bank.

World Bank (2006a) *A New Resolve to Sustain Reforms for Inclusive Growth*. Country Economic Memorandum, 29268-CM. Washington, DC: World Bank.

World Bank (2006b) *Where is the Wealth of Nations? Measuring Capital for the 21st Century*. Washington, DC: World Bank.

World Bank (2008) *Implementing the Extractive Industries Transparency Initiative: Applying Early Lessons from the Field*. Washington, DC: World Bank.

World Economic Forum (2007) *The Global Competitiveness Report 2007–2008*. Geneva, Switzerland: WEF.

Zeufack, A. (2001) *Investissement Privé et Ajustement en Afrique Sub-Saharienne*. Paris: L'Harmattan.

Further Reading

Bolt, K., M. Matete and M. Clemens (2002) *Manual for Calculating Adjusted Net Savings*. Washington, DC: Environment Department, The World Bank. Available at http://siteresources.worldbank.org/INTEEI/1105643-1115814965717/20486606/Savingsmanual2002.pdf, retrieved in July 2008.

Collier, P. (2006) 'Is Aid Oil? An Analysis of Whether Africa can Absorb More Aid', *World Development*, 34, 1482–97.

Cuddington, J. (1989) 'Commodity Export Booms in Developing Countries', *The World Bank Research Observer*, 4, 143–65.

DeLancey, M. and M.D. DeLancey (2000) *Historical Dictionary of the Republic of Cameroon.*. Lanham, MD: Scarecrow Press.

EIU (2007) *Cameroon Country Report*. London, UK: Economist Intelligence Unit.

Fearon, J. (2005) 'Primary Commodities Exports and Civil War', *Journal of Conflict Resolution*, 49, 451–82.

Fouda, S. (1997) 'Political Monetary Cycles and Independence of the Central Bank in a Monetary Union: An Empirical Test for a BEAC Franc Zone Member', *Journal of African Economies*, 6, 112–31.

Gauthier, B. (ed.) (1995) *State Crisis and the Manufacturing Sector in Cameroon*. Monographs on International Business and Economics 95-04. Montreal, Canada: CETAI.

Hotelling, H. (1931) 'The Economics of Exhaustible Resources', *Journal of Political Economy*, 39, 137–75.

IMF (1998) *Cameroon Article IV Statistical Appendix*. IMF Country Report No. 98/17. Washington, DC: International Monetary Fund.

IMF (2002) *Cameroon Article IV Statistical Appendix*. IMF Country Report No. 02/257. Washington, DC: International Monetary Fund.

IMF (2005) *Cameroon Article IV Statistical Appendix*. IMF Country Report No. 05/165. Washington, DC: International Monetary Fund.

IMF (2008) *Cameroon: Fifth Review Under the Three-Year Arrangement*. IMF Country Report No. 08/279. Washington, DC: International Monetary Fund.

Lujala, P. (2007) 'The Spoils of Nature: Armed Civil Conflict and Rebel Access to Natural Resources', *Journal of Peace Research*, 47, 15–28.

Manzano, O. and R. Rigobon (2006) 'Resource Curse or Debt Overhang?' in D. Lederman and W.F. Maloney (eds) *Natural Resources, Neither Curse nor Destiny*. Stanford: Stanford University Press and World Bank.

OMC (2007) *Cameroun: Examen des Politiques Commerciales*. WT/TPR/S/87. Geneva: World Trade Organization.

Omgba, L.D. (2009) 'On the Duration of Political Power in Africa: the Role of Oil Rents', *Comparative Political Studies*, 42: 416–36.

Ross, M. (2004) 'What Do we Know about Natural Resources and Civil War?' *Journal of Peace Research*, 41, 337–56.

Rosser, A. (2006) *The Political Economy of the Resource Curse: a Literature Survey*. IDS Working Paper no. 268. Brighton: IDS.

Sachs, J. and A. Warner (1995) *Natural Resource Abundance and Economic Growth*. NBER Working Paper 5398. Cambridge, MA: NBER.

Shaxon, N. (2007) 'Oil, Corruption and the Resource Curse', *International Affairs*, 83, 1123–40.

Sindjoun, L. (1997) 'Elections et Politique au Cameroun: Concurrence Deloyale, Coalitions Destabilite Hegemonique et Politique d'Affection', *African Journal of Political Science*, 2, 89–121.

World Bank (1988) *Cameroon Adapting Public Finances to a Changing Macroeconomic Environment*. 6 October. Draft Report no. 7451-CM. Washington, DC: World Bank.

World Bank (1991) *Cameroon Structural Adjustment Loan*. Report no. 3089-CM. Release of the second tranche, 1 April. Washington, DC: World Bank.

World Bank (2007) *World Development Indicators*. CD-Rom. Washington, DC: World Bank.

World Bank (2007) *Global Development Finance*. CD-Rom. Washington, DC: World Bank.

Appendix

Table A.2.1 Oil data

	Production (in millions of barrels)		Price (in current US$/barrel)		Extraction cost (in current US$ million)		SNH state mandate cost (in current US$ million)
	WBASP	SNH	BP	WB	WB	SNH	WB
1977	0.3	0.3	12.8	11.6	0.1	0.1	0.1
1978	3.7	4.0	12.9	11.9	2.1	2.3	1.0
1979	14.7	10.0	29.1	28.5	10.2	6.9	9.6
1980	26.2	20.0	33.9	34.0	45.4	34.7	20.3
1981	35.2	30.0	33.1	32.7	83.4	71.1	26.2
1982	41.5	39.0	30.4	30.1	128.3	120.4	28.5
1983	43.3	42.0	27.2	27.3	145.3	141.0	27.0
1984	64.5	55.0	26.5	26.3	214.9	183.1	38.7
1985	64.5	65.0	25.4	25.0	245.0	247.0	36.8
1986	63.4	61.0	13.3	13.2	226.1	217.5	19.1
1987	63.9	59.0	17.0	16.7	208.8	192.8	24.4
1988	59.1	57.0	13.7	13.6	198.7	191.6	18.3
1989	62.6	56.0	16.8	16.4	212.7	190.3	23.5
1990	58.1	55.0	21.9	21.1	189.7	179.4	27.9
1991	53.4	50.0	18.4	17.8	178.3	166.9	21.7
1992	52.0	49.0	17.8	17.5	183.3	172.9	20.8
1993	52.4	46.0	15.6	15.5	173.7	149.2	18.5
1994	48.8	41.7	14.6	14.6	157.1	135.2	16.3
1995	45.5	37.9	15.7	15.8	148.9	124.3	16.4
1996	50.2	38.1	19.0	18.8	167.0	119.8	21.5
1997	52.2	40.6	17.6	17.7	173.1	136.1	21.0
1998	56.8	42.8	11.7	12.0	207.0	156.7	15.6

Table A.2.1 (cont):

	Production (in millions of barrels)		Price (in current US$/barrel)		Extraction cost (in current US$ million)		SNH state mandate cost (in current US$ million)
	WBASP	SNH	BP	WB	WB	SNH	WB
1999	50.2	42.5	16.6	16.6	219.5	183.7	19.1
2000	53.8	41.6	26.2	26.0	224.9	171.3	31.9
2001	51.5	39.4	22.1	22.1	232.3	177.7	25.9
2002	47.2	37.4	22.8	22.7	220.7	174.8	24.5
2003	49.4	35.6	27.2	27.3	238.2	171.9	30.7
2004	48.6	32.7	34.7	34.1	248.1	166.6	37.9
2005	44.2	30.1	49.8	48.7	262.0	178.3	49.1
2006	46.9	32.3	61.6	60.8	317.7	218.8	65.0

World Bank Adjusted Saving Project (WBASP) retrieved July 2008. Extraction= WBASP; unit cost*production according to data source.

State mandate cost is estimated to represent 3.5 per cent of *Société Nationale des Hydrocarbures* (SNH) share of gross rent based on the last 5 years' average (2004–08) of the SNH.

Oil statistics available from www.snh.cm.

3
Learning How to Manage Natural Resource Revenue
The experience of copper in Chile

J. Rodrigo Fuentes

3.1 Introduction

Countries abundant in natural resources face the dilemma of how to manage this source of revenues. The recent boom in commodity prices has put this issue at the top of the agenda in natural resource-rich economies. Chile, for instance, is the largest copper producer in the world, supplying 43 per cent of world copper exports. In 2007, the state-owned corporation, CODELCO, produced one-third of total Chilean copper output, and the revenues from its copper exports accounted for 16 per cent of total fiscal revenues. In the past few years, the government has been under political pressure to distribute more of these revenues across different groups.[1]

Some of the questions that arise naturally are: How is the Chilean government managing this boom in copper revenues? What has been the effect of this windfall over total investment and current government spending? How have soaring prices affected the non-copper sectors? How have the fiscal rule and the stabilization fund for copper helped to manage these revenues? What was the role played by the political economy in the Chilean case? What role does the private sector play? What are some of the threats and challenges to the present and future governments associated with the fiscal expansion experienced in the last 2 years? This chapter focuses on these issues and derives some policy lessons for managing natural resource revenues.

Regarding these questions, we have the following hypotheses. First, the privatization of natural resources has allowed additional investment in the sector. It has enhanced accountability, albeit at the cost of wealth transfers to these investors. Second, the transparency of public finance has helped to monitor copper revenues. Third, the fiscal rule and the stabilization fund have helped in defining the way revenues from copper are spent or saved. Fourth, the stabilization fund, in addition to an outward-oriented economy, has boosted export diversification. Fifth, good quality of institutions has played a major role in achieving the mentioned results.

The literature that studies the role played by the political economy, economic policy and institutions in the exploitation of natural resources normally concludes that said exploitation is harmful for growth. Some papers focus on the fight between rival groups to capture the rents generated by this sector (see, for instance, Lane and Tornell 1996; Hodler 2006), whereas others emphasize that the exploitation of natural resources may contribute to weaken institutions (see Engerman and Sokoloff, 1997, 2000; Leite and Weidmann, 2002; Robinson *et al.*, 2003; Mehlum *et al.*, 2006). Despite this evidence, there are many cases of successful economic performance in natural resource-rich countries. The type of economic result depends crucially on the quality of the institutions and the kind of economic policies in place. For instance, Botswana, Indonesia and Norway belong to the group of good examples, whereas Kuwait, Nigeria and Mexico are less favourable ones. The lessons from these cases are that fiscal discipline and quality of institutions do matter when facing commodity price windfalls.[2]

The plan of the chapter is as follows. Section 3.2 presents a brief history of the role of copper in the Chilean economy, analyses the political economy behind the government's resource management (that is, how early reforms in fiscal discipline and transparency were conducted and how they survived over time) and discusses how the copper reserves have been handled across the decades. In the last respect, Chile was not different from other countries in the 1960s and 1970s; copper resources transited from being in private foreign ownership to a state-owned resource and were subsequently opened up to private investment (for a deeper discussion on this topic, see Meller, 2002). The political economy of the different equilibria is important to understand the present situation.

Section 3.3 covers the role of the private sector in reducing agency problems. The main questions here are: Have the contracts been efficient? Has the economy benefited from private participation in copper operations? Certainly, it has helped to reduce the level of corruption. However, the process of this participation has encountered several problems, starting with needed amendments to the contracts with the investors. We analyse the legal framework established in the early 1980s and the role of the royalty charged since 2006, from an efficiency standpoint. This section also discusses how the political economy was managed in Chile to ensure property right protection and better policies.

Section 3.4 discusses the Chilean fiscal rule aiming to improve the management of resource revenues, which has been successful for macroeconomic stability (Chumacero *et al.*, 2007 provide a discussion on the political economy behind the fiscal reforms that have taken place in Chile). This section also describes the copper price stabilization fund and analyses its performance regarding price smoothing, paying special attention to the recent windfall. As some people have argued, the combination of clear fiscal rules with transparent management is a necessary condition for a well-functioning stabilization fund (see the arguments and the evidence in Davis *et al.*, 2001). We also analyse the timing and composition of government expenditures. In fact, in the recent windfall, the government has saved a large part of the revenues to constitute a Reserve Fund for Pensions and a Fund for Economic and Social Stabilization. The type of instruments used by the government for saving the surplus generated by the high price of copper is part of the analysis. We also discuss the effects on the value of the peso and the competitiveness of other tradable sectors. Section 3.5 provides some final remarks.

3.2 The role of copper and the management of its revenues in the Chilean economy

This section will show some statistics on the Chilean economy that provide a background for further research. The analysis will concentrate on the importance of copper for the Chilean economy and its repercussion over the non-copper sectors, during different time spans. Later, this section will provide a short history of the political economy and economic policy in Chile that will serve as a background to understand how this country has harnessed the revenues from copper.

Before getting into the figures, let us briefly sketch the relevant time periods in the Chilean economic and political system. After the Second World War and until 1973, Chile had a democratic government elected by direct voting. During that period, the state was playing an active role in the economy as a producer in many areas. This intervention in production activity reached its peak in 1973. A good example of this increasing role played by the state was the nationalization of large copper mines that had been exploited by multinationals up to 1971; this was unanimously approved by the parliament. Foreign investors received very little in exchange for their mining investments.

In 1973, after the military coup, the new authorities reorganized public finances, privatized many state-owned companies and gave a main
role to the market as a resource allocation mechanism. It also introduced several reforms in terms of trade and financial openness, liberalized the financial system, privatized pension funds and the health
insurance system, deregulated economic activities, the tax system, and
so on. This government changed the constitution of the country and
modified several laws related to foreign direct investment (FDI) and
mining activities. Despite these modifications, the state-owned company, CODELCO, remained the main copper producer.

In 1990, after the return to democracy, the rules of the game were
unchanged. There was a boom in FDI to the copper sector, increasing
the participation of the private sector in this activity. The ensuing democratic governments have respected fiscal discipline and deepened the
outward orientation of the economy. Fiscal discipline was formalized in
an explicit fiscal rule implemented in the year 2000, complemented
with two the sovereign funds: one for price stabilization (which was
already in place) and intergenerational transfers.

In the following sections, a deeper analysis of this political and economic environment will deal specifically with the management of copper revenues.

3.2.1 Copper, fiscal revenues and export diversification

The main non-renewable natural resource in Chile is copper. It is the largest player in the copper market, with 43 per cent of world copper exports.
The price of this mineral has almost tripled in the past 4 years (Figure 3.1)
compared with the previous 4 years, creating many pressures on the government regarding how to spend the revenues from this windfall.

Figure 3.1 shows both the nominal and the relative price of copper,
deflated by the US wholesale price index. The recent windfall in nominal
prices is historically very high, but relative to world inflation (proxied by
the Wholesale Price Index (WPI) of the USA), the level in the period
2005–07 is similar to that in the period 1965–75. This is very important
because, as will be discussed below, in 1971, the government expropriated
copper mines from their foreign owners for virtually no compensation.

The state-owned firm, CODELCO, is the largest copper producer in
the country; however, its importance has dropped over the last 20 years
(see Figure 3.2). As of today (2009), CODELCO represents only 20 per
cent of total copper extraction.

The above result is due to vigorous FDI in the Chilean mining sector.
Figure 3.3 shows FDI by recipient sector. The accumulated FDI in 1974–

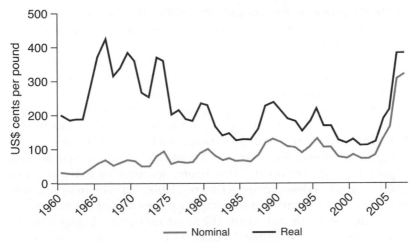

Figure 3.1 Nominal and relative copper price (US$ cents per pound)

*Deflated by USA Wholesale Price Index, base July 2008=100.
Source: Chilean Copper Commission.

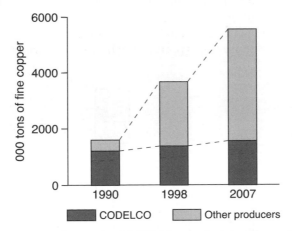

Figure 3.2 Copper production by CODELCO vs. private producers (000 tons of fine copper)

Source: Chilean Copper Commission.

89 was $5 billion. This amount was easily surpassed in the second half of the 1990s. In just 5 years, FDI reached $28.4 billion. This figure has diminished in the 2000s. As Section 3.3 will show, this was the consequence of two legal modifications: a new FDI law passed in 1974 and a new Mining Code approved in 1982.[3] However, the largest inflow of

FDI to the copper sector arrived in the 1990s, after the country returned to democracy and the elected government did not introduce additional modifications to the law.

Until 1994, the mining sector concentrated more than half of the FDI. Although investment in this sector was higher in the following years, its importance was lower on account of the explosive investment in electricity, gas and water supply, and in other sectors (mainly services). It is important to note than, in the 8-year period 2000–07, FDI has not matched the quantity in the second half of the 1990s.

Figure 3.4 shows the shares of FDI and public investment in total copper mining investment. This figure, together with the previous graphs, depicts a clear picture of the correlation between mining investment by private agents and the share in production of the private sector during the 1990s and 2000s. The figure for the last 3 years reflects a large investment in a refinery by CODELCO.

Copper exports and government revenues also show the importance of this commodity to the economy. Owing to the soaring price of copper and large investments in the mining sector over the 1990s, mineral exports increased from $6.5 billion in 1998 to $44.2 billion in 2007. This amount is 65 per cent of 2007 exports, whereas in 1998, it was equivalent to 43 per cent of total exports (Appendix Table A.3.1 shows the importance of mining exports in the balance of payments.)

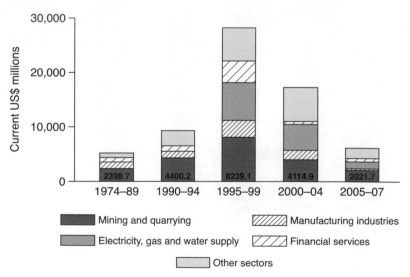

Figure 3.3 Foreign direct investments (in current US$ million)
Source: Foreign Investment Committee.

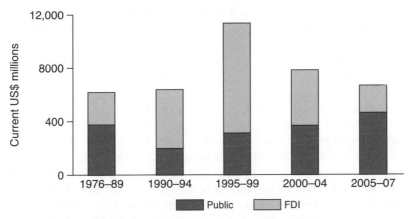

Figure 3.4 Mining investment in Chile (in current US$ million)

Sources: CODELCO, ENAMI and Foreign Investment Committee. Data for 1974–75 for public investment are not available.

Figure 3.5 shows copper's importance in government revenues. The graph closely follows the evolution of the copper price. Today, it accounts for 16.4 per cent of total revenues, which is about the same as that shown for 1990. Nevertheless, it is important to highlight that total government revenue increased 257 per cent over the period 1990–2007, so the contribution of copper is large in real terms. (Appendix Table A.3.2 shows the fiscal balance for 1960–2007.)

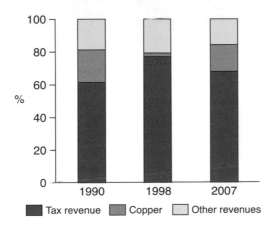

Figure 3.5 Government revenues (in millions of 2007 Chilean $)

Source: The Budget Office of the Ministry of Finance (DIPRES).

It is very common for countries rich in natural resources to experience the phenomenon called Dutch disease, which means that an economy with comparative advantages in natural resources (for example, gas, petroleum or copper, in the case of Chile) generates a real appreciation of its currency, with a subsequent contraction in the export of other tradable products.

Table 3.1 presents the evolution of exports by sectors in three different years. Copper exports are around 50 per cent (when the price is high) of total exports, coming down from 85.5 per cent in 1970. On the other hand, manufacturing products increased between 1970 and 1990 from 12 per cent to become one-third of total exports. This share has been steady in the last 18 years. It is important to consider that manufacturing products are closely related to natural resources such as agriculture and forestry; this is just an indicator of the comparative advantages of the Chilean economy.

One of the main reasons for this export diversification was the unilateral trade openness that took place after 1973, under the military government, and the free trade agreements signed after 1990, when the country had returned to democracy. Back in 1973, there was a large dispersion of the effective rate of protection across sectors, because of high import tariffs (90 per cent on average) and several non-tariff barriers. In 1989, there was a flat rate of 15 per cent import tariffs, with almost all non-tariff barriers abolished; the exception was the price bands set for

Table 3.1 Exports of goods by sectors (share in total exports of goods)

Sectors	1970	1990	2008
Agriculture, timber and fishing	3	11.4	6.0
Mining products	85.5	55.3	58.7
Copper	75.5	45.6	50.4
Others	10	9.7	8.3
Manufacturing products	11.6	33.1	35.3
Food and beverages	2.8	14.7	13.0
Wood products	0.8	4.3	3.3
Paper and pulp	3	4.9	5.1
Chemical products	1	4.7	5.9
Basic metallic industries	2.1	1.1	2.3
Machinery, electric and transportation equipment	1.2	1.7	2.5
Other manufacturing products	0.8	1.7	3.3
Total exports (US$ million)	1,111.70	8,580.30	65,102.90

Source: Author's calculations using Central Bank of Chile information. Figures for 2008 are estimated.

some crops. Starting in 1990, tariffs were cut to 11 per cent and, by the end of the decade, to 6 per cent (flat rate). At the same time, the democratic government was signing free trade agreements with several trade partners, which reduced the average tariff even further.

Another way to see how exports have been diversified over time is by using an index of concentration. Figure 3.6 shows the Herfindhal index calculated over the value of exported goods. The meaning of an index equal to 1 is that the economy is just exporting one good, and as the index decreases, more goods are being exported. As a comparison, the figure also shows the evolution of three other countries; one of them is copper-rich (Zambia, ZMB) and the other two are oil-rich countries (Nigeria, NGA, and Venezuela, VEN). Chile and Venezuela show a steady drop in the index since the late 1970s, at least until 1998. The trend seems to change in the case of Venezuela, as well as in the other two economies, whereas Chile's index stays near 0.1. Note that the drop in the value of the index started in the mid-1970s together with the trade openness process.

In summary, by 2007, the price of copper was booming. This commodity is the main exportable product and is a major source of fiscal revenue. In the last 20 years, private producers have become increasingly important. As a by-product of this process, Chile has developed technology and know-how on the efficient exploitation of copper mines, especially those in the higher mountains.

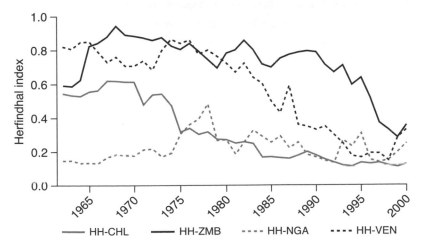

Figure 3.6 Herfindhal index calculated over exported goods

Source: Feenstra *et al.* (2005).

Despite the importance of this commodity in the composition of exports, the economy showed a continuous export diversification process until 1990, and has stayed at that level of diversification since then. It is hard to assess whether the abundance of copper may have prevented other sectors from developing, as the counterfactual is not available. Trade openness together with other reforms helped to set the 'right' price in the economy, which allows the allocation of resources on the basis of comparative advantages.

There are a few examples that are worth mentioning that helped to develop some specific sectors. For instance, Decree Law 701 provided a subsidy to forest certain zones in Chile. The subsidy was for small plantations and decreased over time. Nevertheless, it is important to consider that the subsidy was accompanied by a new rule of law that ensures property rights. Forest investment requires several years to yield rents; therefore, property right protection plays a key role. It is very likely that both the subsidy and property rights protection spurred the development of this sector. Another example is the salmon culture that was developed from a public–private initiative, which made Chile the main exporter of this product.

How were the boom and bust periods in the price of copper related to revenue management by the government? How did the political economy change over time to explain many of these facts? These are the main questions to be addressed next.

3.2.2 The political economy and economic policy

As mentioned earlier, the Chilean economy has experienced profound structural changes in both arenas: political situation and economic policy. From the Second World War until 1973, the country was managed by a representative democracy with two important powers: the executive power (represented by the president of the Republic) and the legislative power (represented by a bicameral system). During this period, the government had an important participation in economic activity and copper was no exception.

In the post-war period, the world became more protectionist against trade flows. Chile did not escape that trend. After the Second World War, the Chilean economy became increasingly inward oriented, with only a couple of timorous attempts at liberalization that failed. This process peaked in 1973, during the government of Salvador Allende, when the economy had high barriers to trade with a huge dispersion of the effective protection rate. The years 1971–73 were basically a socialist experiment: price and interest rate controls, high barriers to trade and financial flows, nationalization of private firms, a large public deficit and multiple exchange rates were the norm.

From 1973 until 1989, a military dictatorship ruled the country. The economic policy changed towards a market-oriented economy with little state intervention. During this period, the constitution was changed, a new mining law and a new environment for FDI was set in place. Several other reforms were put forward in the agenda of the new administration. How was this possible?

Initial conditions are essential for understanding how the process of reform took place in Chile. The socialist experience of 1971–73 did not go well, with the economy ending up with several distortions.[4] Based on that experience and given that the only economic plan available was the one prepared by a group of liberal economists, the new military government (1973–89) implemented a different economic system. It established a market economy, liberalized prices and interest rates, introduced drastic trade reform, privatized state-owned enterprises (SOEs), established a new pension fund system and enforced fiscal and monetary responsibility (for a description of the reforms, see Edwards and Edwards, 1987, and the references therein).

According to Chumacero *et al.* (2007), the principles that governed these reforms – and that are central to understanding the evolution of fiscal behaviour – are:

- secure property rights;
- a subsidiary role for the state;
- fiscal consolidation and orthodox management of monetary and foreign exchange policies;
- systematic reduction in spaces for public discretion and potential arbitrariness, introducing impersonal rules whenever possible;
- trade and financial openness;
- social policies focused on poverty reduction, with means testing and expenditure targeting as the main instruments;
- institutionalization of the 'rules of the game' in such a way that it would not be easy to change them.

Property rights protection is a key building block to stimulate long-term investment, as in the case of natural resources such as forestry and mining; specifically, it diminishes the risk of expropriation. Other important principles for private FDI were trade and financial openness, reducing public discretion and securing the enforcement of the rules of the game. There is little doubt that this big bang scheme of reforms allowed an increase in private investment and the development of macroeconomic stability. These reforms were conducted under a dictatorship, which permitted the passing of many laws in a short period of time. Nevertheless, Latin America is a case of reforms and counter-reforms, so there was a latent risk associated at the end of the military government.

The Constitutional Code approved in the 1980 plebiscite established the current political structure of Chile. It was designed to preserve the continuity of policies when the country returned to democracy. First of all, it established that General Pinochet would retain power for at least another 8 years. After that, a plebiscite would initiate the return to open elections. Moreover, this constitution ensures a strong presidential structure, where the president governs for a 6-year term (later changed to 4 years) with no immediate re-election. If none of the candidates reaches an absolute majority in the first round, the voting is decided in a run-off election between the two most voted candidates a month later.

There is also a bicameral legislature with a Senate and a Chamber of Deputies. The constitutional code designs a system to elect the members in a way that favours reducing the number of competing parties or forming coalitions. Each district elects two members for the Senate and for the Chamber of Deputies, but if any of the coalitions obtains two-thirds of the votes, it wins both seats. There were six senators designated directly or indirectly by the president of the Republic (this was abolished few years later). Pinochet appointed the first group of these senators. Therefore, the Senate was in the hands of the right-wing party, which constituted the opposition to the first elected democratic government in 1989.

Today, there are many parties in place; but they are grouped into two large blocks: right-wing *Alianza* and left-wing *Concertación*. The importance of this scheme is twofold; first, the negotiation process takes place first within each group and then between groups. Second, it diminishes the number of leading political actors, reducing transaction costs and thereby increasing the likelihood of reaching a Pareto-optimal solution (Spiller and Tommasi, 2003). Moreover, senators are elected for an 8-year period and deputies for a 4-year period with the possibility of immediate re-election. This provides strong intertemporal linkages, with the result that any political decision affects the future of the politician and gives incentives for cooperation between both blocks. During the first democratic government after 1989, consensus among political actors was the only available strategy.

The legislature provides checks and balances on the president. However, the legislative agenda is set by the president of the Republic, as it has a veto and urgency options. Changes in many important laws require a supermajority threshold. For instance, this rule has avoided changing the electoral system.

Thus, the political system, set by the Constitutional Code, played a key role in prudent fiscal policy and non-reform reversals during the transition to democracy. The first democratic government did not have incentives to change the economic system, as the economy was growing and performing well, and they realized, after the Argentinean experience a few years earlier, that economic stability was essential to protect democracy. The property rights of investors have been respected, and private investment has flowed to the mining sector over these 20 years of democratic administration. However, there is still discussion over whether there is a fair distribution of the rents from copper between private producers and the state. This is the topic of the next section.

3.3 Contracts with the private sector

The private sector could play an important role in harnessing the revenues from natural resources, when the government correctly handles the contracts to share the rents (if any) from the minerals. The participation of the private sector, mainly multinational companies, helps to finance the capital required in this activity. Shortage of funds is usually a reason for not exploiting natural resources and foreign direct investment can lift this restriction. However, there may be a potential trade-off between how to encourage private sector participation in the exploration and exploitation of mineral resources and how much the society gets from it. In what follows, the section describes the mechanism designed in Chile to provide incentives to private investment. Later, it proposes a tentative answer to the question of whether the Chilean government is benefiting too little from the mineral resources.

3.3.1 Private sector participation in the mining industry in Chile

Private FDI in copper mining (and other minerals) faces a high risk of expropriation; this was actually the case in 1971 when Congress approved the nationalization of large-scale copper mines with compensation to the owners based on the book value of the mines. The government subtracted from this value any profit that exceeded a 'normal' return on investment since 1955. This normal return was set at 12 per cent. In the end, the compensation was practically zero.

After the military coup of 1973, the new government decided to attract FDI by building a new set of rules for it. In 1974, the Decree Law

600 (DL 600) was established as a way to protect and promote FDI. The DL 600 guarantees foreign investors the right to transfer their principal and net profits thereon to other countries. It also establishes the non-discrimination principle between foreign and domestic investors, but opens the possibility for foreign companies to be subject, for a 10-year period, to an invariable effective fixed tax rate of 42 per cent on taxable income. This benefit is extendable to 20 years for investments above US$50 million. Alternatively, foreign companies can waive (only once) this right and ask for application of the ordinary tax law, which is the one applied to national investors; this law can be subject to changes over time. Accelerated depreciation and cumulative losses could be deducted from profits to calculate taxable income.

Despite this effort, FDI to the mining sector did not increase as expected. As with any other investment that matures over a long-term horizon, mining activity requires stable rules of the game and protection to property rights. In that sense, the Organic Constitutional Law of Mining Concessions, enacted in 1982, provided the new environment for mining investment. This law gives guarantees in case of future expropriation; the compensation in that case would be based on the net present value (NPV) of the verified reserves at the time of expropriation. Moreover, the constitutional status of the law makes it difficult to amend. The Chilean Mining Code of 1983 provides additional support to the law of mining concessions. But it was not until the early 1990s that FDI in the mining sector boomed (see Section 3.2). The smooth transition to democracy and the respect granted to property rights by the elected governments may have helped.

According to this law, the state is the absolute, exclusive and inalienable owner of all mines, but it can grant the concession to explore and exploit them or do it itself through CODELCO. The new institutional framework, plus the fiscal regime and political stability, provides the incentive to develop private investment from abroad.[5] In fact, until 2005, there was no specific taxation on mining activities. The investors had to pay taxes according to either the DL 600 or as any domestic investor, depending on their chosen status. Before 2005, the fiscal regime targeted profits rather than revenues and provided the incentives for long-term investment, which is the case in the mining sector (Prat, 2005). It is important to highlight that large-scale projects benefited greatly from the allowance under FDI status, especially the accelerated depreciation of fixed assets, financial cost allowances and losses carried from one year to the next. All these exemptions were very important in the early stages of the mining projects.

In the early 2000s, a debate emerged about the benefits received by the foreign investors, considered by some people to be excessively large relative to their contribution to the state. In 2002, the government enacted the Elusion Law, which primarily sought to eliminate loopholes in the legislation that reduced tax collection. But the debate around mining activities continued until the approval of the current mining law (Law 20,026) in June 2005. This law established a specific tax on mining activities (royalty), starting on 1 January 2006. The royalty was levied on the taxable operating income of the mine operator based on annual sales (Table 3.2).

This tax was not applicable to foreign investors who had signed a DL 600 contract before 1 December 2004, except for the time period of the tax regime in the DL 600 or in case they waived this right. This law modifies the FDI decree law, in the sense that it allows foreign investors developing mining projects to make use of a new tax invariability system. In cases of investment amounts greater than US$50 million, the following rights are granted by the Foreign Investment Committee to the foreign investors for a term of 15 calendar years:

Table 3.2 Royalty tax according to annual sales of mine operator

Annual sales of the mine operator	Rate
1. Mine operator with annual sales equal to or less than the equivalent of 12,000 MFT	Not subject to the tax
2. Mine operator with annual sales equal to or less than the equivalent of 50,000 MFT, and greater than the equivalent of 12,000 MFT	
2.1 Regarding that portion in excess of 12,000 and no greater than 15,000 MFT	0.5%
2.2 Regarding that portion in excess of 15,000 and no greater than 20,000 MFT	1.0%
2.3 Regarding that portion in excess of 20,000 and no greater than 25,000 MFT	1.5%
2.4 Regarding that portion in excess of 25,000 and no greater than 30,000 MFT	2.0%
2.5 Regarding that portion in excess of 30,000 and no greater than 35,000 MFT	2.5%
2.6 Regarding that portion in excess of 35,000 and no greater than 40,000 MFT	3.0%
2.7 Regarding that portion in excess of 40,000 MFT	4.5%
3. Mine operator with annual sales greater than 50,000 MFT	5.0%

Source: Foreign Investment Committee.

- Invariability of the legal provisions in force at the date of signature of the respective contract, regarding the specific tax on mining activities.
- They will not be affected by any new tribute, including royalties, cannons or other similar tax burden, specifically levied on mining activities, established after the signing of the respective foreign investment contract.
- They will not be affected by modifications introduced to the amount or form of calculation of the development and exploration licences in force at the time of the signing of the respective contract, and which could make those licences more onerous.

In summary, the DL 600, which rules FDI, plus the Mining Code approved in the early 1980s, provided the appropriate environment to attract FDI to the mining sector. It is important to mention that the economy was coming out of a complicated political and economic scenario, characterized by a shortage of funds for investment. In that sense, the legal framework and the high copper price allowed for a booming mining sector. However, the tax regime imposed under these codes did not generate the expected benefits for the Chilean state. The law was amended in 2005, when the main change was a new tax based on sales rather than profits, which could affect long-term investment.[6]

Private participation in the exploitation of natural resources under appropriate tax regimes can be an important way to avoid corruption and to harness revenues from that sector. It could be questioned, however, whether large participating multinationals have transferred enough resources to the Chilean state. This is the topic of the next subsection.

3.3.2 Are government revenues from copper production too low?

There are two sources of copper revenues to the Chilean government. On the one hand, profits obtained by the SOE, CODELCO, go to the fiscal wallet after paying 1 per cent of gross revenues to the armed forces. On the other hand, there are revenues provided by specific and general taxes to mining activities.

According to Cantallopts *et al.* (2008), the average contribution of the SOE was 6.6 per cent of total fiscal revenues during 1990–2003, and 17.4 per cent over the period 2004–06. Large private copper mining, in contrast, contributed, on average, 0.4 per cent of total fiscal revenues for 1990–2003 and 4.8 per cent of total fiscal revenues for 2004–07. Figure 3.7 shows the share of fiscal copper revenues in total fiscal reve-

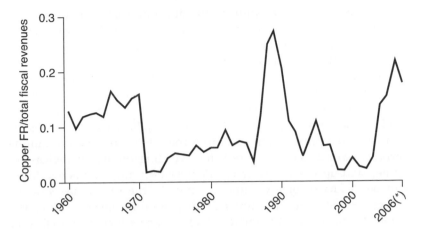

Figure 3.7 Copper fiscal revenues over total fiscal revenues

Source: The Budget Office of the Ministry of Finance (DIPRES), Jofré *et al.* (2000).

nues. The contribution is highly cyclical and is related to the domestic economic environment.

It is necessary to divide in two the question of whether the contribution of private mining to the government was proper. Are there any rents in this sector that should be shared, beyond income taxes? Is anything in mining activities that makes it hard to collect taxes?

Regarding the first question, it seems that copper is relatively abundant around the world (Tilton, 2003), which means that the value added of the mineral is closely related to the capital and labour needed to extract it. However, copper mines have different qualities; that is, the marginal cost of production is different for natural reasons. The world supply curve for copper takes this into account; in this case, the marginal firm has zero profit, whereas the infra-marginal firm obtains positive rents. These rents are the incentives for geologists to explore and search for 'high-quality' mines. If there is competition in this activity, it will dissipate the rents; in case it still generates profit, the government will collect income taxes.

Given the abundance of copper in the world, it is hard to say that there are Ricardian rents associated with copper-mining activities. Tilton (2003) analyses several perspectives and concludes that there is no reason to think that copper will become scarce, at least for many decades. Short-run shortages will increase the price, which will provide incentives to open mines with higher marginal costs and/or generate additional technological progress.

The above conclusion points in the direction that governments can obtain revenues from private mining only through income taxes. Then, what is the best technology to collect taxes from mining activities? One could think that mining is like any other economic activity where there is no need to construct a specific structure to collect taxes. However, the description of the tax incentives in previous pages shows that income taxes have contributed relatively little to government revenues. The explanation for this situation rests on several pillars. One of them is the relatively low price of copper during the 1990s. In addition, mining projects have a long maturity before yielding profits. In the case of Chile, start-up costs, accelerated depreciation and cumulative losses can be deducted for tax purposes; thus, in the earlier stages of the mines' exploitation, the entrepreneurs pay no income tax. Moreover, interests paid are tax deductible, which generates incentives to finance the project with debt rather than equity. This can be a way to elude tax payment, as a financial company can extract profits through interest payments. Note that firms in other sectors are subject to the same rules.

In summary, the low contributions of private mines to government revenues are more related to the tax collection technology than to mineral rents appropriation. In the last few years, because of the high price of copper and the royalty, private investors have paid more taxes. The tax scheme has to include the right incentives for searching for new high-quality minerals and for making innovations that reduce production costs in the sector, and it should not discriminate across activities. The royalty imposed on the mining sector accomplishes the first two ingredients: it does not discourage exploration, but it goes against the non-discrimination principle.

3.4 Fiscal regimes and the political economy of fiscal rules

How was a responsible fiscal rule shaped over time? How and when did it start? How has this reform survived? These are the main issues addressed in this section. The first part of the section describes different fiscal regimes in Chile and their relationship with the price of copper. The second part describes how government expenditure has been managed in order to allow for intergenerational transfers.

3.4.1 Fiscal regimes

There were attempts to balance the fiscal budget after the Second World War up to 1970, but they all failed. This was a period characterized by inward-oriented policies in which the state played an active role in productive activities. The average fiscal deficit in the 1960s was around 2 per cent, which reflects the fiscal policy over that period.

Back in those years, copper was Chile's main export. It accounted for 75 per cent of total exports and 30 per cent of tax revenues. Therefore, it was a very attractive source of resources for the government in office and a supply of dollars for imports. Large private mines characterize this sector. However, between 1966 and 1969, the state of Chile acquired 51 per cent of the total mines' property. This is called the historical Great Mining of Copper (see Meller, 2002).

As described in Section 3.2, starting in the 1970s, the increasing state involvement in productive activities generated a large fiscal deficit that was financed by inflation tax. An important example of the state's participation in productive activities is the constitutional reform to nationalize the large mines still owned by multinationals, unanimously approved by the Congress in 1971.

The military coup of 1973 found the economy with highly distorted relative prices, an almost non-existent financial sector, hyperinflation and a large budget deficit resulting from government expenditures and the losses of SOEs. The fiscal deficit (as a percentage of gross domestic product, GDP) was around 12 per cent (see Jofré *et al.*, 2000), and the average deficit for the entire period was almost 10 per cent. One of the first tasks concerning this matter was to organize the public finances by cutting down fiscal expenditures, changing the tax structure and privatizing SOEs.

A new fiscal institutionalism was established in 1975, when the government enacted the State Financial Administration Law. The law entrusted fiscal responsibility, including all public expenditures and public enterprise deficits, to the hands of the Ministry of Finance and its Budget Office. That same year, the government introduced a 20 per cent value added tax with automatic indexation and elimination of all special preferences. Many SOEs were privatized or restored to their legal owners. The Budget Office was granted the power to enforce fiscal discipline in those companies that still belonged to the state. Regarding copper, CODELCO was created as a SOE in 1974 to manage the large mines that had been nationalized in 1971. Despite the efforts of the government to keep solid fiscal accounts, the deep financial crisis of 1982–83 and the bail out of private banks did not help much in keeping a balance surplus. The cost of the financial crisis was 40 per cent of GDP (see Barandiarán and Hernández, 1999; Sanhueza, 2001), and the average surplus during 1974–99 accounted for 0.5 per cent of GDP.

The plebiscite of 1980 approved a new Constitutional Code, which deepened the fiscal reforms. This constitution gave more control of the budget to the executive. The Congress has to approve the budget, but it cannot introduce new expenditures; it can reduce some items, but not those associated with or committed under permanent laws. Congress also has access to the revenues calculations, but it cannot propose any changes. As will be discussed below, the new constitution established the road map to bring back democracy and its rules of the game.

Under the rules of the new constitution, democracy returned to the country in 1990 after a plebiscite that rejected the option of General Pinochet being president for another 8 years. Fiscal responsibility was a cornerstone for the successful transition to democracy (see Chumacero *et al.*, 2007). The newly elected authorities decided to maintain fiscal austerity, as they considered that good economic performance was a necessary condition for a healthy democracy. Figure 3.8 shows the fiscal balance over five different periods (that coincide with different fiscal regimes), which illustrates the fiscal responsibility described here.

Starting in 2001, the third democratic government announced the application of a new fiscal rule. Government expenditures would be a function of the structural revenues to guarantee a 1 per cent structural surplus. The justifications for this rule (and this number) were, on the one hand, the existence of a structural deficit at the Central Bank of Chile as a result of the private banks' bail out in the 1980s and its exchange rate policy (target zone for nominal exchange rate) in the 1990s. On the other hand, the government faced future contingent

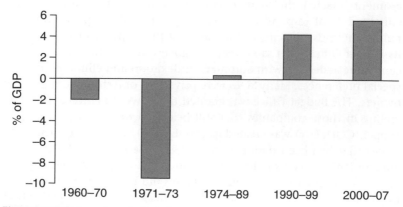

Figure 3.8 Fiscal surplus of central government (% of GDP)
Source: The Budget Office of the Ministry of Finance (DIPRES).

liabilities, arising from the state guarantees to minimum pensions, to university students' loans and to the concession system of infrastructure built by the private sector.[7]

The structural balance refers to the financial result for the central government under a situation where: (1) the tax revenues correspond to those collected in a particular year when the GDP is at its long-term trend level; (2) prices of copper and molybdenum correspond to the long-run equilibrium. The structural balance isolates the cyclical effects of the fiscal balance to estimate a long-term situation of the central government instead of a particular condition. The use of this indicator involves three specific difficulties: the estimation of the long-term GDP and long-term prices of copper and molybdenum. A committee of experts is in charge of estimating both the long-term GDP and the copper price. Because there is no expert committee to estimate the long-term price of molybdenum, the government takes the moving average of the monthly prices of the mineral during the last 4 years as a proxy for the long-term price.

The formula for the structural balance is (see Rodríguez *et al.*, 2007):

$$B_t^* = B_t - \left(NMTR_t - NMTR_t \cdot \left(\frac{Y_t^*}{Y_t} \right)^{\varepsilon} \right) - \left(MTR_t - MTR_t^* \right) - \left(CR_t - CR_t^* \right) - \left(MR_t - MR_t^* \right)$$

where B_t^* is the structural balance in period t; B_t is the effective balance in period t; $NMTR_t$ is the net non-mining tax revenues and social security in-payments in period t; MTR_t is the tax revenues from private mining companies in period t; MTR_t^* is the structural tax revenues from private mining companies in period t; Y_t is the effective GDP in period t; Y_t^* is the trend in GDP in period t; CR_t is effective transfers from CODELCO on account of copper sales in period t; CR_t^* is structural transfers from CODELCO on account of copper sales in period t; MR_t is effective transfers from CODELCO on account of molybdenum sales in period t; MR_t^* is structural transfers from CODELCO on account of molybdenum sales in period t; and ε is the GDP elasticity of non-mining tax revenues.

The indicator of the structural balance has changed since its implementation.[8] The first methodological changes took place in 2004, when the national fiscal statistics adopted the methodology suggested by the IMF (2001), which applied an accrual basis instead of the cash flow basis in use.

Then, in September 2005, the estimation of the fiscal revenue from private mining was modified to include the cyclical effect of the copper price instead of the GDP's cyclical effect. This adjustment better explains the cyclical effect of the government's revenues from private mining, because the evidence shows that they are more correlated with the price of copper than with the GDP trend. In 2006, a new change was introduced to the estimation of the tax revenue from private mining to capture the cyclical effect of the recently approved royalty on mining activities.

Finally, in 2006, the revenues from CODELCO were adjusted, disaggregating copper revenues from molybdenum sales. Originally, molybdenum sales were included as part of copper sales, because its low prices between 2001 and 2005 made them represent only about 8 per cent of total CODELCO revenues. However, since 2005, its price has increased sharply, becoming an import source of revenues for CODELCO and making it necessary to adjust the government's revenues from molybdenum sales with its own price instead of the copper price.

An interesting question is how the fiscal surplus reacts to the price of copper. This chapter does not attempt to model the fiscal surplus, but rather to give some insight about how the fiscal surplus is related to the price of copper. Figure 3.9 shows that there is no correlation between the price of copper (in logs) and the fiscal surplus. This result does not control for anything.

Table 3.3 shows the regression estimation of an equation where the fiscal surplus is a function of the current and lagged price of copper (in

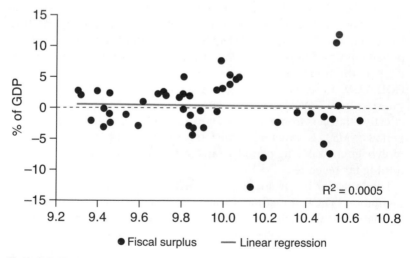

Figure 3.9 Fiscal surpluses and the real price of copper
Source: Author's calculations.

logs), the growth rate of GDP and the lagged value of the dependent variable. The previous discussion allows us to identify at least five fiscal regimes (it could be six, but there are not enough observations to estimate a larger model), so that each variable interacts with a dummy variable that takes the value of 1 under each fiscal regime.

Variables that control for the cycle are not statistically significant even if some of the periods are grouped into one. Regarding the variable of

Table 3.3 The effect of the real price of copper on fiscal surplus

Dependent variable: fiscal surplus over GDP						
	[1]		[2]		[3]	
D6070*real Pcu	1.633		1.881	**	1.994	**
	(2.874)		(0.834)		(0.839)	
D7173*real Pcu	25.640	***	25.688	***	14.575	***
	(9.066)		(8.655)		(3.592)	
D7489*real Pcu	3.509		2.092	**	2.200	**
	(2.422)		(0.878)		(0.884)	
D9007*real Pcu	7.617	***	7.565	***	7.552	***
	(1.860)		(1.763)		(1.784)	
D6070*real Pcu(–1)	0.298					
	(2.881)					
D7173*real Pcu(–1)	–24.175	**	–24.222	***	–12.958	***
	(9.176)		(8.754)		(3.713)	
D7489*real Pcu(–1)	–1.403					
	(2.278)					
D9007*real Pcu(–1)	–5.443	***	–5.416	***	–5.292	***
	(1.953)		(1.861)		(1.881)	
GDP growth			0.049			
			(0.051)			
D6070*GDP growth	–0.056					
	(0.205)					
D7173*GDP growth	0.599		0.545			
	(0.432)		(0.414)			
D7489*GDP growth	0.039					
	(0.071)					
D9007*GDP growth	0.022					
	(0.149)					
FISCAL(–1)	0.669	***	0.679	***	0.707	***
	(0.103)		(0.096)		(0.095)	
Adjusted R-squared	0.860		0.872		0.869	
Log-likelihood	–82.240		–82.757		–84.560	
LM test for AR(2)	0.656		0.845		0.932	
ARCH test	0.123		0.36		0.45	
Number of observations	47		47		47	

t-statistic in parentheses. The parameter is significant at the *10%, **5% and ***1% level.

interest, the coefficient of the current price of copper is positive, which shows that an increase in the price of copper generates contemporaneously a positive effect on the fiscal surplus. The logic is clear: when the price of copper increases, government revenues increase in the same period too, and so does the fiscal surplus. The effect of the lagged value of the price of copper, however, is negative, meaning that, 1 year after a rise in the copper price, the government reduces the fiscal surplus. The pattern of positive and negative effects is statistically significant only in two periods: 1971–73 and 1991–2007. In those periods, part of the saving resulting from the higher prices of copper was reverted in the following year. Even though coefficients are not statistically equal, numerically they are very close.

3.4.2 Government expenditures and intergenerational transfers

Intergenerational wealth transfer is one of the many issues in the extraction of natural resources, especially non-renewable ones. However, this should not be an argument to delay the extraction of the natural resource as it is impossible to predict the future value of the reserves.[9]

There has been a recent boom in the price of copper that has generated substantial revenues for the state. In addition, since 2006, the government has received the royalty on large-scale copper mines. What are the planned uses of those resources?

The revenues from the royalty are financing a Fund for Innovation for Competitiveness, which is administered by the Ministry of Economics. There is a National Council of Innovation for Competitiveness that advises the president of the Republic with proposals on human capital development, dissemination of technologies and innovation policies. The main goal is to duplicate the per capita income by the year 2020. If these policies succeed, they will constitute a source of transfers to future generations.

Regarding other proceeds received by the Chilean government from this windfall in the price of copper, in September 2006, the government implemented the Fiscal Responsibility Law, which included the creation of two Sovereign Wealth Funds (SWFs): the Fund for Social and Economic Stabilization (FESS) and the Pension Reserve Fund (PRF).

The government passed a pension fund reform in 2008, which created a fiscal risk for the future.[10] The present administration created the fund for pensions to transfer part of the fiscal surplus to ensure payment of minimum pensions and solidarity pensions to old people in the future. For this purpose, the government constituted the PRF in

December 2006 with an initial amount of US$604.5 million. By August 2008, the amount accumulated in the fund was roughly US$2.41 billion (around 1.5 per cent of GDP). Under the law, the PRF must be increased by a minimum amount equal to 0.2 per cent of GDP, and a maximum amount equal to 0.5 per cent of the previous year's GDP.

The FESS that the government of Chile established long ago (formerly named the Copper Stabilization Fund) is now being managed as a SWF (Lipsky, 2008). The objective of this fund is to smooth government spending by putting aside fiscal surpluses that are in excess of a structural target, to be used when revenues are low. Assets are expected to accumulate during periods of high copper prices (Walsh *et al.*, 2008). Under the Fiscal Responsibility Law, the FESS may receive all remaining surpluses after contributing to the PRF, although the government may choose to recapitalize the Central Bank of Chile using up to 0.5 per cent of GDP until 2011. By October 2008, the amount in the fund was nearly US$18.8 billion (around 11 per cent of GDP). Table 3.4 shows how SWFs have increased over time under the present windfall in the price of copper.[11]

Table 3.4 Time series of Chile's sovereign wealth funds (millions of US$)

	Sovereign assets[1]	Bank deposits	Agency notes	Total
Mar-07	5216.52	1673.73	247.04	7137.29
Apr-07	5692.84	1269.52	248.20	7210.56
May-07	5641.86	1292.59	199.27	7133.72
Jun-07	6936.54	2719.84	0.00	9656.38
Jul-07	7349.93	2482.55	0.00	9832.48
Aug-07	7211.92	2674.67	0.00	9886.59
Sep-07	7523.36	3382.89	244.29	11,150.54
Oct-07	7853.02	3580.55	352.82	11,786.39
Nov-07	8570.00	3956.00	533.34	13,059.34
Dec-07	9283.19	4216.29	533.12	14,032.60
Jan-08	10,130.22	4134.24	651.68	14,916.14
Feb-08	10,821.29	4140.00	261.24	15,222.53
Mar-08	12,192.70	4999.29	0.00	17,191.99
Apr-08	12,194.46	5046.86	0.00	17,241.32
May-08	11,821.79	5310.53	0.00	17,132.32
Jun-08	13,249.32	5521.06	0.00	18,770.38
Jul-08	14,001.74	5769.07	0.00	19,770.81
Aug-08	13,430.03	5779.80	250.10	19,459.93
Sep-08	13,716.90	5551.50	0.00	19,268.40
Oct-08	15,226.30	3228.10	337.10	18,791.50

[1] Includes bonds, T-bills and indexed bonds.
Source: Ministry of Finance.

Both SWFs are operationally managed by the Central Bank of Chile, which has comparative advantages in the administration of international portfolios. The Central Bank manages both funds as a fiscal agent of the Ministry of Finance, and invests according to the recommendations of a Financial Advisory Committee. The Ministry of Finance makes decisions on withdrawals from the funds, while the Central Bank makes decisions on investment choices, within the limits set forth by the government; in other words, the Central Bank plays the role of an investment bank for the Ministry of Finance.[12]

Since the Central Bank began to serve as a fiscal agent, it has delivered daily, monthly and quarterly reports to the Ministry of Finance and the General Treasury, using measures for performance, risk and compliance with market benchmarks. For its services in managing the funds, the Bank receives the equivalent of 0.48 basis point annually of the average total portfolio maintained from March to December (additional details in Central Bank of Chile, 2007b).

According to Walsh *et al.* (2008), 'Chile's SWFs are being managed transparently, and the government is committed to best practices in this area'. The authorities publish monthly reports about the size, return and portfolio composition of both funds, plus an extensive quarterly report discussing the performance relative to financial developments and established benchmarks. As a result of this communication policy, in 2008, the FESS was ranked in eighth place among 34 non-pension SWFs in 28 countries by the Peterson Institute for International Economics (for details, see Truman, 2008).

Reducing exchange rate volatility, and avoiding Dutch disease and risk diversification are the main reasons for the government to invest the SWFs abroad. Both the PRF and the FESS have been invested, conservatively, in cash and sovereign securities (Table 3.5). However, both of them are being moved towards return-oriented portfolios. Accordingly, the government proposed a new asset allocation for the end of 2008, which would invest both funds in a wider variety of securities. Because the PRF resources are intended to be used in specific pension liabilities, the asset allocation must consider the required liquidity when the liabilities fall due (Walsh *et al.*, 2008).

The ongoing world financial crisis has created no big difficulties up to now. Most of the bank deposits are guaranteed by the financial institutions, and so far the investment banks have shown liquidity shortages, not solvency problems. However, the Central Bank has not renewed the deposits of some of the banks with financial problems. In fact, in 2007 the Financial Advisory Committee recommended to diversify the

Table 3.5 Asset allocation of Chile's sovereign wealth funds (per cent of total assets)

	Current[1]	End-2008 target
Sovereign bonds (nominal)	69	45
Sovereign bonds (inflation-indexed)	1	15
Money market assets	30	5
Corporate bonds	0	20
Equities	0	15
Total	100	100

[1] As of August 2008.

Sources: Ministry of Finance (2008 a, b) and Walsh *et al.* (2008).

funds investing in stocks and corporate bonds, but because of the 2008 crisis, the Ministry of Finance postponed the implementation of this new strategy.

In summary, the recent boom in the copper price generated large revenues for the Chilean government. A big slice of those revenues has been saved and managed transparently through two funds. These funds will be used in periods of low copper price and to ensure minimum pension funds to a large group of retirees in the future. However, an important part of the funds has been used to increase government expenditures in 2009. It is very likely that, this year, the structural fiscal surplus will be a deficit instead of a 0 per cent structural surplus.[13]

3.5 Summary and final remarks

Non-renewable natural resources are sources of wealth, but also a cause of conflict within developing economies. The evidence suggests that the mismanagement of natural resources has caused corruption, low growth and/or Dutch disease. The literature has questioned whether the abundance of natural resources is a blessing or a curse.

This chapter analyses the fiscal behaviour, the political economy and the macroeconomic effects of the exploitation and management of natural resources in Chile, particularly focusing on copper, the main export product in the economy. In the last 2 years, the price of copper has soared, at least up to the current financial crisis. The way that Chile has managed this resource has evolved considerably through time. Starting with the unanimous approval of the nationalization of large-scale copper mines, by the Chilean Senate, in 1971, the Chilean government has gone over a long history of building reputation, legal institutions and policy improvements.

The main characteristics that emerge from this experience are the following. First, the involvement of the private sector is crucial for extracting natural resources in a context of financial capital scarcity. This involvement consequently requires the construction of adequate institutions that enhance private activity. The Mining Code of 1983 gave the incentives for investment, but FDI to the mining sector did not occur immediately. Actually, the combination of this code with a solid transition to democracy was needed to attract private investment flows to the country in the 1990s. It is also necessary that the rules of sharing the rents between the sovereign state and the private investor be transparent and carefully designed. For instance, there was recently a debate in Chile on whether the state has received a fair compensation from copper extraction. For a long time, the state had not had a large share in the copper rents. This was explained by the low price of copper, the allowances permitted by law to calculate income tax, the nature of the mining industry and the fact that there was no royalty charged on mining activities. However, given the abundance of copper in the world, it is hard to find arguments for additional taxes on mining operations.

Second, when the government has a large participation in the resource ownership, the pressure of different interest groups is also large. The Chilean government, for instance, has a large share in the rents of copper, mainly through the state-owned company CODELCO and secondarily via income taxes. The methods that the government created to (partially) resist these pressures are the fiscal discipline (fiscal rule such as 0 per cent of structural surplus over GDP) and the creation of two transparent funds (one for pension claims and another for copper price stabilization). These funds are invested abroad by the Ministry of Finance via the Central Bank of Chile, which is an autonomous entity. Fiscal rules and stabilization funds work well if they rest on a good institutional environment (that is, respect for property rights, transparency and accountability of the government). Building this environment takes time; reputation and credibility are hard to develop. Neutrality of policies could be a way to resist rent-seeking groups and to improve the quality of institutions.

Third, beside the stabilization funds and fiscal discipline, there are complementary policies that may help to avoid a Dutch disease type of phenomena. Although minerals are still 50 per cent of Chilean total exports, which is much lower than the 85 per cent in the 1970s, trade openness (unilaterally and through free trade agreements) has helped to diversify the country's exports.

Acknowledgements

This chapter was written as part of a project funded by the Revenue Watch Institute, which acknowledges the support of the Bill and Melinda Gates Foundation. I would like to thank Paul Collier, Nicolas Depetris Chauvin and Tony Venables for comments on earlier versions of this work, and Roberto Álvarez, José Miguel Sanchez, Salvador Valdés-Prieto and Gert Wagner for helpful discussions on some of the issues. Valuable research assistantship was provided by Karol Fernandez.

Notes

1 Some politicians were lobbying for spending resources before the next presidential election as they saw that the incumbent coalition's probability of losing was high; others wanted to spend extra resources to cover the losses from an inefficient public transportation system in the capital city. Besides, different associations (for example, teachers, healthcare workers and copper-mining unions) were requesting more funds for their specific sectors.

2 The role of natural resources in shaping economic performance has also been studied from the 'Dutch disease' perspective. The literature on this topic distinguishes two streams: (1) the effect of a real appreciation of the domestic currency (due to the discovery of a natural resource commodity or to a price boom) on the rest of the tradables; and (2) the effect of natural resources for long-term growth. The idea is that a boom produced in the natural resources sector crowds out other tradable goods (mainly in the manufacturing sectors) that are an important source of growth (see Corden and Neary, 1982, for the theoretical effects on the tradable sector; and Sachs and Warner, 1995, for theoretical argument and evidence on the growth effect of natural resources). In this sense, natural resource abundance becomes a curse. The key assumption here is that an increase in the productivity of the tradable sector is more growth enhancing than a corresponding increase in the non-tradable or natural resources sectors (Torvik, 2001, presents a general model in which the effect of natural resources on growth is ambiguous).

3 As will be explained later, these laws were enacted under a military government with no democratic participation.

4 For instance, a relative price distortion, almost autarchy in trade and capital flows, a huge fiscal deficit and financial repression.

5 For a more exhaustive review of the Chilean fiscal regime for mining activities, see Prat (2005). About the political game, see Chumacero *et al.* (2007).

6 In October 2010, a new amendment to the Royalty was approved in terms of tax rate and a new period of invariability. Firms need to decide whether they want to be subject to the new law or to the previous one. However, up to now (November 2010), it is not clear how this law will operate. The internal Revenue Service will enact a set of rules to clarify the application of the law.

7 The government guarantees a minimal income to some concessionaires. For details, see Engel *et al.* (2007).

8   For additional details about the methodological changes in the structural balance indicator, see Rodríguez *et al.* (2007).
9   Chile had the experience of inadequate management of a non-renewable resource. Chile's natural nitrate was, from the late eighteenth century to the First World War, the main export product (see Lüders and Wagner, 2003, and the references therein), when competition from synthetic nitrate drove the Chilean minerals out of business.
10 Valdés-Prieto (2008) made a very interesting analysis of the political economy behind the pension reforms. The solidarity pension has existed in Chile since 1952, was reformed in 1963, and was taken as it was in the pension fund reform by the military government in 1981. The present government coalition has blamed the latter as the cause of this liability, but according to Valdés-Prieto (2008), this is a fiscal risk rather than a liability, and it was a legacy of the old system. In the beginning, the motive was to obtain political dividends, but at the time of the windfall, it helped to control pressures for higher fiscal expenditures.
11 There were no explicit policies to avoid the Dutch disease effect of the price of copper. The stabilization fund helps in the sense that it controls government expenditure, which is the main source of Dutch disease. This is important because, when the price of copper rises, firms' benefits increase; part of the benefits go abroad, as they belong to private investors, and part stays in the hands of the government via taxes or CODELCO's profit.
12 In Chile, the Central Bank is independent from the government. This means that it cannot lend money to the central government and it has financial autonomy. Additional details in Central Bank of Chile (2007a).
13 According to figures from the Ministry of Finance, the actual deficit for 2009 was 4.4%, whereas the structural deficit was 3.1%, which reflect the large increase in public expenditure as a percentage of GDP.

References

Barandiarán, E. and L. Hernández (1999) *Origins and Resolution of a Banking Crisis: Chile 1982–86.* Central Bank of Chile Working Paper 57.

Cantallopts, J., P. Perez and R. Molina (2008) 'Análisis Histórico y Estimaciones Futuras del Aporte de la Minería al Desarrollo de la Economía Chilena', *Comisión Chilena del Cobre*, Estudio 28/3.

Central Bank of Chile (2007a) *Monetary Policy in an Inflation Targeting Framework.* Santiago: Central Bank of Chile.

Central Bank of Chile (2007b) *Annual Report.* Santiago: Central Bank of Chile.

Chumacero, R., J.R. Fuentes, R. Lüders and J. Vial (2007) 'Understanding Chilean Reforms' in J.M. Fanelli (ed.) *Understanding Market Reforms in Latin America.* GDN, Palgrave-Macmillan.

Corden, W.M. and J.P. Neary (1982) 'Booming Sector and De-industrialization in a Small Economy', *Economic Journal*, 92, 825–48.

Davis, J., R. Ossowski, J. Daniel and S. Barnett (2001) *Stabilization and Savings Funds for Nonrenewable Resources: Experience and Fiscal Policy Implications.* Occasional Paper 205, International Monetary Fund.

Edwards, A. and S. Edwards (1987) *Monetarism and Liberalization: The Chilean Experiment.* Chicago: The University of Chicago Press.

Engel, E., M. Marcel and P. Meller (2007) *Meta del Superávit Estructural: Elementos para su Análisis*. Santiago, Chile: The Budget Office of the Ministry of Finance (DIPRES).

Engerman, S.L. and K.L. Sokoloff (1997) 'Factor Endowments, Institutions, and Differential Paths of Growth among New World Economies: A View from Economic Historians of the United States' in S. Haber (ed.) *How Latin America Fell Behind: Essays on the Economic Histories of Brazil and Mexico, 1800–1914*. Palo Alto, CA: Stanford University Press, pp. 260–304.

Feenstra, R., R. Lipsey, H. Deng, A. Ma and M. Hengyong (2005) *World Trade Flows: 1962–2000*. NBER Working Paper 11040. Cambridge, MA: NBER.

Hodler, R. (2006) 'The Curse of Natural Resources in Fractionalized Countries', *European Economic Review*, 50, 1367–86.

IMF (2001) *Manual de Estadísticas de Finanzas Públicas*. Washington, DC: International Monetary Fund.

Jofré, J., R. Lüders and G. Wagner (2000) *Economía Chilena 1810–1995: Cuentas Fiscales*. Documento de Trabajo IE-PUC no. 188.

Lane, P.R. and A. Tornell (1996) 'Power, Growth and the Voracity Effect', *Journal of Economic Growth*, 15, 217–45.

Leite, C. and J. Weidmann (2002) 'Does Mother Nature Corrupt? Natural Resources, Corruption and Economic Growth' in G. Abed and S. Gupta (eds) *Governance, Corruption and Economic Performance*. Washington, DC: IMF.

Lipsky, J. (2008) 'Sovereign Wealth Funds: Their Role and Significance'. Speech at the Seminar 'Sovereign Funds: Responsibility with Our Future', organized by the Ministry of Finance, Santiago, Chile, 3 September 2008.

Lüders, R. and G. Wagner (2003) *Export Tariff, Welfare and Public Finance: Nitrates from 1880 to 1930*. Documento de Trabajo IE-PUC no. 241.

Mehlum, H., K. Moene and R. Torvik (2006) 'Institutions and the Resource Curse', *Economic Journal*, 116, 1–20.

Meller, P. (2002) 'El Cobre Chileno y la Política Minera' in P. Meller (ed.) *Dilemas y Debates en Torno al Cobre*. Santiago, Chile: Dolmen Ediciones.

Prat, C. (2005) 'Is it Convenient to Modify the Fiscal Tax Regime to Increase the Earnings of the Chilean State Derived from Private Mining Activities?' Unpublished Dissertation for a Master in Law in Mineral Law and Policy, CEPMLP/Dundee, UK.

Robinson, J.A., R. Torvik and T. Verdier (2003) *Political Foundations of the Resource Curse*. DELTA Working Paper no. 2003-33.

Rodríguez, J., C. Tokman and A. Vega (2007) *Structural Balance Policy in Chile*. Studies in Public Finance. Santiago, Chile: The Budget Office of the Ministry of Finance (DIPRES).

Sachs, J.D. and A.M. Warner (1995) *Natural Resource Abundance and Economic Growth*. NBER Working Paper no. 5398, Cambridge, MA: NBER.

Sanhueza, G. (2001) *Chilean Banking Crisis of the 1980s: Solution and Estimation of the Costs*. Working paper 104. Santiago: Central Bank of Chile.

Spiller, P.T. and M. Tommasi (2003) 'The Institutional Determinants of Public Policy: A Transaction Approach with Application to Argentina', *Journal of Law, Economics and Organization*, 19, 281–306.

Tilton, J.E. (2003) *On Borrowed Time? Assessing the Threat of Mineral Depletion*. Washington, DC: RFF Press, Resources for the Future.

Torvik, R. (2001) 'Learning by Doing and the Dutch Disease', *European Economic Review*, 45, 285–306.

Truman, E. (2008) *A Blueprint for Sovereign Wealth Fund Best Practices*. Policy Brief no. PB08-3. Peterson Institute for International Economics.

Valdés-Prieto, S. (2008) 'The 2008 Chilean Reform to First Pillar Pensions'. Manuscript, Pontificia Universidad Católica de Chile.

Walsh, J., M. Papaioannou, M. Singh and E. Tereanu (2008) 'Chile's Sovereign Wealth Funds: An International Perspective' in IMF (ed.) *Chile: Selected Issues Paper*. Washington, DC: IMF.

Further Reading

Engerman, S.L. and K.L. Sokoloff (2000) 'Factor Endowments, Inequality, and Paths of Development among New World Economies', *Economía*, 3, 41–102.

Ministry of Finance of Chile (2008) *Informe Ejecutivo Mensual: Fondo de Reserva de Pensiones*. August. Santiago: Ministry of Finance of Chile.

Ministry of Finance of Chile (2008) *Informe Ejecutivo Mensual: Fondo de Estabilización Económica y Social*. August. Santiago: Ministry of Finance of Chile.

Republic of Chile (1993) *Decree Law 600: Foreign Investment Statute*. Santiago: Republic of Chile.

Appendix

Table A.3.1 Balance of payments (in US$ million)

Year	Current account	Mining exports	Financial account
1960	−148.1	321.5	76.3
1961	−241.1	305.6	187.6
1962	−181.9	330.9	133.2
1963	−157.8	339.8	107.6
1964	−131.6	363.4	152.1
1965	−56.6	428.5	65.8
1966	−82.2	598.6	168
1967	−127.4	651.3	125.5
1968	−135.3	684.3	294.6
1969	−5.6	925.5	222.5
1970	−102.9	839.8	267.5
1971	−205.5	701.2	−26.5
1972	−404.8	618.2	327.4
1973	−293.6	1048.7	−847.2
1974	−210.8	1623.3	72.4
1975	−491.7	868.2	1537.7
1976	147.7	1233.2	606.5
1977	−551	1161.4	560.1
1978	−1087.9	1218.7	2045
1979	−1189.4	1887.9	2474.9
1980	−1970.6	2124.7	1920.9
1981	−4732.6	1737.8	4630.8
1982	−2304.2	1684.6	2379.8
1983	−117.3	1874.9	1049.1
1984	−2110.5	1603.9	1922.8
1985	−1413	1788.7	1482.8
1986	−1191.2	1757.1	968.7
1987	−735.5	2234.7	890.2
1988	−231.2	3416.2	353.7
1989	−689.9	4021.4	723.1
1990	−484.8	3810.2	533.8
1991	−98.6	3617.3	−291.4
1992	−958.2	3886	587.8
1993	−2553.4	3247.8	2565.7
1994	−1585.3	4242	2142.5
1995	−1345.1	6487.1	1217.5
1996	−3082.7	6843.3	3063.7
1997	−3660.2	7486	3422
1998	−3918.4	6051.9	4160.3
1999	99.5	6777.8	974.7
2000	−897.4	8020.7	450.7
2001	−1100.3	7256.4	1957.9
2002	−580.1	7120.2	1435.7

Table A.3.1 (cont):

Year	Current account	Mining exports	Financial account
2003	−778.7	8795.1	1511.1
2004	2074.5	16,962.3	−1810
2005	1449	23,190.9	−166.1
2006	6838.1	36,976.9	−7054.1
2007	7199.7	43,106.7	−6222.3

Source: Central Bank of Chile. Data before 1973 are constructed with the old balance of payments definitions.

Table A.3.2 Fiscal accounts (millions of 1996 Chilean pesos)

Year	Total spending	Interest spending	Copper revenues	Other revenues	Gross fiscal balance	Primary fiscal balance
1960	1,435,315	0	157,073	1,049,881	−228,361	−228,361
1961	1,510,375	0	122,834	1,163,854	−223,687	−223,687
1962	1,723,105	0	161,460	1,212,460	−349,185	−349,185
1963	1,632,220	0	165,992	1,182,866	−283,362	−283,362
1964	1,565,468	0	172,345	1,196,206	−196,917	−196,917
1965	1,820,579	0	196,556	1,478,755	−145,268	−145,268
1966	2,026,953	0	304,030	1,536,874	−186,049	−186,049
1967	1,952,248	0	278,504	1,607,936	−65,808	−65,808
1968	2,039,767	0	264,053	1,696,764	−78,950	−78,950
1969	2,048,276	0	321,961	1,791,205	64,891	64,891
1970	2,357,675	0	352,285	1,869,200	−136,190	−136,190
1971	3,315,915	0	45,814	2,298,604	−971,497	−971,497
1972	4,208,617	0	57,970	2,617,555	−1,533,093	−1,533,093
1973	3,496,985	0	48,264	2,616,271	−832,450	−832,450
1974	3,712,737	0	133,489	2,914,299	−664,949	−664,949
1975	3,356,459	0	172,560	3,142,169	−41,730	−41,730
1976	3,107,084	0	152,448	2,904,383	−50,253	−50,253
1977	3,411,161	0	154,712	3,130,175	−126,273	−126,273
1978	3,628,208	0	238,942	3,376,092	−13,175	−13,175
1979	3,323,328	0	212,144	3,758,520	647,336	647,336
1980	3,469,715	0	259,728	3,997,846	787,859	787,859
1981	4,095,741	0	280,859	4,212,122	397,240	397,240
1982	4,057,242	0	373,534	3,547,354	−136,354	−136,354
1983	3,845,223	0	221,995	3,272,259	−350,969	−350,969
1984	4,192,453	0	273,045	3,506,753	−412,654	−412,654
1985	4,072,692	0	263,242	3,492,335	−317,115	−317,115
1986	3,896,209	0	138,100	3,623,626	−134,482	−134,482
1987	3,536,013	317,656	455,734	3,445,434	365,155	682,811
1988	3,497,404	383,085	1,023,081	3,141,477	667,154	1,050,240
1989	3,547,356	316,016	1,224,368	3,275,575	952,587	1,268,602
1990	3,491,342	357,518	850,676	3,217,936	577,270	934,788
1991	3,917,945	425,853	482,766	3,870,601	435,422	861,274

Table A.3.2 (cont):

Year	Total spending	Interest spending	Copper revenues	Other revenues	Gross fiscal balance	Primary fiscal balance
1992	4,286,522	310,803	430,281	4,413,399	557,158	867,961
1993	4,696,585	295,094	228,418	4,753,705	285,537	580,631
1994	4,973,114	244,156	431,416	5,002,678	460,981	705,137
1995	4,975,528	197,630	663,449	5,284,329	972,250	1,169,880
1996	5,710,049	165,939	407,026	6,010,253	707,230	873,169
1997	6,064,612	135,012	448,632	6,333,113	717,133	852,145
1998	6,735,632	219,447	136,748	6,607,095	8,211	227,658
1999	7,184,425	110,885	123,302	6,393,368	−667,755	−556,870
2000	7,349,199	158,429	319,394	7,128,215	98,410	256,839
2001	8,237,068	514,292	230,667	9,242,385	1,235,984	1,750,276
2002	8,762,537	539,789	214,749	9,556,023	1,008,235	1,548,024
2003	9,167,524	588,761	450,361	10,154,004	1,436,841	2,025,602
2004	9,766,995	560,583	1,753,488	11,044,878	3,031,371	3,591,954
2005	10,582,360	553,527	2,440,440	13,240,437	5,098,517	5,652,044
2006[1]	11,745,634	539,103	4,431,123	15,629,383	8,314,872	8,853,975
2007[1]	13,167,556	521,302	4,141,791	19,337,478	10,311,713	10,833,015

[1] Data for 2006 and 2007 correspond to accrual basis instead of cash flow basis.

Source: Central Bank of Chile.

4

Oil in Iran
Dependence, distortions and distribution
Massoud Karshenas and Adeel Malik

4.1 Introduction

Since it was first discovered in Iran in the early twentieth century, oil has continued to shape Iran's development trajectory in a significant way. By virtue of being a leading oil exporter in the world, Iran accumulates significant resources from oil. An abiding feature of its economy, in periods both before and after the 1979 revolution, is the close link between the vagaries of global oil markets and domestic economic fortunes.[1] This link has strengthened over time as Iran has become more dependent on oil revenues as a major source of foreign exchange, government revenue and savings.

This chapter traces the impact of oil on Iran's economic development. The influence of oil is mediated, among other things, through government policy, political structures and institutions. However, public policies are also influenced by the nature of the interests they serve. We therefore study Iran's development experience through the political economy lens, focusing not just on outcomes but on deeper political structures that produce and sustain these outcomes. This chapter argues that the story of oil and development in Iran revolves around three inter-related spheres of influence: dependence, distortions and distribution.

Iran's exports are overwhelmingly concentrated in oil, with the result that its economy is driven primarily by developments in the oil sector. At the same time, Iran has an overextended state that frequently disrupts markets and distorts the policy environment. It is one of those rare examples where *dirigisme*, or state-directed development, has run a very long course, surviving well into the twenty-first century. This *license raj* of the Middle East – manifested through planning, protection and economic controls – has been sustained through the continued inflow of oil resources. Without oil, it would have been difficult to sustain these restrictive institutions. Finally, Iran provides a fascinating account of how oil rents are shared with a wide constituency of supporters through a political redistribution of sorts.

The adverse effects of oil specialization that are typically associated with resource-rich economies are very much at work in Iran as well. For instance, Iran is no stranger to such pathologies as growth collapses, a weak tax effort, pro-cyclical fiscal policy, large government, delayed economic reform and an underdeveloped private sector. But Iran does not offer a straightforward demonstration of the resource curse. It started off with relatively favourable initial conditions. The country has a sizeable middle class and has never been directly colonized. From an early stage, Iran had implemented land reforms and made impressive gains in literacy. As a result, Iran enjoyed levels of development that preceded the stellar economic performance of East Asia. During the period 1959–77, for example, real non-oil gross domestic product (GDP) per capita in Iran grew at the rate of about 7 per cent per annum. By early 1970s, Iran's per capita income was twice that of South Korea. Yet, its economic fortunes diverged significantly in later years, with the result that, in 2005, its per capita income in purchasing power parity (PPP) terms was one-third of that in South Korea.[2] Ironically, if there was one country in the Middle East that was better positioned to convert its oil wealth into a blessing, it was Iran. The study of oil and development in Iran is therefore a sobering narrative of lost opportunities.

Oil, however, is not the only factor that greases the wheels of Iran's political economy. In many ways, Iran's development experience is shaped by the confluence of three factors: oil, ideology and isolation. The policies and development outcomes that we analyse in this chapter are as much a product of Iran's distinct ideological heritage, principally the legacy of the 1979 Islamic revolution, and its international isolation. The US sanctions against Iran, the freezing of its assets, the protracted war with Iraq and its continuing economic and political isolation provide an important context that has forced Iran to look inwards and pursue more protectionist policies. Of course, this was reinforced by the political influence of interest groups within Iran who benefited from the country's protectionist policies. A proper analysis of these non-oil influences lies beyond the remit of this chapter, but it is worth recognizing them at the outset.

The discussion in this chapter is organized into six sections. Section 4.2 sets the context for our analysis by providing a brief description of natural resource endowments, institutions and major economic developments since 1960s. Section 4.3 describes arrangements in the oil sector. The macroeconomic consequences of oil are discussed in Section 4.4, whereas the associated political economy issues are developed in Section 4.5. Finally, Section 4.6 offers some concluding remarks.

4.2 The context: endowments, history and institutions

This section will set out the resource and institutional context of the Islamic Republic of Iran. It will define the nature of initial conditions that modulate the context in which oil shapes economic development in Iran.

4.2.1 Resource endowments

Iran is endowed with significant natural resources, which consist mainly of hydrocarbon reserves. The World Bank's wealth estimates indicate that natural capital constitutes about 59 per cent of total wealth in Iran.[3] Oil and natural gas constitute 73 per cent of total natural wealth. It is the fourth largest oil producer in the world, and its proven oil reserves are second only to Saudi Arabia. Current International Energy Agency (IEA) estimates of oil reserves suggest 93 years of production at current extraction rates. Iran also has significant gas reserves, amounting to 15 per cent of proven global reserves – second highest after Russia. The South Pars field, which is one of Iran's largest offshore gas fields in the Gulf and contains 8–10 per cent of world gas reserves, has recently attracted considerable foreign investment. However, Iran's gas sector is less developed compared with its regional competitors, Oman and Qatar.

Although hydrocarbons are the dominant natural resource in Iran, the country is also endowed with mineral deposits, including copper, iron ore, bauxite, coal and gold, among others. 'Around 80m tonnes of minerals are quarried every year from some 1,500 non-metallic and 50 metallic mines' (EIU, 2008). Within the mineral category, the copper industry has assumed growing significance. Iran holds 4 per cent of the world's copper deposits. The reserve at Sar Chesmeh near Kerman is the second largest deposit in the world, containing an estimated one billion tonnes of ore.[4]

4.2.2 The structure of the Iranian state

The political economy of post-revolutionary Iran stems from the unique structure of the Iranian state. Iran has a dual structure of power, whereby the official state, namely the elected parliament and the executive, coexists with the unelected core state controlled by the clergy and headed by the supreme leader. The core clerical state, apart from having control over important state apparatuses such as the judiciary and the armed forces, also screens candidates who can take part in parliamentary and presidential elections, has veto power over the legislation passed by the parliament and exerts considerable influence over the day-to-day affairs of the official government through a variety of informal channels.

Within this institutional architecture, several organizations are assigned the task of supervising, overseeing and coordinating national decision making. For example, a conservative vetting body known as the *Guardian Council* ensures the consistency of parliamentary laws with the Islamic injunctions. Any possible conflicts that might arise between the *Guardian Council* and *Majlis* (the elected parliament) are mediated by another institution of the core state, the *Expediency Council*.

This duality of the state structure complicates our analysis of how core decisions regarding the extraction and use of natural resources are actually made in Iran. It would be oversimplistic to treat the Iranian state as an autonomous and unitary state and analyse the five decision points around: negotiations, contract design, transparency in revenues, and savings and expenditure policies. The dual state structure in Iran translates into a multiplicity of power centres, representing different coalitions of social, economic and religious interests. Various factions attached to these power centres are sustained through elaborate informal networks.

This duality of power structure provides an important context for analysing Iran's political economy. The dual structure sows the seeds of 'embedded factionalism', which generates destructive competition over power and resources (Bjorvatn and Selvik, 2008). The distinct structure of the post-revolutionary state – and its supporting constituencies – has, in turn, a determining influence on how hydrocarbon revenues are channelled to the society. The different economic and political interests that these factions have come to represent are therefore key drivers of macroeconomic policies. It serves as the essential backdrop against which much of Iran's political economy can be explained – be it redistributive fiscal policies, the nature of economic distortions or rents from natural resources.

To see why this state structure is central to explaining Iran's political economy, consider the economic clout of charitable organizations (*Bonyads*) and the Revolutionary Guards (*Sepāh e Pāsdārān e Enqelāb e*

Eslāmi), both of which operate in semi-autonomous public domains and are indirectly controlled by the core state. They receive significant public funding and are broadly exempt from public accountability. Although the core unelected state has no direct budgetary influence, it has significant indirect stakes in these semi-public organizations. For example, these semi-public organizations are crucial vehicles for dispensing patronage to various political constituencies. In short, the core state is believed to control vast economic assets through these 'shadow' economic forces. Its economic interests are reflected in a variety of public policies from the terms at which bank credit is allocated to the pace of economic reform and the nature of 'privatization' of public assets. Many of these stories will form an essential part of ensuing discussions in this chapter.

4.2.3 Growth cycles and institutional changes since the 1960s

This section will provide a brief overview of the key political economy developments of Iran since the 1960s. For this purpose, we will define the economic history of Iran in three distinct periods, namely the pre-revolution period (1960–78), the decade of revolution and the Iraq war (from late 1979 to the late 1980s), and the period since the end of the Iran–Iraq war. Each period can in turn be divided into various subperiods according to different criteria. Figure 4.1 shows one such categorization based on cycles in GDP growth.

A description of the salient features of economic development in each phase will form a useful backdrop for analysing the management of oil revenues and its consequent impact on economic growth.

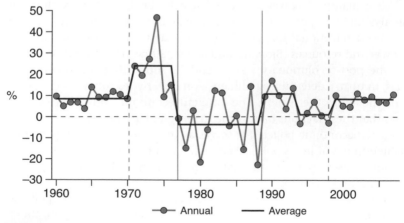

Figure 4.1 GDP growth cycles, 1960–2007

4.2.3.1 The pre-revolution era

The period prior to the 1979 revolution can be viewed as consisting of two subperiods (see Figure 4.1). One is the long period of sustained economic growth during the 1960s up to the oil price boom of 1972–74. During this period, GDP growth in Iran was among the highest achieved by any country at that time on a sustained basis. It is also remarkable that such high growth performance in Iran was achieved with relative price stability and low inflation (consumer prices index (CPI) inflation was 1.7 per cent a year during the 1960s). This was made possible by a steady growth in oil export volumes, of over 12 per cent a year, giving rise to a stable flow of foreign exchange proceeds. This helped to sustain the rapid pace of import-substituting industrialization (ISI). Growth in the pre-revolution era was also driven by: (1) generous investments in infrastructure and heavy industry; (2) land reforms; and (3) higher educational investments. These became the enabling conditions for sustained growth.

The second subperiod in this phase coincides with the oil price hike of 1972–74 and the mismanagement of oil revenues by the government, which led to an overheated economy and a subsequent recession that began as early as 1976. This also ushered in the end of the long secular trend of growing oil export volumes which began in the mid-1950s. Iranian oil production reached its peak in 1976. The economic system in this phase can be characterized as a mixed market economy, akin to the systems commonly prevalent in other developing countries at the time. Public investment was conducted within the framework of 5-year development plans, and was mainly concentrated in infrastructure and heavy industry.

Government planning in this period was complementary to private sector activities, and public incentives became instrumental to private sector growth. A strong ISI strategy was pursued behind high tariff walls and concessionary development finance. Development banks provided targeted credit subsidies and relevant technical assistance. A new class of industrialists emerged who energetically introduced many new industries and technologies in close association with foreign capital. The land reform programme during the 1960s also undermined the established absentee landlordism, opened the agricultural sector to commercial farming and increased the mobility of labour.

After having grown on a sustained basis for nearly two decades since the mid-1950s, oil exports slumped in the second half of the 1970s. The end of the oil era had tested the industrialization strategy of the 1960s. The absence of significant productivity improvements and the lack of solid institutional foundations made growth unsustainable. A complicating factor was the macroeconomic mismanagement that followed after the oil boom of the early 1970s. Oil windfalls led to a major spending drive that proved inflationary, but also facilitated rent-seeking activities with associated inefficiencies. The time had come for economic reform and the adoption of a new development strategy, which should have implied a change from a top-down development strategy to one in which the new industrial class was assigned a greater strategic role, in both economic and political terms. Whether the Shah's regime was capable of such a move is a question of historical interest only as, with the onset of the 1979 revolution, events took a dramatically different turn.

4.2.3.2 The phase of revolution and war

The second period begins after the revolution in 1979 and the subsequent war with Iraq which continued during much of the 1980s. The external context was adverse during this period, in terms of both falling oil prices and the changing geostrategic context. The drastic fall in oil exports precipitated an economic decline. By 1988, real per capita national income had declined by 50 per cent from its peak in 1976. Iran's status in the western community switched from being a friend to being a foe, inviting sanctions and international isolation. This brought profound changes in Iran's political economy and shaped the contemporary economic and political structures in important ways. The foundations of the dual state structure, where the elected parliament coexists with the unelected core state, were laid in this period (see Section 4.2.2 for background).

At least three developments are noticeable during this post-revolution period. First, there was a large-scale nationalization of the banking, industrial and services sector. Second, the Iranian state assumed an overextended role in the economy by imposing direct controls over the market. Third, as a necessary consequence of international isolation and domestic economic intervention, the post-revolution years saw an emergence of entrenched interest groups.

At the time of the revolution, almost all of the modern large-scale enterprises in industry and services, including the banks, were taken over by the state. A large part of these assets was transferred to semi-private charitable institutions (*Bonyads*), which have come to dominate the economy by accumulating vast assets in recent years. They operate under the auspices of the office of the supreme leader and, apart from their dominant control of the large-scale non-government enterprise sector, they also wield considerable political power. They obey neither the laws of public enterprises nor those of the independent private sector. These charities are exempt from taxation, and their accounts are not publicly disclosed. By the end of this period, the large-scale enterprises were predominantly controlled either by the government or by the semi-official *Bonyads*.

This appears to be in line with the economic system envisaged in the constitution of the Islamic Republic, where the private sector was assigned a relatively minor role. The expanded role of the state in the economy was not solely confined to a shift in the balance from private to public ownership. It was also manifested in an intricate system of direct controls over the operation of markets, from foreign exchange controls and the maintenance of a system of multiple exchange rates to the control of interest rates and allocation of bank credits, as well as rationing and direct price controls in a large number of product markets.

By the mid-1980s, the black market exchange rate had a 2000 per cent premium over the increasingly overvalued official exchange rate. The twenty-fold premium in the parallel exchange market was indicative of the enormous subsidies that the oil sector provided to those who benefited from the government's foreign exchange rationing system. Similar subsidies were granted through the subsidization of consumer products and key producer inputs, such as energy. By the end of the decade, the prices of some key products such as energy and bread had fallen to well below 10 per cent of international prices (see, for example, Karshenas and Pesaran, 1995). Some of this came about as a result of the exigencies of running a war economy, but over time, the resulting price distortions gave rise to entrenched interest groups, which made the task of reform difficult in later years.

4.2.3.3 *The post-war period*

The third phase began with the ending of the Iran–Iraq war. In many ways, this constitutes the pragmatic phase of the Islamic Republic. It began with a partial liberalization and economic reform programme, combined with a large reconstruction and investment effort undertaken by the government. Economic planning, which had been abandoned during the war years, was reinstated with the first 5-year plan of the Islamic Republic under President Rafsanjani. Privatization of state enterprises appeared on the policy agenda. A significant reform was the unification of the exchange rate in March 1993.

Even partial reform effort proved short-lived, however. Unbridled expansion of bank credit and unsustainable foreign borrowing led to the abandonment of the reform programme. The bulk of foreign debt in 1993 was in short-term commercial credit. In the presence of US sanctions, the government faced difficulties in rescheduling these debts, forcing it to reintroduce trade and foreign exchange restrictions. By December 1993, the foreign exchange unification policy was effectively given up. The rest of the 1990s was a period characterized by economic retrenchment and repayment of the public debt accumulated during the boom in the early 1990s.

At a deeper level, however, there has been limited reform in the basic economic structure of the Iranian state that emerged during the first decade of the revolution. If anything, there has been a considerable shift of economic power from the official elected government – the 'legal rational' arm of the state – towards the less transparent and more murky and informal core state, with the independent private sector being increasingly marginalized. Since the early 1990s, the process of privatization has continued with ups and downs. This process received a major push under President Khatami's third 5-year plan, which ratified an ambitious privatization programme despite opposition from sections of the core state. By and large, the privatized government enterprises have, however, either been taken over by the semi-public *Bonyads* or sold via public offering in the Tehran stock exchange with majority shares being controlled by government-owned banks and other public or semi-public institutions. Privatization has, however, posed a limited challenge to the government's dominant role in the economy. In many cases, privatized assets have simply been transferred from the state to semi-public organizations.

Privatization continues to remain on the policy agenda, with greater constitutional and political support being accorded to the process.[5] A new executive order by the supreme leader in 2006 has directed the government to privatize government enterprises by the end of the fifth development plan (2014). Government ownership will be limited to a few strategic activities such as upstream oil and gas, selected banks and a few companies in the utilities and transport sectors. The majority of shares will be sold to non-government foundations at 50 per cent discount and will be managed on behalf of the poor (IMF, 2007).

Despite the variable economic record, there are two favourable trends that have gained strength since the 1960s, and therefore deserve a proper mention. These relate to the important demographic and social changes in Iran. Besides the introduction of land reforms, the 1960s saw the introduction of family law and a vigorous campaign for family planning. In the pre-revolution period, the population grew at an annual average rate of 2.8 per cent, but it slowed down during the 1970s. Although the rate of population growth initially increased after the revolution because of war and the pro-natal policies of the government, it has subsequently fallen as a result of the resumption of an effective family planning programme. The population growth rate, which had risen to 3.9 per cent in the 1980s, has fallen to 1.5 per cent since the early 1990s. This has had important implications for the country's demographic profile and labour force dynamics. Another underlying factor has been a steady improvement in education and health indicators. Mean years of schooling increased from about 1 in the early 1960s to 3.4 in the early 1980s, 5.1 in 2000, and close to 6 in 2008.[6] In the early 1970s, mean years of schooling were well below international norms; by the year 2000, however, Iran had achieved levels of education that were more commensurate with its per capita income.

4.3 Oil sector arrangements

Iran was the first country in the Middle East where oil was discovered and exported in the early twentieth century. Iran was also the first country where oil was nationalized in the early 1950s. The National Iranian Oil Company (NIOC) was the first national oil company in the Middle East set up at that time to manage the oil industry on behalf of the government. With the defeat of the oil nationalization movement in effect up to the early 1970s, the major part of the oil reserves was under the control of foreign oil companies under the commonly prevailing 50:50 profit-sharing agreement. From the early 1970s, along with other oil-exporting countries in the Middle East, effective control of all oil reserves was taken over by the NIOC, which operated under production-sharing agreements with foreign oil companies up to the 1979 revolution.

Since the 1979 revolution, production-sharing agreements have been replaced by the so-called *buy-back agreements*, a mixture of service contract and limited production-sharing agreement. These agreements grew out of Iranian sensitivity about retaining local control of the country's natural resources while at the same time attracting the skills and resources of foreign firms. As part of these contracts, a 'foreign investor develops the designated field according to a previously agreed budget, hands over the facility once production starts and is reimbursed, with an agreed profit margin, from the proceeds of the field's output over a fixed period'.

The design of these buy-back agreements is believed to have led to underinvestment in the oil sector. The relatively inflexible terms of the buy-back agreements, together with strict constitutional limits on local control of the oil fields, has caused delays in the completion of projects. Negotiations with foreign firms have been further prolonged by a dearth of suitably qualified professionals in the oil ministry and NIOC. Buy-back contracts can also lead to considerable inefficiency and limit technology transfer by forcing the foreign oil companies to take only a short-term interest in the oil projects at the expense of long-term efficiencies.

Overall, Iran has not fully exploited its potential for attracting foreign resources for oil sector development. Officially recorded foreign investment in the oil sector constitutes no more than 0.01 per cent of GDP. The inflexibility of Iran's distinct contracting arrangements, together with a hostile international environment, has impeded efforts to expand oil production. Three constraints are particularly note worthy: (1) the war with Iraq; (2) US sanctions since 1997; and (3) growing domestic demand for fuel.

Oil production peaked in 1976 and subsequently declined after the 1979 revolution and the war with Iraq in the 1980s. Soon after the revolution, oil production dropped from 5 million to 1.5 million barrels/day (bbl/d). Production has picked up since the end of the Iraq war, but remains well below the pre-revolution levels (see Figure 4.2). In recent years, the country has been struggling to raise oil production, bringing it up to 3.8 million bbl/d. But even to maintain these production levels, Iran needs to add approximately 300,000 bbl/d of output every year, which requires substantial new investments to upgrade Iran's ageing fields.

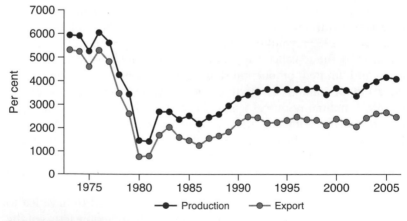

Figure 4.2 Crude oil production and exports

Direct US sanctions against foreign investment in Iran's energy sector have been another key inhibiting factor.[7] US sanctions have slowed down the development of oil fields, even though Iran has been successful in attracting resources from non-US sources (mainly Europe and China). The impact of US sanctions has been estimated to cost the Iranian economy to the tune of 1.1 per cent of GDP annually (Torbat, 2005). Iran has neither the skills nor the requisite financial resources to fully compensate for this underinvestment in the oil sector.

Iran's capacity to invest in the energy sector is strained by growing domestic demand for subsidized fuel and limited local refining capacity. This has drained both government revenues and the exportable surplus of oil. Crude oil exports have stagnated since the early 1990s. A growing population at home and subsidized provision of fuel have raised domestic demand for oil. On average, domestic oil consumption has grown annually at the rate of 4.3 per cent during the period 1999–2006. Owing to a lack of domestic refining capacity, Iran needs to import more than 50 per cent of its petrol. Imports of refined oil have therefore increased from 60,000 bbl/d in 1990 to well over 260,000 bbl/d. Recently, Iran has encouraged the substitution of gas for oil in domestic consumption in order to release a greater exportable surplus of oil.

Regardless of these external and domestic constraints to the extraction of oil, revenues accrued from the sale of natural resources are recorded and disclosed with relative transparency. Oil, gas and other mineral resources are treated as national wealth, and revenue from these are consistently recorded in budget documents and balance of payment accounts. There is also no direct evidence of any large-scale misappropriation or illegal diversion of oil revenues. In this respect, Iran fares markedly better than many of its peers in the resource-rich Middle East, where the distinction between public and private wealth is more often blurred. There is no evidence of crude misappropriation of oil revenues. Issues of transparency arise indirectly through channelling of rents to favoured interest groups. Macroeconomic policies often serve as convenient tools for such political redistribution. We will spell this out more clearly in subsequent sections.

4.4 Oil and the macro-economy

Oil is a central driver of macroeconomic developments in Iran. There are three key aspects of the role of oil in Iran's economy: a provider of government revenue, a source of foreign exchange and a supplement to domestic savings. These three aspects of the contribution of oil revenues – government finance, savings and foreign exchange contributions – and the problems they pose for the management of the economy are the subject of this section. Figure 4.3 traces the evolution of the share of oil in total exports, savings and government revenues since 1959.

Historically, the Iranian economy has shown a high degree of dependence on the proceeds from oil exports. As shown in Figure 4.3, crude oil exports have consistently constituted over 80 per cent of foreign exchange revenues over the past five decades. The contribution of oil revenues to the government budget has also been consistently high. In fact, as shown in Figure 4.3, during the more recent growth period of 1999–2007, the share of oil revenues in total government revenues has been well above the early growth phase of 1960–71. Oil revenues have also made a sizeable contribution to national savings. This was particularly evident during the two oil booms in the 1970s and 2000s. Oil's contribution to exports, government revenues and savings has also shown considerable volatility since 1959, closely tracking movements in oil prices. Cycles in the domestic economy are therefore directly linked to developments in the oil sector. The next section will separately examine the effect of oil on the national budget, savings and investment.

4.4.1 Oil and the budget

Oil's most direct channel of influence on the domestic economy is its effect on the government budget. Table 4.1 presents the evolution of different aspects of the central government budget since 1965. An

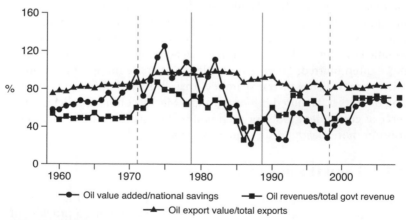

Figure 4.3 Share of oil in exports, government revenue and national savings

important clarification to note here is that data on oil revenues in the 1980s and 1990s are not strictly comparable with other decades. This is because oil revenues during these two decades were converted in highly overvalued official exchange rates. This generated hidden subsidies and transfers to those who had access to foreign exchange at official rates. With the unification of the exchange rate in 2002, however, these subsidies have been made explicit. Notwithstanding these caveats, the evidence provided in Table 4.1 confirms the observation we made earlier: oil revenues dominate the trends and cycles in government revenues. Furthermore, unexpected increases in oil revenues have often led to a spending bonanza.

What stands out from Table 4.1 is the extremely undeveloped fiscal machinery of the government, as indicated by the very low and declining share of taxes in GDP. This enhances the country's dependence on oil revenues. Few people pay direct income taxes; their share in GDP is a paltry 1 per cent. The main contribution to tax revenues comes from corporate and import taxes. Even corporate taxes remain low, and have

Table 4.1 Central Government Budget, 1965–2007 (% of GDP)

	1965–67	1975–77	1985–87	1995–97	2005–07
Total revenues	20.6	43.3	14.1	22.1	30.2
Oil revenues	10.5	33.3	5.4	14.0	21.2
Tax revenues	8.4	8.3	6.6	5.0	6.1
Corporate tax	–	3.2	2.4	2.1	2.2
Income tax	–	1.0	1.0	1.1	0.9
Wealth tax	–	0.3	0.3	0.2	0.3
Import tax	–	3.0	1.5	1.1	2.0
Sales and consumption tax	–	0.8	1.4	0.4	0.7
Other revenues	1.7	1.8	2.1	3.2	2.6
Expenditure	23.6	49.6	21.6	22.4	28.3
Current	14.8	30.8	16.8	15.2	19.7
Development	8.9	18.8	4.8	7.2	6.6
Budget deficit/surplus	–3.0	–6.3	–7.5	–0.3	1.8
(% of non-oil GDP)	–3.7	–10.0	–8.0	–0.3	2.5
Non-oil balance	–13.5	–39.5	–12.9	–14.3	–19.4
(% of non-oil GDP)	–16.4	–63.8	–13.8	–16.9	–26.6

The consolidated budget of the central government includes the stabilization fund and net transfers to state-owned enterprises, but excludes the budget of municipalities and local governments financed by local taxes.

Source: Central Bank of Iran and IMF (2007).

actually declined as a share of GDP since 1977. This is surprising in the face of a growing corporate sector and a shrinking share for the agricultural sector. A partial explanation for this may have to do with the growing role of charitable foundations (*Bonyads*) that dominate Iran's corporate sector yet remain outside the tax net. In 2008, the government attempted to reform the tax system by introducing a 3 per cent value added tax, but this has been resisted by protest marches and the closure of the bazaars in some major cities.

Another notable aspect of the dependence of public spending on oil revenues relates to the speed with which unexpected increases in oil revenues are translated into government expenditures. Despite the existence of long-term expenditure plans, increases in government revenue, over and above those budgeted within the development planning framework, were immediately translated into increased public expenditures. This tendency of government expenditures to closely track movements in oil revenues is common across both the pre- and the post-revolution periods.

An important institutional development for Iran's fiscal regime was the establishment of the Oil Stabilization Fund (OSF) in 2000. The primary objective of the OSF was to collect surplus petroleum receipts for smoothing out the effect of unexpected oil price fluctuations. A secondary objective was to promote investment in priority sectors. At least 50 per cent of the fund's balances are set aside as foreign exchange loans to the private sector through commercial banks. In principle, government withdrawals from the OSF for budgetary purposes are discouraged, requiring ratification by the parliament. In practice, the OSF is frequently raided to meet budgetary needs. Table 4.2 presents OSF accounts

Table 4.2 Oil Stabilization Fund (OSF) operations, 2000–06 (in US$ billion)

	2000	2001	2002	2003	2004	2005	2006
Total inflows	5.9	1.8	5.9	5.8	10.4	13.0	21.6
Total outflows	0.0	0.8	5.1	5.4	9.4	11.5	23.0
(Transfers to the central govt budget)	0.0	0.4	4.5	5.3	7.5	7.8	17.8
(Net domestic onlending)	0.0	0.1	0.6	0.1	1.8	2.1	5.3
Valuation adjustments							0.3
OSF balance	5.9	1.0	0.8	0.4	1.0	1.5	−1.1
Memorandum items:							
OSF stock of foreign exchange deposits at the Central Bank	5.9	7.0	7.8	8.1	9.1	10.7	9.5
OSF stocks of domestic loans	0.0	0.1	0.7	0.8	2.6	4.8	10.0

Source: IMF (2008).

for the period 2000–06. A striking finding from Table 4.2 is that over 80 per cent of the funds have been transferred to the central government budget since the creation of the OSF.

In 2006 alone, withdrawals by central government were equivalent to the entire assets of the OSF at the end of 2006. By the end of 2007, the OSF had foreign exchange deposits of about US$22 billion and a domestic loan portfolio of US$14.4 billion. With the recent rapid increase in oil prices, the transfer of funds from the OSF to the current budget has increased rapidly, standing at over US$20 billion in 2007. In fact, 90 per cent of the actual budget deficit in 2007 was financed through OSF withdrawals (Farzanegan and Markwardt, 2009). Considering that the rise in oil revenues over this period is mainly attributable to higher oil prices rather than an expansion in output or exportable surplus, this high degree of reliance on OSF funds, apart from leading to short-term inflationary pressures, is a recipe for fiscal crises and more serious instability in the medium and long run.

The apparently similar spending responses of the pre- and post-revolution governments to oil price booms can convey the misleading impression that the underlying political economy has remained unchanged. Quite the opposite; prior to the 1979 revolution, the government was a highly centralized and unified technocratic entity, which had a relatively high degree of autonomy from underlying societal forces. Many of the economic problems during that era were associated with top-down planning that is characteristic of a centralized state. It was also responsible for the overheating of the economy during the 1973–74 oil boom, as the technocrats did not have the power to stand up to the grandiose dreams of the Shah when he ordered a quadrupling of the size of the fifth development plan.

The political economy of the Islamic Republic is markedly different, however. The dual power structure of post-revolutionary Iran introduces critical differences in the resource allocation mechanisms between the two regimes. A different set of fiscal priorities is now shaping patterns of public spending. For example, the core clerical state now controls vast economic assets and often uses them as a means for rewarding its supporters through employment generation and charitable transfers.

An important change in the structure of the budget during the post-revolution period is the decline in the share of government development expenditure and the relatively large increase in the share of current expenditures (Figure 4.4). This is not an unexpected result for the war years of the 1980s, when both the drastic cut in oil revenues and the war

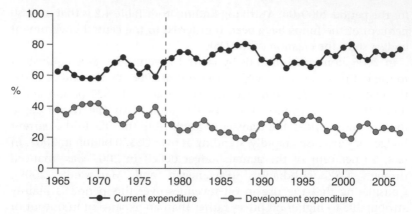

Figure 4.4 Share of current and development expenditure in the government budget

effort had strained public finances. Development expenditures did pick up after the war, returning roughly to pre-revolution levels.

But this surge proved short-lived. The share of current expenditures in government spending has grown since the mid-1990s. Perhaps more surprisingly, the share of development expenditures has remained low despite growing oil revenues since 1999. This may partly be a result of the new interpretation of Article 44 of the constitution, which prevents the official government from engaging in industrial and commercial investments. However, this still does not explain the underinvestment in infrastructure, especially electricity generation activities.

What explains this rising share of current expenditures? These growing expenditure commitments reflect, in part, the political compulsion to create public employment and to maintain generous public subsidies. For example, food subsidies have more than doubled, increasing from about 1.4 per cent of GDP in 2000 to about 3 per cent in 2007.[8] This was a period when public development spending did not exceed 5 per cent of GDP, on average. Implicit subsidies arising from the underpricing of energy and other public utility services have been an even more important drain on government revenues. Recent International Monetary Fund (IMF) estimates indicate that implicit subsidies in the oil and gas sector amounted to roughly 20 per cent of GDP in 2007 (IMF, 2008).[9] Even though most oil-rich states tend to subsidize the domestic price of oil, Iran has one of the lowest oil prices in the region.

Under these conditions, the growing share of current expenditures has not necessarily meant an improvement in the quality of public service provision. On the contrary, the quality of public sector health and educational services appears to have been deteriorating, as those who can afford it appear to be increasingly resorting to private health and educational services. Figure 4.5 shows how public spending per student has been declining as a share of per capita GDP during the post-revolution period.

4.4.2 Oil, savings and investment

Like other macroeconomic outcomes, savings and investment behaviour in Iran is mainly driven by developments in the oil sector. This is vividly demonstrated in Figure 4.6, which shows how aggregate savings

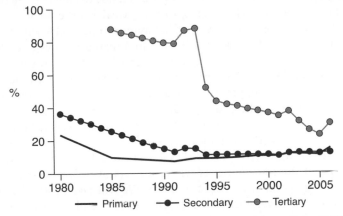

Figure 4.5 Public expenditure per student (percentage of per capita GDP)

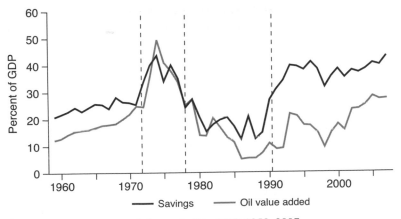

Figure 4.6 Savings rates and share of oil in GDP, 1959–2007

(as a share of GDP) have closely tracked the share of oil value added in GDP.[10] Excluding the exceptional years, principally the first oil boom in the early 1970s and the Iran–Iraq war, the considerably high savings rate during the period 1991–2007 stands out in Figure 4.6. How can these high and rising savings rate since the 1990s be explained relative to the historical norm? Preliminary estimates indicate that a major part of savings is generated by the private sector, aided by the rapid population transition that Iran has witnessed since the 1990s. Household savings have risen in response to a young and rapidly growing labour force combined with rapidly declining birth and dependency rates.

The dependence of savings on oil revenues tends to alleviate the need to mobilize domestic savings. This, in turn, weakens the prospects for financial sector development. Saving behaviour in Iran is closely tied to two broader issues: the mechanisms for mobilizing savings and their allocation to investment opportunities. Iran's distinct institutional set-up, especially the nature of its financial system, holds the key to explaining these saving patterns. By and large, banks are government owned, and their lending and credit allocation policies are broadly reflective of government priorities. The state has often used these banks as vehicles for selectively allocating credit to preferred production sectors, regions and activities. With such profound state intervention, Iran is one of the few countries where aspects of financial repression continue to shape financial development. We will take up the issue of financial sector development in greater detail while analysing the investment process in Iran.

4.4.2.1 Investment

Figure 4.7 traces the evolution of aggregate savings, investment and fixed investment, all expressed as a share of GDP.[11] As expected, investment rates have been very erratic. Some peculiar features of the investment patterns can be quickly noted:

- Investment rates have been generally higher during the 1990s relative to the 1960s.
- Despite higher investment rates in the 1990s, GDP growth has been well below that achieved during the 1959–73 period. This raises important questions about the efficiency of investments in the 1990s, which is surprising given the availability of a more educated labour force relative to the 1960s.
- While investment has been high during the 1990s, it has remained significantly below its potential, especially bearing in mind the high saving and growth rates during this period.

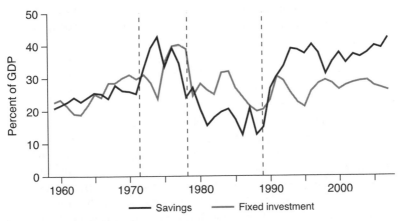

Figure 4.7 Savings and investment rates, 1959–2007

Overall, Iran has enjoyed respectable levels of investment. For instance, the share of gross fixed capital formation in GDP was 36.9 per cent in 2007. But the story on investment is more complicated than the aggregate statistics tend to reveal. If the Central Bank statistics are to be believed, the higher share of aggregate investment during the past two decades has mainly been driven by private investment. This is not always borne out by data from the Central Statistical Office (CSO): the ratio of private to public investment has generally been lower according to the CSO data.

Lurking behind this apparent discrepancy between official statistics is the role of parastatals in the Iranian economy. Investment expenditures by the quasi-state institutions (e.g. *Bonyads*) are often treated as private investment even though, for all practical purposes, these investments are directly or indirectly controlled by the 'core' state, albeit in a haphazard and uncoordinated manner. A significant part of what is considered to be private investment is thus effectively public investment. Overall, public expenditures remain a key driving force for private economic activity. Even when undertaken by purely 'private' agents, investment is shaped mainly by government expenditures and policies. The Iranian government has shaped private investment through the allocation of cheap credit by the banking system, the provision of subsidies, exchange rate policies and various protective measures in the product markets.

The investment process cannot, therefore, be properly analysed without due mention of the overextended role of the Iranian state, afforded in large part by oil revenues. Oil has sustained a large government and its interventionist policies. The state has played an overarching role in shaping the non-oil economy through its policies and institutions. It would be fair to say that public policies have more often been a cause for distortions rather than development. They have hindered the growth of a vibrant private sector. Despite the growing industrial share in GDP, the manufacturing sector accounts for a small proportion of GDP (less than 11 per cent).

Iran has failed to exploit its full potential for private industrial development. Although the manufacturing sector is weak, it has a non-negligible presence, especially when compared with Iran's other oil-rich neighbouring states in the Middle East. Iran has significant stakes in the steel and petrochemicals industries; in fact, it has the largest steel industry in the entire Middle East. It also has a heavily protected car industry that has recently formed joint manufacturing ventures with foreign motor manufacturers.

Despite this industrial presence, Iran's non-oil economy rarely provides the sort of cushion that is required to deal with the vagaries of the oil markets. Oil continues to play a decisive role in shaping the non-oil sector. A cursory look at the macro data confirms this. Trends in aggregate investment, for example, have mirrored movements in oil prices. High and rising oil prices have tended to drive market sentiment and raise investment levels. All oil booms, including the most recent one, confirm this pattern. Even though Iran's investment levels are not very low by regional comparison, the private sector is unlikely to be the main driver of these investments. Iran's private sector is weak, uncompetitive and lives under the shadow of a dominant state sector. This explains why relatively high saving and investment levels have not translated into commensurate growth rates. The principal explanation for this has to do with the low efficiency of investments.

Industrial inefficiencies have increased dramatically under the Islamic Republic. The efficiency of capital has fallen drastically over the last four decades: from an annual growth of 4.7 per cent during 1960–76, growth in total factor productivity was reduced to 1 per cent annually during 1989–2002 (IMF, 2004: 12).[12] Old industries in the public sector and the semi-public institutions are badly in need of restructuring. The continued existence of these inefficient industries is incompatible with the objectives of export diversification and growth in the non-oil economy. The World Bank estimates on the wealth of nations tend to confirm this low productivity of capital. Intangible capital, which is the main source of wealth generation in developing societies, plays little part in the growth of the economy (World Bank, 2006: 29).

This is archetypical of resource-rich societies, which produce too little given their potential, and have lousy investment that reinforces the resource curse (van der Ploeg, 2008).

These industrial inefficiencies have tended to persist, thanks to the easy availability of oil resources. Oil revenues have allowed the Iranian state to compensate for organizational and production inefficiencies, mainly by injecting public resources in the guise of subsidies or direct investment. Although the effect of such inefficiencies may be cushioned in the short run through the availability of oil revenues, they can make development unsustainable in the long run. The nature of structural change in an oil economy such as Iran is crucial for sustainable development. A crucial aspect of structural change is the extent to which industry, agriculture and other sectors can replace the role of oil as the main provider of foreign exchange revenues. To a large extent, this depends on industrial strategies and policies adopted by the government.

In the discussion below, we attempt to offer possible reasons for the low efficiency of productive capital and the absence of a vibrant private sector. We will consider the role of (1) an inhospitable policy environment; (2) a heavily intervened and poorly functioning banking system; and (3) the dominance of quasi-state actors, such as *Bonyads*.

Inhospitable policy environment   State intervention in the economy has a long history in Iran. Evidence suggests that this interventionist stance proved more detrimental in the wake of the first oil boom in the 1970s. In much of the developing world, ISI policies were systematically dismantled in the late 1980s. In the case of Iran, international isolation and the Iran–Iraq war tended to strengthen the interventionist stance. The peculiar political economy interests that emerged from the revolution have also inhibited economic reform. Nationalization of the private sector after the 1979 Islamic revolution, import compression and overvalued exchange rates during the war years also proved unhelpful. Taken together, these interventionist and inward-looking policies created an inhospitable environment for private sector development.

In the pre-revolution era (1963–79), Iran followed the fashion of the time: import substitution policies (ISI). Growth of private enterprises during this period was mainly a result of government protection and subsidies. Thus, the investment process was directly or indirectly driven by the public sector. But, as with the experience of other developing countries, ISI policies were associated with rent-seeking and corruption – problems that intensified after the first oil boom. Against the backdrop of ISI policies and pervasive government intervention, a sudden increase in oil prices led to a policy and institutional collapse. The ISI policies pursued during the 1963–79 period had the paradoxical effect of increasing the economy's dependence on the oil sector. At the same time, the highly protected manufacturing sector, which grew rapidly behind tariff walls, did not have the incentive to export, nor did it develop the efficiency required to compete in international markets (see Karshenas, 1990: ch. 7; Pesaran, 1992).

Private investment received a major blow after the 1979 revolution. A significant part of the industrial and banking sector was nationalized and transferred to the public sector. The state's control extended to all major sectors of the economy. This not only squeezed the private sector, but also resulted in unproductive investments. But, perhaps more importantly, the policy environment continued to deteriorate after the revolution. The policy of import compression introduced as a response to foreign exchange shortages after the Iraq war and the introduction of various forms of subsidies strengthened the protection given to the domestic manufacturing sector. At the same time, import restrictions affected private sector growth. The effect of a prolonged war with Iraq and continued western sanctions against the regime is that Iran has become more inward looking over time. This has had a further debilitating effect on the private sector.

Another factor producing a distorted policy environment was the system of multiple exchange rates during the war years. Iran had two exchange rates until 2002: an official exchange rate that was accessible to government departments, connected firms and individuals; and a black market rate that applied to the rest of society. As Figure 4.8 shows, the gap between official and black market exchange rates was sizeable. This became a source of several economic distortions. It contributed, for instance, to the opacity of public sector accounts, as state-owned enterprises were allocated foreign exchange at the official rate. The exchange difference constituted a hidden subsidy for these organizations, and unlevelled the playing field for private sector firms. The overvalued exchange rate that resulted from this multitier system further harmed the competitiveness of the private sector.

Politicization of financial and monetary policies   Coupled with a relatively loose fiscal policy, Iran has had a high rate of credit expansion. This has resulted in excessive growth of monetary assets and unprecedented levels of inflation. Iran's financial and monetary policies are ultimately driven by the demands for political redistribution. Over time, Iran's financial sector, which is largely state owned, has become a

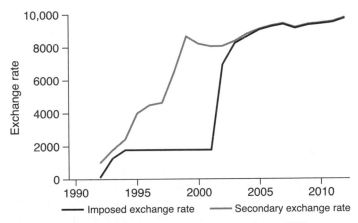

Figure 4.8 Official and black market exchange rates (rials per US$)

major conduit for transferring oil rents to chosen groups in society. Iran is perhaps one of the very few countries that are still subjected to a state of financial repression. Bank lending rates have remained well below the inflation rate. The government and the central bank have proved incapable of controlling the rate of credit expansion under political pressure from different interest groups. For example, the influential semi-public corporations have preferential access to credit. Monetary authorities face consistent political pressure to extend subsidized credit to favoured groups. In 2007, the President directed the banking system to lower lending rates to 12–13 per cent.

Under direction from the government, low-interest loans are extended to agriculture, tourism and small businesses. It is not clear whether this concessionary credit is used to expand productive opportunities or is simply recycled through the banking system to earn a high interest premium. The subsidized credit is allegedly subject to abuse. Regardless of the use these subsidized loans are put to, overexpansion of bank credit to preferred sectors and inefficient loss-making enterprises has become a major source of economic instability, fuelling inflationary pressures and compounding macroeconomic problems. This stems in part from the central bank's inability to exert appropriate supervision and control over credit expansion under pressure from different interest groups.

Given the high levels of inflation, real interest rates remain low, implying a weak relation to the scarcity of capital that prevails in Iranian economy. The politicization of the banking system has resulted in an excessive growth in money supply. Between 2003 and 2007 alone, the rate of domestic credit expansion has increased from 30.3 per cent to 41.6 per cent per annum. Lax credit policies have led to limited banking competition, low profitability of the banking system, and inadequate mobilization and inefficient allocation of savings. Lack of robust competition renders these banks inefficient, pushing up the cost of capital for the private sector.

Role of Bonyads *and other charitable organizations* An important new element introduced in the post-revolutionary period was the greater involvement of the public sector in industrial production. This is reflected in the growing prominence of semi-public organizations, known as *Bonyads* or religious charities. The principal rationale of these charitable organizations was to meet the ideological needs of the Islamic state, with the promotion of distributive justice as one of its avowed aims. Although their primary objective is to advance the welfare of the poor, they have gradually turned into private monopolies that survive on state patronage. *Bonyads* can arguably be described as disguised state-owned enterprises.

Over time, these charitable organizations have turned into a key instrument in Iran's populist macroeconomic policies. Their legal status is not well defined: they are neither public organizations nor fully private. Given their charitable status, the *Bonyads* are eligible for an entire gamut of state favours, giving them an edge over other private organizations. *Bonyads* receive budgetary transfers; they are exempt from taxes and have preferential access to bank credit and foreign exchange at below market rates.

No wonder these charitable organizations have increasingly dominated private economic activity, operating in every conceivable business. A notable feature of these organizations is their opacity. Very limited information exists on their business operations, investment strategies and associated investment returns. Although it is hard to get precise estimates, it is believed that there are more than 300 such organizations. In the 1980s, their budget was equivalent to nearly half the total national budget. The largest charitable foundation is the Foundation of the Oppressed and War Veterans (MJF). The MJF has over 200,000 employees, 350 subsidiaries and an estimated value of US$3 billion, which is equivalent to 10 per cent of Iran's GDP. During the period 1981–90, government resources allocated to the foundation increased at an annual rate of 29.3 per cent (Wiig, 2009).

The *Bonyads* operate under the auspices of Iran's Supreme Leader and evade regular parliamentary oversight. They also evade all forms of supervision, accountability and independent financial audit. They are scrutinized neither by the government nor by shareholders. Ideally, the budget of semi-public foundations should be presented to the parliament as a supplement to the government budget with their credit position with the banking system separated from the accounts of the proper private sector. But this is rarely done. There is a serious lack of information regarding the functions and performance of these organizations. Their accounts are not publicly disclosed and, in the absence of credible data, it is almost impossible to evaluate the costs and benefits of their various programmes. It is not known, for instance, how well targeted their assistance programmes are. Shortage of credible and independently verifiable data on these organizations precludes an objective assessment of their programmes.

During the 1990s, *Iran's Revolutionary Guards Corps* (IRGC, or *Pāsdārān* for short) has emerged as another significant economic player. The *Revolutionary Guards* are an offshoot of the Iranian Army, created after the 1979 revolution. Like the *Bonyads*, the IRGC enjoys an extralegal status that affords them indemnity from public scrutiny as well as taxes. This new military–business complex controlled by the *Guards* now enjoys considerable economic and financial muscle. The Guards' foray into economic activity can be traced back to the end of the Iraq–Iran war, when one of the military's construction agencies, the *Khatam-ol-Anbiya* (KOA), was converted into a commercial entity and provided a wider role for post-war reconstruction. The KOA is now slated to be the third wealthiest conglomerate in Iran, with about 60 subsidiaries and 35,000 employees. The conglomerate has growing business stakes in the construction, engineering and telecommunication sectors (Wiig, 2009).

Enjoying strong ties with the core clerical state, *Bonyads* and *Pāsdārān* have both thrived under state patronage. Their growing control of the market and their preferential access to state favours prevent the emergence of a truly private sector. They undermine competition and distort private incentives for wealth generation. The economic activities of these quasi-state actors may hold the key to explaining the notoriously low efficiency of investment in Iran. The commercial and charitable functions of these foundations, although said to be formally separate, are not compatible with the aims of economic efficiency and commercial profitability. In the last decade, *Bonyads* are also believed to have been important obstacles to economic reform, as they represent powerful political and economic constituencies in the Islamic Republic.

Perhaps more importantly, these charitable foundations provide an interesting window into the workings of Iran's distinct political economy. They are a product of the country's dualistic power structure and a manifestation of the financial influence that Iran's unelected core state enjoys. The *Bonyads* and *Pāsdārān* serve as convenient conduits for distributing state favours and public employment to ideological supporters of the regime, many of whom are drawn from lower socio-economic groups. In this milieu, these charitable trusts help to consolidate political authority. They have become important tools for the socio-economic mobility of the lower and middle classes who had previously supported the revolutionary regime (Saeidi, 2004).

The dominant role of *Bonyads* has not been challenged by the privatization process. Some assets of these charitable organizations have been privatized, but this has not dented their economic clout. In some instances, they have, in fact, been beneficiaries of the privatization process: shares of national companies undergoing privatization have also been sold to *Bonyads* and *Pāsdārān*. Even if successfully privatized, the lack of credible information on these organizations will hamper accurate perception formation of investors and market participants, including those in the stock market.

4.5 The political economy of oil

The preceding sections demonstrate the central role of oil in shaping Iran's economy. It is clear that the core aspects of macroeconomic policy – be it budget spending, public finance, investment or savings – are ultimately determined by what happens in the oil markets. Superficially, with regard to the broader effects of oil specialization, Iran is no different from other resource-rich countries. It shares many of the same pathologies of oil: an overextended public sector, insufficient taxation, pro-cyclical fiscal policy, low profitability of investment, a weak private sector and slow pace of economic reform, to mention a few.

Although oil's impact on Iran's economy is not too dissimilar from other resource-rich countries, the political economy processes that generate these outcomes are clearly different. A discussion of the effect of oil on Iran's development would therefore be incomplete without reference to its associated political economy. It is important to look beyond macroeconomic policies and their outcomes, as they are ultimately shaped by the underlying distributional conflicts in society. They can be partly seen as vehicles for distributing oil rents to favoured sections of society.

To clarify these themes, this section will briefly pose three inter-related questions: What are the specific political economy dimensions at work in Iran's case? How are rents from oil distributed to the wider society? Are there any major differences in the way Iran has responded to the two oil booms of the 1970s and the 2000s?

As suggested earlier in this chapter, the political economy of post-revolution Iran is crucially determined by the structure of the Iranian state. The two central pillars of Iran's power structure – the official elected state and the core clerical state – create an 'embedded factionalism'. This generates conflicts over the distribution of resources and becomes the political basis of macroeconomic populism, manifested through cheap credit, consumer subsidies and generous public spending. Expansionary monetary and fiscal policies in Iran can then be viewed as tools to resolve distributional tensions arising from the competing claims of powerful interest groups. These include, for example, urban consumers, public and private producers and groups associated with the religious establishment.

Iran's distinct political economy also provides a likely explanation for its low efficiency of investment and its weak private sector. As discussed earlier, the bulk of investment in Iran is channelled through semi-public charitable organizations, such as *Bonyads* and *Pāsdārān*, which have amassed considerable economic muscle through state patronage without being subjected to market pressures. Given that their investment operations are largely non-transparent, it is difficult to provide a definitive view of how economically and socially efficient these investments are. These quasi-state actors are, however, important means for providing jobs, contracts and other material rewards to political loyalists, serving as instruments for transferring oil rents to supportive political constituencies. This is the political backdrop against which Iran's Islamic commercial conglomerates have come to acquire growing economic and financial clout.

One of the peculiarities of the oil-exporting economies lies in the fact that oil revenues can, in some cases, allow the capture of rents on a magnitude, and for a duration, that may be unsustainable in non-oil economies. Despite being a major oil producer, however, the scale of rent flows from oil falls short of its actual potential in Iran. This is mainly a consequence of the country's inability to increase its oil production in the face of persistent underinvestment in the exploration and extraction of oil resources. Despite this, oil revenues have historically served as the main source of government revenue. This has permitted distortions and rigidities in the economic structure to continue for a longer period than would have been possible without access to oil resources. A steady flow of oil revenues has helped to sustain a plethora of market distortions. Economic and financial repression, for instance, has run a longer course in Iran than in many other developing countries. Oil provides an important explanation for the persistence of these economic distortions.

We next turn to a brief discussion of how oil rents are distributed to the wider society. As the previous section has shown, Iran's ubiquitous business conglomerates that operate at the margins of the public and private sector are convenient means for channelling rents to various interest groups. The use of the financial system to allocate credit on preferential terms is yet another mechanism for transferring rents to political clients. Oil resources are also distributed more widely to society through a range of implicit and explicit subsidies.

In Iran, the oil rents are combined with regulatory rents, which emanate from excessive state intervention; say, for example, price controls, high trade barriers or the system of multiple exchange rates. Had it not been for oil, it would have been difficult to sustain these regulatory rents. Regardless of whether these rents originate in the oil sector or from misguided state regulation, they tend to benefit groups that enjoy preferential access to public resources. Over time, this has led to strong clientelistic ties that have reinforced and perpetuated the rent-generating activities of the state.[13]

Recent literature on rent-seeking has concentrated on the economic cost of this phenomenon: the opportunity cost of resources that are devoted to access such rents and the resources spent in lobbying for rent-generating policies. Earlier economic literature had concentrated on the static efficiency losses of these interventions, such as the misallocation of resources between different activities. In addition to these two sources of allocative inefficiency, however, are the dynamic inefficiencies that arise from the presence of supernormal profits in certain economic sectors, which tend to persist as a result of continued state protection.

Such dynamic inefficiencies can result in long-term economic distortions which, apart from directing resources to the protected sector, exert a detrimental effect on its productive efficiency. There is limited incentive on the part of producers in the protected sectors to rationalize their production and management methods, or to embark on inventive activities, which is essential for a successful integration of the domestic economy with the international market place. Although quantitative measures of these different sources of efficiency loss in the case of Iran are not available, the latter source of dynamic inefficiencies associated with rent-seeking can be particularly significant in the context of long-term economic development.

To sum up, the manner in which oil rents are accumulated and distributed deserves a more nuanced explanation. Relative to the extreme cases of bad governance in Africa and the Middle East, oil rents are not pilfered at source, but captured in the process of distribution. Oil rents are distributed to a wide class of beneficiaries in Iran, many of whom hail from the middle and lower income groups. The problem in Iran, however, is less to do with the concentration of oil rents in a few hands, but more with the efficiency implications of the manner in which they are distributed.

4.5.1 Are policy responses different between the two booms?

Given the significance of natural resources and the associated political economy, it is pertinent to pose the following questions: Has Iran managed its latest oil boom any better than the one in the 1970s? Are there discernible patterns of continuity and change? We begin with the clarification that the two periods are not strictly comparable. For one thing, oil revenues have, on average, been lower in real terms and more volatile in the post-revolution period. Iran has also faced greater economic and political isolation on the international stage. Despite these confounding factors, a comparison of the two oil price booms appears to be useful.

At face value, oil price hikes in the two periods have not led to widely divergent macroeconomic outcomes. Oil booms in the 1970s and 2000s were both associated, for instance, with resurgence in economic growth. Both periods witnessed spending and investment booms. However, a comparison across the two periods presents a picture of both continuity and change. There is a surprising continuity in the interventionist stance: the state has continued to play an overstretched role in the national economy in both periods. Oil continues to dominate the Iranian economy, and macroeconomic policy remains largely pro-cyclical.

These apparent similarities mask considerable differences. Although the recent increase in oil prices has led to a resumption in economic growth, allowing Iran's GDP to grow by around 6 per cent annually, growth numbers are still considerably lower than those in 1970s. And if we consider the earlier period, 1962–71, Iran's GDP grew twice as fast. Unlike the 1960s, however, growth in the recent period has been accompanied by double-digit inflation rates. Investment performance has also differed across the two oil booms. There has been a collapse in the efficiency of investment since the inception of the 1979 revolution. The chaotic transition brought by the revolution and the destructive consequences of war with Iraq certainly had a role to play. But productivity did not pick up even after the war. The average annual productivity growth during the post-war decade was a mere 1 per cent, which is nearly four times lower than the corresponding figure for the pre-revolution period (Mojaver, 2009).

Although the government followed a strategy of import-substituting industrialization behind high tariff walls and other protectionist barriers in both periods, there are significant differences between the two periods in terms of institutions and agents of accumulation. Clearly, the underlying political economy is radically different across the two oil booms. Compared with the centralized political dispensation in the 1970s, twenty-first-century Iran operates under a dual power structure, where the unelected core state commands vast economic resources and engages in widespread political redistribution. There are also critical differences in the resource allocation mechanisms. During the second oil boom, Iran has witnessed a growing share of current expenditures, especially on subsidies and other fiscal transfers, but a falling proportion of development spending. Economic controls are more extensive in the second period, although these are partly a response to an adverse external environment.

Importantly, the nature and demands of political redistribution are different in post-revolutionary Iran. Credit subsidies and parastatals have assumed a growing significance in the second boom. In a divided power structure, oil has intensified populist policies and fuelled greater factional competition for resources, leading to a different configuration of elites. Bazaar merchants, religious elites and political factions within the state have now gained increasing prominence. The Islamic Republic needs to cater to a wider constituency, with the result that the base for rent distribution is arguably wider than the centralized technocratic structures of the 1970s. However, it is also associated with greater economic inefficiency than in the 1970s.

Oil has not been an unmitigated disaster for Iran; it has facilitated progress on several fronts. Even if fundamental reform has been difficult to introduce, there have been some notable advances. For example, the adverse effects of the oil windfalls in the 1970s did generate some social learning. As a result, the fiscal response was slightly better, with Iran achieving a more balanced budget and a relatively higher government saving. Despite facing significant obstacles, the economic reform programme in the 1990s was successful in dismantling some economic controls and introducing privatization. Two areas of relative success have been the unification of the exchange rate and the setting up of an oil stabilization fund (OSF) in 2000 intended to smooth out the effect of oil revenue fluctuations on government expenditure.

The need for the OSF was driven home by the painful experience of the boom and bust episodes in the early 1990s and the extreme vulnerability of the regime in the face of international isolation. The OSF accumulates above-budget receipts and, as noted earlier, it has yielded some respectable savings. One of the aims of the OSF is to strengthen the non-oil private sector: up to half the fund can be used to promote private sector exports in the non-oil sector. These noble objectives apart, the OSF is frequently 'raided' to meet current spending needs.

Learning from the experience of the 1990s, Iran has utilized oil revenues to write off expensive public debt and unify exchange rates. The more conservative fiscal stance of the government relative to the early 1990s, combined with a sustained increase in oil prices, paved the way for exchange rate unification by the Central Bank. Iran has also made massive investments in education, resulting in an increase in the literacy rate from 43 per cent in 1975 to 75 per cent in 1996. Surprisingly, oil has facilitated critical reforms in both periods. In the pre-revolution period, oil windfalls helped the successful execution of land reforms, and in the post-revolution period, oil facilitated the unification of exchange rates. In the arena of international trade, quantitative restrictions were replaced by equivalent tariffs, although average tariff rates remain some of the highest in the Middle East.

4.6 Concluding remarks

This chapter has attempted to develop a political economy narrative of oil and development in the Islamic Republic of Iran. Iran was the first country in the Middle East to discover oil, and it is the fourth largest oil producer in the world. Oil exploration and extraction has, however, slowed down since the 1979 revolution. In this regard, four factors have played their hand adversely: the imposition of US sanctions, war with Iraq, growing domestic demand for fuel and Iran's inflexible contracting arrangements. The unfortunate result of this has been a chronic underinvestment in the oil sector. Presently, Iran finds it difficult even to maintain existing levels of oil production. Although production shortages are a serious concern, government commitments regarding oil contracts are generally credible, and oil revenues are publicly disclosed with relative transparency. There is no evidence of any large-scale diversion of oil resources at source.

There is no simple linear explanation for how oil has shaped Iran's development trajectory. Iran has had a varied development experience, with periods of growth as well as regression. In the period preceding the first oil boom in the 1970s, Iran witnessed a 'comprehensive' programme of economic and social modernization, dubbed by the government as the 'white revolution'. This was a period of sustained growth, enabled by land reforms and massive investments in physical and human capital.

The oil shock in the 1970s, however, disrupted Iran's economic advance and subjected the development strategy of the 1960s to a severe test. The oil shock led to an erosion of the quality of governance and a collapse in macroeconomic management. In the face of oil windfalls, the quality of spending deteriorated, building up strong inflationary pressures. The centralized development strategy under the Shah, combined with the substantial oil windfalls in the 1970s, subverted the authority of the government technocrats precisely at a time when measured and rational decision making was essential.

The 1979 revolution brought a dramatic change in the external and domestic context of Iran. Internationally, the country faced growing economic and political isolation. The ensuing war with Iraq and a slump in global oil prices further weakened Iran's position. In the face of these adverse external circumstances, Iran became more inward looking, extending its reach to all areas of economic activity. The Islamic regime introduced a new *dirigisme* that involved nationalization of the banking, industrial and services sector and a series of direct market interventions.

However, the most far-reaching consequence of the revolution was political, not economic. The structure of the Iranian state that emerged after the revolution involved a duality of power structures in which the elected official state cohabits with the core clerical state. This multiplicity of power centres creates an inherent factionalism that can sometimes lead to intense competition for resources. This is the political backdrop that mediates oil's impact on economic development. Oil remains a central driving force in the Iranian economy. It is the principal source of foreign exchange, government revenue and savings. No wonder, then, that developments in oil markets shape the workings of the Iranian economy in a profound manner.

The central budget is the principal medium through which oil revenues are expended. Higher oil prices have frequently led to spending booms. The result: volatility in the oil markets is often reflected in the volatility of budget spending. This correlation between the central budget and oil prices is further strengthened by a weak tax effort. The share of taxes in GDP is both low and declining. Macroeconomic policy has become more populist in nature, reflected in the growing share of current expenditures in the central budget. A range of explicit and implicit subsidies is used to pass on the oil rents to consumers and other special interest groups.

We next analysed the effect of oil on savings and investment behaviour. A key finding here relates to a high, and rising, savings rate. A favourable demographic profile, with the active labour force forming a growing share of the population, provides one explanation for this high savings rate. Investment rates have also been quite substantial, especially since the mid-1990s. These high savings and investment rates, however, do not translate well into economic growth. Putting together the figures on growth, savings and investment reveals one of the most striking findings on Iran: the low productivity of investment. There is strong evidence to suggest that Iran has witnessed a collapse in the efficiency of investment, especially since the advent of the revolution. The problem in Iran is not one of low investment levels, but unproductive and inefficient investments. For much of the past thirty years, total factor productivity in Iran has been either negative or very low.

The low efficiency of investment is even more puzzling in the face of two further trends: (1) the growing share of the industrial sector in GDP; and (2) a high proportion of private investment in aggregate investment. This begs the question: Where has all the investment gone? A closer inspection can help to reconcile the facts on investment with reality. First, even though the industrial sector has grown in size, the manufacturing sector has a relatively insignificant presence in the Iranian economy. Second, the distinction between public and private investment is blurred in Iran. A significant part of the private sector is simply an extension of the 'core' and 'unaccountable' state sector. So, what goes around as private investment is essentially neither private nor public investment in the normally understood sense of these terms. For example, investment by Islamic conglomerates of *Bonyads,* which is sometimes referred to as private investment and sometimes as disguised public investment, is neither subject to public sector transparency and accounting rules nor akin to arms-length and taxable private sector activities.

The issue of investment efficiency is closely related to the nature of the investment process, especially the operations of commercial charitable organizations, such as *Bonyads* and *Pāsdārān,* which draw considerable financial and political support from Iran's religious establishment. The investment operations of these parastatals are largely non-transparent. For one thing, very little is known about the nature and returns on their investments. Their legal status grants them immunity from taxes and public disclosure. Rather than acting as profit-maximizing agents, these conglomerates thrive on state patronage. The phenomenal rise of these parastatals may have come at the expense of private entrepreneurial activity. They unlevel the playing field and erect entry barriers for younger and smaller firms.

A proper analysis of investment and spending decisions, and, more generally, macroeconomic trends, is complicated by Iran's dual political structure. Many of Iran's pressing economic problems – whether it is populist macroeconomic policies, abuse of the financial system, low efficiency of investment or economic distortions – have their basis in the political economy. The state's control of the banking system, its exchange rate policies, the use of direct and indirect subsidies and the operation of Islamic charities are all different mechanisms for political redistribution. The *Bonyads* offer a particularly dramatic illustration. These semi-official commercial ventures can be viewed as vehicles for distributing oil rents in the guise of credit, contracts and jobs to political clients. They offer valuable opportunities to incumbent religious elites for economic and political entrenchment.

Iran offers an interesting case where rents are captured not at their source but in the process of distribution. Arguably, such redistribution does not just line the pockets of a few. It trickles down to some wider segments of society, including those selected from the lower and middle rungs of the income ladder. But this can have grave implications for efficiency and can even compromise equity in the long run – for example, by refusing equal opportunities and a level playing field to aspiring small or young firms.

Acknowledgements

This contribution written as part of a project led by the Oxford Centre for the Analysis of Resource Rich Economies, Department of Economics, University of Oxford. The authors wish to thank Meysam Ahmadi for excellent research assistance and Tony Venables, Paul Collier, Homa Katouzian and participants at the Oxford conference in June 2009 for their valuable comments. We are also grateful to S.M. Ali Abbas at the IMF for providing useful research material.

Notes

1 A closer inspection of economic cycles – and of boom and bust episodes – reveals a strong association between oil prices and growth fluctuations in Iran. For more detailed evidence on this, see Hakimian (2008), Karshenas and Hakimian (2005: 72–74), and Farzanegan and Markwardt (2009).

2 Figures from the 2006 World Development Indicators.
3 The corresponding figure for the Middle East and North Africa region is 0.36. http://web.worldbank.org/WBSITE/EXTERNAL/TOPICS/ENVIRONMENT/ EXTEEI/0,,contentMDK:20872280~pagePK:210058~piPK:210062~theSitePK: 408050,00.html.
4 The statistics on mining resources are based on Economist Intelligence Unit (2008).
5 Privatization sat uneasily with Article 44 of the constitution, around which forces opposed to privatization congregated. The *Expediency Council* announced a re-interpretation of Article 44 in 2004 with far-reaching effects. According to the new interpretation, all government enterprises, including heavy chemicals and petrochemicals, telecommunications, electricity generation and all the downstream activities in oil and gas, mining, banking and insurance, etc. are to be privatized.
6 Own calculations based on data from the Central Statistical Office.
7 The sanctions apply to any company investing US$20 million or more per year in an Iranian project.
8 Furthermore, despite rising oil prices in international markets, the domestic price of oil has not been adjusted upwards. The fiscal burden of explicit oil subsidies has therefore grown.
9 Implicit subsidies for the domestic users of natural gas alone account for approximately 9 per cent of GDP.
10 Iranian national account statistics are measured on production and expenditure sides and do not report the income side. Aggregate national savings are derived as a residual, and should therefore be treated with caution, as residuals could embody substantial measurement errors.
11 Data based on reports from the Central Bank and the Central Statistical Office.
12 The incremental capital output ratio (ICOR) also reduced from 5–6 per cent to approximately 2.5 per cent (IMF, 2004).
13 It is important to note that government subsidies that are introduced on economic grounds, e.g. on grounds of economies of scale and learning, need not generate any rents in the private sector, as subsidies of this type are supposed to make enterprises, which would otherwise be loss making, become viable.

References

Bjorvatn, K. and K. Selvik (2008) 'Destructive Competition: Factionalism and Rent-seeking in Iran', *World Development*, 36, 2314–24.
Economist Intelligence Unit (2008) *Country Profile 2008: Iran*. London: EIU.
Farzanegan, M. R. and G. Markwardt (2009) 'The Effects of Oil Price Shocks on the Iranian Economy', *Energy Economics*, 31, 134–51.
Hakimian, H. (2008) 'Institutional Change, Policy Challenges and Macroeconomic Performance: Case Study of Iran (1979–2004)', Working Paper No. 26. Washington, DC: The International Bank for Reconstruction and Development/The World Bank, on behalf of the Commission on Growth and Development.
IMF (2004) *Islamic Republic of Iran: Selected Issues*. IMF Report 04/308. Washington, DC: International Monetary Fund.

IMF (2007) *Islamic Republic of Iran: 2006 Article IV Consultation*. IMF Report 07/100, March 2007. Washington, DC: International Monetary Fund.

IMF (2008) *Islamic Republic of Iran: Selected Issues*. IMF Report. Washington, DC: International Monetary Fund.

Karshenas, M. (1990) *Oil, State and Industrialization in Iran*. Cambridge: Cambridge University Press.

Karshenas, M. and H. Hakimian (2005) 'Oil, Economic Diversification and the Democratic Process in Iran', *Iranian Studies*, 38, 67–90.

Karshenas, M. and H. Pesaran (1995) 'Economic Reform and the Reconstruction of the Iranian Economy', *Middle East Journal*, 40, 89–111.

Mojaver, F. (2009) 'Sources of Economic Growth and Stagnation in Iran', *Journal of International Trade and Economic Development*, 18, 275–95.

Pesaran, M.H. (1992) 'The Iranian Foreign Exchange Policy and the Black Market for Dollars', *International Journal of Middle East Studies*, 24, 101–25.

Saeidi, A.A. (2004) 'The Accountability of Para-governmental Organizations (*bonyads*): The Case of Iranian Foundations', *Iranian Studies*, 37, 479–98.

Torbat, A. (2005) 'Impacts of the US Trade and Financial Sanctions on Iran,' *World Economy*, 28, 407–34.

van der Ploeg, R. (2008) 'Comment on "Asset Accounting and the Sustainability of Extractive Economies – the Case of Iran" by Atkinson et al. 2008'. Mimeo, Oxford University.

Wiig, A.K. (2009) 'When the Poor become the Masters: The Political Economy of Iran's Revolutionary Guards'. Mimeo. Oslo: Norwegian Defence Research Establishment.

World Bank (2006) *Measuring the Wealth of Nations*. Washington, DC: World Bank.

Further Reading

Esfahani, H. S. and F. Taheripour (2002) 'Hidden Public Expenditures and the Economy in Iran', *International Journal of Middle East Studies*, 34, 691–718.

Pesaran, H. (2000) 'Economic Trends and Macroeconomic Policies in Post-revolutionary Iran' in Parvin Alizadeh (ed.) *The Economy of Iran: Dilemmas of an Islamic State*. London: I.B. Tauris.

5

Kazakhstan
Public saving and private spending

Akram Esanov and Karlygash Kuralbayeva

5.1 Overview

This chapter examines the way in which Kazakhstan handled key decisions in managing its vast natural resource wealth in 2000–08 and the extent to which resource revenues were harnessed for sustained growth. We find that the hydrocarbon sector spurred strong economic growth during this period by boosting domestic demand and propelling growth in such non-tradable sectors as construction and financial services. In addition, our analysis indicates that prudent macroeconomic policies pursued by the government had been at the core of this robust expansion with more than two-thirds of oil revenues amassed in the Oil Fund. Notwithstanding sound macroeconomic policies, the private sector remained under-regulated and took excessive risks by over-borrowing abroad, which led to a consumption boom. The government lacked policies aimed at curbing the excessive risktaking behaviour of the private sector which, to a great extent, jeopardized the sustainability of Kazakhstan's growth potential and the government's prudence. We refer to this phenomenon as a Ricardian curse of the resource windfall.

5.2 Introduction

Using the case of Kazakhstan, this chapter examines how the Central Asian state handled key decisions in managing its natural resource wealth and whether resource revenues were harnessed for sustained growth when the country faced major oil revenue inflow since its independence. Kazakhstan is a former Soviet republic with a population of approximately

15 million people. The country covers an area of 2.7 million square kilometres, stretching from the Caspian Sea in the west to the Altay Mountains in the east, and from the plains of western Siberia in the north to the deserts of Central Asia in the south. Located at the junction of Asia and Europe, it is the only landlocked country with substantial hydrocarbon reserves in its subsoil. After the demise of the Soviet Union in 1991, the Central Asian state gained independence and started its transition towards a market economy.

The transition process has proved to be difficult and uneven. According to most estimates, Kazakhstan experienced a cumulative decline in gross domestic product (GDP) of around 40 per cent in 1991–95. In 1996, however, the economy started to stabilize and showed early signs of economic recovery by registering positive growth for the first time since the Soviet demise. Yet, the Russian financial crisis adversely affected the Kazakh economy, and real GDP contracted by 1.9 per cent in 1998 before resuming growth in 1999. At the turn of the century, Kazakhstan emerged as one of the most vibrant, fast-growing economies in the post-communist region. In 2000–07, the economy expanded at an average annual rate of 10.2 per cent (Table A.5.1), and per capita income in purchasing power parity (PPP) terms increased from US$4811 in 2000 to US$11,086 in 2007, second only to Russia in the Commonwealth of Independent States. The hydrocarbon sector served as an engine of this robust growth by boosting domestic demand and propelling growth in the non-tradable sectors, including the construction and financial sectors. During this era, growth acceleration has been accompanied by prudent macroeconomic policies. The government contained inflation, maintained fiscal discipline, stabilized exchange rates and saved a large portion of oil revenues in the National Oil Fund, which aided the transparency of the windfall revenue management process in the country. However, the global liquidity crisis that started in the middle of 2007 has severely affected the Kazakh economy by turning the boom phase of the cycle into the bust. The global financial crisis had a negative impact on the economy primarily through the financial sector, which had been under-regulated during the boom phase and became increasingly vulnerable to negative shocks stemming from the international economy. The banks, underpinned by the strong macroeconomic performance and favourable external conditions, borrowed excessively abroad and extended credits to the construction, property and consumer sectors at home. The heavy dependence of local banks on external funding and high exposure to the property sector amplified the vulnerability of the private sector to the global liquidity crisis. This behaviour of the private sector put at risk prudent government policies and the entire economy, which we label as a Ricardian curse of the resource windfall.

The objective of this chapter is to give a detailed account of key decision points in handling natural resource wealth in Kazakhstan and to analyse whether these decisions facilitate the transformation of resource endowment into sustainable economic development. The analysis covers the period from 2000 to 2008 marked by rising international oil prices. These favourable market conditions brought enormous windfall revenues to the government of Kazakhstan, while posing significant challenges for macroeconomic policy-making. We focus on two main issues in the policy-making process: resource revenue generation and revenue management. In examining revenue generation strategy, we analyse the government's development strategy and the fiscal and regulatory framework designed in the petroleum sector. The discussion of revenue management issues focuses on the saving and spending policies of the government. To assess macroeconomic performance, we also identify the main sources of economic growth and examine the role of the petroleum sector in those developments.

The rest of the chapter is organized as follows. Section 5.3 analyses macroeconomic developments by identifying key drivers of the recent economic growth and main patterns in the dynamics of external balance. Section 5.4 provides an overview of the oil sector and investigates the revenue generation process in the sector. Section 5.5 examines the revenue management strategy of the government. Section 5.6 examines how the financial sector developed in Kazakhstan. Section 5.7 discusses main anti-crisis initiatives of the government. Section 5.8 concludes.

5.3 Macroeconomic developments

In order to assess the degree to which the government of Kazakhstan has managed to harness oil revenues into sustained economic growth, we look first at the macroeconomic developments in the country over the period 2000–08. We describe patterns of economic growth across sectors and explain why growth has been uneven across different sectors. This exercise is expected to identify key drivers of economic growth and shed light on the role of the natural resource sector in spurring unbalanced growth. We also examine macroeconomic developments over the last decade by analysing key patterns in the dynamics of the balance of payments and investment.

5.3.1 Structure and sources of growth

Over the period 2000–07, Kazakhstan experienced strong economic growth largely underpinned by high international energy prices. As shown in Figure 5.1, this robust economic growth started to show some signs of slowing down in 2008, reflecting a decline in international oil prices and the spread of the global financial crisis.

This strong economic performance, however, has been accompanied by uneven growth performance across different sectors, which, in turn, altered the structure of the economy. In particular, as Table 5.1 demonstrates, the mining sector (oil and mineral extracting sectors) experienced the highest growth of 21 per cent in 2000, albeit the pace of the growth has decelerated substantially since then, reflecting the capacity constraints in the sector. The financial sector has expanded rapidly over the past 8 years, registering double digit growth rates since 2001. The annual growth rate of the financial sector averaged 26 per cent during this period. Only the construction sector comes close to the financial sector in terms of growth performance. This sector grew, on average, by 22 per cent annually between 2000 and 2007. Among the main sectors of the economy, the growth rate in agriculture was the lowest. The agriculture sector grew, on average, by slightly more than 5 per cent per annum, and the growth has been very volatile, sliding into negative territory twice during this period. In 2005–07, the growth performance of agriculture improved considerably, suggesting that recent changes in government policies have started to bear some fruit. Manufacturing and trade have also shown strong average growth of about 10 per cent

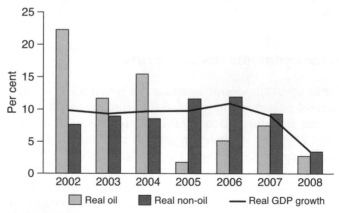

Figure 5.1 Real GDP growth

Source: IMF Country Reports.

Table 5.1 Real output growth by sectors, 2000–07 (%)

	2000	2001	2002	2003	2004	2005	2006	2007
Agriculture	–3.2	17.1	3.2	2.2	–0.1	7.1	6.0	8.5
Mining	21.0	14.4	16.3	10.3	12.9	2.4	7.5	2.6
Manufacturing	14.0	13.7	7.6	7.9	10.1	7.1	7.9	6.6
Construction	14.0	27.4	19.5	9.8	14.4	39.5	36.4	16.4
Trade	5.0	13.5	8.6	10.2	10.5	9.3	9.8	13.5
Finance	8.3	18.2	16.6	18.3	25.3	34.9	42.1	43.5
Total output by sectors	9.6	13.9	9.9	9.6	10.1	10.3	11.5	10.3

Source: ADB data and authors' calculations.

per year. Overall, the total output by sectors expanded at an average rate of 10.7 per cent per annum during the period 2000–07. Only two sectors – the financial sector and construction – have outperformed the total output growth in terms of average growth rate per year.

In 2005–07, the growth in the construction and finance sectors was mostly driven by excessive borrowing by the banking sector in the global capital markets, which turned out to be unsustainable, resulting in negative growth of the sector in 2008, after the economy had been severely hit by the global liquidity crisis. In contrast, the mining sector, which had made a significant contribution to the country's real GDP growth since 2000, continued to demonstrate positive growth in 2008. The growth in the mining sector since 2000 has been mostly driven by the expansion of the hydrocarbon industry. In 2000–07, oil production in the country demonstrated a strong 11 per cent compound annual growth rate (CAGR) (see Figure 5.2). In 2007, Kazakhstan produced approximately 1.45 million barrels per day (bbl/d), a 3.3-fold increase from 434,000 bbl/d in 1995 and a twofold increase from 743,900 bbl/d in 2000. It is expected that the oil sector will remain an important growth driver in the country in the medium term. Our estimates, for example, suggest that oil production will double by 2016 from its 2006 production level and will reach almost 2,500,000 bbl/d. The growth prospects of the oil industry in the country are closely tied to the development of the Kashagan project discussed in Section 5.4.

5.3.2 Balance of payments

Turning to the analysis of key trends in the balance of payments, this chapter seeks to quantify the response of the private sector to the oil boom and identify important developments in the oil industry. As

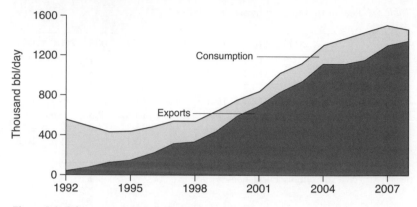

Figure 5.2 Oil consumption and exports
Source: Statistical Agency of the Republic of Kazakhstan.

Figure 5.3 demonstrates, the trade balance has been rising steadily as a result of the favourable pricing for Kazakhstan's export commodities and higher export volumes. The trade balance surged to US$33.5 billion (25.4 per cent of GDP) in 2008 from near US$1 billion (4.4 per cent of GDP) recorded in 2001. Yet, with the exception of 2008, a positive trade balance had been absorbed by a negative services and income balance. Within the income balance, gains investors received on their foreign direct investment (FDI) had been a major item that adversely affected the current account balance. The income of foreign direct investors amounted to US$16.6 billion in 2008, compared with US$10.3 billion in 2007 and only US$1 billion in 2002. The interest paid on debt borrowed by Kazakh banks also increased, negatively affecting the current account balance. Owing to the massive borrowing by Kazakh banks in 2006 and 2007, interest on debt capital increased to US$3.9 billion in 2008 from US$0.8 billion in 2005 and US$0.4 billion in 2004. As a result of these developments, the average current account deficit stood at 2.5 per cent of GDP in the period 2000–08, which is significantly smaller than the current account deficit of 7.9 per cent of GDP registered in 2007 and somewhat greater than the current account surplus of 5.3 per cent of GDP recorded in 2008.

This relatively large current account deficit was financed by two main items: net FDI and external borrowing by the Kazakh banks, mostly in 2006 and 2007 (see Figure 5.4). Net FDI inflows amounted to US$10.7 billion in 2008, up from US$6.6 billion in 2006, reflecting robust investment inflows to the extractive industries. Enormous external borrowing

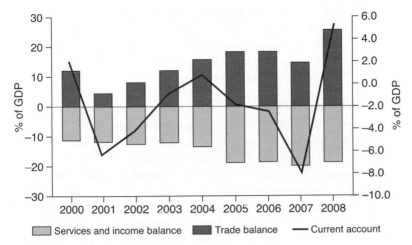

Figure 5.3 Current account and its key components

Source: National Bank of Kazakhstan.

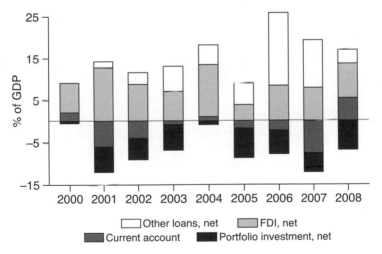

Figure 5.4 Balance of payments: key components

Note: Other loans represent mostly borrowing by banks.

Source: National Bank of Kazakhstan.

by Kazakh banks in 2006 and 2007 contributed to the sizeable capital account surplus in those years. In particular, net 'other' medium- and long-term loans (mostly loans attracted by banks) increased sharply to US$14.6 billion in 2006, up from only US$2.9 billion in 2005. Since the second half of 2007, increments in the banks' liabilities have been on a downward trend, reflecting the banks' difficulties in borrowing in the international capital markets, so that net 'other' investment inflows were down to US$11.7 billion in 2007 and further declined sharply in 2008 to US$4.4 billion from the peak recorded in 2006.

5.3.3 Investment trends

A close inspection of investment patterns across sectors also clearly confirms that the mining and property sectors were the main drivers of the strong boom in the economy in 2001–07.

In particular, the composition of investment in fixed capital across sectors as a percentage of total investment in 2001–07 demonstrates that a lion's share of capital investment went to the mining sector. The mining industry received about 24.5 per cent of the total investment in 2007. Table 5.2 also illustrates that the second biggest investment receiver was the property sector, which received 21.1 per cent of the total capital investments in 2007. The share of the construction sector

Table 5.2 Kazakhstan: sectoral composition of capital investment at current prices, 2001–07

	2001	2002	2003	2004	2005	2006	2007
Total investment	100	100	100	100	100	100	100
Agriculture, hunting and forestry	1.7	1.4	1.3	2.0	1.6	1.1	1.2
Mining industry	51	41.5	35.5	27.0	22.3	22.8	24.4
Manufacturing industry	9.8	9.4	9.9	11.8	10.9	10.6	9.4
Electricity, gas and water	4.4	2.5	2.1	1.6	1.4	1.4	1.9
Construction	2.2	4.6	6.2	8.9	12.3	12.6	12.2
Trade, car repair and household goods	3.2	4.3	4.4	5.3	4.7	4.4	3.0
Hotels and restaurants	0.7	0.3	0.3	0.5	0.3	0.3	0.2
Transport and communication	14.5	11.1	12.3	11.4	8.1	8.3	8.3
Financial sector	1.4	0.9	0.9	1.0	1.3	1.5	1.9
Property	5.1	12.6	14.4	17.8	25.3	23.4	21.1
Public sector	1.4	9.7	11	11.2	10.6	12.0	14.8
Education	1.3	0.7	0.7	0.5	0.4	0.4	0.6
Health and social sectors	1.2	0.4	0.2	0.3	0.2	0.3	0.3
Other municipal, social and personal services	2.1	0.6	0.8	0.8	0.5	0.8	0.6

Source: Kazakhstan NSA data and authors' calculations.

in total capital investment grew dramatically during this period from 2.2 per cent in 2001 to 12.2 per cent in 2007, whereas the share of the property sector in the total capital investment increased by about four-fold during the same period. This is not surprising, given the high real return to capital,[1] which stood in the vicinity of 25 per cent during this period. Over this period, the share of the manufacturing sector in total capital investment has not changed much. However, the share of the transportation and communication sectors in total investment fell from 14.8 per cent in 2001 to 8.3 per cent in 2007. Furthermore, in 2001–07, the share of capital investment allocated to the public sector increased dramatically from 1.4 per cent in 2001 to about 15 per cent in 2007 as the government increased its spending on large infrastructure and diversification projects.

5.4 Oil sector and revenue generation

The above-mentioned analysis of macroeconomic developments implies that the oil sector was behind the robust economic growth of the country in 2000–07. The next step is to scrutinize the government's strategy towards the development of the extractive sector. It is important to determine whether this strategy could also lead to widespread social and economic development in the medium and long term. In addressing these issues, we focus on two crucial components of the policy-making process: revenue generation and revenue management policies adopted during this period. First, we elucidate the revenue generation strategy by analysing the petroleum development strategy and the fiscal regime designed by the government in the hydrocarbon sector. Next, we turn to the question of the government's revenue management strategy and focus on saving and spending policies.

5.4.1 Oil endowment

Kazakhstan is endowed with significant oil and gas reserves. In terms of oil reserves, it ranks second only to Russia among the former Soviet states, and its energy reserves are approximately equal to such smaller Organization of Petroleum Exporting Countries (OPEC) members as Libya and Nigeria. Specifically, BP (2008) estimates Kazakhstan's proven oil reserves at 39.8 billion barrels (3.2 per cent of proven world reserves) in 2007. At the current production level, the country has a reserve-to-production (R/P) ratio of 73.2 years, close to that of the Middle East (R/P ratio of 82.2 years), and significantly greater than the world average of 41.6 years and the Russian average of 21.8 years.

Having the Caspian Sea region's largest recoverable crude oil reserves, Kazakhstan produces more than half the regional oil production, which is currently equal to 2.8 million barrels per day (Table 5.3). The other regional producers include Azerbaijan, Uzbekistan and Turkmenistan. Kazakhstan's oil deposits are concentrated in the western part of the country, mostly near, and under, the Caspian Sea.

According to some estimates, Kazakhstan had proven gas reserves of 1.9 trillion cubic metres (tcm) in 2007, comparable to Iraq's proven natural gas reserves. At the current level of production, 27.3 billion cubic metres (bcm) per year, the R/P ratio is equal to 69.8 years. Although current gas production is low, it is expected to reach 43 bcm by 2010 and 62 bcm by 2015, according to some estimates from Kazakhstan's Ministry of Energy and Mineral Resources. Overall, oil production, rather than gas production, had a pronounced impact on the economic development of the country at the turn of the twenty-first century.

5.4.2 Oil market structure

At present, the market structure of Kazakhstan's oil and gas industry is still in flux. Over the past two decades, global factors, along with Soviet legacies, have shaped the development of the Kazakh hydrocarbon industry. In this section, we examine whether the government policies

Table 5.3 Summary of principal oil fields

Field	Ownership (%)	Legal structure	Reserves recoverable	Share in country's production 2007(%)
Tengiz	Chevron, 50; ExxonMobil, 25; KMG, 20; LukArco (Russia–UK), 5	Joint venture	6–9 billion bbl	20
Karachaganak	ENI (Italy), 32.5; British Gas, 32.5; Chevron, 20; Lukoil, 15	PSA	8–9 billion bbl of oil; 47 Tcf of natural gas	17
Kashagan	ExxonMobil, 16.81; KMG, 16.81; Shell, 16.81; Total, 16.81; ENI, 16.81; Conoco (USA), 8.39; Inpex (Japan), 7.56[1]	PSA	13 billion bbl of oil equivalent	NA

[1] As of October 2008, according to the new agreement (see Box 5.1).

Source: EIA (2008), Yenikeyeff (2008).

since independence have been designed to maximize government revenues and enhance the efficiency of the oil sector. We address these issues by analysing key factors that determined the fiscal regime and the regulatory framework in the petroleum sector and by discussing the implications of these government policies for revenue generation in the sector. In our analysis, we distinguish between two broad phases in terms of the evolution of the ownership structure in the oil industry: *first-generation contracts* 1993–99 and *second-generation contracts* 2000–08.

5.4.2.1 First-generation contracts *1993–99*

The first phase covering 1994–99 witnessed recovery from the collapse of the Soviet economic system, impeded by low world commodity prices and the consequences of the Russian crisis. This period was also marked by large-scale privatization of the principal enterprises in the main industrial sectors of the economy and, in particular, in the petroleum sector. Privatization of most large enterprises was accomplished in an extraordinarily short period of time, mostly in 1995–97, and in less than 3 years,[2] the extensive transfer of ownership of the enterprises to foreign firms had been accomplished.

There are several key factors that account for sweeping privatization of the country's main enterprises in the petroleum sector and the immediate opening up of the oil fields to foreign investors. In 1994–99, the main priority of the government was to arrest the escalating economic collapse. The challenges of the early transition period had been further aggravated by the industrial structure inherited from the Soviet period. In particular, the industrial structure in the country had been characterized by: (1) the presence of large, very specialized enterprises and their dependence on enterprises in other parts of the former Soviet Union; (2) the prevalence of outdated industrial infrastructure in need of substantial investment; and (3) the absence of immediate buyers for the intermediary products or raw materials of Kazakh exports. In addition, other domestic constraints,[3] including the absence of alternatives to natural resource sources of export revenues and the lack of managerial and technical expertise at the local level, partially explain why the government sold the majority of stakes in key enterprises to foreign investors. By the beginning of 1998, the government of Kazakhstan had dramatically reduced the presence of the state in the principal industrial enterprises, which led to the emergence of international companies as the main actors in the petroleum sector of the economy.

The most prominent contracts signed during this period determined the ownership structure of the oil industry that has prevailed since then. Specifically, in April 1993, the government of Kazakhstan signed a 40-year joint venture agreement with Chevron to develop the gigantic Tengiz oil field, by then the country's largest active field and the world's fifth largest, with estimated recoverable oil reserves at 6–9 billion bbl (EIA, 2008). In 1997, the government of Kazakhstan also signed two significant production-sharing agreements (PSAs). The first was with the international consortium to develop the giant Karachaganak oil and gas condensate field located onshore in western Kazakhstan. The second momentous PSA was with another international consortium to exploit the Kashagan oil deposit in the Caspian Sea shelf. The residual shares in each of these contracts had been given to the state-owned company KazMunaiGaz (KMG, formerly KazakhOil).

Strong growth in oil production recorded in the 2000s was possible due to the successful expansion of the Tengiz oil field (developed by TengizChevrOil – TCO) and Karachaganak. However, after 2013, Kashagan is expected to be the main driver of oil output expansion. Commercial oil production from Kashagan was due to start in 2005; however, because of cost overruns and various delays, the new schedule is set for 2013 (see Box 5.1). The development of the Kashagan field is critical for the country's oil ambitions. Kazakhstan has the potential to become one of the world's top oil producers by the end of the next decade[4] if commercial production starts as projected at Kashagan.

Box 5.1 Kashagan dispute – key facts

- Kashagan oil field is the largest field discovered in the world in the last 30 years.
- Initially, Kashagan was due to start commercial production in 2005. The first announcement of the delay in oil production was announced in 2005. At that time, the international consortium paid to the government of Kazakhstan a US$150 million fine for delaying the start of oil production at the field until 2008.
- At the end of July 2007, the second announcement of the cost overruns and delays was made, with an estimated twofold increase in the costs of the project and postponement of the commencement of commercial production until 2010.
- In response, in August 2007, the Kazakh government and the Agip KCO began negotiations over the development of the oil field.

- The dispute over the field was finally resolved on 13 January 2008 with the agreement that allows the Kazakhstan state oil company to double its stake in the project. Under the new agreement, KazMunaiGaz's stake in the consortium has been raised to 16.6 per cent at the expense of all other partners. Each big shareholder – Eni SpA, Exxon Mobil, Total SA and Royal Dutch Shell plc – also holds 16.6 per cent, down from 18.5 per cent. The stakes of the two remaining shareholders, ConocoPhillips and Inpex of Japan, have also been reduced.
- Kazakhstan is expected to pay US$1.78 billion for the increase in its stake, a figure that is well below the actual market value of the additional stake in the project.[5] In addition, the government of Kazakhstan will receive between US$2 billion and US$4 billion (depending on world oil prices) from the consortium over the life of the contract (which will not be extended beyond 2041) as compensation for the delay in the flow of oil revenues from Kashagan due to the delay in production.
- The expected cost of the project over its 40-year life is US$136 billion.
- The projected peak output from Kashagan is expected to add 1.5 million barrels per day (bbl/d) to the world markets by end-2020.
- The new projected start of oil production at Kashagan is 2013.
- The final production-sharing agreement (PSA) for the Kashagan oil field was signed on 31 October 2008. The amendments to the PSA include a new floating royalty structure, which assumes that the government will receive 3.5 per cent of output when global oil prices are above US$45/bbl, 7.5–8 per cent over US$130/bbl and 12.5 per cent over US$195/bbl. The PSA is not subject to the new tax code that came into effect in January 2009.

In summary, the current ownership structure of the petroleum industry, characterized by an extensive involvement of the multinationals, has mostly emerged during the first phase. Nevertheless, in subsequent years, the government has made efforts to 'rebalance' previously signed agreements and introduce tougher tax conditions on new projects – *second-generation contracts* – which we discuss next.

5.4.2.2 Second-generation contracts *2000–08*

The period 2000–08 was marked by buoyant economic growth, spurred mostly by rising commodity prices. During this period, the government began to embrace a more protectionist view concerning developments in the energy sector and undertook some key steps to increase local presence in these sectors. As a result, the contracts signed after 2000, described as second-generation contracts, have been designed to reflect this new approach towards the development of the natural resource sector.

The favourable development in world commodity prices since 2000 provided an impetus for the government to exert more control over the exploitation of its natural resources. Some government officials started to embrace a more protectionist view concerning developments in the energy sector and to look for ways to increase local presence in the oil and gas sectors. Such tendencies were sparked by beliefs that the government lost control over the country's energy sector during the privatization process of the 1990s. For this reason, the government began to implement various reforms to enhance tax collection revenues generated by the mineral extracting industries and gain parity with western oil giants in the oil and gas development ventures. In 2004–05, the government introduced tougher fiscal terms by amending tax regulations. A major change in the legislation, for example, granted the government of Kazakhstan pre-emptive purchase rights in any energy project shares under sale (Kaiser and Pulsipher, 2007). This amendment helped the state to buy part of the British Gas share of the Kashagan project and legitimize the government's bid for a 33 per cent share in Canadian-based PetroKazakhstan. In 2004, the government also introduced legal changes that further expanded the participation of the state oil company KMG in new ventures. As argued above, contracts signed in the first decade since independence were skewed in favour of multinationals with residual shares in projects being allocated to KMG. From 2000, however, the government has made efforts to expand the power of KMG as an investor and partner in several joint projects.

This trend of increasing local presence in the industry has continued with a number of recent developments in the petroleum sector. First, Kazakhstan's government has successfully renegotiated participation in the Kashagan offshore project (see Box 5.1). Second, in November 2007, President Nursultan Nazarbayev signed a bill that would allow the government to change or revoke natural resource contracts deemed to threaten national security. Third, Kazakhstan has developed new tax schemes for the oil, natural gas and mining sectors (see Box 5.2), which came into effect from January 2009.

Box 5.2 Tax code 2008 – key proposals (as of January 2008)

- The objective is to simplify and streamline tax administration, align tax accounting with international standards and shift the burden of taxation more on the subsoil and raw materials sectors.
- Key proposals include: (1) replacement of royalty payments with a mineral extraction tax; (2) replacement of the current 'rent' tax with an export duty on oil and natural gas producers; and (3) introduction of an excessive profit tax for energy and mining companies.
- New PSAs will not be contracted from January 2009 onwards.
- Some of the tax provisions (referred to as 'stable' tax regimes) specified in contracts concluded earlier on subsoil use would be cancelled, excluding the Tengiz field and projects currently operating under PSAs.
- The export duty is based on a formula that depends on global oil prices.[6]
- The mineral extraction tax rates are expected to be imposed at a gradually increasing scale. In 2009, its range is 5–18 per cent of global crude oil prices, depending on the company's annual production volume. In 2010, the range will increase to 6–19 per cent; from 2011, it will be 7–20 per cent.
- The tax rate for exported natural gas is set at 10 per cent of its market value, whereas gas sold to domestic markets would be taxed at 0.5–1.5 per cent of market value.
- The excess profit tax: the government intends to tax that portion of the net income of the oil, natural gas and mining companies that is in excess of 25 per cent (it was previously 20 per cent) of their expenses, with the sliding progressive scale of tax rates from 0 per cent to 60 per cent applied to 'excess' income.
- A gradual reduction in the corporate income tax rate from 30 per cent in 2008 to 20 per cent in 2009, 17.5 per cent in 2010 and 15 per cent in 2011.

5.4.3 Fiscal regime – implications for revenue generation

In the previous section, we argued that the first-generation contracts mostly determined the current oil market structure. However, since 2000, the government has undertaken a targeted approach in 'rebalancing' contractual arrangements with the industry and increasing the government's take of oil revenues. Evolution of the fiscal regime,

reflected in the changes in petroleum legislation and tax codes discussed above, implied more progressive terms for the contracts signed
in the period 1993–99 and tougher tax terms for projects signed after
2000. Existing empirical evidence confirms these trends (Jojarth, 2007;
Wood Mackenzie, 2007). Wood Mackenzie (2007) concludes that fiscal
changes introduced by the Kazakh authorities since 2001 have been
some of the most successful across the global oil industry. Out of the 29
surveyed oil-producing countries, Kazakhstan recorded the fifth largest
increase in state take in the percentage of pretake net present value
from its 2002 terms to its 2007 terms. In the next section, we attempt to
shed light on the evolution of fiscal terms by calculating export revenues and the government's take of those revenues.

The government's approach to exerting more control over the petroleum industry and increasing its hydrocarbon revenues is counteracted
by the fact that the bulk of oil production in Kazakhstan after 2015 will
be delivered from the fields currently operating under the PSA agreements (Kashagan and Karachaganak, mostly). PSAs prevail over any
existing or future laws whose provisions are in conflict with the contract signed under the PSA. The government of Kazakhstan used the
PSA arrangement with foreign investors mostly to establish favourable
investment terms and attract foreign capital in the first years after independence. However, over time, as the bargaining power of the government improved, the government has successfully renegotiated the
terms of the contracts unaffected by the changes in petroleum legislation. The renegotiation of the Kashagan project is an example of this
trend.[7] At the same time, the Kazakh authorities decided not to favour
PSA arrangements any more. According to the new tax code (see Box
5.2), PSA will not be contracted from January 2009.

Recent developments in the Kazakh oil industry fit well with Moran's
(1974) '*dynamic balance of power theory*', or the '*dynamic bargaining model*'.[8]
The theory states that resource-rich countries ascend a bargaining learning curve in their negotiations with multinational companies and do better for themselves in the future. Our discussion of recent changes in
petroleum legislation and tax codes, renegotiations of existing contracts
in the oil sector and the government's reluctance to employ PSA arrangements in dealing with foreign investors in the future, point to the fact
that Kazakhstan has progressed on the learning curve. It is important to
note, however, that the negotiations between multinational companies
and developing countries are quite complex, and that 'learning-by-doing'
is only one aspect of contract negotiations. Nevertheless, we contend that
the theory describes quite accurately this aspect of the contract negotia-

tions process between the government of Kazakhstan and multinational companies, confirming the significance of learning. We find that the government has advanced in its overall level of skills to deal with various aspects of the oil industry and has demonstrated the ability to negotiate skilfully with multinational companies.

In terms of the legal structure of the current projects in the petroleum sector,[9] about 60–70 per cent of oil production in Kazakhstan is undertaken through joint venture agreements, for example the development of Tengiz and other older, smaller offshore fields. As Karachaganak, Kashagan and most recent offshore contracts are written under a PSA framework, they should represent a greater share of oil production in the country after 2015.

5.5 Oil revenues and the government's revenue management

5.5.1 Revenues in the oil sector

The oil sector in Kazakhstan has generated enormous (net) revenues.[10] Both surging oil prices and growing oil production have contributed to a significant increase in the magnitude of export revenues in the last decade. The amount of total revenues generated in the oil sector has been growing steadily since 2000, reaching US$40.7 billion in 2008, almost 20 times higher than the 2000 level. In terms of GDP, the amount of total revenues has grown from 14.3 per cent of GDP in 2000 to 24.7 per cent of GDP in 2007 and to 32 per cent of GDP in 2008. The (net) export revenues and oil budget revenues have exhibited a similar trend. The size of (net) export revenues has increased from US$2 billion in 2000 to a record high level of US$35 billion in 2008.

To shed light on the progressivity of the fiscal terms, which we discussed above, we calculate the ratio of the government's take to the total (net) export revenues generated in the oil sector. As shown in Table 5.4, the government's take of these massive revenues has undergone only slight changes in relative terms and fluctuated, on average, by 50 per cent of the total export revenues during this period. This pattern, however, does not corroborate the progressivity in fiscal terms introduced by the government, as some studies suggest (Wood Mackenzie, 2007). We offer two explanations for this pattern. One possibility is that the bulk of production in the oil sector in 2000–08 derived from major projects that operated under the contracts signed in 1993–99. In particular, such projects as Tengiz and Karachaganak have special tax provisions, referred to as 'stable' tax regimes, which are not subject to changes in petroleum legislation and are less likely to be affected by changes in tax codes. Another explanation is that the most 'aggressive' change in the tax burden of the oil sector has been introduced by the recent tax code effective from January 2009. This means that our analysis focusing on the period 2000–08 does not capture the impact of this amendment in the government's take. In future research, it is necessary to analyse the implications of the new tax code for the government's ability to capture resource revenues.

As Table 5.4 shows, over time, the government of Kazakhstan has put greater emphasis on saving its hydrocarbon revenues. The National Oil Fund (National Fund of the Republic of Kazakhstan, or NFRK) has become a major vehicle for saving oil revenues. The NFRK was created in 2001 with the aim of reducing the negative impact of volatile oil prices on the economy and saving some portion of oil revenue windfalls for future generations. As Table 5.4 illustrates, the government has generated about US$46.9 billion in revenue from the oil sector since

Table 5.4 (Net) export and budget revenues from the oil sector, 2000–07

	2000	2001	2002	2003	2004	2005	2006	2007	2008
In US$ billion									
(Net) total revenues	2.6	2.1	2.7	4.7	9.5	15.5	22.9	25.7	40.7
(Net) total export revenues	2.0	1.7	1.9	3.5	7.2	13.2	19.2	23.3	35.0
Oil budget revenue	0.6	1.5	1.1	1.8	3.0	6.0	8.1	9.9	14.8
Receipts of the Oil Fund		1.3	0.7	1.5	1.0	3.1	6.1	9.3	13.7
As a percentage of GDP									
(Net) total revenues	14.3	9.4	10.8	15.2	22.1	27.1	28.5	24.7	31.7
(Net) total export revenue	11.1	7.5	7.7	11.2	16.7	23.1	23.9	22.4	27.2
%									
Oil budget revenue/ (net) total export revenue ratio	29.8	88.0	56.7	52.9	42.0	45.8	42.3	42.4	42.3
Oil fund receipts/oil budget revenue ratio		88.7	65.1	81.7	33.0	51.3	74.9	94.3	89.9
Memorandum items:									
Kazakh crude oil export (US$/bbl)	20.2	17.3	16.9	20.8	28.7	43.7	56.9	60.9	86.4
Brent crude oil price (US$/bbl)	28.5	24.4	25.0	28.8	38.3	54.53	65.1	72.4	98.9

Source: Statistical Agency of Kazakhstan, Ministry of Finance and authors' calculations.

2000, with about US$36.3 billion being saved in the NFRK. This amount is equal to about 78 per cent of the total oil revenues accrued to the budget, indicating that the authorities have pursued a prudent fiscal policy and have managed to save a substantial portion of the oil windfall. Next, we examine the NFRK institutional design.

5.5.2 National Oil Fund (NFRK)

The rules governing the NFRK were originally quite complex, but they have been changed over time to simplify the process of oil wealth accumulation, stabilize the level of government spending and provide some control over the long-term level of the fund. According to the new methodology introduced in mid-2006, all payments from the pre-identified extractive sector companies go first to the NFRK and, from there, the so-called annual guaranteed transfers are transferred to the budget in accordance with the predetermined guidelines. The total size of funds annually directed from the NFRK to the budget is calculated on the basis of the formula, which is a combination of two well-known approaches on how to save and how much to consume out of oil revenues:[11] the bird-in-hand (BIH) rule, and the permanent income hypothesis (PIH) rule.[12] In particular, the annual amount spent out of oil revenues for a given year is calculated by the following formula:

$$G = A + bNFRK_{t-1}{}^*ER$$

where G is the guaranteed transfer to the budget, A is a fixed part of the transfers (predetermined), b is a coefficient reflecting returns to the National Fund investments for a predetermined period, $NFRK$ are investments of the National Fund of the Republic of Kazakhstan, and ER is the exchange rate.

By selecting the parameters for the rule, the government decides how much of the oil windfall to spend and leaves the residue to be saved. The parameters of the formula and, thus, the amount of guaranteed transfers, are specified by the government at the time of formulating the federal budget. In addition, the guidelines specify that the total amount of transfers cannot exceed one-third of the assets of the NFRK. This clause is inserted to avoid complete depletion of the NFRK. It is further stipulated that the guaranteed transfers have to be used only for development projects, and they are mostly channelled through such state-owned development institutions as Kazyna and Samruk.

The new rules facilitated the stabilization of government spending and the saving of oil revenues in the NFRK. As displayed in Table 5.5, the

Table 5.5 The National Oil Fund

	2001	2002	2003	2004	2005	2006	2007	2008
US$ billion								
Receipts	1.345	0.715	1.539	1.024	3.113	6.145	9.300	13.737
Capital gains	0.672	0.053	0.027	0.099	0.335	0.595	0.783	–0.550
Withdrawals	0.051	0.001	0.003	0.004	0.005	0.007	2.117	8.937
Net inflows	1.293	0.713	1.536	1.021	3.108	6.138	7.183	4.800
Stock	1.293	2.007	3.543	4.564	7.672	13.810	20.993	25.793
Stock (% of GDP)	5.84	7.92	11.45	11.37	14.23	18.15	21.42	20.8
Memorandum items:								
Exchange rate (KZT/US$)	146.78	153.29	149.14	135.97	132.9	126	122.5	120.3

Source: Ministry of Finance.

introduction of the new rules resulted in a significant jump in revenue accumulation in the NFRK. In 2004, the NFRK received approximately US$1.4 billion, whereas the amount received from the oil sector increased by more than four times and reached US$6.1 billion in 2006. This trend continued in subsequent years, and an increase in the stock of the Fund in 2007–08 amounted to US$13.5 billion, equal to the stock of the assets accumulated in the NFRK by the end of 2006 over the span of 6 years.[13]

In terms of the asset management strategy, the current arrangement is that the Ministry of Finance (MoF) owns the Fund, whereas the National Bank of Kazakhstan (NBK) manages it. NFRK assets have two components: stabilization and savings. The revenue accumulated in the stabilization portfolio (which represents 75 per cent of the NFRK balance) was invested in liquid assets (fixed income securities), whereas the proceeds collected in the savings portfolio (25 per cent of the NFRK balance) had to be invested in less liquid, high-return, long-term securities (equities). Prior to 2009, the revenue accumulated in the NFRK had been invested in overseas funds. In 2009, however, the government revised the NFRK asset investment strategy in order to provide support to the domestic economy in the face of the global liquidity crisis. The key elements of the government's anti-crisis measures are discussed in Section 5.7.

5.5.3 Government spending policy

In terms of public spending priorities, the period 2000–08 can be divided into three subperiods (World Bank, 2005). The first subperiod lasting from 2000 to 2003 was marked by a cautious change in public spending priorities. The government implemented tight fiscal policies, and oil windfalls were mostly saved in the NFRK. As Table 5.6 demonstrates, on average, about 79 per cent of the total oil revenues accrued to the budget in 2001–03 had been accumulated in the NFRK. This period has seen a significant fall in current expenditures as a share of GDP from 20.2 per cent in 2000 to 17.2 per cent in 2003, whereas capital expenditures have almost tripled from 1.7 per cent of GDP in 2000 to 5 per cent of GDP in 2003. The capital spending focused on improving infrastructure, supporting rural and agricultural development, the capitalization of development funds and support of enterprises within the industrial policy framework.

The second subperiod, from 2004 to 2005, stands out in terms of its lax fiscal policy stance. This era saw a full percentage point increase in recurrent expenditures, while the capital expenditures declined slightly as a percentage of GDP. In general, total expenditures as a share of GDP increased significantly from 17.4 per cent in 2004 to 25.6 in 2005. Much of the spending increase was used to support housing and the energy sector. Furthermore, some of the increase in government spending went to finance development programmes as Kazakhstan started to implement an active industrial policy to diversify its economy. The creation of several national development agencies, such as the Kazakhstan Development Bank, the Investment Fund, the National Innovative Fund and the Small Business Development Fund, can be considered as a first step in implementing the long-run national development strategy. In addition, the government has reformed the tax system and reduced tax for non-resource industries, while increasing its non-oil budget deficit. Relatively loose fiscal policy implemented in these 2 years was mirrored in how much had been saved in the NFRK. The fraction of the oil budget revenues saved in the NFRK amounted to only 42 per cent during these 2 years, whereas the government saved about 78 per cent of the total resource revenues in 2001–08.

The promotion of human capital development has been a hallmark of the 2006–08 subperiod. Although retaining most of the previous priorities, the government has identified investment in education. In addition, the government launched new welfare programmes designed to improve the well-being of citizens. Raising oil prices allowed the government to increase spending without jeopardizing its saving policy, with the bulk (86 per cent) of oil budget revenues being saved in the NFRK. In 2003–07, the energy sector was a clear winner in terms of attracting public funds.

Table 5.6 Government spending, percentage change in real terms, 2001–07

	2001	2002	2003	2004	2005	2006	2007	Average
Agriculture	10.2	91.7	7.4	41.3	20.4	−1.8	13.4	26.1
Transport and communication	4.5	18.2	6.5	41.2	24.7	11.5	55.0	23.1
Housing	27.2	30.4	−27.8	19.4	195.3	−6.1	28.2	38.1
Social sector	4.20	7.84	−0.44	4.60	39.80	1.67	6.33	9.9
Industry and construction	5.1	−40.1	−11.0	−26.5	14.5	16.0	23.2	−2.7
Energy	NA	NA	26.7	7.0	148.3	18.6	26.5	45.4
Total expenditure	8.2	18.6	−1.4	11.6	61.5	−9.0	7.8	13.9
Total expenditure (% of GDP)	17.5	19	17.1	17.4	25.6	21.1	21	19.8

Source: Statistical Agency of Kazakhstan and authors' calculations.

Public spending on the energy sector grew, on average, about 45 per cent per year during this period. In addition, in 2001–07, the average increase in government spending on housing was 38 per cent per year. Given that total expenditures during this period rose only about 14 per cent per year, on average, the housing sector received more attention from the government, compared with other sectors, excluding the energy sector. The government also increased its spending on agriculture, on average, by 26 per cent annually, and this spending trend helped to keep the sector from excessive contraction. Average public expenditures on transport and communication rose annually by about 23 per cent. Government expenditures on this sector more than doubled as a share of GDP, growing from 1 per cent in 2001 to 2.3 per cent in 2007. Spending on the social sector grew about 10 per cent per annum, on average, in 2001–07.

Kazakhstan's cautious spending approach is mirrored in the government's general fiscal balance. As seen in Table 5.7, despite the fact that the state budget had been executed with a modest deficit of around 1 per cent of GDP during this period, at the consolidated level, Kazakhstan operated with an approximate 5 per cent of GDP surplus, giving the government a substantial degree of flexibility to deal with the adverse consequences of the global financial turmoil. Consistent with the policy of saving most of the hydrocarbon revenues in the NFRK, the government had also paid back external debts to smooth out public expenditures and to reduce future debt obligations. The total external debt of the government stood at only 1.6 per cent of GDP at end-2008 compared with the stock of almost 20 per cent of GDP 7 years previously (Table 5.8).

Table 5.7 Kazakhstan: budget and the National Oil Fund balance (as a percentage of GDP)

	2001	2002	2003	2004	2005	2006	2007	2008
Balance	5.6	2.9	4.1	2.0	5.9	8.4	5.2	1.5
State	−0.2	0.0	−0.9	−0.3	0.6	0.8	−1.7	−2.1
National Oil Fund	5.8	2.9	5.0	2.4	5.3	7.6	6.9	3.6

Source: Ministry of Finance.

Table 5.8 Total government debt: external and internal (as a percentage of GDP)

	2001	2002	2003	2004	2005	2006	2007	2008
External government debt	17.3	14.2	11.5	7.7	4.2	2.9	1.8	1.6
Internal government debt	2.8	3.3	3.7	4.1	3.9	3.7	4.1	5.2
Total government debt	20.1	17.5	15.2	11.8	8.1	6.6	5.9	6.8

Source: Ministry of Finance.

5.5.4 Government development policy

Whether the country's enormous resource endowment turns out to be 'blessing or curse' depends not only on the choice of appropriate saving and spending policies, but also on broader development policies adopted by the government in response to the resource boom. Appropriate government spending and saving policies help to achieve macroeconomic stability, stabilize the level of government spending and smooth oil price volatility. Yet, the ultimate goal of the government's resource management policies should be the growth of the non-oil private sector. If there is growth in the non-oil economy, then there should be investment by the private sector, implying an appropriate balance between consumption and investment decisions by individuals.

A wide array of factors affect the way the public resource management strategy can influence private sector behaviour – consumption and investment – in response to the oil boom. As Collier *et al.* (2010) argue, there are four channels through which the government can allocate resource revenues and impact the private sector response. They can be disbursed to the private sector through citizen dividends or through the tax/benefit system. Resource revenues can also be retained as public financial assets, but lent to the private sector either by government lending (through development banks) or by reducing existing public debt. They can be used to increase public consumption, or they can be retained as government financial assets and lent to foreigners by establishing a sovereign wealth fund. Although all these four alternatives have been employed by the government of Kazakhstan, resource revenue has been mostly allocated through the fourth option – by retaining almost all oil revenues as public assets and lending abroad. The small fraction of oil revenues – guaranteed transfers from the NFRK – had been circulated to the non-oil economy, but primarily through state-owned development institutions. This strategy of resource allocation had been in line with the overall development strategy adopted by the government, which assigned a special role to the state in generating economic growth.

The government-led development policy has been pursued in a systematic and targeted way. The government of Kazakhstan launched a set of various development initiatives and established different development institutions to implement these initiatives. For example, the first comprehensive development strategy of the government was announced in October 1997 and has become known as 'Kazakhstan 2030: Prosperity, Security, and Improvement of Welfare of Citizens of Kazakhstan' or simply *'Kazakhstan – 2030'*. This policy document has been followed by a series of development strategies adopted in 2003. In particular, the announcement of *'Innovative Industrial Development Strategy for 2003–2015'* (hereafter IID) signalled that the government was committed to further economic diversification, and the export-led industrialization model was chosen as a way of achieving its development objectives.[14] As an investment arm of the government, the Kazakhstan Investment Fund, Kazakhstan Development Bank, Kazakhstan Innovation Fund and Export Insurance Corporation were set up by the government to implement the IID.

In 2006, President Nazarbayev created two national development agencies to provide prudent management of state assets and revenues. The first, the Kazyna Sustainable Development Fund, consolidated all previously created development agencies. The main task of this Fund was to enhance innovative economic development to boost the nation's industrial competitive edge and assist the government with the implementation of its diversification strategy. The second institution, the Samruk State Holding Company, was charged with the task of enhancing the efficiency and accountability of state asset management. By mid-2007, the Kazyna Fund had invested about US\$2 billion in various development projects, and the Samruk had started representing the state in major national companies.

Thus, the state-owned development agencies have been the main conduits of the implementation of development strategies in the country, with negligible private sector participation in this process. The government policies have focused on isolating the domestic economy from a large part of resource revenues by investing the bulk of oil revenues in overseas funds and by disbursing the rest of the oil revenues in a targeted and controlled way. The country's private sector has not had much access to resource revenues, providing little recycling of oil money in the non-oil economy. However, the private sector anticipated the continuation of prudent government policies characterized by the stable macroeconomic situation, a reduction in government debt, cautious public spending of resource revenues and the perceived continuation of a favourable situation in global markets for the main export of the country. They increased their current consumption through borrowing because they anticipated that lower taxes in the future would pay for their debt. Their behaviour, using economist's terms, would correspond to the behaviour of the individual in the Ricardian world, and these individuals would be called 'Ricardian' ones. In the case of Kazakhstan, therefore, interaction of the public and private sectors through four main channels has been altered by the expectations of the private sector. The private sector was also motivated in its behaviour by favourable credit ratings (mostly due to the oil windfall), and has become increasingly exposed to risks related to foreign borrowing. The government, on the other hand, lacked policies aimed at discouraging the excessive risk-taking behaviour of the private sector. As we discuss in the next section, various measures adopted by the authorities to limit private sector external borrowing had a negligible effect. Thus, the government had little control over the consumption/investment balance of the private sector, further encouraging the excessive consumption and unproductive investment (into residential and commercial property) of the private sector. The private sector behaviour has greatly jeopardized the sustainability of Kazakhstan's growth potential and the government's prudence. The financial sector, whose main parameters are discussed below, was a major channel through which Ricardian consumer behaviour affected the country's growth prospects.

5.6 Financial sector

As argued above, the finance and construction sectors were the main contributors to economic growth in the country in 2005–07, outperforming the mining sector. From the balance of payment data, we also learned that the flow of massive external liabilities was a major source of banking sector growth in the late 2000s. To unravel the link between the sector's growth and enormous external borrowing further, we turn to an analysis of the parameters of the financial system.

5.6.1 The banking sector

Kazakhstan is a former Soviet republic in which the government placed a high priority on banking sector reform. By the end of 1997, substantial reforms in the structure of the financial system had been accomplished, and a major financial collapse was avoided.

In the short time span, Kazakh banking had caught up very quickly with most advanced emerging economies. Its total assets tripled in 5 years and reached 92 per cent of GDP by the end of 2007, up from 36 per cent of GDP at the end of 2003 (Conrad, 2008). This spectacular performance placed Kazakhstan in the middle of the group of emerging peers and made it a leader in the Commonwealth of Independent States (CIS). In particular, the average ratio between assets and the GDP amounted to 60–100 per cent in East European countries, with the Czech Republic (104 per cent in 2007 and 100 per cent in 2003) and Hungary (109 per cent in 2007 and 50 per cent in 2003) as leaders, suggesting that the Kazakh banking performance was quite outstanding, even by East European standards. On this measure, the CIS countries were far behind Kazakhstan. The ratio between assets and the GDP was 87 per cent in 2007 and 39 per cent in 2003 in Ukraine, and 61 per cent in 2007 and 42 per cent in 2003 in Russia.

Kazakh banking is one of the most penetrated banking systems, with loans of 70 per cent as a share of GDP at the end of 2007. Other postcommunist states with advanced banking systems lag behind. For example, loans made up 69 per cent of GDP in Hungary in 2007 and 44 per cent of GDP in 2003. In Ukraine, loans constituted 60 per cent of GDP in 2007, compared with 25 per cent in 2003. In Russia, loans made up 40 per cent of GDP in 2007 and 22 per cent of GDP in 2003. The main driver behind the high penetration of the Kazakh banking system has been corporate lending, which amounted to 49 per cent of GDP in 2007, with the trade and construction sectors being the largest borrowers from Kazakh banks. The main reason behind this development was the inability of local firms to raise needed resources on the undeveloped domestic debt market, compelling the banks to play a role as conduits in facilitating financing for them.

A major reason for the rapid expansion of the banking sector in the country was the extremely strong reliance on foreign funds. As a result of more advanced banking reforms relative to restructuring in the enterprise sector in the first decade following independence, domestic

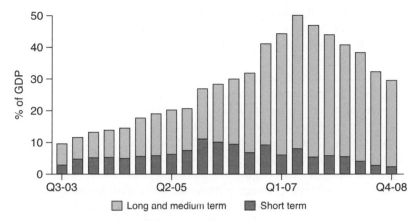

Figure 5.5 The external debt of the banks
Source: National Bank of Kazakhstan.

funds were insufficient to support business growth in the banking sector. Local funding sources remained limited, underdeveloped, short term and volatile. The deposit base, albeit increasing, remained thin in such a sparsely populated country as Kazakhstan. To support their business growth, Kazakh banks over-borrowed from abroad, in part because of the country's rapid integration into international capital markets and opened access to external funding for the banks. The global capital markets, characterized by a 'glut of saving' and low interest rates, facilitated these processes. At the same time, the development of the oil sector in an environment of high commodity prices, by contributing to high economic growth and a robust fiscal position, had also improved market sentiment towards the country and encouraged lending by foreign investors.[15] A sharp increase in external borrowing by the banks peaked in Q2 2007, amounting to US$45.9 billion (50.2 per cent of GDP), and it has been on a downward trend since the start of the global liquidity squeeze in mid-2007 (Figure 5.5).

Banks have used external borrowing to fund aggressive credit expansion in the economy. The stock of domestic credit to the private sector more than doubled in 2 years, amounting to 59 per cent of GDP at the end of 2007, up from 35.2 per cent of GDP at end-2005. It was a pure arbitrage opportunity for Kazakh banks, by borrowing in international capital markets and lending at higher rates in the domestic markets, supported by the strengthening currency. The average return on equity increased to 15 per cent in 2007 from 6 per cent in 2001, which further increased the willingness of banks to borrow and foreign investors to lend (Conrad, 2008). Our own estimates suggest that the return on capital has been remaining high in the country, at about 25 per cent since 2004 (see Section 5.5), which also explains why sectors such as construction and property attracted a large share of fixed investments.

As long as credit was cheap, this significantly contributed to the property boom in Almaty and Astana, the two main cities in the country, and to the high exposure of Kazakh banks to the construction and retail sectors. Credit supported by rising income has spread rapidly throughout the population in recent years. Credit growth was extremely high until August 2007 (Figure 5.6). Mortgages, car loans, construction loans and unsecured consumer credit grew especially rapidly in 2006 and 2007. The share of mortgage loans in the total loans extended by banks surged from 1 per cent in 2002 to 9.4 per cent in 2007. The share of consumer loans increased from 4.7 per cent in 2002 to 16.6 per cent in 2007, and construction sector loans were up from 6.4 per cent in 2002 to 17.2 per cent in 2007, suggesting that the share of construction loans and credit accounted for at least 43 per cent of the banks' loan portfolio in 2007 (Conrad, 2008).

Because of the over-reliance on foreign funding, Kazakh banks and the financial system in the country have been hit hard by the global liquidity squeeze that started in the middle of 2007. Despite growing concerns about the risks related to external borrowing, Kazakhstan's authorities were unable to curb the booming expectations of the private sector. Various measures adopted by the authorities to mitigate vulnerabilities in the banking sector had only a partial impact, as some shortcomings in the regulatory environment had not been addressed (IMF, 2006, 2007). The excessive borrowing by Kazakh banks had therefore been compounded by weaknesses in the regulatory framework.

Overall, the current strains of the banking sector in Kazakhstan exposed the weaknesses of the business model that pushed itself over the edge by relying excessively on cheap and easy money. Rather than following the more time-consuming strategy of building up its deposit base, the private sector took advantage of fast, easy and cheap money, and brought its consumption forward. This was the result of the behaviour of Ricardian individuals who fully anticipated their future shares in resource revenues and thus adjusted their consumption accordingly. Such behaviour of the private sector, however, was not optimal from the social perspective, resulting in a 'Ricardian' curse of the resource windfall (van der Ploeg and Venables, 2008).

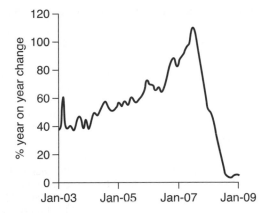

Figure 5.6 Domestic credit growth
Source: National Bank of Kazakhstan.

However, the exuberance of the private sector came to a halt in the middle of 2007 when the US sub-prime crisis erupted. In response to the tightening lending conditions on the global capital markets, Kazakh banks markedly slowed down their lending activity. In addition, uncertain market conditions have brought to the fore the issue of the quality of bank assets, which resulted from the ongoing correction of the property and house price bubble in the country. As the banking sector problems worsened, threatening to deepen a likely recession in the economy, the government of Kazakhstan was forced to step in and embark on a set of anti-crisis measures, which are discussed in the following section.

5.7 The anti-crisis measures of the government

The government of Kazakhstan responded swiftly to changes in the international capital markets to provide support and liquidity for its weakened financial system. The government proposed a comprehensive anti-crisis programme that specified the timetable for the implementation of the government's initiatives and identified funding sources and agencies responsible for the realization of each component of the programme. The key elements of the anti-crisis programme are summarized in Table 5.9. The programme's total value is estimated at almost US$20 billion, or 15 per cent of 2008 GDP. The strong fiscal

Table 5.9 Kazakhstan: government anti-crisis initiatives as of 14 January 2009

Measure	Funding source	Key dates
Bank recapitalization programme: purchases of ordinary and preferred shares (up to 25%) as well as provision of subordinated loans to the four largest banks	US$3.5 billion, out of US$5 billion channelled from the Oil Fund in 2008 for capitalization of Samruk–Kazyna	Purchases of ordinary shares by 15 April 2009; purchases of preferred shares by 1 June 2009 Provision of subordinated loans by 1 September 2009
Distressed asset fund aimed at acquiring non-performing loans (NPLs) from banks[16]	US$430 million (allocated in the 2008 budget); US$570 million (envisaged as expenditure in the 2009 budget)	Purchases of the NPLs totalling KZT70 billion (US$580 million) by 1 February 2009 Decision on the necessity of the placement of the remaining funds (KZT50 billion (US$420 million)) by 1 April 2009
Property support		
	Samruk–Kazyna will issue securities in the amount of KZT480 billion (US$4 billion) to sell to the Oil Fund	To be implemented by 30 January 2009
	Samruk–Kazyna will issue securities (KZT 480 billion) to be placed at the Kazakh Stock Exchange to attract pension fund money	The placement to be implemented by 15 October 2009
Support to small- and medium-sized enterprises		
Implemented through extending credits to the enterprises that will be channelled through banks	Samruk–Kazyna, KZT 240 billion (US$2 billion)	Agreements with the banks should be signed in February 2009
Realization of investment and innovative projects		
	US$1 billion out of US$5 billion channelled from the Oil Fund for capitalization of Samruk–Kazyna in 2008	Implementation of the projects started from June 2009

Table 5.9 (cont):

Measure	Funding source	Key dates
Support to the agriculture industry		
	KazAgro will issue securities (US$1 billion) to be sold to the Oil Fund	To be implemented by 1 March 2009
Other measures		
Banking sector: lower reserve requirements	Central bank	US$2.9 billion, effective as of 18 November 2009
Total above		US$19.4 billion

Source: www.government.kz

position has provided the government with some flexibility to pledge its support to stabilize the economy, whereas the government has decided to rely upon the NFRK for financing its programmes.

To consolidate the government's anti-crisis measures, the government created a new state-owned Samruk–Kazyna Welfare Fund through the merger of the state asset management company, Samruk, and the state development fund, Kazyna, in October 2008 (see also Section 5.5). To finance some of the anti-crisis initiatives of the government, the Samruk–Kazyna Fund was expected to issue securities to be sold to the NFRK. This strategy would imply that oil money accumulated in the NFRK would be invested in domestic assets, marking a departure from the previous NFRK investment strategy, that is the investment of oil revenues in overseas funds.

5.8 Conclusion

In this chapter, we have examined key decision points in managing natural resource wealth in Kazakhstan in 2000–08. As our analysis shows, the government of Kazakhstan demonstrated considerable prudence in managing its natural resource wealth by saving the bulk of oil revenues in foreign assets. A parallel development has been a reduction in sovereign external debt, a fall in currency mismatches and improvements in the liquidity position of the government. The incumbent authorities have largely managed to insulate the domestic economy from a large part of resource revenue inflows by accumulating a greater portion of oil revenues in overseas funds and investing the rest into the economy in a targeted and controlled manner through state-owned institutions. In addition, during this period, the government maintained good macroeconomic performance. Yet, the private sector's response to the oil boom went beyond what could have been anticipated by the government. The private sector's expectations became intertwined with the government revenue management policy in a complex way, resulting in massive external borrowing by the banking sector. As a result, government prudence has been undermined by private sector profligacy, leading to the costly bail out of the banking sector and putting at risk the country's growth potential.

Excessive reliance of the Kazakh banks on external funding highlights the fact that most of the oil money appears to have ended up outside the banking system and thus has lent little support to banking asset growth and investment by the private sector in the non-oil economy. Only in recent years has the government announced significant tax cuts for the non-oil sector, suggesting that the non-extracting sector savings in taxes would be spread throughout the economy, supporting the banking sector of the country in the future. The investment of most public oil revenues in overseas funds also raises the issue of the optimal size of the Oil Fund (van der Ploeg and Venables, 2009). Kazakhstan is a capital-scarce country and should use resource revenues primarily to build assets within the country, often to alleviate absorption constraints in the non-traded sector, rather than to acquire foreign financial assets, which on average yield a lower return. In view of these constraints, the government has been planning to adopt a new financial system framework that would focus on access of the banks to the country's internal financial resources, including NFRK revenues, rather than reliance on external borrowing.

In summary, the experience of Kazakhstan in managing its oil revenues demonstrates that the government's prudence in handling resource revenues might be insufficient if the appropriate regulatory framework, which controls the consumption/investment balance of the private sector, is missing.

Acknowledgements

This research is part of the project funded by the Revenue Watch Institute with the support of the Bill and Melinda Gates Foundation. We are grateful to Anthony Venables and Paul Collier for helpful feedback. We also acknowledge the participants in the Revenue Watch Institute conference, Oxford, UK, 12 December 2008, for insightful comments and suggestions, and Kassymkhan Kapparov for research assistance. The views expressed in this chapter are solely those of the authors and do not necessarily reflect the views of the Revenue Watch Institute.

Notes

1 The real rate of return to capital is calculated as the ratio of the capital share in income to the real capital–output ratio plus the difference in the price of the capital and the price of the output minus the depreciation rate.

2 For an overview of foreign investment in the extractive industry, see Peck (1999, 2004).

3 See, for example, Esanov *et al.* (2001), Jones Luong and Weinthal (2001) and Peck (1999, 2004).

4 The prospects for oil production depend heavily on export capacity, which might be unable to meet increased production.

5 The below-market price paid by the government of Kazakhstan for an additional stake in the project is considered as a bargain price that the major oil companies received in 1997, the year the contract on Kashagan was signed. This reflects the fact that the state is re-asserting its negotiating position with international oil companies.

6 When the export tax was first introduced in May 2008, it was reviewed quarterly, and it was set up at US\$109.9/tonne (US\$15/bbl) and US\$27.4/tonne (US\$3.6/bbl) for those who pay royalties. In mid-September 2008, the government nearly doubled it to US\$203.8/tonne (US\$27.8/bbl) and to US\$121.32/tonne (US\$17.37/bbl) for those who pay royalties. The initial rate was based on the average oil price in Q1 2008, whereas the September rate was based on the Q2 2008 average oil price.

7 Some observers have compared the Kashagan dispute with the problems of Royal Dutch Shell at the Sakhalin II project off the east Russian coast, where a consortium led by Shell eventually relinquished control over the project to Russian Gazprom. However, the Kashagan phenomenon and the recent developments in the Kazakh oil industry should be considered in the context of local politics and should not be confused with the 'resource nationalization' seen in other oil-exporting countries.

8 Hosman (2009) was the first to apply Moran's theory to the case of Kazakhstan.

9 Boadway and Keen (2008) review the principal tax instruments for the petroleum and hard minerals sectors as well as some of the central design issues dealing with time, uncertainty and time consistency.

10 (Net) total (export) revenues are calculated as the difference between total (export) revenue, which is equal to the total volume produced (exported) multiplied by the export price, and the cost of production and transportation. In Kazakhstan, oil is produced from different fields, with quality and production costs varying across fields. Moreover, oil is exported using different pipelines, implying different transportation costs. In our calculations, we averaged production and transportation costs across different oil fields and transportation routes.

11 On PIH and BIH approaches, see Collier and Venables (2008).

12 van der Ploeg and Venables (2008) examine how to spend and when to save a resource (or aid) windfall in a model of a developing country by incorporating two market imperfections: credit-constrained households and the upward-sloping supply curve of foreign debt. They demonstrate that policy actions based on the PIH in a heavily indebted country with a small windfall are not optimal. Only if the windfall is large, relative to initial debt, is it optimal to build a sovereign wealth fund, following the conventional PIH prescription.

13 Arguably, the surge in oil prices during that period and an increase in export volumes also contributed to the trend in 2007 and most of 2008.

14 The IID was a comprehensive plan with detailed targets for industrial development. In particular, the document targeted 8.4 per cent annual growth for processing industries until 2015, at least a threefold increase in labour productivity during this period, compared with 2000, a twofold reduction in GDP energy intensity and a threefold increase in the 2000 level of GDP by 2015. The cost of the programme was estimated at US$1.2 billion per annum in 2002 prices.

15 Kuralbayeva and Vines (2008) demonstrate how an emerging oil-exporting country could face Dutch party effects in an environment with high commodity prices, resulting from lower interest on external borrowing and, thus, higher external debt.

16 The Kazakh authorities seem to have abandoned the idea of creating a distressed asset fund on account of the difficulties in valuing the distressed loans issued by Kazakh banks. On this point, see the 2009 archives of the Silk Road Intelligencer at http://silkroadintelligencer.com/archives/.

References

Boadway, R. and M. Keen (2008) *Theoretical Perspectives on Resource Tax Design*. Paper presented at the OxCarre 2nd annual conference, December 2008, University of Oxford.

BP (2008) *Statistical Review of World Energy 2008*. Retrieved from www.bp.com/statisticalreview.

Collier, P. and A. Venables (2008) *Managing Resource Revenues: Lessons for Low Income Countries*. OxCarre research paper no. 2008–12, University of Oxford.

Collier, P., F. van der Ploeg, M. Spence and A. Venables (2010) *Managing Resource Revenues in Developing Countries*. IMF Staff Papers.

Conrad, J. (2008) *Three Dimensions of the Banking Crisis in Kazakhstan*. CWRD discussion paper no. 2.

Energy Information Administration (EIA) (2008) *Country Analysis Briefs: Kazakhstan*. Available at http://www.eia.doe.gov.

Esanov, A., M. Raiser and W. Buiter (2001) *Nature's Blessing or Nature's Curse: The Political Economy of Transition in Resource-based Economies*. EBRD working paper no. 66, London.

Hosman, L. (2009) 'Dynamic Bargaining and the Prospects for Learning in the Petroleum Industry: The Case of Kazakhstan', *Perspectives on Global Development and Technology*, 8, 1–25.

IMF (2006) *Republic of Kazakhstan: 2006 Article IV Consultation*. IMF country report no. 06/244. Washington, DC: International Monetary Fund.

IMF (2007) *Republic of Kazakhstan: 2007 Article IV Consultation*. IMF country report no. 07/235. Washington, DC: International Monetary Fund.

Jojarth, C. (2007) *Turning Oil Wealth into Development: Azerbaijan and Kazakhstan*. Unpublished manuscript, Stanford University.

Jones Luong, P. and E. Weinthal (2001) 'Prelude to the Resource Curse; Explaining Energy Development Strategies in the Soviet Successor States and Beyond', *Comparative Political Studies*, 34, 367–99.

Kaiser, M. and A. Pulsipher (2007) 'A Review of the Oil and Gas Sector in Kazakhstan', *Energy Policy*, 35, 1300–14.

Kuralbayeva, K. and D. Vines (2008) 'Shocks to Terms of Trade and Risk-premium in an Intertemporal Model: the Dutch Disease and a Dutch Party', *Open Economies Review*, 19, 277–303.

Ministry of Finance of Republic of Kazakhstan. Retrieved from http://www.minfin.kz.

Moran, T. (1974) *Multinational Corporations and the Politics of Dependence: Copper in Chile*. Princeton, NJ: Princeton University Press.

Peck, A. (1999) 'Foreign Investment in Kazakhstan's Mineral Industries', *Post-Soviet Geography and Economics*, 40, 471–518.

Peck, A. (2004) *Economic Development in Kazakhstan: The Role of Large Enterprises and Foreign Investment*. London: Routledge Curzon.

Silk Road Intelligencer (2009). Online Reports. Retrieved from http://silkroadintelligencer.com/archives/.

van der Ploeg, F. and A. Venables (2008) *Harnessing Windfall Revenues: Optimal Policies for Resource-rich Developing Economies*. OxCarre research paper 2008–09, University of Oxford.

Wood Mackenzie (2007) *Government Take: Comparing the Attractiveness and Stability of Global Fiscal Terms*. Retrieved from http://www.woodmacresearch.com/cgi-bin/wmprod/portal/energy/productMicrosite.jsp?prodID=218.

World Bank (2005) *Getting Competitive, Staying Competitive: The Challenge of Managing Kazakhstan's Oil Boom*. World Bank report no. 30852-KZ.

Yenikeyeff, S. (2008) *Kazakhstan's Gas: Export Markets and Export Routes*. Oxford Institute for Energy Studies. NG 25, November 2008, Oxford.

Further Reading

National Bank of Republic of Kazakhstan. Retrieved from http://www.nationalbank.kz.

National Statistical Agency of Republic of Kazakhstan. Retrieved from http://www.stat.kz.

Raballand, G. and F. Esen (2007) 'Economics and Politics of Cross-border Oil Pipelines – the Case of the Caspian Sea Basin', *Asia Europe Journal*, 5, 133–46.

World Bank (1997) *Kazakhstan: Transition of the State*. Washington, DC: World Bank.

Appendix

Table A.5.1 Kazakhstan: selected economic indicators

	2000	2001	2002	2003	2004	2005	2006	2007	2008
National accounts, population and unemployment									
Real GDP growth (%)	10.0	13.1	9.8	9.8	9.2	9.4	10.6	8.7	3.2
Nominal GDP (US$ billion)	18.3	22.1	24.6	30.9	43.2	57.1	81.0	104.2	132.2
Population (million)	14.9	14.9	14.9	14.9	15.0	15.1	15.2	15.4	15.6
GDP per capita (US$)	1,227	1,490	1,659	2,080	2,887	3,789	5,325	6,765	8,475
Unemployment (% of labour force, end-year)	12.8	10.4	9.3	8.8	8.4	8.1	7.8	7.3	7.5
Prices, interest rates and exchange rates									
CPI inflation (% year-on-year change, December over December)	9.8	6.4	6.6	6.8	6.7	7.6	8.4	18.8	9.5
CPI inflation (% change in average index for the year)	13.4	8.5	6.0	6.6	7.1	7.9	8.7	10.8	17.1
Exchange rate (KZT per US$, average)	142.2	146.8	153.3	149.1	136.0	132.9	126.0	122.5	120.3
Refinancing rate (%, end-year)	14.0	9.0	7.5	7.0	7.0	8.0	9.0	11.0	120.3
Money supply and credit									
Broad money supply (M2, % of GDP)	11.2	10.4	13.2	15.0	20.0	20.0	27.6	27.7	24.7
Broad money supply (M2, % year-on-year change)	22.5	16.3	47.4	39.2	69.5	29.0	85.7	25.7	8.3
Domestic credit (% of GDP)[1]	11.1	15.9	18.5	21.9	26.4	35.2	47.8	59.3	50.2
Domestic credit (% year-on-year change)[1]	88.4	79.9	34.8	44.6	53.6	72.6	82.3	55.2	2.8

Balance of payments

Exports (goods and non-factor services, % of GDP)	56.6	45.9	47.0	48.4	52.5	53.5	51.5	49.8	57.7
Imports (goods and non-factor services, % of GDP)	49.1	47.0	47.0	43.0	43.9	44.7	40.4	42.9	37.4
Current account balance (US$ billion)	0.4	-1.4	-1.0	-0.3	0.3	-1.1	-1.9	-7.2	6.9
Current account balance (% of GDP)	2.0	-6.3	-4.2	-0.9	0.8	-1.8	-2.4	-6.9	5.3
Net FDI inflows (US$ billion)	0.9	0.4	2.2	2.2	5.4	2.1	6.6	7.9	10.7

Foreign debt and reserves

Foreign debt (US$ billion)	12.7	15.2	18.8	23.4	33.5	44.2	73.8	96.7	107.8
Public (US$ billion)[1]	4.0	3.8	3.5	3.6	3.3	2.4	2.3	1.9	1.6
Private (US$ billion)[2]	8.8	11.4	15.3	19.8	30.2	41.8	71.4	94.8	106.2
Foreign debt (% of GDP)	69.5	68.6	76.4	75.7	77.7	77.4	91.0	92.8	81
Central bank gross FX reserves (US$ billion)	2.1	2.5	3.1	5.0	9.3	7.1	19.1	17.6	19.4
Central bank gross non-gold FX reserves (US$ billion)	1.6	2.0	2.6	4.2	8.5	6.1	17.8	15.8	17.4
National Oil Fund of Kazakhstan (US$ billion)		1.2	2.0	3.5	4.5	7.6	13.8	21.0	25.8

[1] To the public and private sectors.
[2] Includes intercompany debt.

Source: National Bank of Kazakhstan, Statistical Agency of Kazakhstan, Ministry of Finance.

6

The Developmental State
Malaysia

Zainal Aznam Yusof

6.1 Introduction

Malaysia, as an upper middle income and relatively resource-rich country, has been presented as a case of successful development. Over the
period 1957–2006, the economy grew at about 6 per cent per annum,
and per capita income increased by slightly more than 21 times (US$266
in 1957 and US$5742 in 2007). Apart from economic growth, its distri-
bution record has been more than satisfactory. Absolute poverty has
been reduced from about half in 1970 to 3.6 per cent in 2007. The ethnic diversity of the country has long been a major concern. Malaysia is
a plural society with sharp economic cleavages between the Bumiputera
(sons of the soil) and the Chinese and Indians. But, despite these imbalances, it has, overall, managed to contain the extreme tendencies and
pressures on sensitive race relations that can be endemic in a multi-
ethnic society. Growth and development in a divisive society, it appears,
have been associated with equity and security.

Over the 50 years of post-independent development, from 1957
when it gained independence from British rule, the economy has diversified beyond agriculture and primary commodities, such that manufactured goods now account for a much larger share of gross domestic
product (GDP) and total exports. Ethnic economic imbalances became
more and more important following the May 1969 racial riots and
moved to the forefront of policy-making. The over-riding objective of
the New Economic Policy (NEP), an affirmative action policy launched
in 1971, maintained in the National Development Policy (NDP) and
the National Vision Policy (NVP), which succeeded the NEP in 1990,
was to promote national unity through the eradication of poverty
irrespective of race and the restructuring of Malaysian society so as to
reduce the identification of race with economic function and geographical location. The redistributive objective was to be achieved through a

wide range of direct redistribution policies to assist the Bumiputera to obtain parity with the non-Bumiputera in income and wealth. Growth with equity continues to be the guiding development strategy.

There has been increasing interest in examining the growth performance of resource-rich economies. Evidence has been accumulating that there could be a resource curse, i.e. the growth of resource-rich economies has been hampered by their natural wealth, whereas non-resource-rich economies have better growth records.[1] Much work has been initiated to probe into the likely determinants of the resource curse. Malaysia has been identified as a relatively resource-rich economy that has escaped from the resource curse and has a good growth record. This case study on government and the management of revenue from resources will focus on the revenue and expenditure related to natural resources. The areas and issues that will be given attention will include the mechanisms (the economic and politics that can impinge on the mechanisms) and the principles of resources management, covering the stages from extraction through revenue flows to expenditure. Issues that will be considered include contracts (licensing, contracting and taxation regimes), transparency and accountability. Although the focus will be on the savings and investment decisions, some attention will be given to the ethnic diversity of Malaysia and the management of resource revenues in an ethnically diverse economy. The utilization of financial resources for distributive purposes, or in the interest of affirmative action, is of special interest. The issue of how resources are being utilized for distributive purposes to reduce ethnic economic imbalances will also be incorporated. The aim is to derive some lessons/messages for policies from the Malaysia (and other) case studies.

The chapter is structured as follows. Section 6.2 highlights the growth and structural changes in the economy over the last 40 years. Sections 6.3–6.5 report on the sources of revenue of agricultural commodities, rubber, oil palm and forestry, oil and gas and the management of the hydrocarbon sector. Section 6.6 deals with savings and investment. Natural resources and diversification are dealt with in Section 6.7. Some of the lessons on managing revenues are taken up in Section 6.8. Section 6.9 forms the conclusion.

6.2 Growth, Dutch disease and diversification

The economic growth of the Malaysian economy has been sustained at a more than satisfactory level. The post-war growth of the Malaysian economy can be divided into four broad phases: 1957–70, 1971–90, 1991–2000 and post-2000. The racial riots of May 1969 were a turning point and led to the introduction of the NEP, an affirmative action policy, in 1971, the publication of the Second Malaysia Plan, 1971–75, and the Outline Perspective Plan (OPP) 1971–90.

Growth, structural changes and the key sources of revenue, and some key features are shown in Table 6.1. Over the 40-year period 1967–2007, the economy grew at about 6 per cent per annum. Economic growth in 1998 contracted by more than 7 per cent, the most severe single recession year, following the effect of the Asian financial crisis in 1997–98. The financing of growth depended far more on internal financing, and the economy hardly relied on external financing to any significant extent. A running fiscal deficit was a common feature of growth; the fiscal deficit of the federal government was higher in the 1970s and up to the early 1980s, but the size of the fiscal deficit was reduced from the mid-1980s onwards.

Over the 40-year period, the external side of the economy has remained generally strong, and the international reserves of the Central Bank have been increasing. The overall balance of payments, with some exceptional years, has registered a higher surplus, especially in the post-2000 years, due mainly to improvements and an increasingly larger current account surplus; the current account surplus has increased from 9 per cent of gross national product (GNP) in 2002 to 16.3 per cent of GNP in 2007. The services account, historically, has recorded a deficit.

Structural changes and the diversification of the economy were reflected in the changing composition of sectoral GDP and exports. Agriculture's share of GDP has declined whereas manufacturing's share has increased. The sources of revenue have also been changing. Resource revenues, particularly from oil and gas, have been increasing, and oil revenue has financed about 40 per cent of federal government development expenditure. Public development expenditure has been growing as a share of GDP. The privatization strategy, which was implemented from the mid-1970s onwards, sought to reduce the role of the government in the economy, but the decline in public investment, as a share of GDP, has not been significant.

Malaysia, at independence, was largely an economy dependent on agriculture and mining. Rubber production and tin mining were the

Table 6.1 Growth, revenues and expenditure – highlights

	1970		1980		1990		2000		2007		Average annual growth (%)			
	US$ million	Share of GDP (%)	US$ million	Share of GDP (%)	US$ million	Share of GDP (%)	US$ million	Share of GDP (%)	US$ million	Share of GDP (%)	'71–'80	'81–'90	'91–'00	'01–'07
GDP (current prices)	3592	n/a	25,429	n/a	45,716	n/a	93,790	n/a	186,720	n/a	22.3	6.4	8.4	10.5
GDP	10,451	n/a	25,820	n/a	45,716	n/a	90,829	n/a	128,790	n/a	9.6	5.9	7.2	5.1
GDP per capita	1027	n/a	1757	n/a	2434	n/a	3902	n/a	4920	n/a	5.8	3.4	5.6	3.4
GNP (current prices)	3781	n/a	23,149	n/a	42,189	n/a	86,182	n/a	183,365	n/a	20.8	6.6	8.4	11.5
GNP	11,002	–	23,505	–	42,189	–	83,462	–	126,475	–	8.2	6.1	7.9	6.2
GNP per capita	1011	–	1694	–	2331	–	3586	–	4654	–	5.6	3.3	5.2	3.8
Agriculture	2994	28.8	5711	22.6	6799	14.9	7810	8.6	13,685	10.2	7.2	1.9	3.4	8.8
Mining and quarrying	1277	12.3	3911	15.4	5929	13.0	9370	10.3	20,057	15.0	12.3	4.8	7.7	12.2
Construction	388	3.7	1187	4.7	1730	3.8	3561	3.9	3663	2.7	12.6	4.5	8.6	0.4
Manufacturing	1525	14.7	4819	19.0	10,493	22.9	28,033	30.9	37,392	28.0	12.8	8.3	11.2	4.3
Services	4205	40.5	9691	38.3	20,806	45.5	42,056	46.3	58,897	44.1	9.3	8.0	8.2	5.0
Exports (goods and services)	4093	39.4	14,031	55.4	32,812	71.7	108,822	119.8	147,293	110.2	14.4	9.1	14.5	4.6
Imports (goods and services)	3639	35.0	13,420	53.0	31,912	69.7	91,372	100.6	120,206	89.9	15.4	9.6	12.3	4.2
Manufacturing exports[1]	780	9.1	2846	11.9	17,332	39.3	83,660	89.2	143,353	74.0	16.2	20.0	18.9	3.1
Current account balance	8.0	0.2	–279	–1.2	–919	–2.1	8487	9.0	30,322	15.6	–	–	–	–
Government revenue	779	20.3	6273	26.1	10,924	24.8	16,280	17.4	42,242	21.8	11.4	5.8	4.4	9.6
Oil-related revenue[2]	2.1	0.05	1242	5.2	2768	6.3	3387	3.6	16,099	8.3	133.7	10.5	3.4	21.3
Government expenditure	938	24.4	8001	33.3	13,216	30.0	22,234	23.7	49,602	25.6	12.6	6.2	6.2	7.1
Operating expenditure	702	18.3	4636	19.3	9260	21.0	14,881	15.9	37,353	19.3	9.4	7.6	5.7	8.8
Development expenditure	235	6.1	3365	14.0	3955	9.0	7353	7.8	12,249	6.3	20.6	5.6	7.8	4.2
Fiscal balance	–154	–4.0	–1668	–6.9	–1272	–2.9	–5188	–5.5	–6239	–3.2	–	–	–	–

[1] Manufacturing exports data starts in 1975.

[2] Data for oil-related revenue starts in 1971.

Source: Economic Planning Unit (2001b).

two key economic activities that contributed much to growth. The growth of commercial agriculture and tin mining started in the early nineteenth century under British colonial rule. Increasing demand for natural rubber arose from the growth of the automobile industry, and British plantation companies invested on a large scale in British Malaya in the late nineteenth century (Drabble, 1973).

Diversification has been successful. Over the period 1948–52, rubber accounted for almost 70 per cent of the total output value of the major agricultural commodities and, for the period 1963–67, its share declined to about 65 per cent of total agricultural output, whereas it fell from 38 per cent to 15 per cent as a share of GNP (Lim, 1973). The successful diversification strategy comprises a number of elements, especially through research and development (R&D), and the role of the Rubber Research Institute of Malaysia (RRIM) was crucial in this regard. Replanting schemes for rubber, essentially, were programmes for the re-investment of the profits of rubber estates and rubber smallholdings.

The decision to increase the cultivation of oil palm in the 1960s was a significant policy change and a key component of agricultural diversification. Public and private investment in oil palm estates gained momentum from the 1960s (Khera, 1976). The Federal Land Development Authority (FELDA) spearheaded the diversification into oil palm cultivation; palm oil acreage increased from about 99,000 acres in 1960 to 335,000 acres in 1970, a more than threefold increase in acreage. Palm oil production increased from about 90,000 tons in 1960 to 396,000 tons in 1970.

The structural transformation of the economy over the period 1970–2007, after 50 years of independent economic growth, is shown in Table 6.1. The key structural change was the continued decline in agriculture and the rise in importance of manufacturing and services. Agriculture's share of GDP fell from about 28.8 per cent in 1970 to 14.9 per cent in 1990 and 10.2 per cent in 2007. Meanwhile, manufacturing's share of GDP increased from 14.7 per cent in 1970 to 22.9 per cent in 1990, and to 28 per cent in 2007. The corresponding figures for services were 40.5 per cent, 45.5 per cent and 44.1 per cent respectively.

Industrialization was fuelled by a combination of state intervention in the economy and the growth of public enterprise, the use of fiscal policy and incentives to attract foreign direct investment (FDI) and the provision of industrial infrastructure and low-cost labour. The early import substitution phase gave way to an explicit export-oriented industrialization strategy and, within less than 20 years, the economy had to adapt to a labour shortage economy and a new phase of industrial deepening towards relying much less on labour-intensive manufacturing industries.

Commodity exports have played, and still do play, an important role in fuelling economic growth. Tin, rubber and then palm oil were the major commodity exports and, by the mid-1970s, the export of petroleum gained greater prominence. The rapid growth of manufactured exports, beginning from the late 1970s, has contributed much to the rise in the trade share of GDP; by the latter half of the 2000s, manufactured exports accounted for more than 80 per cent of total exports (Figure 6.1).

Penang island played an important part as an industrial base and cluster for the growth of the electronics and electrical industries, beginning with the assembly and export of semiconductors, and subsequently for the manufacture of other products and then in research and design. Resources were also channelled to provide the infrastructure for industrial development in Penang and beyond Penang. Industrial estates were developed with factories, industrial premises and utilities for manufacturing enterprises located in the industrial estates. Industrial Free Trade Zones (FTZs) and warehouses were developed for the export-oriented industries to facilitate the movement of inputs for manufacturing enterprises. The Penang Development Corporation (PDC) was the leading agency in attracting major transnational corporations (TNCs) into the island, the provision and support of training facilities to meet the demand of manufacturing enterprises and the development of the island as a centre for manufacturing growth.

Figure 6.1 Growth, trade and exports

Source: Bank Negara Malaysia.

The growth experience of Malaysia shows a relatively successful adoption of an export-led growth strategy with manufactured exports not being crowded out by economic windfalls from natural resources. How did Malaysia avoid 'Dutch disease'? How was it possible that revenues from oil were not detrimental to the growth of manufactured exports? The Dutch disease phenomenon has to do with the failure to sustain growth following the experience of economic windfalls, with sizeable capital inflows resulting from the booms in resource revenues, particularly revenue from oil, and with the adverse effects on manufactured exports as the exchange rate appreciates. The essence of Dutch disease is the adverse impact of natural resource discoveries on the competitiveness of existing economic activities, specifically manufacturing. In the Dutch disease model, there are three sectors: a tradable natural resource sector, a tradable non-resource manufacturing sector and a non-traded sector (Sachs and Warner, 1995).

Distortions in the economy were kept to a minimum. Malaysia's economy is very open, with trade accounting for more than 200 per cent of GDP. This openness has been held on to for a very long time; the trade account is open and there is convertibility in the current account. The capital account is very open with the exception of 1998–2005; capital controls were imposed following the Asian financial crisis, and the exchange rate (the ringgit) was pegged at RM3.80 to the US$. It was unpegged in July 2005 and is now under a managed float on the basis of a basket of currencies. Protection in the economy during the import substitution phase and after was kept low and was not as extensive as in other developing economies; the overall level of effective tariff protection was low.[2] With no severe macroeconomic imbalances for prolonged periods, and conservative fiscal prudence and monetary policy, inflation was kept to a remarkably low level and has averaged less than 2 per cent per annum over the last 50 years. These factors helped, with a few exceptional years, to sustain a stable growth path and to avoid the Dutch disease.

The transformation of the real and financial sides of the economy accelerated in the 1970s and continued in the 1980s through the turbulence and stresses of the two decades. Monetary policy in the 1980s fostered greater discipline among the financial institutions and ensured adequate liquidity for private investment. With the accumulation of foreign reserves, overall during 1960–80, there were no saving–investment and foreign exchange gaps to be bridged. Also, there was financial deepening, as shown in rising financial assets/GNP and M2/GNP ratios over the 1960–87 period, and the lengthening of maturities for financial instruments.[3]

For about 10 years after independence, Malaya operated under a pegged exchange rate system. During the 1960s, the economy operated under the system of the Currency Board, with the Malaysian dollar being pegged directly within a very narrow band to the pound sterling. On 12 June 1967, the Central Bank took over the power of issuing currency and allowed the Bank to manage the level of the exchange rate of the Malaysian dollar.[4] In May 1973, new policy changes ended the interchangeability of the currencies of Malaysia, Singapore and Brunei. The termination of interchangeability and the floating of the currency were major decisions, and enabled the Central Bank to pursue independent foreign exchange market operations. With the floating of the currency, the broad exchange rate policy stance was to maintain an orderly market; the Bank would intervene in the foreign exchange market to moderate day-to-day fluctuations in the value of the ringgit and not to fight the underlying trend dictated by the market.

One implication of Dutch disease is that windfall gains from natural resource discoveries will lead to an appreciation of the exchange rate and the stifling of growth in manufactured exports and growth of manufacturing. The evidence suggests that exchange rate behaviour did not dampen industrial growth and growth of manufactured exports. The nominal exchange rate, using the ringgit value to the US$, was fairly stable for most of the 1960s, and from the 1970s, the exchange rate started to appreciate up to the early 1980s (1982–83). From then on, it went through a phase of depreciation up to the early 1990s (1991–92). When the real exchange rate (RER) is used, the RER index showed that there was significant depreciation of the RER from 1987 to mid-1993, a depreciation of about 25 per cent, and this was instrumental in helping the growth of an export-oriented industrialization strategy (Athukorala, 2001). From 1993 to 1997, and just before the outbreak of the financial crisis, the exchange rate appreciated by about 20 per cent. The selective liberalization of the capital account to facilitate capital outflows has moderated the RER appreciation arising from the increasing flows of FDI into Malaysia (Menon, 2001). As a response to the financial crisis in 1997–98 and a sizeable depreciation in the currency, capital controls were imposed and the ringgit was pegged at RM3.80 to the US$ in 1998. The ringgit was de-pegged in July 2005, and the exchange rate system has moved to a managed float against a basket of currencies. Since the unpegging, the ringgit has been appreciating and, by end-February 2007, the ringgit nominal effective exchange rate (NEER) has appreciated by about 4 per cent (Bank Negara Malaysia, 2007).

6.3 Resources, revenue and growth – agricultural commodities

6.3.1 Rubber – investment and diversification

In the post-war period, revenue from the exports of tin and rubber accounted for the largest source of revenue. Revenue from these resources has declined in importance. Over the 16-year period from 1946 to 1962, taxes from both exports contributed 90 per cent of total revenue and have remained at this level. The commercial cultivation of rubber began in the late nineteenth century (Drabble, 1973; Coates, 1987). The rubber industry has a history of production and price controls. The International Rubber Regulation Schemes to secure higher rubber prices by controlling exports, new planting and replanting were introduced in the 1930s. In Malaya, estates and smallholders were allocated export quotas, and export coupons were issued to the smallholders; production by smallholders was substantially under-assessed; their basic export quotas were lower than their share of net exports.[5] In the 1950s, synthetic rubber started to dominate the rubber market. Consumption of synthetic rubber was substantial in the US, and it increased in the UK and other industrial countries. In 1950, synthetic rubber accounted for about a quarter of world total consumption and, by 1960, it had increased to 47 per cent.

In the 1950s (1951–60), Malaya replanted 679,000 acres with an average of 67,900 acres per annum. The replanting was financed by grants from the government raised through export taxes. Replanting with new high rubber clones increased yields/productivity and reduced labour costs. The Rubber Industry Board operated the Rubber Replanting Scheme, which was introduced in 1952. Two rubber replanting schemes – Fund A for the estates and Fund B for the smallholders – were established. The Federal Land Development Authority (FELDA) achievements show the progress in investment in smallholdings. Operating on an estate basis, FELDA's holdings are plots of 10 acres each. Over the period 1956–66, more than 80 per cent of FELDA's acreage was under rubber, and the remaining 20 per cent was under oil palm. Rubber acreage continued to decline, and rubber and cocoa land was converted to oil palm and other uses. Rubber acreage continues to fall, and about 1.3 million hectares were under rubber over the 2001–05 period.

Investment in R&D contributed to the rise in productivity of rubber and agricultural diversification. Established in 1926, the Rubber Research Institute of Malaysia (RRIM) played a key role in raising the productivity of the rubber industry in Malaysia. Revenue and margins increased substantially with higher yielding clones. The diversification and investment in high-yielding clones in rubber estates is shown in Table 6.2. Rubber estates have increasingly replanted their acreage with higher yielding planting materials; in 1955, about three-tenths of the tapped acreage was under high-yielding planting material, and this acreage increased to about 91 per cent by 1970.

Rubber exports as a share of total exports have declined and, by 2006, they were estimated to have accounted for 1.4 per cent of total exports. Revenue from export duty for rubber has been declining from 3.3 per cent in 1970 to an estimated 0.8 per cent in 1995.

6.3.2 Palm oil – diversification and investment

Before Malaysia became the world's leading producer of palm oil, West Africa was the most important producing region for palm oil (Lim, 1967). A new phase commenced in 1957 when the government became more active in investing in palm oil through the FELDA. Before the Second World War, oil palm was entirely an estate crop. In the first half of the 1970s, about 288,000 acres were newly planted with palm oil by FELDA. Almost 90 per cent (3.6 million hectares) of the total planted acreage in 2005 was matured acreage, compared with 86 per cent in 1990 and 75 per cent in 1970. Revenue from palm oil, like rubber, has been fluctuating.

Palm oil prices peaked in the early and mid-1980s reaching US$1,562 per metric tonne and have declined since the peak, reaching an average

Table 6.2 Percentage share of unselected seedlings and high-yielding clones in acreage tapped and production rubber estates, 1955, 1960, 1965 and 1970

	1955	1960	1965	1970
Acreage tapped				
Unselected seedlings	69.7	51.7	28.0	8.8
High-yielding	30.3	48.3	72.0	91.2
Total	100.0	100.0	100.0	100.0
Production				
Unselected seedlings	50.3	33.9	13.6	2.6
High-yielding	49.7	66.1	86.4	97.4
Total	100.0	100.0	100.0	100.0

Source: Lim (1967).

price of US$578 per metric tonne in 1975. As a share of total revenue, export duties from palm oil have not been very sizeable and have stayed, on average, below 1 per cent for much of the 1970s. Palm oil export duties' share of total revenue of US$8.8 increased to 3.5 per cent in 1985 (US$31).

6.3.3 Constituencies for diversification

The agricultural diversification of the economy, from raising the productivity of rubber and from the cultivation of rubber to that of oil palm, began in earnest sometime in the early 1950s, even before independence in 1957. What was the support and constituency for the utilization of resources for economic diversification? Economic and political factors, as well as institutional developments, help to explain the support for agricultural diversification. First, falling rubber prices, the gloomier prospects for natural rubber and competition from synthetic rubber made it imperative that the productivity and competitiveness of rubber be raised.

Second, the economic interests and livelihood of the smallholders, with farms of less than 100 hectares in size, played a key part in the growing demand for the diversification of the agriculture sector. Third, the impending political changes and the anticipation of Malaya being granted independence by the late 1950s played a part in the speedier implementation of agricultural and rural development programmes, and the continuing push for diversification.[6] Fourth, foreign plantation interests were also party to agricultural diversification through the rubber replanting programmes and the subsequent diversification into palm oil production.

In the 1970s, resource nationalism became more apparent. Foreign investment in plantation and mining was targeted for corporate takeovers and the restructuring of their ownership structure, through the Foreign Investment Committee (FIC), to enhance Malaysian, especially Bumiputera, ownership. In 1970, foreign ownership of share capital accounted for 67 per cent of the total, 75.3 per cent in agriculture, mainly rubber, and 72.4 per cent in mining. By 1990, foreign ownership of share capital was reduced to 25 per cent. The government avoided any kind of nationalization; the accepted and declared policy was restructuring of the corporations through growth. Agricultural diversification must also be linked to the development strategy of exploiting land resources through massive land development schemes to provide land to the landless and those with uneconomic land holdings, and the building of institutions.[7]

6.3.4 Forest natural resources

Malaysia is rich in biodiversity, and its forests are an important source of livelihood and revenue, although the revenue is not as important as the revenue from oil and gas. Malaysia's tropical rainforests comprise evergreen rainforest with different types of natural forests, ranging from beach and lowland rainforests to montane forests (Jomo *et al.*, 2004). Natural forests cover approximately 20 million hectares, or 61 per cent, of Malaysia's total landmass of 32.9 million hectares (Table 6.3).

As conservation of natural forests and sustainable forest management are part of the government's policy, the annual allowable cut rate (ACR), or coupe, was reduced to 272,800 hectares per year during the period 2001–04. Concessions for a fixed period govern the exploitation of forestry resources. A stumpage fee, i.e. the price at which the government sells the timber to the concession holder, is a key part of the forest utilization contract.[8] The evidence also suggests that both Sabah and Sarawak had depleted their natural capital more rapidly than they built up their physical capital stocks in the 1980s (Vincent and Rozali, 1997).

A key institutional development that evolved in response to the need for a coordinated and common approach to forestry development was the establishment of a National Forestry Council in 1971 and a National Forestry Policy in 1998. The creation of the Permanent Forest Estate (PFE) (forest reserve) has made an important contribution to the growth of forestry resources. The adoption of a national forestry policy has helped to slow down the rate of deforestation since the early 1980s, despite the growing pressure to convert forest lands to plantation agriculture (Figure 6.2).

In evaluating the overall outcomes of forest resource exploitation and management in Malaysia, several key issues can be raised. Although

Table 6.3 Status of forest lands in Malaysia, 2006

Region	Land area	Natural forest	Plantation forest	Total forest area	Forest area as a percentage of land area
				Area (millions hectares)	
Peninsular Malaysia	13.2	5.9	0.1	6.0	45.4
Sabah	7.4	4.1	0.2	4.3	57.4
Sarawak	12.4	9.8	0.0	9.8	79.1
Malaysia	33.0	19.8	0.3	20.1	60.8

Source: Forestry Department, Peninsular Malaysia (2007).

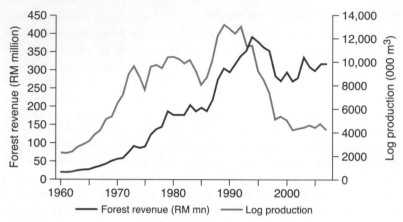

Figure 6.2 Forest revenue collection and log production (Peninsular Malaysia)
Source: Forestry Statistics Peninsular Malaysia, Various years.

the country's forest cover remains relatively high, the quality of the logged-over forests may have declined sharply, thereby affecting future timber yields. Over the five decades of forest management history, the cutting cycles prescribed for Peninsular Malaysian forests have been progressively reduced from 100 years to 80 years under the Malaysian Uniform System (MUS), and to 35–40 years in the more recent Selective Management System (SMS). Although the reduction in cutting cycle takes into consideration the advancements in harvesting and processing technology, as well as the increase in utilization efficiency (use of small logs and branches as well as higher mill recovery), the shortening of the growing period entails a sacrifice of the quality of wood produced, especially the heavy hardwood species. The reinvestment into reforestation activities may have been too low, as indicated by the ratio of silvicultural cess collection to expenditure.

6.4 Petroleum and gas

6.4.1 Early history and growth

In July 1882, oil was discovered in Baram, a small town near Miri in the East Malaysian state of Sarawak.[9] In December 1910, oil was discovered in Miri and commercial production started in 1911. In Sabah, the other East Malaysian state, the Central Borneo Company was granted a prospecting lease in 1889, but this lease, and subsequent leases, to the Labuan Exploration Company (1918) and Shell (1934, 1952 and 1989) were less successful in finding commercial onshore deposits. The origins and foundation of Malaysia's petroleum industry can be traced back to the early 1970s (Bowie, 2001). From the early 1970s, especially with the oil crises in 1973 and the Organization of Petroleum Exporting Countries (OPEC) oil shock that tripled world prices for crude oil, there was much concern over the ownership and control of national resources. In mid-1974, the Petroleum Development Act (PDA) was enacted and, on 17 August 1974, a National Oil Corporation – Perbadanan Petroleum Nasional or Petroliam Nasional Berhad, or Petronas – was established under the Companies Act. The PDA 1974 vested Petronas with the ownership and control of the country's petroleum resources.

Malaysia has two hydrocarbon basins: the Northwest Borneo basin covers the coasts of Sabah, Sarawak and Brunei and is mainly offshore, whereas the Malaysia basin covers the South China Sea from the southern end of the Gulf of Thailand and is also mainly offshore. Offshore exploration in the late 1960s, with Esso and Continental Oil being granted exploration leases off the east coast in 1968, and Mobil for the Straits of Malacca in 1971, however, proved to be promising. In 1970, Esso discovered oil off Terengganu.

6.4.2 Revenue from oil and gas

Revenue collected by the federal government from oil and gas increased from US$154 million in 1975 to an estimated US$16.1 billion in 2007. As revenue from oil and gas increased relatively faster than the amount of revenue collected from other sources, revenue from oil and gas, as a proportion of total revenue, as shown in Table 6.4, rose from 7.8 per cent in 1975 to 37.8 per cent in 2007.

There are three sources of revenue from oil and gas: (1) direct tax; (2) indirect tax; and (3) non-tax revenue. Direct tax revenue from oil and gas is derived from the petroleum income tax (PITA), i.e. income tax on companies whose revenues are petroleum based. In the case of indirect taxes from oil and gas, these are in the form of export duties on petroleum and petroleum-related products. Dividends from Petronas to the federal government are an important source of revenue, and petroleum royalties are also another non-tax revenue.

Dividends (45 per cent) and income tax from petroleum (42 per cent) account for the bulk of revenue from oil and gas. Non-tax revenue collected in the form of dividends from Petronas in 2007 reached US$7.2 billion, while petroleum royalties amounted to US$1.3 billion. Non-tax revenue from oil and gas, therefore, amounted to US$8.5 billion to account for 62 per cent of the total non-tax revenue collected by the

Table 6.4 Federal government revenue from oil and gas, 1975–2007 (US$ million)

Type of oil and gas revenue by year	1975	1980	1990	2000	2007
Petroleum income tax	124	782	978	1582	6825
Petroleum export duties	0	305	707	262	740
Petronas dividend	0	0	851	1079	7247
Petroleum royalty and gas	30	155	232	464	1277
Total revenue from oil and gas	154	1242	2768	3387	16,089
Percentage share of total government revenue	7.8	19.8	25.3	20.8	37.8
WTI US$ per barrel (Dec)	11.16	37.00	27.34	28.46	91.73
Total government revenue	1975	6273	10,924	16,280	42,601

Source: Ministry of Finance, Economic Report. Various years.

federal government in 2007. In 2007, the federal government collected total revenue of about US$16.1 billion from the oil and gas sector, which is about 37 per cent of the total revenue of US$42.6 billion collected in 2007. The revenue from the oil and gas sector helped to finance about one-third of the total federal government expenditure of US$48 billion in that year. The size of the contribution of the oil and gas sector to the federal government revenue was equivalent to 8.5 per cent of GDP at prices current in 2007.

With the intensification of the exploration for, and development of, oil and gas, production of crude oil rose from 98,000 barrels per day (bbl/d) in 1975 to 725,000 bbl/d in 1998, to a lower level of 690,000 bbl/d in 2007. Production of natural gas also increased sharply, from 1658 million standard cubic feet per day (mmscfd) in 2001 to 6439.6 mmscfd in 2007. Malaysia's crude oil and natural gas reserves have improved further in recent years.

Malaysia is a net exporter of crude oil. Higher domestic production volume of crude oil and gas relative to domestic consumption volume has raised oil exports. Exports of crude oil increased from US$303.7 million in 1975 (3.24 million metric tones) to an estimated US$14.5 million in 2007 (17.64 million metric tonnes). In the case of liquefied natural gas (LNG), its export value rose from US$2.9 billion in 2001 to US$7.2 billion in 2007.

Petronas' profit before tax rose from US$7.6 billion for the financial year ending March 2001 to US$3 billion for the financial year ending March 2007. Therefore, petroleum income tax collected increased sharply from US$134.5 million in 1975 to US$6.6 billion in 2007. Rising development expenditure, as well as the need to contain the overall federal government's financial deficit to a prudent level, necessitated increasing the payment of dividend from Petronas to the government. Dividends paid to the government by Petronas rose from US$374.5 million in 1985 to US$7 billion in 2007, made possible by Petronas recording rising profits. In 2007, the dividends paid to the government were about half (51.7 per cent) of its net profit of US$13.5 billion. This form of financing is non-inflationary, while allowing Petronas to continue to have adequate funds to finance investment for capacity expansion.

6.4.3 Changing composition of oil revenues

The composition of oil revenue has undergone significant changes. In 1975, petroleum income tax and petroleum royalty accounted for 80.5 per cent and 19.5 per cent of total revenue respectively. By 2007, Petronas dividends accounted for the largest portion of revenue collected, i.e. 45 per cent, followed by PITA at 42.4 per cent, petroleum royalty at 7.9 per cent and petroleum export duties 4.6 per cent, as shown in Table 6.5.

During the 2008 financial year, the crude oil price increased to US$101 per barrel from US$65 per barrel (mid-July oil price reached US$145 per barrel). For the financial year up to March 2008, Petronas recorded profits of US$33 billion, out of which US$20.3 billion was paid to the government, accounting for 44 per cent of the total revenue of the government. The US$20.3 billion is inclusive of royalties, corporate income tax, petroleum income tax, export duty and dividends. Since its inception in 1974, Petronas has paid a total of US$120.8 billion to the government, equivalent to about half of the total development expenditure of the 5-year development plans, from the third to the ninth Malaysia plans.

A special dividend of US$1.8 billion, out of the US$8.7 billion, was paid to the government in 2008 (Table 6.6). Petronas' total assets increased to

Table 6.5 Share by types of oil and gas revenue, 1975–2007 (percentage share of total oil and gas revenue)

	1975	1980	1990	2000	2007
Petroleum income tax	80.5	62.9	35.3	46.7	42.4
Petroleum export duties	0.0	24.5	25.5	7.7	4.6
Petronas dividend	0.0	0.0	30.7	31.9	45.0
Petroleum royalty and gas	19.5	12.5	8.4	13.7	7.9
Total revenue from oil and gas	100.0	100.0	100.0	100.0	100.0

Source: Ministry of Finance, Economic Report. Various years.

Table 6.6 Petronas payments to the federal and state governments, 2008

Payments	US$ billion
Royalty to federal government	1.4
Dividends	8.7
Taxes (petroleum and corporate)	7.5
Export duties	0.6
Total payments to federal government	18.1
Royalty to state governments	1.4
Total	37.7

Source: Petronas.

US$98.7 billion in financial year 2008 compared with US$85.7 billion in 2007, and shareholders' funds rose to US$60.3 billion from US$49.7 billion over the period. According to Petronas, it needs about 30–35 per cent of its annual profits for re-investment compared with 52 per cent for oil majors and more than three-quarters (77 per cent) for other national oil companies. The smaller reinvestment requirement results from the mature acreages of the country's oil fields and the prudent steps that Petronas had taken in building the country's oil and gas infrastructure.

6.4.4 Petronas, globalization and leadership

Petronas had its beginnings in the early 1970s when 'economic nationalism' was riding a wave in Malaysia. Following the NEP, an affirmative action policy, the government pushed for greater Malaysian ownership and control, especially in the plantation and mining sectors, where foreign ownership and control had been dominant for a long time.[10] On the international side was the oil embargo, which was initiated by Arab oil producers in OPEC on 17 October 1973 and lasted until March 1974, following the war with Israel, with cutbacks in production and export restrictions to the US and its allies in Europe. Ownership of oil and gas resources had become a major issue for Malaysia, as well as other oil-producing countries, and was the backdrop and motivating factor for the establishment of Petronas. Increasingly, in the 1970s and 1980s, countries in the Middle East, Africa and Asia started moves to gain control over their oil and gas resources.

Petronas received the approval of parliament and was formally established on 17 August 1974. Established through the PDA under the Companies Act, Petronas is granted exclusive ownership of petroleum resources in Malaysia. Petronas formulated the policies and guidelines for investment in the upstream and downstream businesses. As a wholly owned government company, Petronas functions commercially with a board but, under Section 3 of the PDA, a controversial section, it is subject to the 'control and direction of the Prime Minister . . .' and not accountable to parliament.

As Petronas has been vested with the exclusive ownership of petroleum resources in Malaysia, no other government-owned enterprise has interests in the petroleum sector. The contribution by Petronas to the revenue of the government through its dividends is usually subjected to discussions and negotiation between the oil corporation and the Ministry of Finance. Activities of the independent private oil corporations, such as Shell and Exxon, come under the purview of Petronas, particularly on the basis of the production-sharing contracts (PSCs). Petronas made the strategic push to expand globally sometime in the 1990s, and its first overseas operation was in Myanmar.[11] Now it has investments in more than thirty countries. What made Petronas go global? Who initiated this move to expand investment overseas? The strategic decision to invest overseas did not have the unanimous support of the management of Petronas. There were early dissenting views within Petronas on the corporation's move to expand and invest overseas.[12] Others were also of the view that overseas exploration and production should not be a priority for Petronas and, as a national oil corporation (NOC), it should not expand internationally. Those who had reservations over Petronas' overseas ambitions wanted the corporation to focus on developing national/domestic oil and gas resources. They were also concerned over the availability of financial, technological and human resources for such ambitious ventures and the need to build up its exploration and production (E&P) capabilities. Global corporate changes involving the oil majors also posed competitive barriers to Petronas; in the second half of the 1990s, there were mergers between the oil companies resulting in 'super oil majors'.[13]

As Petronas grew and consolidated its position vis-à-vis the oil majors, it grew more inward looking and cautious; the political leadership pushed for the restructuring of Petronas and risk-taking in its overseas ventures. The top leaders of Petronas who were appointed by the government were tasked with overseeing the restructuring of Petronas and initiating changes and strengthening it for expansion overseas.[14] The first initiative to move overseas was made in 1990, but there was resistance from the staff to the idea of expanding overseas.[15]

Initially, the global strategy of Petronas was to venture into regions that were in close geographical proximity to Malaysia. The targets for oil and gas reserves led to a focus on 10–15 countries with hydrocarbon resources, the number of blocks that Petronas need to acquire, and the technical and human capital resources that would be required.[16] Political leadership also buttressed the globalization of Petronas' operations. Leadership at the highest level was also instrumental in pushing Petronas to go global. Prime Minister Mahathir Mohamed pushed Petronas to move overseas and was a consistent advocate of going global.

Several factors can be cited for the relative success of Petronas as a national oil corporation. First, the capability and integrity of the senior management was, and continues to be, a key asset of Petronas. The government, generally, made sound decisions in the choice of Petronas' early senior management to provide the leadership and to build up the oil corporation. Petronas was staffed by experienced senior officials with the appropriate backgrounds in finance, planning, laws and experience in the corporate sector; they were individuals with integrity. Second, its establishment as a company under the Companies Act, and not as a statutory body, allowed the oil corporation to function as a commercial enterprise, unencumbered by bureaucracy and by the parliamentary process. The board considers and approves the finances of Petronas. Its independence from the central bureaucracy also meant that it had the freedom to utilize its profits for further investments in exploration and development. Third, the political leadership, generally, shielded the oil corporation from political interference and provided the support for its push to venture globally.[17]

6.5 Management of the hydrocarbon sector

6.5.1 Entering negotiations

The rights of individual states to enter into contracts with the private sector are constrained by the constitution, which demarcates the rights of the federal and state governments. The discovery of offshore oil in the mid-1970s led to changes in the distribution of power and rights over resources between the federal and state governments and the power to enter into contracts. The Petroleum Development Act, 1974, which received the Royal Assent on 30 July 1974, established Petroleum National Berhad or Petronas, a state-owned enterprise and the national oil company. Rights over oil were centralized. Petronas has exclusive rights of ownership, exploration and production, and the corporation comes under the purview of the Prime Minister. Petronas has entered into a number of production-sharing contracts (PSCs) that have replaced the system of concessions. Vesting powers of ownership over petroleum resources to Petronas and operating it commercially were risky decisions to take.[18]

An appreciation of some of the key political factors and developments in the years up to the early 1970s concerning Sabah and Sarawak would provide a better understanding of the policy on the development of the oil industry in Malaysia and of the evolution of oil rights. Sabah, Sarawak and, later, Terengganu were the oil-producing states. The inclusion of Sabah and Sarawak into the federation of Malaysia in 1963 introduced extra strain and problems for the federal government, and led to a number of incidents that pressured and tested the leadership of the federal government. Relations between the federal government and Sabah, Sarawak and, later, Terengganu tended to be fractious, and part of the reason for this was the differences in views over the sharing of the oil revenues.

6.5.2 Contract design

A crucial decision had to be made on the nature and the detailed design of the contract, as it would determine the size of the rent capture from oil resources. The experience of Pertamina in Indonesia was closely assessed, and the main features of the Pertamina model were adjusted to suit the conditions in Malaysia. Some of the basic contract issues are captured in Figure 6.3 (Vincent and Rozali, 1997). The price of oil is p, and MPC is the marginal production cost (exploration, development and production) of producing an extra barrel of oil. MPC + MDC is the full marginal cost, which includes the marginal depletion cost (MDC) of user costs. The intersection point between p and MPC + MDC (at B) represents the optimum production level, i.e. at q. If government imposes taxes, and there are other constraints and risks, oil could be produced either too quickly or too slowly and, in the extreme case, producers could maximize as much oil in the current period while covering MPC, i.e. at qSR. In the more general case, investors require a higher rate of return for riskier countries, so that MPC is shifted upward to MPC′ and production is lower at q''. The imposition of MPC taxes, e.g. royalty on each barrel of oil, can reduce production; the price received by the company is reduced, and the long-term optimal production will be at q'', with a lower level of production. The practice of 'high grading' will prevail as oil fields that are smaller, costly but viable without the tax, will be left undeveloped.

Prior to the mid-1970s, the exploration for, and production of, petroleum resources were governed by the system of long-term oil concessions. Since then, exploration, development and production activities

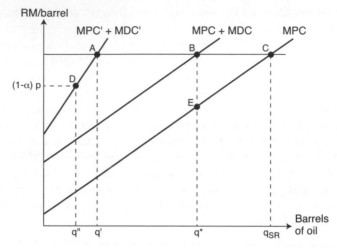

Figure 6.3 Economics of oil extraction
Source: Vincent and Rozali (1997).

have been governed by the PSCs. Under the contract, the PSC contractor will provide all the financing and shoulder the burden of the risk of exploration, development and production for a share of the total production. There are two broad areas of the PSCs. First, it defines and grants wide-ranging powers to Petronas and curtails that of the oil companies who are now contractors. Investment plans, annual work programmes, information on oil resources, investment and production subcontractors have to be submitted to Petronas for approval. Second, the fiscal regime of the PSC is spelt out in detail, and the contract covers the duration, cost oil, royalties, profit oil, research, excess proceeds tax and bonuses. Initially, the contracts were for 24 years, with 5 years for exploration, 4 years for development and 15 years for production.

An assessment of the PSCs suggests that Malaysia 'succeeded in minimizing the capture and repatriation of rents by international oil companies . . .' (Vincent and Rozali, 1997). The PSC can be divided into two types, i.e. the 'first-generation' PSC and the 'second-generation' PSC (Table 6.7). The revisions made to the PSCs in the mid-1980s prevented the slide in investment in exploration and development. It is an open question whether the second-generation PSCs provided sufficient incentive for production. By the mid-1990s, it was noted that the oil and gas reserves that were discovered did not lead to actual production. Three likely factors could explain this outcome (Vincent and Rozali,

Table 6.7 Comparison of first- and second generation production-sharing contracts (PSCs)

Contract feature	First-generation PSC	Second-generation PSC
Royalties	10% of gross production	Same
Cost oil	20% of gross production	Up to 50% of gross production
Profit oil split (Petronas:contractor)	70:30	1. First 50 million barrels First 10,000 bbl/d: 50:50 Next 10,000 bbl/d: 60:40 Above 20,000 bbl/d: 70:30 2. Remaining oil: 70:30
Bonuses	Signature Discovery Production	None
Research cess	0.5% of contractor's cost of profit oil	Same
Participation by Petronas Carigali	None	15% carried interest during exploration phase with 15% option to participate upon commercial discovery

Source: Vincent and Rozali (1997).

1997): (1) the sliding scale for profit oil encouraged the contractor to maintain daily and overall production at a low level; (2) a higher tax burden compared with other sectors is imposed by the petroleum income tax; and (3) the export tax, akin to a windfall tax, increases high grading and reduces profits.

The PSCs were widely considered by the oil companies to be more stringent when compared with Indonesia and Philippines. In the early 1980s, the second-generation PSCs were introduced, and they eased the stringency of the first-generation PSCs. More liberal treatment was accorded in the new PSCs in 1985, and cost oil share was raised upwards to a maximum of 50 per cent and a sliding scale to profit oil was introduced. The liberalization measures attracted investment and, between 1986 and 1990, twenty-five PSCs were signed. Despite the liberalization, the rent captured by the Malaysian PSCs was higher than in a number of other countries and was classified as 'very tough', and rent captured annually by the federal government has been estimated at 'more than two-thirds'.

A helpful way to assess the PSCs is to consider them from the three issues of: (1) rent capture; (2) high grading; and (3) risk sharing, taking into account different oil field sizes (Vincent and Rozali, 1997). Using the net present value as the measure of economic rent, government's rent capture has been high, especially under the first-generation PSCs. Changes were made to the PSCs by the end of the 1990s. A new PSC based on the 'revenue over cost' concept (the R/C PSC) was introduced in 1997 to encourage investment in Malaysia's upstream sector. The PSC term for deep water blocks is shown in Table 6.8. Up to 2007, Petronas had signed more than sixty PSCs with international petroleum companies, enabling them to participate in the exploration, development and production of oil and gas in the country.

Petronas does not enjoy complete independence. Although Petronas has more independence in exploration and development, including negotiations for PSCs, it has some constraints in deciding on the quantum of dividends that are to be allocated to the government annually. It also has less independence in making decisions or subsidies for petro-

Table 6.8 Deepwater PSC terms

Main features	Beyond 1000 m water depth	Between 200 and 1000 m water depth
Royalty	10%	10%
Cost recovery		
Oil	75%	70%
Gas	60%	60%
Profit split	Petronas:contractor	Petronas:contractor
Oil	First 50,000 BOPD 14:86	
	Next 50,000 BOPD 18:82	
Gas	Above 100,000 BOPD 37:63	
	Above 300,000 MMBLS 50:50	
	Cumulative production	
	Up to 2.1 TSCF 40:60	
	Above 2.1 TSCF 60:40	
Contract period (years)		
Exploration	7	7
Development	6	6
Production	25	25
Signature bonus	Waived	Waived
Discovery bonus	Waived	Waived
Production bonus	Waived	Waived
Research cess	0.5%	0.5%
Petronas Carigali's participation	Minimum 15%	Minimum 15%

Source: Petronas.

leum products and for the pricing of gas. Oil revenues have also been utilized to subsidise the price of gas to industrial users. According to Petronas, the higher oil prices in financial year 2008 also meant that Petronas' subsidy to the gas sector increased to US$5.9 billion, compared with US$4.5 billion in 2007 (*Star*, 16 July 2008). Since 1997, the cumulative gas subsidy had increased to US$21.3 billion. The independent power producers (IPPs) accounted for more than half (58.7 per cent or US$2.2 billion) of the total gas subsidy for the power sector (US$3.8 billion).

There are two aspects of revenue utilization from oil and gas: (1) the revenues that have been channelled from Petronas to the federal government; and (2) the oil revenues of Petronas that the corporation utilizes for its own developmental programmes. Cumulatively, petroleum revenue from the petroleum income tax (PIT) amounted to RM52 billion for the Eighth Malaysia Plan, 2001–05, or some 22.4 per cent of total federal government revenue from income taxes, or 11.3 per cent of total federal government revenue (Economic Planning Unit, 2005). With its revenue of US$29.8 billion in 2007, Petronas incurred capital expenditure of US$3.8 billion, with about 65 per cent (US$2.5 billion) taken up by exploration and production, and logistics and maritime costs (US$60.9 million) chalking up the second highest amount of capital expenditure (Petronas, 2007).

Over the 2004–07 period, it incurred a cumulative total capital expenditure of US$20.9 billion or almost US$5.4 billion per annum. Investment in exploration and production is the largest sector of Petronas' investment and, over the same period, the cumulative capital expenditure for exploration and production had reached about US$13.1 billion, about US$3.3 billion per annum, or about 69.5 per cent of total capital expenditure. Capital expenditure in logistics and maritime was the second largest sector for its investment and was followed by capital expenditure in oil and petrochemicals. As costs rise and as more investment will be in deepwater oil fields, the total costs of investment will increase.

Petronas has invested domestically and overseas in a wide range of activities. It has interests in more than thirty countries in exploration and the development of oil fields, to augment its crude oil and gas reserves. Almost 40 per cent of its revenue in 2007 was from overseas. It now has over 100 affiliates and associated companies. It is involved in a wide range of petroleum activities from upstream exploration and production of oil and gas to downstream oil refining, marketing and distribution of petroleum products, trading, gas processing and liquefaction, gas transmission pipeline operations, marketing of liquefied natural gas, petrochemical manufacturing and marketing, shipping, automotive engineering and property investment. Its first overseas operation was in Vietnam in 1991.

Overseas investments have boosted Petronas' international reserves to 6.31 billion barrels of oil equivalent (boe) in 2007 (5.94 billion boe in 2006). With a reserves replacement ratio (RRR) of 3.2 times its international E&P operations, it is one of the highest in the industry. International reserves accounted for 23.4 per cent of Petronas' total reserves in 2007. International oil production in 2007 reached 581,700 boe per day (432,000 boe in 2006), which was slightly more than a third (34 per cent) of Petronas' total oil production for the year compared with 27 per cent in 2006. The share of international oil production is increasing.

6.6 Savings and investment

Financing from non-inflationary resources was a key feature of macroeconomic policy. State intervention in the economy became more pervasive in the 1970s with the implementation of the NEP, an affirmative action policy. Fiscal policy was expansionary. Although foreign borrowings increased, they were not significant. With continuing expansionist state programmes in the 1980s, especially heavy industries programmes, there was a greater demand for finance. Foreign borrowings increased significantly, and with the global recession and much slower growth, the fiscal deficit increased in the early 1980s, increasing to 18.7 per cent of GNP in 1982, more than double the level of 1979. Adjustments, including the repayment of external debt, were made to correct the macroeconomic imbalances. Growth slowed to 5.2 per cent for the first half of the 1980s.

A number of key trends in savings and investment can provide a useful background to the utilization of financial resources for economic growth, and the contribution of oil revenues to the financing of investment. A contrast between the pre-1990 and post-2000 period will also highlight the underlying trends in savings and investment. First, Malaysia is a high saver with rising incomes. The gross national savings rate has been rising and ranging from 37 per cent to 38 per cent of GNP in recent years. The post-2000 period has recorded more years of surplus in the S-1 gap. Second, public investment has been growing at a fast pace, especially in the post-1970 period when the state became more interventionist, in the interest of affirmative action. By 1980, government expenditure had increased to a third of GDP, remained at 30 per cent by 1990 and then fell to about 25 per cent by 2007. Third, with high national savings, there has been a steady reliance on utilizing domestic sources of financing, from non-inflationary sources. Foreign direct investment has supplemented financial needs for growth, but there has been no reliance on external loans. Fourth, there have been more years of fiscal deficits than surpluses but, on average, the fiscal deficit has been kept to a manageable and sustainable level. Fifth, on the external side, there were, generally, no persistent serious imbalances in the balance of payments, but the pre-2000 period was marked by running current account deficits. The current account was in surplus for the post-2000 period. Sixth, the overall balance of payments remained strong and recorded a surplus from 2002 to 2005. The current account surplus was large with a stronger goods surplus and an average of 13 per cent of GNP for 2001–06. Net outflows were recorded for the financial account, and overseas FDI has been growing. The services account was in deficit for 2004 and 2005. With a savings rate higher than domestic capital formation, the savings–investment gap has therefore been in surplus for the 2001–06 period.

The Malaysian approach to managing revenues and the economy does not include the use of a stabilization fund. Despite its dependence on volatile revenues from resources, it saw no need for a stabilization fund. Although Khazanah Nasional is not seen as a sovereign wealth fund, the United Nations Conference on Trade and Development (UNCTAD) has cited and classified Khazanah Nasional as a Malaysian sovereign wealth fund. Khazanah Nasional is under the control of a number of large and leading corporations under state ownership and control, and it has sizeable and growing investment overseas, ranging from infrastructure and plantations to manufacturing industries.

The savings and investment decisions of Petronas would be better understood against the macroeconomic background of the economy and the principles governing the management of revenues. Over the period 1960–80, it could be generalized that Malaysia did not have a financing problem, as it had adequate domestic financial resources to finance investment without recourse to serious external financing (Lin, 1993). In more recent years, Malaysia has continued to sustain high levels of national savings and investment.[19] As shown in Table 6.9, it maintained an average national savings rate of 37 per cent of GDP and an investment rate (gross capital formation) of 22 per cent of GNP.

Over the 1971–90 period, the fiscal deficit amounted to US$36.2 billion. To finance the deficit, the bulk (73 per cent) was sourced from

Table 6.9 Resource balance, savings and investment (US$ million)

	1970	1980	1990	2000	2005	2006	2007
Public gross domestic capital formation	225	2794	4915	11,481	14,438	17,043	20,796
Public savings	n/a	n/a	7994	14,577	18,655	28,845	33,739
Deficit/surplus	n/a	n/a	3079	3096	4216	11,803	12,943
Private gross domestic capital formation	389	4682	9344	13,180	11,684	13,997	16,512
Private savings	n/a	n/a	5346	18,572	27,492	19,550	31,548
Deficit/surplus	n/a	n/a	–3998	5392	15,808	14,059	15,036
Gross domestic capital formation	614	7476	14,259	24,661	26,123	31,039	37,308
(as a percentage of GNP)	5.3	14.5	33.8	29.8	20.9	20.8	21.8
Gross national savings	681	7026	13,340	33,148	46,147	56,901	65,287
(as a percentage of GNP)	18.0	30.4	31.6	40.1	37.0	38.1	38.1
Balance on current account	8	–279	–919	8487	20,024	25,862	27,979
(as a percentage of GNP)	0.1	–0.5	–0.8	10.3	16.1	17.3	16.3

n/a, not available.

Source: Department of Statistics, Malaysia and Bank Negara Malaysia.

domestic borrowing (US$26.4 billion) and foreign borrowing (US$8.4 billion), and the rest from the use of accumulated assets and receipts (Economic Planning Unit, 1991). The deficit during the period 1991–2000 was financed by domestic borrowings and accumulated assets and special receipts (Economic Planning Unit, 2001a).

National savings over the post-1970 period grew substantially. In the 1970s, the public sector became more active, largely because of its developmental programmes through its NEP, the affirmative action policy. Gross national savings averaged about 26.5 per cent of GNP in the 1970s. There was a recession in the early 1980s (1982) and the late 1990s (1998), with the latter being more severe, when the economy contracted by 7.8 per cent in 1998. With the global recession in 1981–82, fiscal stimulus was initiated to cushion the impact of the recession, but this led to a sharp increase in the fiscal deficit of the public sector to 18.7 per cent of GNP in 1982. As imports accounted for a significant proportion of federal government expenditure, the sharp increase in public expenditure contributed to a rising current account deficit in the balance of payments.[20]

Demand for funds by the government to finance its heavy industry projects increased in the early 1980s, but its timing was poor because of the global recession and tight liquidity position, and this led to increased foreign borrowings. The overall fiscal deficit increased from 8.3 per cent of GNP in 1979 to 18.7 per cent of GNP in 1982, and net foreign borrowings increased to 47 per cent of the overall deficit in 1982. Structural adjustment policies were then implemented to contain the sizeable fiscal deficit, and it was reduced to 3.9 per cent of GNP in 1988. Prior to the 1980s, the size of the fiscal deficit was smaller. With the implementation of adjustment programmes in 1983, foreign borrowings declined between 1982 and 1986 and the external debt was prepaid. Fiscal consolidation and privatization in the second half of the 1980s contributed to a reduction in the role of government; total expenditure to GNP fell from about 58 per cent in 1981–82 to about 44 per cent in 1986–87.

The post-2000 period is somewhat different from the pre-1990 period. Economic growth, following the 11 September terrorist attacks, has slowed down, averaging about 4 per cent per annum for 2001–07. To counteract the downturn, stimulus packages were implemented, but the fiscal deficit has not increased substantially, and the federal government deficit averaged about 4 per cent of GDP for the period 2001–07. Private investment growth has been anaemic. The external side has strengthened, with increasing current account surpluses for the same period. Although the current account was in deficit for most of the pre-1990 period, with the exception of 1982, when the current account deficit peaked at 14.1 per cent of GNP, it was not very large or unsustainable. As savings were in excess of investment, there was no saving–investment gap and gross national savings averaged more than 30 per cent of GNP.

When the public sector as a whole is taken into account, including the non-financial public enterprises (NFPEs), the development expenditure increased to US$121.9 billion and operating expenditure to US$152.7 billion. The NFPEs, which includes Petronas, accounted for more than half of the total development expenditure. A total of US$58.9 billion in development expenditure was expended for 2001–05. The public sector accounts performed better in 2004–05 due to the better performance of the NFPEs in 2004–05. With higher earnings, including from oil and gas activities and higher crude oil prices, an overall surplus of US$1.8 billion (1.4 per cent of GDP) was recorded for 2005.

Where have expenditure and investment been channelled to? What are the sectoral breakdowns of expenditure? About 78–80 per cent of development expenditure has been channelled to the economic and social sectors (Table 6.10). Education, training and transport have the

Table 6.10 Federal government development allocation and expenditure by sector, 2001–10 (US$ million)

	2MP[1]			3MP[2]			4MP[3]			5MP[4]	
	Allocation	Expenditure	%	Allocation	Expenditure	%	Allocation	Expenditure	%	Allocation	Expenditure
Economic	2323	1894	50.6	8003	5893	54.4	12,812	11,934	60.5	9108	8668
Agricultural development	871	686	18.3	2807	2029	18.7	3401	3209	16.3	2813	2774
Mineral resource development	0.3	0.2	0.01	9.1	6.9	0.1	12.3	11.9	0.1	16.3	16.3
Commerce and industry	634	548	14.6	1848	1409	13.0	2807	2685	13.6	1508	1508
Energy and public utilities	144	109	2.9	839	687	6.3	2128	1946	9.9	1477	1358
Social	593	492	13.1	2386	1579	14.6	4401	4244	21.5	3426	3319
Education and training	337	266	7.1	935	672	6.2	2060	1995	10.1	2201	2159
Health	84	70	1.9	230	230	2.1	325	314	1.6	372	353
Security	432	391	10.4	2739	1533	14.2	3295	3190	16.2	1119	957
General administration	73	57	1.5	374	202	1.9	357	345	1.8	470	425
Total	4379	3743	100.0	15,945	10,828	100.0	20,864	19,713	100.0	14,123	13,370

[1] Second Malaysia Plan, 1971–75.
[2] Third Malaysia Plan, 1976–80.
[3] Fourth Malaysia Plan, 1981–85.
[4] Fifth Malaysia Plan, 1986–90.
[5] Sixth Malaysia Plan, 1991–95.
[6] Seventh Malaysia Plan, 1996–2000.
[7] Eighth Malaysia Plan, 2001–05.
[8] Ninth Malaysia Plan, 2006–10.
[9] Inclusive private finance initiatives.

Source: Economic Planning Unit, Malaysia Plans. Various issues.

biggest development expenditure allocations. The bulk of the federal government expenditure, financed through its own operating surpluses and dividends from NFPEs, such as Petronas, as well as individual savings with financial institutions and social security institutions, are largely for the improvement and development of human capital.

Revenues have also been utilized to support the regime of subsidies, and they now form a sizeable portion of the federal government's operating expenditure. Overall, subsidies have taken up about US$7.8

	5MP[4]	6MP[5]			7MP[6]			8MP[7]			9MP[8]	
	%	Allocation	Expenditure	%	Allocation	Expenditure	%	Allocation	Expenditure	%	Allocation[9]	%
	64.8	78,417	10,558	50.6	119,990	13,251	47.6	17,561	17,241	38.5	26,514	41.4
	20.8	17,547	2417	11.6	19,437	2286	8.2	2008	2041	4.6	3427	5.4
	0.1	144	19	0.1	167	11	0.0	13	12	0.0	41	0.1
	11.3	13,213	1542	7.4	20,875	3162	11.4	3009	2680	6.0	5874	9.2
	10.2	11,846	1624	7.8	18,113	1557	5.6	2478	3352	7.5	6341	9.9
	24.8	38,795	5164	24.8	70,497	8788	31.6	17,452	18,277	40.8	25,260	39.5
	16.1	20,369	2787	13.4	36,347	5541	19.9	10,546	11,520	25.7	14,710	23.0
	2.6	6612	909	4.4	13,262	1047	3.8	2503	2504	5.6	3370	5.3
	7.2	29,238	4186	20.1	32,708	3271	11.8	4269	5807	13.0	7409	11.6
	3.2	7103	934	4.5	17,098	2510	9.0	2869	3460	7.7	4790	7.5
	100.0	153,553	20,841	100.0	240,293	27,820	100.0	42,151	44,785	100.0	63,972	100.0

billion (2001–05), which was about 7.5 per cent of total operating expenditure (US$104.4 billion). Subsidies for petroleum products form a significant portion of total subsidies, and recent estimates for 2007 show that these have reached about US$10.2 billion – U$12.5 billion, if sales taxes forgone are taken into account – compared with an estimated US$3.8 billion for 2005.

Pressures have been increasing for the government to gradually remove the current practice of subsidising the retail price of a number of petroleum products. The amount of subsidy provided by the government has increased sharply and, in 2005 alone, the subsidy amount was estimated to have increased by 39 per cent to US$1.8 billion.

The management of revenue, including revenue from oil and gas, is guided by two key principles. First, to ensure that operating expenditure does not exceed the level of revenue collected, or expected to be collected. Underlying this principle is the need to ensure that the current account balance of the federal government financial position continues to record surpluses, or at least, is in balance. Second, when the federal government is in overall financial deficit, i.e. in the event that the surplus in the current account is insufficient to finance the amount of planned development expenditure, the gap must be financed through non-inflationary sources. Non-inflationary financing would include the issuance of government securities for savings institutions to invest, such as by the Employee Provident Fund (EPF), as well as by the banking system. These two principles were closely adhered to in managing revenues and expenditures.

6.7 Natural resources and diversification

6.7.1 Growth and diversification

The consensus on the experience and record of resource-rich economies has generally been discouraging, giving credence to the notion of a 'resource curse'. A key theme of the Malaysian case study has been the successful diversification of the economy from a dependence on agricultural commodities to one that is more industrialized, with manufactured exports accounting for about 80 per cent of total exports and about 30 per cent of GDP. Revenue from natural resources, especially from oil and gas in the second half of the 1970s, has been utilized to achieve this transformation. Macroeconomic policies, as well as industrialization policies, supplemented by a liberal approach to FDI, have contributed to the successful diversification of the economy. Diversification can be divided into two broad types: (1) intra-diversification involving the upgrading of agriculture from rubber into the cultivation of palm oil; and (2) extra-diversification involving fostering the growth of non-agricultural sectors.

How was revenue from resources deployed for diversification and growth in the new sectors? First, the emphasis on agriculture and rural development that was carried through in the post-independence period helped the drive for diversification. The finding that the level of absolute rural poverty was very high, with the Malays accounting for the bulk of the poor, galvanized efforts to reduce poverty through the diversification and modernization of agriculture and rural development. Allocation of development expenditure in the 5-year plans consistently gave high priority to raising productivity and the modernization of agriculture.

Second, close attention was given to utilizing revenue from tin and especially rubber for development purposes. In formulating the 5-year plans, especially the early 5-year plans, rubber prices and the revenue from rubber made sizeable contributions to the size of the development plans and, in the years of low rubber prices and revenue, the size of the development expenditure had to be scaled down appropriately.

Third, revenues were used for raising the productivity of rubber estates and smallholders through incentives and subsidies. Part of the revenue was used for R&D and to develop high-yielding clones. Rubber replanting grants for estates and smallholders were the incentive for the estates and smallholders to replant their rubber acreage with the high-yielding rubber clones.

Fourth, the diversification from the cultivation of rubber into palm oil was also part of the response to the competition from synthetic rubber and the pessimism over the long-term price trends for rubber. Revenue was used for R&D, through the imposition of a cess for oil palm cultivation and the development of land development schemes for the cultivation of oil palm. The FELDA land development schemes, particularly from the 1970s, spearheaded the diversification into oil palm cultivation. The Palm Oil Research Institute Malaysia (PORIM), the counterpart to the Rubber Research Institute Malaysia (RRIM), provided the R&D inputs for the diversification into palm oil.

Fifth, the pace of and emphasis on diversification picked up from the late 1970s and accelerated in the 1980s with the push for an export-led growth of manufacturing industries and the restructuring of the economy away from agriculture. This industrialization phase of diversification coincided with the accelerated development of oil and gas resources and the establishment of Petronas in the mid-1970s. Labour-intensive industries, particularly textiles, clothing and, most significantly, the electronics and electrical industry, were the new sources of growth. Some heavy industries, especially the national car, were promoted. Financial resources were utilized for infrastructure development, promoting export-promoting zones and warehouses. Fiscal incentives were used to attract FDI, especially that involved in manufactured exports. Manufactured exports became a major contributor to economic growth, accounting for more than 70 per cent of total exports by the late 1980s, with the non-resource-based industries dominating exports. Within manufacturing too, there was intra-sector diversification; in the early years of manufacturing growth, the main source of growth came from the processing of resources and, subsequently, non-resource-based industries overtook the growth of resource-based industries.

6.7.2 Affirmative action

Revenues were also used for affirmative action. Affirmative action in Malaysia was governed by the two-pronged New Economic Policy (NEP). Launched in 1971, it was aimed at eradicating poverty irrespective of race, and restructuring society to correct the identification of race with economic function. Essentially, it sought to reduce racial economic imbalances through improving the economic status of the Bumiputera, the largest ethnic group. Absolute poverty has fallen from about half in 1970 to about 3.6 per cent in 2007, but the target of at least 30 per cent ownership of wealth by Bumiputera has not been achieved. The quota was the most widely used restructuring policy instrument, as well as subsidies. Development expenditures for education and entrepreneurial programmes were used for distributional purposes. And government procurement is an additional distributional policy instrument. The development expenditure allocation for poverty alleviation (US$1.2 billion) and restructuring of society (US$2 billion) for the Ninth Malaysia Plan 2006–10, for example, amounted to US$3.3 billion.

Expectations were raised that the resource revenues generated by Petronas from the mid-1970s and the activities of Petronas itself could be used to further the affirmative action programmes of the government. There are two components of affirmative action that are related to the oil revenues from the operations of Petronas. First, the financial contributions from Petronas to the revenue of the federal government for affirmative action programmes. Second, the support by Petronas to encourage the growth of Bumiputera entrepreneurs and businesses in petroleum, including petroleum-related, services.

Bumiputera participation was promoted through licensing and registration, contracting/procurement and for the development of vendors, dealerships, Malaysianization of manpower of the production-sharing contractors and training. More than half the upstream contracts from May 2000 to 2006, and downstream contracts, were awarded to Bumiputeras. The Bumiputera companies under the vendor development programmes were involved in a wide range of business activities including the manufacture and supply of plastic lubricant containers, spiral wound gaskets, heavy duty plastic bags, LPG cylinders, scaffolding, air intake filters, conventional flanges and shale shaken screen, and service and cleaning of heat process equipment. A sizeable number of Bumiputera dealers operated Petronas stations in Malaysia. Bumiputera employment in Petronas and Bumiputera manpower for the PSCs is substantial. Petronas has also invested in the Institut Teknologi Petronas, Universiti Teknologi Petronas and Petronas Management Training Sdn. Bhd, and has also provided education sponsorship for more than 14,500 candidates in engineering, medicine and accountancy.

Petronas' involvement in bailing out Bumiputera Malaysian Finance (BMF) and, in a few other cases, when it intervened to provide financial support for government-linked agencies in the early 1980s, has raised concern over the corporation's activities. In 1984, as the Bank Bumiputera Malaysia Berhad (BBMB) was not in a position financially to help out BMF, as part of the financial restructuring of BBMB, Petronas took over BBMB. Petronas had to assist and bail out BBMB for the second time in 1989, when the bank incurred losses of US$419.8 million after having to make provisions of US$0.5 billion, following the guidelines of the Central Bank on the treatment of non-performing loans. Petronas provided the US$419.8 million as a capital contribution to BBMB. In 1991, Petronas sold BBMB for US$0.4 billion to the Ministry of Finance Inc.

6.8 Some lessons on managing resource revenue

This case study has highlighted the achievements of Malaysia in sustaining a relatively high level of economic growth and per capita income. Resource revenues have been important in financing growth. What are the highlights of the Malaysian case study? What are the lessons that can be drawn from its growth experience and managing of resource revenues? First, macroeconomic policies and resource revenues were instrumental in the diversification of the economy from one that was based on primary commodities and agriculture to a more industrialized economy. Growth was increasingly fuelled by the rapid expansion in manufactured exports.

Second, maintaining macroeconomic stability was assisted by the pursuit of a few conservative principles in managing revenue and expenditure. There was heavy reliance on maximizing self-financing, using non-inflationary sources of financing, operating expenditure should be covered by current revenue and a tighter oversight and control on the costs of development projects and, generally, of fiscal prudence.

Third, industrial policies have played an important role in financing the growth of the manufacturing industries and the diversification of the economy, and FDI has made an important contribution to financing growth. Maintaining a more open economy, gradual liberalization, providing infrastructure support and the availability of labour have attracted FDI largely to the export-oriented industries, especially up to the late 1990s. External debt, particularly long-term debt, was kept at a low level, and debt was often refinanced when the financing markets made it sensible to do so.

Fourth, the constitution of the federation seems, so far, to have provided a reasonably strong framework for the governance and politics of oil and forestry resources. The case study suggests that a strong central government has been a key factor in accounting for the relative success of managing resource revenue in Malaysia. Petronas being accountable only to the Prime Minister was an additional manifestation of the centralization trend. As for forestry resources, the introduction of the laws for forestry with their push for sustainable development and international standards for the exploitation of forestry resources were initiated and supported by the central government, but there is room for improvement in the implementation of the federal government legislative initiative in the various states.

Fifth, the case study has also highlighted the issues and problems that can surface in managing resource revenues in a federal system of government. Although there are benefits of centralizing the disbursement of oil and gas revenue, the changing political climate calls for a search for a middle ground that would be acceptable to both sides. The central government is likely to accede to the demand for a higher percentage of the oil royalty for the oil-producing states. Kelantan, the state on the east coast under the rule of PAS, the Islamist party, has recently been calling for a share of the oil revenue from oil production off the coast of Kelantan (*Malaysian Insider*, July 2009). Federal–state relations involving the sharing of revenue are expected to be more contentious.

Sixth, greater independence, an enhanced capacity and capability of the agency responsible for the development of the oil and gas resources and political support are necessary qualities that would enhance the chances of managing oil and gas revenues successfully. Petronas made the sound decision to build up its human capital and to attract qualified and educated manpower, thus raising its capacity.

Seventh, there is also the persistent concern that Petronas' involvement in non-core activities will dilute its resources and focus on the oil and gas industry. The corporation's stand on transparency by international standards has not been exemplary and has attracted a low grading from a survey by Transparency International. Petronas will have to respond to these demands for greater transparency, and the government will have to reconsider the appropriateness and desirability of making Petronas accountable only to the Prime Minister rather than to parliament.

Eighth, the successes in the management of forestry resources have been more mixed and, although there have been improvements, there have also been lapses at the level of the states in pursuing sustainable forestry development. Rent capture would also be increased if the biodiversity value of timber resources is taken into account.

Ninth, leadership has played a key part in guiding the growth and development of Malaysia and specifically in managing its economic resources (Yusof and Bhattasali, 2008). The strength and decisiveness of the leadership had much to do with the longevity in the rule of the Alliance and the Barisan Nasional (BN) that succeeded it. With such a long reign, there has been continuity in the ruling government's vision, strategies and policies. The long rule of the BN with a two-thirds majority meant that the leadership was assured of being in power, thus enabling it to have a longer perspective on development. The technocratic leadership, especially in the formative years of the nation, has also provided some strength to governance.[21] However, the loss of the BN's two-thirds majority in parliament arising from the March 2008 general elections has ushered in a more contentious political climate, and challenges to the rule of BN are expected to escalate.

6.9 Conclusion

Countries that are rich in natural resources are not guaranteed to grow at a higher rate than resource-poor countries. Malaysia, a middle-income country that is relatively well endowed with natural resources, has recorded satisfactory rates of growth for the past 50 years, raising its living standards, as well as substantially reducing the level of absolute poverty. It has, therefore, avoided the resource curse. It has managed its revenue resources reasonably well to sustain economic growth. The Malaysian case study has also highlighted the importance of the governance of resource revenue, leadership and the key role of the constitution in providing the framework for the utilization of resource revenue for economic growth.

A key feature of the Malaysian growth story is that it succeeded in using its resources for the diversification of the economy. Diversification was important for raising the economy from a low-income economy to a middle-income economy. Over a period of about 30 years, the economy has been transformed from one that was dependent on agriculture and the export of commodities to one that is more industrialized, and with manufactured exports accounting for the bulk of total exports. Agriculture's share of GDP fell while that of manufacturing increased. The intra-sectoral diversification drive involved the channelling of resources, within the agriculture sector, from rubber to the cultivation of oil palm. With the dismal prospects for rubber prices and the competition from synthetic rubber, support was given to and resources channelled for the cultivation of palm oil from the late 1960s. The state played a key role in the diversification into palm oil through investments in the development of large land development schemes, the rehabilitation of uneconomic farms and support for smallholders to diversify into palm oil and to private sector plantations. Replanting schemes, using new high-yielding rubber clones, also complemented the diversification into palm oil.

The other push involved diversification of the economy to become more industrialized. An aggressive push was initiated in the late 1960s to develop labour-intensive industries, and this export-led growth strategy saw the growth of, initially, the electronics and electrical industries. Penang island in the north played a key part in the diversification of the economy. Manufactured exports overtook the exports of agricultural commodities. FDI, through investments by TNCs, played a crucial role in the growth of the electronics and electrical industries and other export-oriented manufacturing industries; manufactured exports of electronics and electrical products accounted for the bulk of manufactured exports. Fiscal policies, which included the granting of generous tax holidays, accelerated depreciation allowances and export incentives, supported the diversification push. Resources were also used to develop industrial clusters by having free trade zones (FTZs) and industrial estates. The diversification of the manufacturing sector has now entered a new phase. Losing its comparative advantage in low-cost labour for manufacturing industries, there is the push now to move up the value-added chain and to develop more skill- and knowledge-intensive manufacturing industries to meet the challenge from new competitors.

Acknowledgements

I would like to thank Dr Zamros Dzulkafli, Mr Ng Teck and Dr Yeah Kim Leng for providing research assistance in the preparation of this chapter. The preliminary findings were initially presented at the Oxcarre Workshop at Oxford University in May 2008. A revised draft was presented at the Oxcarre Workshop at Oxford University in December 2008. The views and comments of the participants at the two workshops have been reflected in this chapter. I would also like to thank Tony Venables and Paul Collier for their suggestions and useful comments. Special thanks are extended to Dato' Nasaruddin, Vice President, Corporate Planning, Petronas, and Akmal Hisham Tak, Senior Manager, Corporate Projects, Group Strategic Planning, Corporate Planning and Development Division, Petronas, and senior officials of the Forestry Department. They are in no way responsible for the views expressed in this chapter. All remaining errors are my own.

Notes

1 For examples of work on the resource curse, see Sachs and Warner (1995), Torvik (2007), Sala-i-Martin and Subramaniam (2003), Collier (1998, 2006, 2007), Collier and Goderis (2007) and Hausmann and Rigobon (2002).

2 There have been some differences of opinion over the level and trends in the effective level of protection. For a summary, see Hoffman and Tan (1980).

3 The financial assets/GNP ratio was 0.55 per cent in 1960 and 2.7 per cent in 1987, and the M2/GNP ratio was 0.27 in 1960 and 0.75 in 1987.

4 The par value of the old Malaysian dollar, which was established at 0.290299 grammes of fine gold by agreement with the IMF, was retained for the new Malaysian dollar.

5 Arguments have been advanced that the under-assessment of smallholders' rubber was either deliberate or due to ignorance. Foreign-owned estates were concerned that indigenous smallholders would overtake the estates.

6 For political developments in post-war Malaya, see, for example, Means (1976) and Lau (1991).

7 Internal rates of return to settler investment were higher than internal rates of return to the government or public investment (see Thiam, 1975).

8 On forest concessions, see for example Gray (2000) and Rusli et al. (2002).

9 The British resident advisor in Baram, Sarawak, wrote in his diary that oil had been discovered in wells that had been dug by local people. Charles Hose, the next resident, conducted further explorations.

10 Razaleigh Hamzah, the first chairman of Petronas, has reported that the first discussions with Prime Minister Abdul Razak on the formation of a national

oil company started in 1972. In 1974, he was instructed by the Prime Minister to establish a national oil company that would own and control the country's oil resources. A proposal for Pernas, a government corporation involved in promoting the Bumiputera in industry and commerce, to acquire concessions and older oil fields that had been relinquished by Shell was not pursued.

11   Myanmar was Petronas' first foray overseas through Carigali in 1990, but the exploration block was not a success, and Petronas retracted from the Myanmar venture.

12   Rastam Hadi, former managing director of Petronas, for one, was not in favour of such a move and pressed for Petronas to focus on national/domestic operations within the nation's own waters.

13   Exxon and Mobil merged to become ExxonMobil; BP took over Amoco (American) and Arco (American); Total (French) merged with Elf (France) and Fina (Belgian) to form Total-Fina and Elf; Chevron (American) merged with Texaco (American); and Conoco (American) merged with Phillips (American).

14   McKinsey and Co. were engaged to help Petronas with its reorganization. Azizan Zainul Abidin, the chairman who succeeded Bashir Ismail, oversaw the elaboration of Petronas' mission statement and shared values, and strengthened its operations and corporate culture. These were outlined to the general managers' workshop in August 1988. These corporate values and mission included an increase in communication, recognition of excellence, loyalty, integrity, team spirit and an open management style (see Aris, 2008).

15   Hassan Merican, former CEO of Petronas, has been quoted: 'We faced a lot of resistance. Questions were asked; Why should we go overseas? Why do we need to globalize when we are doing well domestically . . . We got . . . a core group who subscribed to the idea, and worked internally to convince others that this was the way to go . . .' (Aris, 2008: 200).

16   One target was to source about 30 per cent of its revenue from overseas operations by 2005.

17   There have been accusations of Petronas' resources being utilized to bail out government-owned interests such as those involving Bumiputera Malaysian Finance (MBF), and its resources being diverted to non-oil sectors.

18   Tengku Razaleigh, who was appointed the first chairman of Petronas, and Ananda Krishnan, a corporate figure and 'oil entrepreneur', were influential in persuading Tun Abdul Razak, the Prime Minister, to set up a national oil corporation. Ananda Krishnan was also involved in oil exploration in Indonesia and was familiar with Pertamina. Others who were involved included Raja Tun Mohar and Rama Iyer.

19   There is some evidence to suggest that, over the period 1970–92, there was an inverse correlation between savings and investment ratios for Malaysia, with a more volatile current account (Fry, 1993).

20   On the relationship between savings and investment, see Fry (1993).

21   See Ness (1967), Esman (1972) and Ahmad (2003). On early administration in Malaya, see Gullick (1958).

References

Ahmad, A.S. (2003) *The Malayan Bureaucracy: Four Decades of Development.* Petaling Jaya: Prentice Hall.

Aris, A. (2008) *The Quintessential Man. The Story of Tan Sri Azizan Zainal Abidin.* Kuala Lumpur: Crestime Holdings Sdn. Bhd.

Athukorala, P. (2001) *Crisis and Recovery in Malaysia: The Role of Capital Controls.* Cheltenham: Edward Elgar.

Bank Negara Malaysia (2007) *Annual Report 2006.* Kuala Lumpur: Bank Negara Malaysia.

Bowie, P. (2001) *A Vision Realised: The Transformation of a National Oil Corporation.* Kuala Lumpur: Orilla Corporation Sdn. Bhd.

Coates, A. (1987) *The Commerce in Rubber: The First 250 Years.* Singapore: Oxford University Press.

Collier, P. (1998) *The Political Economy of Ethnicity.* Paper prepared for the Annual World Bank Conference on Development Economics, Washington, DC, 20–21 April.

Collier, P. (2006) *Africa: Geography and Growth.* Oxford: Centre for the Study of African Economies, Department of Economics, Oxford University.

Collier, P. (2007) *Laws and Order for the Resource Curse.* Oxford: Oxford University.

Collier, P. and B. Goderis (2007) *Commodity Prices, Growth and the Natural Resource Curse: Reconciling a Conundrum.* Paper presented at the Oxcarre Launch Conference, Oxford University.

Drabble, J.H. (1973) *Rubber in Malaya 1876–1922: The Genesis of the Industry.* Kuala Lumpur: Oxford University Press.

Economic Planning Unit (1991) *Second Outline Perspective Plan, 1991–2000.* Kuala Lumpur: Government Printer.

Economic Planning Unit (2001a) *Eighth Malaysia Plan, 2001–2005.* Kuala Lumpur: Government Printer.

Economic Planning Unit (2001b) *Third Outline Perspective Plan, 2001–2010.* Kuala Lumpur: Government Printer.

Economic Planning Unit (2005) *Ninth Malaysia Plan, 2006–2010.* Kuala Lumpur: Government Printer.

Esman, M.J. (1972) *Administration and Development in Malaya: Institution Building and Reform in a Plural Society.* Ithaca: Cornell University Press.

Forestry Department Peninsular Malaysia (2007) *Forestry Statistics Peninsular Malaysia 2006.* Kuala Lumpur: Perniagaan Normahs.

Fry, M. (1993) 'Saving, Investment and Current Account: A Malaysian and East Asian Perspective' in Al' A. Ibrahim (ed.) *Generating A National Savings Movement.* Proceedings of the First Malaysian National Savings Conference, Kuala Lumpur, 8–10 July.

Gray, J. (2000) *Forest Concessions: Experience and Lessons from Countries Around the World.* IUFRO International Symposium on Integrated Management of Neotropical Forests by Industries and Communities, 4–7 December.

Gullick, J.M. (1958) *Indigenous Political System of Western Malaya.* London: University of London.

Hausmann, R. and R. Rigobon (2002) *An Alternative Interpretation of the 'Resource Curse': Theory and Policy Implications.* NBER Working Paper Series, Working Paper 9424.

Hoffman, L., and T.S. Ee (1980) *Industrial Growth, Employment and Foreign Investment in Peninsular Malaysia*. Kuala Lumpur: Oxford University Press.

Jomo, K.S., Y.T. Chang, K.J. Khoo, *et al.* (2004) *Deforesting Malaysia: The Political Economy and Social Ecology of Agricultural Expansion and Commercial Logging*. London: Zed Books Ltd.

Khera, H.S. (1976) *The Oil Palm Industry of Malaysia: An Economic Study*. Kuala Lumpur: Penerbit Universiti Malaya.

Lau, A. (1991) *The Malayan Union Controversy 1942–1948*. Singapore: Oxford University Press.

Lim, C.-Y. (1967) *Economic Development of Modern Malaya*. London: Oxford University Press.

Lim, D. (1973) *Economic Growth and Development in West Asia 1947–1970*. Kuala Lumpur: Oxford University Press.

Lin, S.Y. (1993) 'The Savings and Investment Gap: An Independent Estimate of National Savings' in Al' Alim Ibrahim (ed.) *Generating A National Savings Movement*. Proceedings of the First Malaysian National Savings Conference, Kuala Lumpur, 8–10 July.

Malaysian Insider (2009) *Ku Li Says Petronas Must Pay Kelantan Oil Royalties*. 26 July.

Means, G.P. (1976) *Malaysian Politics*. London: Hodder and Stoughton.

Menon, J. (2001) 'Internationalisation of the Malaysian Economy, Extent and Implications of Openness to Trade' in C. Barlow (ed.) *Modern Malaysia in the Global Economy*. Cheltenham: Edward Elgar.

Ness, G.D. (1967) *Bureaucracy and Rural Development in Malaysia: A Study of Complex Organisations in Stimulating Economic Development in New States*. Berkeley, CA: University of California Press.

Petronas (2007) *Annual Report*. Kuala Lumpur: Petronas.

Rusli, M., A.G. Awang Noor, M. Shukri, M.N. Kamaruddin and M.O. Shawahid (2002) *Forest Concession Policy: Past Research and Future Direction*. Proceedings of the Regional Symposium on Environment and Natural Resources, 10–11 April, Hotel Renaissance, Kuala Lumpur, Vol. 1, 223–333.

Sachs, J.D. and A.M. Warner (1995) *Natural Resource Abundance and Economic Growth*. NBER Working Paper Series, Working Paper 5398.

Sala-i-Martin and A. Subramaniam (2003) *Addressing the Natural Resource Curse: An Illustration from Nigeria*. NBER Working Paper Series, Working Paper 9804.

Thiam, T.B. (1975) 'Returns to Investment in Land Development from Settler and Government Viewpoints' in S. Chee and K.S. Mun (eds) *Malaysian Economy Development and Policies*. Kuala Lumpur: Malaysian Economic Association.

Torvik, R. (2007) *Why Do Some Resource Abundant Countries Succeed While Others Do Not?* Paper presented at the Oxcarre Launch Conference, Oxford University, 12–13.

Vincent, J.R., R.M. Ali, *et al.* (1997) *Environment and Development in a Resource-Rich Economy Malaysia Under the New Economic Policy*. Harvard Institute for International Development and Institute of Strategic and International Studies (ISIS) Malaysia.

Yusof, Z.A. and D. Bhattasali (2008) *Economic Growth and Development in Malaysia: Policy Making and Leadership*. World Bank Commission on Growth and Development.

Further Reading

Ahmad, E. and R. Singh (2002) *Political Economy of Oil Revenue – Sharing in a Developing Country: Illustrations from Nigeria*. IMF Working Paper.

Alesina, A. and E. La Ferrara (2004) *Ethnic Diversity and Economic Performance*. NBER Working Paper Series, Working Paper 10313.

Bank Negara Malaysia (1989) *Money and Banking in Malaysia, 30th Anniversary Edition 1959–1989*. Kuala Lumpur: Bank Negara Malaysia.

Bank Negara Malaysia (1994) *Money and Banking in Malaysia, 35th Anniversary Edition 1959–1994*. Kuala Lumpur: Bank Negara Malaysia.

Economic Planning Unit (1971) *Second Malaysia Plan, 1971–1975*. Kuala Lumpur: Government Printer.

Edwards, C.T. (1970) *Public Finance in Malaya and Singapore*. Canberra: Australian National University Press.

Forestry Department Peninsular Malaysia (2000) *Forestry Statistics, Peninsular Malaysia, 2000*. Kuala Lumpur: Perniagaan Normahs.

Forestry Department Peninsular Malaysia (2005) *National Forestry Act 1984 (Act 313)*. Kuala Lumpur: Syarikat Percetakan Ihsan.

Holzhausen, W. (1974) *Federal Finance in Malaysia*. Kuala Lumpur: Penerbit Universiti Malaya.

Ismail, A.H. (1975) 'The Smallholding Sector and the New Economic Policy' in S. Chee and K.S. Mun (eds) *Malaysian Economy Development and Policies*. Kuala Lumpur: Malaysian Economic Association.

Johnston, D. (2008) 'Changing Fiscal Landscape', *The Journal of World Energy Law and Business*, 1.

Khera, H.S. (1975) 'The State and Peasant Innovation in Rural Development: The Case of FELDA Oil Palm Schemes' in S. Chee and K.S. Mun (eds) *Malaysian Economy Development and Policies*. Kuala Lumpur: Malaysian Economic Association.

Leete, R. (2007) *Malaysia from Kampung to Twin Towers: 50 Years of Economic and Social Development*. Kuala Lumpur: Oxford Fajar Sdn. Bhd.

Ministry of Finance (2003) *Economic Report 2003/2004*. Kuala Lumpur: Percetakan Nasional Malaysia Berhad, various issues.

Petronas (2007) *Corporate Profile*. Kuala Lumpur: Petronas.

Poh, L.Y. and A. Hinrichs (2005) *An Analysis of the Forest Revenue System in Terengganu, Peninsular Malaysia*. Kuala Lumpur: Perniagaan Normahs.

Rogers, M.L. (1986) 'Electoral Organisation and Political Mobilisation in Rural Malaysia' in B. Gale (ed.) *Readings in Malaysian Politics*. Petaling Jaya: Pelanduk Publications (M) Sdn. Bhd.

Rudner, M. (1979) 'Agricultural Policy and Peasant Social Transformation in Late Colonial Malaya' in J.C. Jackson and M. Rudner (eds) *Issues in Malaysian Development*. Kuala Lumpur: Heinemann Educational Books Asia Ltd.

Shamsul, A.B. (1986) 'The Politics of Poverty Eradication: The Implementation of Development Projects in a Malaysian District' in B. Gale (ed.) *Readings in Malaysian Politics*. Petaling Jaya: Pelanduk Publications (M) Sdn. Bhd.

Simandjuntak, B. (1965) *Malay Federalism 1945–1963*. Kuala Lumpur: Oxford University Press.

Wafa, S.H. (1975) 'Strategies and Policies of Land Development in Malaysia' in S. Chee and K.S. Mun (eds) *Malaysian Economy Development and Policies*. Kuala Lumpur: Malaysian Economic Association.

Walde, T.W. (2008) 'Renegotiating Acquired Rights in the Oil and Gas Industries: Industry and Political Cycles Meet the Rule of Law', *The Journal of World Energy Law and Business*, 1.

Wood, M. (2007) Upstream Radar Report – *Executive Briefing*.

7
Management of Resource Revenue
Nigeria

Olu Ajakaiye, Paul Collier and Akpan H. Ekpo

7.1 Introduction

Between the onset of oil revenues in Nigeria from 1970 to 2003, Nigerian gross domestic product (GDP) grew at only 1.9 per cent. Not only was this rate below the world average, it was even below population growth. Indeed, as this was a period of unprecedented global prosperity, Nigeria was one of the few countries in the world whose GDP declined absolutely in per capita terms. Manifestly, whether or not oil contributed to this absolute decline, the country did not manage to harness its oil for sustained growth. Hence, the key natural resource issue is why this opportunity for accelerated growth was so resoundingly missed. In view of the gulf between the huge opportunity constituted by the oil discoveries and the dismal outturn, this is arguably the overarching socio-economic issue facing Nigerians. Not only do Nigerians, as other societies, need to understand their recent past but, as the opportunity constituted by oil continues, only by learning from past mistakes can that future be different.

The question as to what went wrong can be answered at several different levels: technical, political and social. In this chapter, our focus is on the key decisions with respect to oil rent management and utilization that explain the lack of growth, rather than on detailed dissection of what happened in the economy. Major political decisions are not taken in a vacuum, but reflect pressures from interest groups. Thus, our explanation will be in terms of the political economy that shaped decisions. Much political economy can be best understood through narrative. Outcomes are path dependent: that is, they cannot be understood other than in terms of a particular sequence, with choices and exogenous shocks leading to outcomes that then inexorably trigger other choices. However, the key decision failures in Nigeria occurred so consistently over several decades that it is more plausible to see the entire period until 2003 as facing structural political problems. Rather than being path dependent, choices were continuously consistent with the same, unchanging set of forces. Outcomes may only have been path dependent within a limited range determined by this deeper constant structure.

7.2 The outcomes of key decisions

For the depletion of natural assets to be converted into sustained development, a series of decisions have to be got sufficiently right. It is useful to think of these decisions as forming a chain made up of five links. The analogy of a chain is helpful because all these links need to hold in order to achieve sustained growth: growth through the depletion of natural assets poses a 'weakest link' problem. Evidently, as Nigeria failed to harness oil for growth, this chain broke. In this section, we set out the chain and consider where along it Nigerian decisions went wrong. The first link in the chain is that natural resources must be discovered. Second, the people living in the neighbourhood of the extraction must then be fully compensated for any environmental costs and be confident that they will get a just share of the benefits over and above this compensation. Third is the value of resources extracted to be captured by the government through taxation. Fourth, sufficient of this value should go into asset formation that the depletion of extractable assets is fully offset. Finally, the process of domestic investment must be sufficiently efficient that the return on investment is at least as high as that available elsewhere in the world. To varying degrees, none of these decisions was adequate in Nigeria, but some failures were more severe than others.

7.2.1 Discovery

The first link, the discovery process, was sufficiently well handled that, even by 2008 after 40 years, proven oil reserves were around 36 billion barrels (Table 7.1). Given prevailing world prices of around $70 per barrel and typical costs of extraction, the potential rents from these reserves are of the order of $2 trillion. Nigeria has evidently discovered a lot of oil.

The first significant discovery was prior to Independence. In 1956, the then Shell–BP struck oil in commercial quantity at Oloibiri (in today's Bayelsa State), and oil production began in 1958 in the Oloibiri

Table 7.1 Proven reserves

Year	(000 million barrels)
1988	16
1998	22.5
2008	36.22

Source: BP.

oil field. Other multinational corporations were also attracted to oil prospecting. In 1955, Mobil started prospecting activities following the withdrawal of a monopoly given to Shell by the British Colonial Administration. Texaco, Gulf Oil, Safrap, Agip and American Petroleum entered the oil business between 1961 and 1963. Upon Independence, the new government granted licences to oil-prospecting companies, both foreign and domestic (Orubu, 2002). A long-term oil-pricing contract was signed with British Petroleum. However, this did not anticipate the hike in oil prices of 1974. The terms of the long-term contract thereupon were considered untenable by the government. In the ensuing dispute, the assets of British Petroleum were nationalized. This episode ended the credibility of long-term pricing contracts. Presently, the oil exploration and exploitation business is dominated by multinationals such as SPDC, TotalFinaelf, Chevron Texaco, Exxon Mobil, Agip, Stafoil-BP and Pan Ocean.

Successive Nigerian governments have shown an interest in oil exploration and exploitation, prioritizing local content and local skill development. The government established its own oil company, the NNPC, which, through a subsidiary, participates directly in the business of oil prospecting. The NNPC oversees development in both the upstream and downstream sectors of the industry. It has created several subsidiaries, namely Integrated Data Services Ltd, Eleme Petrochemicals Company Ltd, the Kaduna Refinery and Petrochemicals Company Ltd, the National Engineering and Technical Company Ltd, Nigerian Petroleum Development Company Ltd, the Pipelines and Product Marketing Company Ltd and the Kaduna, Port Harcourt and Warri Refineries and Petrochemicals Ltd. Each subsidiary handles a specialized area in the industry. SPDC accounts for over half of the total crude oil production in the country.

A second approach has been partnerships with international oil companies through joint venture agreements and production-sharing contracts. These arrangements are provided in the legally binding Joint Operating Document, which includes clauses that empower the NNPC to take over the operation of any joint venture after giving appropriate notification to the operator of such a venture. These changes were meant to facilitate the indigenization of the upstream end of the industry as the need arose. In the joint venture, the Nigerian government, through the NNPC, usually holds a minimum of 60 per cent participation.

A third approach was to enact laws to compel the oil companies to train Nigerians to take over strategic positions in the industry. For example, the Petroleum Decree of 1969 required a holder of an oil-mining licence to ensure that Nigerians in managerial, professional and supervisory grades reach at least 75 per cent of the total number of people employed by the company within 10 years (Okojie and Oaikhenan, 2005).

Despite these three approaches, in practice, relatively little domestic capacity has been established. Although there are several joint venture partnerships (JVP) and Joint Operating Agreements (JOA), Garba and Garba (2001) noted:

> In all seven JVAs, the government is a non-operator. Therefore, although OPEC fixes Nigeria's production quota, the operators make most of the technical decisions, especially with respect to input–output plans and the operating budget. The federal government – the non-operating partner – is, however, liable for the decisions made by the operators in the same equity proportions that they share costs and output.

It is, therefore, not surprising that, in contract matters, the oil companies seem to have an edge; one official said that, most of the time, it is difficult to verify the claims of the oil companies because of lack of capacity on the part of the NNPC.

Although capacity development has been limited, the more fundamental outcome, the achieved rate of extraction, has trended down rather than up. This has reflected both poor design of the incentive regime for extraction, and social turmoil in the Niger Delta. Production, currently under 800 million barrels, has seldom exceeded the early peak of 823 million barrels extracted in 1974. Further, production has often fallen well below these levels, sometimes inefficiently coinciding with periods of very high prices. For example, during the early 1980s, oil production fell below 400 million barrels due to over-aggressive pricing by the Nigerian oil ministry. Similarly, as oil prices rose in the period post-2004, oil production fell, this time due mainly to political disturbance in the Niger Delta. Nevertheless, given the poor use made of the oil that has been extracted, it is difficult to see the lack of further discovery and extraction as being binding problems. Indeed, given the way oil has been used, it is fortuitous that more of it was not extracted.

7.2.2 Fair treatment for the locality of extraction

The second link, the just treatment of the neighbourhood in which the extraction took place, was a spectacular failure: the Niger Delta erupted into so much violence that eventually it substantially reduced production. The nature of the failure was partly environmental and partly political. In different phases, different approaches were tried. Periodically, military force was used to repress dissent. There were also periods in which political accommodation was attempted.

The Niger Delta Region (NDR) includes nine oil-producing states (Abia, Akwa Ibom, Bayelsa, Cross River, Delta, Edo, Imo, Ondo and River States) with a total land area of about 75,000 km^2 and 185 local government areas. The NDR contains the world's third largest wetland with the most extensive freshwater swamp forest and rich biological diversity. Half the area is traversed by creeks and dotted with small islands, whereas the remainder is a lowland rainforest zone. The region consists of minority ethnic groups with about 13,329 settlements.

The NDR is heavily invested in the oil and gas industry but, despite the fact that this is a non-renewable resource, economic diversification has not received adequate attention. Consequently, the vibrant agricultural sector of the mid-twentieth century upon which the region depended for government revenue and foreign exchange earnings in the 1960s and 1970s has been virtually abandoned. Instead, 85 per cent of the population now relies on the informal sector characterized by low productivity and wages for their livelihood (UNDP, 2006: 3).

Meanwhile, the NDR produces the oil wealth that accounts for the bulk of Nigeria's foreign exchange earnings. Ironically, the area remains the most backward and underdeveloped part of the country. Stakeholders have consistently drawn attention to the extreme poverty in the region, and have always urged the federal government to pay more attention by at least allocating more resources to the area. Some parts of the region even attempted secession (in fact, seceded) even before the Biafran war. The secession was popularly known as the 12-day revolution led by Isaac Adaka Boro. In view of the persistent neglect, the NDR was perceived as a conquered territory until very recently when violence erupted in the region.

Four phases are discernible in the evolution of violence in the Niger Delta. First is the period of colonization, during the prevalence of palm oil. The second phase was the discovery of oil and gas and the subsequent inhuman exploration and production processes. The third phase is the period of prolonged environmental degradation of the NDR as a result of oil exploitation. This era saw the destruction of the means of livelihood of the people of the Niger Delta. This led to the suppressed provocation of the people for a long time. The fourth phase is the emergence of resistance to oppression by the people in the Niger Delta.

The current conflict and violence in the Niger Delta started in the early 1990s after nearly four decades of oil exploitation. The petroleum sector had by this time created enormous wealth for Nigeria as a nation. However, the benefits were slow in trickling down to the majority of the people in the NDR whose environment had, over time, been devastated by oil production activities. Environmental degradation of the soil, air and water resulting from oil production had forced a lot of the Niger Delta people to abandon their traditional agricultural and fishing practices. Hence, as oil production raked in the petrodollar for Nigeria, the average Niger Deltan became poorer and poorer with time.

In the early 1990s, the Movement for the Survival of Ogoni People (MOSOP) was formed. This organization championed agitations for the rights of the Ogoni people. This led to conflict between the Ogonis and the oil companies to the extent that both parties carried out acts of violence against each other. Eventually, MOSOP issued an ultimatum to the oil companies (Shell, Chevron and NNPC) demanding $10 billion in accumulated royalties, damages, compensation and the immediate stoppage of environmental degradation of their region, as well as negotiations for mutual agreement on all future drilling in the area.

The Nigerian government responded by banning public gatherings and declaring that disturbances to oil production were acts of treason. This crisis led to the murder of four Ogoni chiefs by a section of MOSOP. On 10 November 1995, nine activists from MOSOP, including Ken Saro-Wiwa, were sentenced to death by a special tribunal set up by the late General Sani Abacha. They were subsequently hanged. During this period, 30 Ogoni villages were razed by soldiers, 600 people were detained and at least 40 killed. This figure eventually rose to 2000 civilian deaths and the displacement of about 100,000 internal refugees.

The late 1990s saw an increase in the number and severity of clashes between militants from the Ijaw ethnic group and those of Itsekiri origin. The bone of contention has been the true owner of the city of Warri, the largest metropolitan area in Delta State between the Ijaw, the Itsekiri and the Urhobo. In December 1998, the All Ijaw Youth Conference crystallized the struggle of the Ijaws for petroleum resource control with the formation of the Ijaw Youth Council (IYC) and the issuing of the Kaiama Declaration. In its declaration, the IYC, urged the oil companies to suspend operations and withdraw from Ijaw territory. In response, the Ijaws in Bayelsa and Delta States were attacked by two warships, and over 10,000 Nigerian troops and many civilians were killed, beaten and raped. The Odi massacre also saw many civilians killed by Nigerian soldiers. Subsequent actions by the Ijaws against the oil industry included both non-violent actions as well as attacks on oil installations and foreign oil workers.

By 2003–04, the ethnic unrest and conflicts of the late 1990s as well as clashes with government troops had metamorphosed into an increasing level of militarization in the Niger Delta. Local and state officials did not help matters as they offered financial support to the militant groups they believed would enforce their political agenda. The convergence of militant groups in the region saw the emergence of the Niger Delta People's Volunteer Force (NDPVF) led by Mujahid Dokubo-Asari and the Niger Delta Vigilante (NDV) group led by Ateke Tom. The major militant groups are under the Movement for the Emancipation of the Niger Delta (MEND). There are, however, over 100 other smaller militant groups. In May 2009, the Joint Task Force (JTF) undertook military operations against militants operating in the NDR. In 2009, the government announced an amnesty, an allocation of 10 per cent of oil revenues to be distributed in some way directly to the people of the Delta, and offered economic integration to those members of violent groups who came forward. To date, this has quelled the violence but, in practice, neither the distribution of money nor the attempt at integration of the combatants has been implemented.

7.2.3 Taxation

The third link in the chain, the taxation of oil extraction, was the least problematic. Initially, taxation was determined through the Oil Mineral Ordinance of 1959. This was followed by enacting the Petroleum Profit Tax Act, which made the profits of the oil companies taxable. The Act stressed the calculation of royalty and petroleum profit tax on the posted price of the commodity. The tax rate was raised to 55 per cent in 1973 and 67.75 per cent in 1974, while the royalty was raised from 12.5 per cent to 16.67 per cent over the same period. It was raised further to 85 per cent in 1985. Very substantial rents accrued to the government through the taxation of oil companies. This stage has attracted much attention because of the emotive nature of transactions between international oil companies and the government of a poor country. At the margin, there is evidence that the companies periodically took advantage of the lack of expertise and scrutiny within the government, for example a belated audit undertaken in 2004 revealed substantial underpayment of taxes. But the margin of inefficiency in taxation is dwarfed by mistakes elsewhere in the decision chain.

Oil revenues rapidly became the dominant source of government revenue (see Figures 7.1 and 7.2 and Appendix Table A.7.1 for the underlying data). By 1974, they exceeded 80 per cent and, even at the trough of world oil prices, they were seldom below 70 per cent. The failure to build other sources of revenue had two implications. One was that government revenues were highly exposed to the volatility of oil prices. As a result, both democratic and military governments were periodically forced into crisis measures. Thus, in 1982, the Shagari government introduced austerity measures under an Economic Stabilization Act; in 1985, the Buhari government introduced a National Economic Emergency Decree; and in 1986, the Babangida government introduced a structural adjustment programme. The other implication was that, in terms of political economy, the government lacked a revenue interest in developing a prosperous non-oil economy.

7.2.4 Spending, saving and investment

The fourth link, offsetting the depletion of oil by the accumulation of other assets, is undoubtedly the most comprehensive decision failure. Because policy changed abruptly in 2003, just in time for the recent oil boom, it is best to evaluate asset behaviour in two phases, the long

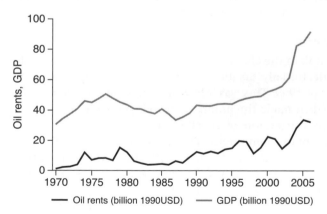

Figure 7.1 Oil rents and GDP, 1970–2006

Source: World Bank, Genuine Saving Project and UNSTATS.

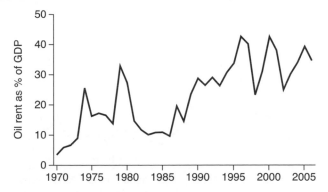

Figure 7.2 Oil rents, 1970–2006 (% of GDP)

Source: World Bank, Genuine Saving Project and UNSTATS; authors' calculations.

period 1970–2003 and then the brief, better managed boom that started in 2003.

Over the period 1970–2003, the cumulative oil rents to the government were around $345 bn (expressed in $1990). On top of this, around $34 bn of external debt was accumulated ($31 bn in $1990). As the debt could not have been accumulated without the oil as implicit collateral, the two can be thought of as a package amounting to around $376 bn (in $1990). So much for asset depletion – less oil and more debt – now consider the other side of the balance sheet, the accumulation of assets (see Figures 7.3 and 7.4 and Appendix Table A.7.2 for the underlying data). Total gross fixed investment (GFKF) cumulated to only $311 bn. However, much of this would have occurred even without the oil. If, for example, we take as a highly cautious counterfactual that GFKF would have remained flat at its 1970 level, it would still have cumulated to $239 bn. Hence, even at the most generous estimate, only around $72 bn of the oil debt windfall was invested domestically, or about 19 per cent.

The early years of oil revenues were also years of post-war recovery. Hence, there was a natural focus on reconstruction. Additionally, there was massive expenditure in human capital development, with the government embarking on training Nigerians at home and abroad on various scholarship schemes. There was also considerable investment in the health sector when several primary, secondary and tertiary healthcare facilities were established. There was also some focus on infrastructure with the construction of paved roads, international airports and sea ports. As the civil service expanded, there was also large investment in public housing for them.

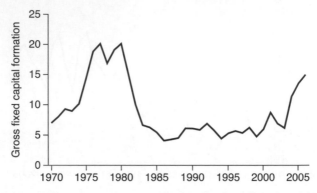

Figure 7.3 Gross fixed capital formation, 1970–2006 (billion constant 1990 US$)
Source: UNSTATS.

With the onset of the first oil boom, a notable absence was any discussion of the need for precautionary savings. On the contrary, debts were accumulated, although even the size of the fiscal deficits is uncertain for some years during this period (see Figure 7.5 and Appendix Table A.7.3 for the underlying data). During the subsequent mini-boom in oil prices of 1991 (as a result of the first Gulf War), the Babangida military government did establish a Stabilization Fund to be used for the smoothing of revenues. This suggests that there was indeed a degree of learning from the adverse consequences of past volatility. However, the scale of the fund was little more than token: a mere 0.5 per cent of the Federation Accounts proceeds were paid into the fund. Further, the

Figure 7.4 Gross fixed capital formation, 1970–2006 (% of GDP)
Source: UNSTATS.

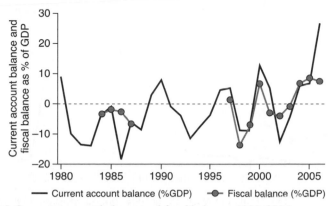

Figure 7.5 Current account balance and fiscal balance, 1980–2006

Source: IMF (GFS, Article IV Consultation Reports, WEO Dataset) and UNSTATS.

management of the fund suffered from the now endemic problems of arbitrary and discretionary decision processes, gross indiscipline, unprecedented corrupt practices and, above all, the lack of any checks and balances. Consequently, the fund was not able to serve the intended purposes when the oil boom was over in the mid-1990s. The Stabilization Fund was closed in 2002 when the Supreme Court ruled on a resource control suit instituted by some state governments, declaring the payments of 0.5 per cent into a Federal Account illegal.

Potentially, in a poor society, many types of expenditure that are normally classified as recurrent, such as health and education, may, nevertheless, sustainably raise incomes. However, throughout the period, the structure of Federal Government recurrent expenditure was dominated by transfers, and administration took the lion's share of recurrent expenditure. Recurrent expenditure on social and community services was relatively low, whereas recurrent expenditure on economic services was less than 10 per cent of the total almost throughout the period. The bulk of transfers were in the form of external debt servicing, reflecting the prior accumulation of debt, spent largely on public consumption.

By way of contrast, in the brief boom of 2004–06, oil rents cumulated to around $94 bn, external debt was eliminated, and GFKF was $3 bn above counterfactual. Foreign exchange reserves rose from $7 bn in 2003 to $42 bn in 2006. The debt elimination was helped by a write-down of around $22 bn, a massive concession won thanks to the good international reputation of the economic reform team (see Figure

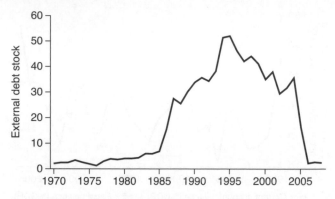

Figure 7.6 Total external debt stock, 1970–2006 (billion constant 1990 US$)
Source: UNDATA (1970–2005) and IMF Article IV (2006–08).

7.6 and Appendix Table A.7.2 for the underlying data). Hence, the underlying numbers were that oil rents were $94 bn and the government accumulated assets of around $49 bn (including spending on buying back debt). A reasonable interpretation is that, during this period, the government used around half the oil revenue for asset accumulation. Indeed, for the first time in its existence, the country received a sovereign rating by two leading international rating agencies – Fitch Ratings and Standard and Poor's. Nigeria was rated 'BB', which puts it in the group of emerging economies. During this period, Nigeria exited from the Paris and London debts.

7.2.5 The quality of investment

The final link, achieving an adequate return on domestic investment, was in a sense moot as, prior to 2004, so little of the oil revenues were used for asset accumulation, and since 2004, most of them were used for the repurchase of external debt (on advantageous terms). However, potentially, more might have been invested domestically had the return on domestic investment, both public and private, been higher. In fact, investment decisions were the outcome of discretionary political processes leading to a preponderance of grandiose projects and a high incidence of corruption. The quality of the civil service was undermined so that, despite a huge expansion in its numbers, poor project selection was compounded by poor implementation. A lot of public money went into establishing all kinds of industries owned and controlled by the government. The government took over what was then known as the commanding heights of the economy.

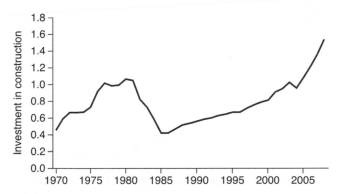

Figure 7.7 Construction, 1970–2008 (billion constant 1990 US$)
Source: UNSTATS.

The private investment climate was correspondingly difficult. Further, the priority for economic development strategy was import substitution so that private investment was encouraged into activities that were dependent upon continuing subsidy. These industries remained dependent upon subsidies and protection, contracting during periods of real exchange rate appreciation.

The final component of an efficient investment process is for the construction sector to be cost-effective so that the unit costs of capital are kept low. However, the Nigerian construction sector appears to have had very high unit costs. Partly, this was because construction projects became prime vehicles for corruption. However, this was compounded by the boom–bust nature of macroeconomic management. Instead of

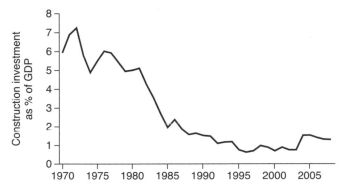

Figure 7.8 Construction, 1970–2008 (% of GDP)
Source: UNSTATS.

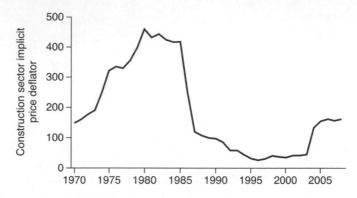

Figure 7.9 Construction sector implicit price deflator, 1970–2008

Source: UNSTATS (authors' calculations).

smoothing the economy, macroeconomic policy exaggerated the oil booms and busts. This resulted from a policy of borrowing during the booms. As a result, during the slumps, the government had to make net repayments of debt because of the inability to borrow on world markets once large debts had been accumulated and oil prices were low. This pattern of exaggerated booms and busts crowded construction demand into brief periods of boom. Thus, the peak output of the construction sector over the entire period 1970–2003 occurred in 1980–81, after which it fell to less than half its peak level (see Figures 7.7 and 7.8). This crowding of demand inevitably produced high unit costs precisely at the times when most construction projects were being implemented (see Figure 7.9). Thus, such evidence as there is suggests that, until the reforms post-2003, the process of investing was highly inefficient.

7.3 The political economy of decisions

In this section, we analyse what went wrong during the period 1970–2003, and why decisions started to go right thereafter, in terms of underlying socio-political structures that shaped decisions. Any such analysis of Nigeria faces a potential difficulty: the performance of the Nigerian economy changed dramatically around 2003. Whereas in the long period 1970–2003, it grew at only 1.9 per cent (a decline in per capita terms), during the period 2003–06, it grew at 9.6 per cent. If economic performance was indeed determined by underlying socio-political structures, then this structural break in economic performance could only be accounted for by a correspondingly dramatic change in socio-political structure. Normally, such structures change only slowly, with the exceptions being revolutions. Hence, if the lack of growth was indeed attributable to socio-political structures, either the period of rapid growth was accounted for by socio-political revolution, or it was merely a temporary spurt attributable to exceptionally favourable external events. Otherwise, socio-political structural explanations for the persistent failure to grow are unsustainable.

Our analysis of the decision chain has led to two political questions, one concerning the Delta and the other the choice between assets and consumption. These are, to a considerable extent, distinct questions. That concerning the Niger Delta is primarily a question as to the spatial distribution of costs relative to benefits: why did this region not receive benefits more commensurate with its costs? In contrast, the asset question is fundamentally intertemporal: why were the interests of the future not better protected? However, although they are distinct questions, they may, nevertheless, have a common answer.

7.3.1 Political power and economic decisions prior to 2003

We have observed the remarkable difference between the pre-2003 and post-2003 periods. The key failures occurred prior to 2003. Hence, the pertinent overarching socio-political question is where, during this period, did effective power lie? In terms of both leaders and the form of polity, 1970–2003 was a rapidly changing mosaic. It included two periods of democracy (1979–83, 1999–2003), two of military rule (1970–79 and 1983–99) and a brief period of a caretaker civilian administration (1992–93). Within the military periods, there were further changes due to coups, and within each of the democratic periods, there were elections. However, the underlying power structure is less complicated than these changes might suggest: in essence, during the entire 34 years, effective power rested with a relatively small number of people who held senior positions in the Nigerian military.

All elites face a fundamental choice between adopting economic policies that promote the growth of the economy and those that redistribute public revenues in their own favour. This choice is determined in part by a trade-off between long-term and short-term benefits: over a sufficiently long period, higher growth will benefit everyone. But it is also determined by how much, within any particular time period, the elite can gain from redistribution relative to growth. For the military elite and their civilian collaborators, both considerations conspired to favour redistribution over growth. First, because the oil revenues were large relative to the economy, the pay-off to redistribution was enormous. Second, given the erratic changes in regimes and personalities, the long term (which favoured growth) had to be heavily discounted by the risk of loss of power.

As an example of policy priorities, one of the key chosen uses of the revenues was to relocate the capital from Lagos to Abuja. Although the military elite and their civilian collaborators benefited directly from the disbursement of oil revenues, indirectly the macroeconomic effects of the oil windfall did much to disadvantage ordinary citizens in the country. The country had been an important agricultural commodity exporter, and the major cities were manufacturing centres, primarily for local demand but also for the neighbouring countries. Both these activities were essentially destroyed by the appreciation in the real exchange rate that made them uncompetitive. Hence, although individual members of the elite group became very wealthy, the country as a whole did not benefit significantly from the oil windfall.

The resource boom generated rents and created an incentive for economic agents to engage in rent-seeking activities (the voracity effect) as opposed to innovations that could encourage growth. The availability of huge oil revenues and weak political and administrative structures gave rise to a high incidence of corruption; emphasis was more on oil taxes and less on direct personal income taxes, thereby weakening the incentive and capacity of the people to hold the government accountable. As a result, policies were structured so as to generate opportunities for the accumulation of personal wealth by the politically powerful. For example, one of the military leaders, General Abacha, is believed to have amassed around $4 bn abroad in his 6-year period of office. Abacha's conduct was not isolated. Astoundingly, the United Nations Office on Drugs and Crime estimates that, over the entire period 1960–99, approaching $400 bn was stolen. By 2001, Nigeria was next to bottom on the global corruption index of Transparency International. The judicial and police system was also implicated: prior to 2003, there was not a single successful prosecution for major public sector corruption. The mechanics of personal enrichment on such a scale shaped economic policies, although they varied according to changing opportunities: as one route closed, another would open. Thus, during the first oil boom, with public revenues being large, the dominant mechanism was probably through the non-competitive awarding of construction contracts. Marwah (2010) estimates that, during the construction boom of 1975–84, some 80 per cent of expenditure on construction contracts was to 'ghost' firms that had neither the capacity to nor the intention of undertaking construction and so were, unambiguously, scams.

In the ensuing oil slump, foreign exchange was rationed, and so its non-market allocation became the predominant device. The elite had an interest in the consumption of imports over production, and so consistently favoured an overvalued exchange rate, dressed up in the nationalist rhetoric of a 'strong Naira'. The overvalued exchange rate also induced massive capital flight. As foreign exchange was liberalized, the political rents passed to the control of unsecured loans by the banks. Each of these devices imposed indirect costs on the economy that far exceeded the amounts looted. With public investment determined more by the scope for embezzlement than by public need, investment choices lacked economic rationale. For example, far more projects were started than could be completed, because kickbacks accrued on the awarding of contracts rather than on their completion. Thus, by the 1990s, the skyline of Abuja was littered with uncompleted, yet abandoned, projects. A particularly damaging abuse of authority was the repeated embezzlement of funds intended to provide Nigeria with electric power. Nigeria suffers from acute power shortages, which limit productive activities, yet a recent audit by the Nigerian authorities finds that some $16 bn has been looted from the sector over the decades. The rationing of foreign exchange damaged both non-oil exports and all activities that depended upon imported inputs. Similarly, the political manipulation of the banks limited the normal contribution of the financial sector to growth.

7.3.2 The political economy of reform, 2003–present

If the failure to harness oil for growth during the period 1970–2003 is to be explained by the dysfunctional private interests of the military, why did growth increase post-2003? We suggest that it was, indeed, a combination of socio-political revolution and fortuitous external conditions. The socio-political revolution did not coincide with the change in polity from military to democratic rule. The latter occurred in 1999 without fundamentally shifting power because, during his first term, the civilian president, Obasanjo, was, to a considerable extent, subject to the goodwill of the political class that held sway while he was in prison and had been instrumental in his assumption of power in 1999 and retaining it in the 2003 election. Only once he had been re-elected for a second term was President Obasanjo in a position to shift power from the erstwhile political class. This he did decisively. Competent and decisive reformers were placed in charge of the Ministry of Finance, Public Procurement, and the Central Bank. This was, indeed, the crux of socio-political revolution.

Finance Minister Ngozi Nkonjo-Iweala radically increased the accumulation of assets. There was a determination to insist on rules rather than discretion and allow agencies that managed the economy to be free from political interference. The impressive asset of figures noted in Section 7.2.4 were thus the result of deliberate policy action rather than merely fortuitous. The chosen instrument was that the minister announced a benchmark dollar price of oil per barrel to be used in estimating revenue flowing into the budget. At times when the actual world price was above this benchmark, the surplus was declared as 'excess' and accrued into a special fund (the Excess Crude Account), rather than being spent. In the first year, all this saving thus accrued as foreign exchange. In subsequent years, part of the fund was used to finance infrastructure. As the benchmark price was set conservatively, the Excess Crude Account thus served two conceptually distinct functions: the medium-term objective of smoothing volatility in world prices and the long-term objective of devoting a substantial proportion of the revenues from oil to the accumulation of other assets. However, in this approach, everything depended upon the setting of the benchmark price for oil. This was done annually by the Finance Minister without clearly articulated underlying principles. After a long legislative struggle, it was enshrined in law as the Fiscal Responsibility Act. The legislation thus gave a prudent finance minister considerable power to prevent either the government or the legislature from spending too much on consumption. However, it depended entirely upon the decision of the finance minister. An imprudent finance minister could, in principle, set a high benchmark price and run down accumulated reserves. Hence, the institution was not fully robust against individuals.

The underlying motivation for this prudent structure of rules was that the new managers of the economy were convinced that:

> . . . the beginning of lifting the curse for any resource rich (oil-producing) country is the realization that the revenue bonanza should not be used to increase current consumption but as a spring board to economic development through boosting real living standards by financing a higher level of investments and core public goods like massive infrastructure.
>
> Usman (2009)

Accordingly, complementing macroeconomic prudence, an economic reform package known as the National Economic Empowerment and Development Strategy (NEEDS) was developed to change the struc-

ture of the economy (National Planning Commission, 2004). This identified priorities for investment spending, notably infrastructure.

The socio-political revolution at the federal level created tensions
with the states, which were still largely under the control of patronage
politics. Managing oil revenues in the context of a federation where
the centre controls major sources of revenue (including oil), yet the
sub-national governments (State and local governments) have the predominant expenditure responsibilities, has posed political problems.
Although managers of the economy at the federal level insisted on
saving the 'excess' of oil revenues (the excess of actual receipts over a
reference price set by the Finance Minister), sub-national governments
preferred to receive and spend their half of oil revenues, as provided for
in the country's constitution. Further, failure to manage the injection
of oil revenue into the economy would threaten macroeconomic stability, risking sharp exchange rate appreciation and consequent damage
to the non-oil tradable sectors of the economy. Thus, the preference of
patronage politicians for spending was juxtaposed against the need
both for long-term asset accumulation and for short-term macroeconomic management of a large but temporary boom.

In addition to reliance upon rules, the reformers committed to
improving information for ordinary citizens. Nigeria was an early signa-
tory of the Extractive Industries Transparency Initiative (EITI), going
further than the international commitment by releasing information on
revenues paid to each state, as well as those received by the federation.

Overseeing public procurement, Oby Ezekwesili introduced comprehensive competitive tendering for all public projects, a move that
reduced costs by around 40 per cent. As with the asset accumulation,
this change was institutionalized by legislation through a Public
Procurement Act. However, as with the Fiscal Responsibility Act, this
only applied at the federal level. As half of all oil revenues accrued
directly to the states, rules can only apply comprehensively if each state
passes its own Fiscal Responsibility Act and Public Procurement Act. To
date, only seven states have enacted their own Fiscal Responsibility
Acts, and only one has a Public Procurement Act.

At the structural level, the medium-term plan known as NEEDS,
2003–07 was prepared under the leadership of Professor Chukwuma
Soludo, the economic adviser to the president and CEO of the National
Planning Commission, and launched at the beginning of the second
term of the Obasanjo government (National Planning Commission,
2004). Inevitably, it was essentially a federal government plan, and the
reforms embedded in it could only be effective if the state governments

developed and implemented complementary reform agendas. NEEDS had five components. First, there was an attempt to diversify the economy by revisiting agriculture and prospecting for solid minerals. However, in practice, there was no political will to diversify the economy. There were properly articulated strategies, but none was effectively implemented. Second, the budget was derived from both a medium-term economic framework (MTEF) and a medium-term sector strategy (MTSS) in an attempt to strengthen public expenditure management in the system. Third, there was a desire for better coordination of monetary and fiscal policy in an attempt to promote macroeconomic stability. Fourth, as noted above, there was an enhanced information flow as the Federal Ministry of Finance published monthly allocations to states and local governments in daily newspapers and on its web page, thereby fostering transparency and accountability. Finally, there were efforts to fight corruption.

In 2004, Chukwuma Soludo was elevated to the position of governor of the Central Bank. There, he dramatically reformed the banking system, consolidating it from over 60 banks to 25, all with high minimum capital requirements. Unfortunately, corrupt lending practices were so ingrained in the banks that, even though these 25 started as adequately capitalized, within 5 years, 12 of them were effectively bankrupt.

The final institutionalized component of reform was the fight against corruption. As a consequence of the terrorist attack of 11 September 2001, the United States constituted a Financial Action Task Force, which produced a list of countries where governance was inadequate to ensure that they could not be a conduit for terrorist finance. Nigeria was placed on this list. In response, President Obasanjo was determined to implement the reforms that would enable Nigeria to get off the list. He steered through the legislature a new Economic and Financial Crimes Commission (EFCC) to tackle financial and related crimes, and the Independent Corrupt Practices and Other Related Offenses Commission (ICPC) to fight corruption in public office. EFCC successfully prosecuted over 250 people in the brief period 2003–07. The ICPC has also recorded remarkable successes as far as its mandate is concerned. Despite these remarkable efforts, corruption still prevailed. For instance, according to www.icpcnigeria.com (2004), Mr Nuhu Ribadu (2010), the former chairman of EFCC, was quoted as saying:

. . . the amount of oil wealth illegally siphoned off is down from about 70 per cent two years ago, due to new controls on central government finances. But the Nigerian regions, which control about half of the nation's revenue, have failed to keep up with the pace of central reform. At the federal level, there has been a big improvement. The very big guys who steal now are the State Governors. Things have improved; about 70 per cent used to go to waste and corruption, but the number now is maybe 40 per cent.

Evidently, during 2003–08, external economic conditions were also uniquely favourable for Nigeria. Oil revenues soared, and there was correspondingly greater interest in prospecting. Although the global crisis of 2008 initially hit oil revenues, by 2010, they had recovered to historically high levels. The intervening fall in revenues could readily be weathered given the large reserves accumulated during 2003–08. Hence, the structural break in the external environment in 2003, followed by a temporary wobble in 2008–09, coincides closely with the changes in political power.

The structural break in outcomes, notably the change from stagnation to rapid growth, can reasonably be seen as the response to these joint changes in internal politics and external opportunities, although it is not possible to quantify their distinct contributions.

7.3.3 Political power and decisions concerning the Niger Delta

We now turn to the other major policy failure: the Niger Delta.

Even before the discovery of oil, the colonial administration, through the Wilkins Commission Report of 1957, recognized that the region was characterized by abject poverty and backwardness arising from gross neglect, marginalization, domination and oppression, and called for the development of the area using its vast marine resources. The recommendations of the Wilkins Commission were not based on oil wealth although oil had been found in Oloibiri in 1956, implying that the problem of under-development of the NDR predates the emergence of oil in Nigeria. The emergence of oil in the region and the massive destruction of the livelihood of the majority of the people escalated the problem. Subsequent governments continued this pattern of neglect, as the people of the NDR watched their resources being used to develop and modernize other parts of the country.

Several other resource-rich countries have faced similar problems of social disturbance in the region of extraction, although few have been as severe as that in the Delta. First, consider the menu of possible approaches to the problem: typically, three approaches can be followed. One is to allocate to the oil-producing areas a disproportionate share of the oil revenues. Such an approach is, however, potentially socially costly in that it diverts revenue from other areas which, by definition, are getting less. Further, once the principle is established that oil-producing areas are entitled to a disproportionate share of the revenues, there is no natural limit to their claims short of being given the entire revenues. A second approach is to suppress dissent by military force. A third approach aims to minimize legitimate local grievances while making local claims to a disproportionate share of revenue appear greedy. For this approach to be feasible, the government must commit to the principle of generous compensation of environmental costs, combined with a mechanism for implementing it, while transparently allocating the revenues so as to benefit future generations of Nigerians across the country.

Whereas the North was the strongest region politically, the Delta was the weakest. The region had fought and lost a secessionist war and so was only in the Federation as a defeated entity, although efforts were made towards reintegration and reconciliation. Further, it was natural that, facing the accumulating security problems of the Delta, Nigeria's military rulers should be biased towards resolving them by means of military containment. The action could readily be conceptualized as a repeat of the military's 'finest hour': holding Nigeria together in the face of revolt from the South-East. Hence, it is not surprising that the actual choices were a combination of the first and the second approaches. The Delta was given a disproportionate share of the revenues, but not sufficient to satisfy its sense of entitlement. Further, the oil revenues accruing to the Delta were received by the local political elite who generally did not share them with ordinary citizens. Nevertheless, politicians could blame the lack of benefits on the Federation, deflecting popular frustration from their own failings. Meanwhile, in response to escalating informal violence, the military was periodically used to maintain order. The third approach was not attempted: environmental costs went uncontrolled and uncompensated, whereas uses of the oil revenue were not transparent, were not devoted to future generations and were not equitable. It is not difficult to see why this third approach was not attractive to the Northern elite. Environmental compensation would have been costly and would have favoured a region with which the Northern military had little sympathy, whereas transparent allocation of the revenues to nationally equitable investment would have fundamentally undermined its core objectives.

Even the socio-political revolution of 2003 failed to provide an effective solution to the Delta problem. Some elements of the third approach were indeed adopted, notably transparency in budgeting and, as we have seen, a radical new respect for the interests of future generations. By the time this approach was being followed, the reputation of the Federal Government may have been so utterly eroded in the Delta that credibility would have taken many years to re-establish. Further, although President Obasanjo was a civilian by this stage, his career had been as a general in the army, and so his instinctive solution to violence in the South-East was military repression.

The demands of politicians from the Delta have ranged from a significant increase in the derivation component of the revenue allocation formula to outright ownership and control of oil resources in the area. The National Political Conference held in 2005 offered to recommend an increase in the derivation component of the Federation Account from 13 per cent to 17 per cent, although the NDR delegates were demanding an immediate increase to 25 per cent and a programmed increase to 50 per cent in the medium term. The demand by NDR delegates was rejected by the conference, thus creating a stalemate that brought the conference to an abrupt end. Meanwhile, militancy in the area has increased so much that it has resulted in reduced crude oil production.

The federal government intervened from time to time by establishing regional agencies such as the OMPADEC (Oil Minerals Producing Areas Development Commission), which later became the N7C (Niger Delta Development Commission). However, these agencies have not had the desired impact, partly because of underfunding and lack of focus but, more importantly, a lack of good governance in the communities in the NDR. State and local governments in the NDR appear irrelevant – the resources received from the federal government are not channelled into providing infrastructure and other amenities necessary to create an environment for economic and commercial activities. The resources are only used to modernize state capitals while vast areas of the region are neglected. The government of President Musa Yar' Adua further responded to the problem by setting up a Niger Delta Technical Committee to advise on the best way of transforming the NDR. In addition, the administration established a Ministry of the Niger Delta to allow the presidency to place more emphasis on the economic development of the region.

However, these interventions by the federal government have not dampened the desire of the NDR people to secure greater control over their resources. Therefore, stakeholders in the NDR continue to argue that resources, oil inclusive, belong to the community in which they are found, and that resource ownership and control go beyond increasing the derivation parameter in the revenue allocation formula. It allows the owners of the resource(s) to participate in the whole gamut of activities including the decision on how to distribute the revenue. NDR stakeholders are also arguing that the deductions from crude oil sales in order to arrive at the net oil revenue before the derivation formula is applied are unacceptable. In addition, they argue for the establishment of trust funds necessary to compensate the people of the region for the long period of neglect and also to provide for the needs of future generations in the NDR communities. Specifically, there is a call for the creation of two trust funds, one for short-term smoothing and the other for long-term intergenerational equity. Both funds would have first charge on the Distribution Pool Account.

Thus, although 2003 marked a socio-political revolution that changed economic decisions, it did not have an equivalent effect on decisions concerning the Delta. The region continued to be marginal to the interests of the politically powerful. Potentially, however, the equivalent socio-political revolution for the Delta occurred in 2010 with the accession to the presidency of Goodluck Jonathan, who was from the Delta and had previously been a deputy governor in the region. On assuming full office, he announced that his foremost priority was to ensure peace in the Delta.

7.4 Resources and revenues at state level

Nigeria's federal structure consists of 36 states, a federal Capital Territory (Abuja) and 774 local governments. At present, revenues for the country are placed in a distributable pool (Federation Account) and shared among the three levels of government vertically and horizontally, based on the prevailing revenue allocation formula. Ekpo (2008) has stated that, in Nigeria, all levels of government depend on oil revenue with its inherent volatility. Similarly, Ajakaiye (2008) showed that the portion of the Federation Account revenue that can be directly and effectively influenced by the Nigerian authorities was below 15 per cent, implying that at least 85 per cent of government revenue is actually exogenously determined. On the other hand, all levels of government have high recurrent expenditure dominated by personnel costs leaving very little room for adjustment to external shock without deleterious effects on stabilization either in terms of running high deficits with the adverse effects on inflation and/or retrenchment with the adverse effects on unemployment and poverty situation (Ajakaiye, 2008).

Overall, around half of all oil revenues are now managed at the level of states and local governments. However, this level of decision-taking is much less researched than the federal level. With 36 states, it is not possible to cover them all. Instead, we focus on two pairs of states with interesting contrasts.

We first contrast two oil-producing states in the Delta. Akwa Ibom State was created in 1987 as part of strategy of minimizing ethnic tension rather than viability. The state is part of the NDR and has both agricultural and oil resources. It depends on oil revenue from the centre and has not generated enough internal revenue to finance its development needs. Between 2000 and 2005, state-generated revenues amounted to only around 10 per cent of total revenues and, as oil revenues rose, state-level tax revenues declined. The state is suffering from low revenue collection efforts, which may limit the incentive and the capacity of the people of Akwa Ibom State to hold their government accountable. Government expenditures exceeded government revenues. Over the period 2000–04, (the last complete data), total expenditure was some 25 per cent above total revenue. Further, the situation appeared to be deteriorating. Whereas in 2000 revenues had significantly exceeded expenditures, by 2004, expenditure was almost double revenue. Evidently, in some form or other, the state was accumulating debts. The composition of expenditure was, however, quite heavily skewed towards capital, which accounted for 40 per cent of total spending. Akwa Ibom is one of the states that have developed a medium-term plan (SEEDS), and government officials confirm that, since 2004, government spending decisions were guided by the State SEEDS document. However, there are indications that the planning approach is from top to bottom. Officials insist that there is too much money at the federal level and prefer a situation in which the state exploits its natural resources and pays a royalty to the federal government. This position is not surprising based on the fact that the state is one of those championing the struggle for resource control. There is no indication that the state has passed its own Fiscal Responsibility or Procurement bill. Also, there are no indications that the state is considering savings out of its Federation Account proceeds, which are largely oil revenue.

Cross River State is also an oil-producing state in the Niger Delta, but it contrasts sharply with Akwa Ibom. Notably, it has established a Reserve Fund by law. The law requires the government to set aside the sum of N600 million annually. The state government has been complying with this law, and there are stringent conditions needed to draw down from the fund. The Reserve Fund is invested to generate interest for the state.

Our next pair of states is the two major city states of Nigeria. Kano State depends heavily on the centre for revenue to finance its development objectives. Between 2000 and 2005, federal transfers constituted 86 per cent of revenue sources. However, Kano is a major centre of commerce, the second most industrialized state in Nigeria and the economic nerve centre of the North. It has over 300 large and medium-sized industrial establishments and thousands of small-scale industrial and commercial activities. Yet, not only was internally generated revenue low, it was in decline. Expenditure was more closely matched to revenue than in Akwa Ibom, although over the period for which we have data (2002–05), expenditures exceeded revenues by 10 per cent. In terms of the composition of government expenditure, capital accounted for around 37 per cent. Kano has also developed a medium-term plan (SEEDS), and government officials confirmed that the state's spending decision had been based on it. The budget process is from the top to the bottom. According to state officials, poverty alleviation constitutes a key priority. There is no indication that the Kano State government has passed its own Fiscal Responsibility or Procurement bill. Also, there are no indications that the state is considering saving part of its Federation Account proceeds.

In contrast to Kano, Lagos State has been following a policy of sharply increasing state-level taxation. By 2010, internally generated revenues were estimated to account for around 67 per cent of the total. The shift in the composition of revenues was matched by a massive shift in the composition of expenditures. Whereas in 2004 capital spending accounted for only 20 per cent of the total, by 2010, it had risen to 60 per cent. There was a strong emphasis on improving urban infrastructure. These radical changes were complemented by both borrowing from banks and issuing bonds. However, indebtedness remained modest at only around 8 per cent of state GDP. In terms of governance, the state legislature was set to pass both a Fiscal Responsibility Act and a Public Procurement Act.

These two pairs of contrasting vignettes suggest that, at the state level, the range of decision-taking varies widely. In some states, decision-takers are managing oil revenues responsibly and using them to develop the economy, whereas in others, practices remain essentially the same as those that characterized the entire society during the pre-reform era of 1970–2003.

7.5 Conclusion

Although overall Nigeria has not succeeded in harnessing oil for development, the story of decision-taking is not as discouraging as this might imply. Around 2003, there was a remarkable structural break both in economic performance and in the underlying structures of political power. These are clearly related. The shift of power from the military elite with little interest in the development of the economy to economic reformers resulted in dramatic changes in priorities. The savings rate out of oil revenues rocketed from a derisory level to being prudent. Macroeconomic management was transformed from amplifying the magnitude of shocks to dampening them. Governance of spending was transformed from being secretive and discretionary to being transparent and rule based. The key reforms were then institutionalized at the federal level through legislation and, at the time of writing, look to be robust to changes in personalities.

However, around half of all oil revenues are managed at the state and local level. This is a constitutional requirement over which the federal government has no control. The socio-political revolution that shifted power from a rent-seeking military to reformers happened at the federal level rather than across the entire society. This has left the struggle for good management of the oil revenues to be fought state-by-state. Some states remain under the control of the pre-2003 power structure. In these states, practices appear to be a continuation of pre-2003 federal practices. In other states, the power structure has shifted and, in some instances, the quality of economic decisions is now ahead of that at the federal level. This is likely to generate wide differences in economic outcomes between states. Although each state has, constitutionally, the power to set its own policies and rules, these emerging differences in performance are likely to generate internal pressures for reform in the lagging states. This may be a practical model for the good management of oil in federal political systems.

Although economic decision-taking in the management of oil revenues has thus improved markedly, the treatment of the oil-producing region has not. The shift in power that enabled economic decisions to change does not extend to shifting approaches to the Niger Delta. Possibly, the accession in 2010 of a president from the Delta constitutes the analogous shift in power that will enable this intractable problem to be resolved. Inevitably, however, the prolonged delay has made the process of reaching a reasonable settlement far more difficult.

Acknowledgements

Prepared for the Oxford Centre for the Analysis of Resource Rich Economies (OxCarre), University of Oxford, funded by the Revenue Watch Institute with support from the Bill and Melinda Gates Foundation. The research assistance of Dr O.J. Umoh, Dr Udoma Afanghide, Mr Lawrence Udofia and Mr Paolo Falco are hereby acknowledged.

References

Ajakaiye, O. (2008) 'Towards Securing Fiscal Policy Coordination in Nigeria' in P. Collier, C.C. Soludo and C. Pattilo (eds) *Economic Policy Options for a Prosperous Nigeria*. New York: Palgrave Macmillan.

Ekpo, A.H. (2008) 'The Nigerian Economy: Is it at the Crossroads?' Presidential address, Nigerian Economic Society, Ibadan.

Garba, G. and K. Garba (2001) 'Market Failure, State Failure and Air Pollution in Nigeria: A Theoretical Investigation of Two Cases' in G. Garba (ed.) *Natural Resource Use: the Environment and Sustainable Development*. Ibadan: Nigerian Economic Society.

Marwah, H. (2010) 'Revisiting African Economic History using Construction Data: Nigeria c. 1970–1985'. mimeo, Oxford University.

National Planning Commission (2004) *National Economic Empowerment and Development Strategy (NEEDS)*. Abuja: National Planning Commission.

Okojie, C.E. and H. Oaikhenan (2005) 'Importance of Oil and Gas to the Nigerian Economy' in A.A. Owosekun *et al.* (eds) *Contemporary Issues in the Management of the Nigerian Economy*. Ibadan: NISER.

Orubu, C.O. (2002) 'The Development and Contribution of the Petroleum Industry to the Nigerian Economy' in M.A. Iyoha and C.O. Itsede (eds) *Nigerian Economy: Structure, Growth and Development*. Benin City: Mindex Publishing.

Ribadu, N. (2010) *Show Me the Money*. Washington, DC: Center for Global Development.

Usman, S. (2009) 'Nigeria: Scorching the Resource Curse'. Paper presented at the London School of Economics and Political Science.

Further Reading

Collier, P., C. Soludo and C. Pattillo (eds) (2008) *Economic Policy Options for a Prosperous Nigeria*. New York: Macmillan.

United Nations Development Programme (2006) *Niger Delta Development Report*. Abuja: UNDP.

Appendix

Table A.7.1 GDP, oil rents, gross capital formation, construction and debt (nominal – current $)

Year	GDP (bn current $)	Oil rents (bn current $)	Gross fixed capital formation (bn current $)	Construction (bn current $)	Total external debt stock (bn current $)
1970	11.12	0.41	3.18	0.66	0.84
1971	13.49	0.85	4.25	0.92	0.96
1972	16.18	1.09	5.01	1.17	1.08
1973	21.14	1.96	5.53	1.27	1.78
1974	32.69	8.76	7.65	1.63	1.88
1975	39.76	6.52	13.07	2.34	1.69
1976	48.44	8.43	18.69	3.08	1.34
1977	54.16	9.17	20.27	3.34	3.15
1978	60.59	8.44	20.35	3.49	5.09
1979	74.80	25.18	21.96	3.92	6.24
1980	93.18	26.11	29.36	4.90	8.92
1981	114.48	17.16	40.32	4.51	11.42
1982	112.51	13.69	35.95	3.71	11.97
1983	113.24	11.65	26.05	3.12	17.56
1984	112.37	12.58	15.98	2.49	17.77
1985	111.51	12.53	13.34	1.72	18.64
1986	56.37	5.58	8.54	1.10	22.21
1987	34.82	7.11	4.74	0.54	29.02
1988	41.77	5.96	4.96	0.55	29.62
1989	37.75	9.00	4.43	0.52	30.12
1990	42.61	12.54	6.07	0.54	33.44
1991	39.91	10.65	5.48	0.50	33.53
1992	36.22	10.66	4.62	0.35	29.02
1993	35.33	9.39	4.79	0.36	30.74
1994	28.28	8.76	3.16	0.29	33.09
1995	28.77	9.76	2.17	0.21	34.09
1996	30.78	13.33	2.44	0.18	31.41
1997	32.17	13.13	3.55	0.22	28.45
1998	33.41	7.54	4.33	0.31	30.29
1999	34.06	10.57	2.34	0.30	29.13
2000	46.39	20.06	3.26	0.30	31.35
2001	44.14	17.16	3.35	0.37	31.04
2002	59.12	14.90	4.14	0.40	30.48
2003	67.66	20.44	6.70	0.46	34.70
2004	87.85	30.32	6.49	1.25	37.88
2005	112.25	44.62	6.13	1.64	22.18
2006	145.43	50.91	12.02	1.95	3.50

Source: World Bank, Genuine Savings Project and UNSTATS.

Table A.7.2 GDP, oil rents, gross capital formation, construction and debt (real – 1990$)

Year	GDP (bn 1990 $)	Oil rents (bn 1990 $)	Gross fixed capital formation (bn 1990 $)	Construction (bn 1990 $)	Total external debt stock (bn 1990 $)	GDP deflator (1990 =100)
1970	30.20	1.11	7.04	0.44	2.27	37
1971	34.57	2.17	7.91	0.57	2.46	39
1972	37.19	2.51	9.34	0.66	2.49	44
1973	40.59	3.77	8.90	0.66	3.42	52
1974	45.65	12.24	9.87	0.66	2.63	72
1975	44.76	7.34	14.22	0.72	1.90	89
1976	47.67	8.30	18.66	0.92	1.32	102
1977	49.94	8.45	20.04	1.02	2.90	108
1978	47.57	6.63	18.40	0.98	4.00	127
1979	44.89	15.11	16.90	0.98	3.75	167
1980	43.34	12.15	19.37	1.06	4.15	215
1981	40.64	6.09	20.16	1.04	4.05	282
1982	40.21	4.89	15.63	0.83	4.28	280
1983	38.18	3.93	10.25	0.73	5.92	297
1984	37.41	4.19	6.56	0.60	5.92	300
1985	40.52	4.55	6.19	0.41	6.78	275
1986	36.98	3.66	5.38	0.41	14.57	152
1987	33.00	6.74	4.11	0.45	27.51	105
1988	35.49	5.06	4.29	0.50	25.17	118
1989	37.78	9.01	4.38	0.52	30.15	100
1990	42.61	12.54	6.07	0.54	33.44	100
1991	42.34	11.30	6.05	0.56	35.57	94
1992	42.53	12.52	5.87	0.59	34.08	85
1993	43.42	11.53	6.81	0.62	37.77	81
1994	43.81	13.57	6.11	0.63	51.27	65
1995	43.68	14.82	4.51	0.65	51.76	66
1996	45.86	19.86	5.33	0.66	46.79	67
1997	47.14	19.24	5.80	0.70	41.70	68
1998	48.42	10.93	5.51	0.74	43.91	69
1999	48.65	15.10	5.35	0.77	41.61	70
2000	51.24	22.16	6.26	0.80	34.64	91
2001	53.50	20.80	4.90	0.90	37.63	82
2002	55.53	13.99	5.89	0.94	28.63	106
2003	61.28	18.51	8.85	1.02	31.43	110
2004	81.95	28.28	6.73	0.95	35.34	107
2005	84.77	33.69	6.02	1.07	16.75	132
2006	91.16	31.91	11.36	1.20	2.19	160

Source: World Bank, Genuine Savings Project and UNSTATS.

Table A.7.3 Fiscal balance and current account balance

Year	Fiscal balance (% GDP)	Current account balance (% GDP)
1980	N/A	8.85
1981	N/A	−10.01
1982	N/A	−13.67
1983	N/A	−14.06
1984	−3.37	−4.40
1985	−2.01	−1.15
1986	−2.80	−18.75
1987	−6.94	−5.96
1988	NA	−8.96
1989	NA	2.77
1990	NA	7.62
1991	NA	−1.19
1992	NA	−4.34
1993	NA	−12.04
1994	NA	−8.12
1995	NA	−4.25
1996	NA	4.15
1997	1.20	4.79
1998	−14.00	−9.24
1999	−7.40	−9.03
2000	6.40	12.48
2001	−3.30	4.60
2002	−4.20	−13.01
2003	−1.30	−6.02
2004	6.30	5.53
2005	8.10	6.46
2006	7.00	26.52

NA, not available.

Source: IMF (GFS, Article IV Consultation Reports and WEO Dataset) and UNSTATS.

8
The Contest for Control
Oil and gas management in Russia

Valery Kryukov, Anatoly Tokarev and Shamil Yenikeyeff

8.1 Introduction

The oil and gas sector has traditionally played a highly important role not only in the Russian mineral complex, but also in the domestic economy. Currently, the hydrocarbon sector accounts for 60 per cent of Russian export revenues and contributes over 45 per cent to the federal budget. As a result, this sector has been a driving force behind the economic development of the entire country and especially so for the oil- and gas-producing regions.

Since the collapse of the Soviet Union in 1991, Russian policies and legislative efforts in relation to natural resource management have been at the cornerstone of domestic political and economic processes. Unfortunately, the Russian government has been unable to promote a system of adequate mechanisms for motivating oil and gas companies to develop hydrocarbon resources in a socially effective way. This results not only from the complexity of creating modern hydrocarbon resource management systems, but is also a result of a clash of diverse interests within the federal centre, regions, oil and gas companies and their owners.

This chapter seeks to examine decision-making processes and procedures in relation to natural resource management and the use of hydrocarbon revenues in Russia in the 1990s and the 2000s. As Russia is a federal state, relations between the federal government and the resource-rich regions have played the main role in shaping a system of resource management, licensing and taxation.

In this respect, Russia has gone through two stages of development:

- 1992–2001 The formation of a decentralized model, based on the active participation of the resource-rich regions and non-governmental organizations (NGOs), representing diverse interest groups; emergence of new private corporate entities;
- 2002–present Transition to a highly centralized bureaucratic model

of resource management in the oil and gas sector dominated by the federal government; the state has increased its political and economic presence in the oil and gas sector by securing direct control over key rents and corporate assets (such as Gazprom and Rosneft).

The first period was characterized by the substantial control of hydrocarbon rents by certain individuals, as well as newly formed independent financial–industrial groups. The subsequent period has been characterized by the strong will of government (primarily at the federal level) to establish the basis for a modern system of resource management as well as an economically efficient use of hydrocarbon revenues.

In the 1990s, the main government agenda was to implement policy reforms vital for the establishment of a new resource management system in Russia. In the government's opinion, the main task of the new system was to ensure the accumulation of a bulk of resource rents into the state budget (at the federal as well as the regional level). The World Bank and the International Monetary Fund (IMF) also proposed similar policies to the Russian government. The essence of these proposals was to consolidate the largest part of oil and gas revenues into the state budget, which could then be used to promote social stability and to support less competetive sectors of the national economy. The idea was to provide a chance for the uncompetitive sectors to utilize state money in order to overcome the transition period to a market economy. The oil and gas sector, on the other hand, could be financed through loans provided by the international financial institutions (such as the above-mentioned IMF, World Bank, as well as the European Bank for Reconstruction and Development).

As of 2002, the federal centre started to implement a policy of strengthening its role in the oil and gas sector, but stopped short of improving the economic and long-term efficiency of the existing resource management system.

Overall, this period saw a notable attempt by the government to promote a highly centralized system of planning, adopting and implementing decisions regarding the natural resource sector. As part of this process, the federal centre effectively curtailed most of the excesses of the previous period, associated with the decisive role of regional authorities and financial–industrial groups in Russia's political and economic system (Kryukov and Tokarev, 2007). However, although the current system has managed to correct the excesses of the 1990s, it has failed to form a modern and effective model of resource management.

The successful utilization of oil and gas revenues, collected through designated taxation and accumulated into the national budget and into special funds, illustrates the level of public efficiency of a resource management system. Rates of savings, investments and consumption are key indicators used to examine the efficiency of an existing system. Unfortunately, in the Russian case, it is highly problematic to establish and assess such indicators in a transparent and comparable manner. In Russia, oil and gas revenues (apart from the share accumulated in special funds) are transferred into a common financial pool composed of federal or regional budgets. Once transferred, it is difficult to establish relations between the income and expenditure segments of these budgets.

In the authors' opinion, it is more accurate to compare such figures on the basis of:

- oil and gas income and the size of socially oriented expenditures in the relevant budget;
- oil and gas income and the level of debt repayment.[1]

In contrast to the data problems inherent within Russia's federal and regional budgets (as described in Section 8.4.3), special funds present an improved situation due to the relative clarity and transparency of the available data. However, these funds were formed at the federal level only in 2004, making the previous historical period a challenging one to examine.

8.2 Evolution of natural resource management in Russia

8.2.1 Development of natural resources and the decision-making processes

Since the collapse of the Soviet Union in 1991, oil, gas, diamonds, precious metals, nickel and aluminium have been the main commodities generating considerable economic rents during the transition period of the Russian economy (Yenikeyeff, 2011).[2] In the 1990s, oil was contested by the federal centre and by the regions as the main commodity generating considerable rents during volatile economic conditions, thus ensuring a certain degree of social stability and political survival of the ruling elites.

The division of authority rights over mineral resources in Russia has been one of the main outcomes of the centre–periphery bargaining game of the early 1990s. For example, in 1990–1991, the Parliaments of Russia's ethnic republics (including oil-rich Tatarstan, Bashkortostan, Komi and Udmurtia) adopted Declarations on State Sovereignty, proclaiming their sole jurisdiction over local natural resources. This claim was subsequently included within the ethnic republics' constitutions and relevant local legislation.[3] The Federation Treaty of 31 March 1992 also declared all natural resources to be the property of local populations.[4] Although the Russian Constitution of December 1993 abolished this principle, four ethnic republics (Tatarstan, Bashkortostan, Udmurtia and Yakutia) continued to assert their 'sovereign' authority over local natural resources. In response, the federal legislation on natural resources vaguely defined federal and regional authority over the subsoil in order to pacify the separatist regions. Thus, divergent views on the role and place of the federal centre and the regions in the resource management system found their way into the legislation.

On the one hand, the legislation established the principle of joint jurisdiction over natural resources (the 'two-keys' system), whereas on the other hand, it envisaged the division of ownership rights over the subsoil in accordance with the administrative–territorial state hierarchy. In this context, the 1992 federal law 'On Subsoil' introduced the concept of the division of all the subsoil into three categories: federal; regional; and municipal.

The result of this 'spontaneous' arrangement regarding rights over subsoil use (which concerned not only oil and gas, but also other mineral resources, such as diamonds, gold and iron ore) was the legislative reinforcement of joint jurisdiction. This principle asserted the existence of equal rights for both the federal government and a given region in their dealings with subsoil issues. It is important to note that this approach ensured that a given resource-rich region would receive a portion of resource rents (Kryukov *et al.*, 2004).

Therefore, the law 'On Subsoil' served as the legislative foundation for the resource management system. This normative legal base was founded on the principles of:

- fee-based subsoil use;
- equal access to fields for all relevant state agencies;
- licensed rights to subsoil use;
- transparent distribution of rents. Particularly important is that, until 2001, the law 'On Subsoil' defined not only the methods by which rental incomes were to be collected, but also the proportion of their distribution between the federal government and the resource-rich regions where the mineral resources were produced. The federal government received 40 per cent and the regions 60 per cent, of which half was set aside for the municipal government and half for the regional budget;

- joint jurisdiction between the federal government and a given resource-rich region.

In the 1990s, the Russian oil and gas sector also experienced major institutional changes through the formation of a completely new corporate environment in the oil and gas sector. During this period, the assets of the former state enterprises, responsible for exploration, production, refining and distribution of petroleum products, were consolidated under an umbrella of newly established vertically integrated companies. The new oil conglomerates made sure to secure under their control the key industrial assets essential for incorporating the entire technologically linked chain of oil production, refining and petroleum product sales. Several companies were established on this principle, including private corporate entities, such as Lukoil, Surgutneftegaz and Yukos, as well as the state oil company, Rosneft, which managed a large share of the state's oil industrial assets. At the same time, the assets of the state pipeline system were transferred under the control of the state company, Transneft, whereas the assets of the Ministry of Gas Industry were incorporated under the umbrella of the newly established state gas concern, Gazprom. Apart from these vertically integrated companies, several other (partially integrated) regional companies were established, such as Tatneft, Bashneft and KomiTEK. The formation of these regional oil companies without federal involvement was possible because of the political weakness of the federal centre at this time, as well as the growing strength of regional elites in some key resource-rich Russian provinces, such as Bashkortostan, Tatarstan, Udmurtia and Komi Republic.

The economic and financial potential of the large vertically integrated oil companies was considerably greater than that of many regions, making them highly influential at the federal level. At the same time, partially integrated regional oil companies were fully controlled by regional administrations and local governors.

As soon as all regional heads began to be elected by popular vote, federal companies began to experience the full-scale control of provincial authorities over new oil fields that the companies sought to develop and over the existing oil resources that they had initially received. The regions flexed the power afforded to them under the 'two-keys' system to extract concessions from the oil companies operating in their territories in the form of various social, financial, constructional and environmental projects. The oil giants provided credit to local agricultural and industrial producers, established grants to educational organizations, built roads, hospitals and houses, and sold petroleum products to local consumers at discounted prices. In other words, regional elites used the 'two-keys' system to extract resources from federal oil companies to maintain local socio-economic stability and thus voter satisfaction.

As the federal government was not directly involved in the management of Russia's natural resources in the 1990s, resource-rich regions became the driving force behind the development of a joint jurisdiction system. In this respect, the legislative and executive bodies of these regions adopted relevant laws and administrative procedures, and also established relevant regional executive agencies to oversee the subsoil use.

Legislators in some resource-rich territories sought to transform the fundamental principles of natural resource use. A few pre-existing norms and procedures were abolished, namely the free-of-charge access to resources, the anonymity of the owner and the lack of control systems and effective administration in the regions' efforts to promote the efficient use of natural resources. For example, in the Tyumen region, legislators and the majority of oil and gas companies facilitated intensive discussions on the following issues (Shafranik and Kryukov, 2000):

- utilizing regional authority to ensure a stable revenue flow from the oil and gas sector into local and regional budgets;
- implementation of strict environmental regulations for areas of oil and gas production;
- establishment of legal limits on the development and expansion of oil and gas operations in regions where traditional forms of economic management were practised by indigenous people of the north (Kryukov and Tokarev, 2005);
- participation in the decision-making processes involving the examination and implementation of development plans for new oil and gas fields.

Later in the 1990s, the lack of detailed procedures on conflict resolution between the centre and the regions over resource management issues, and the absence of a civil system of social norms and legal procedures in general, led to the inefficiency of the joint jurisdiction system in Russia. In 2001, the federal government introduced new administrative reforms aimed at the 'harmonization' of regional and federal laws, and the centralization of decision-making regarding resource management.

However, the highly centralized system of resource management introduced after 2001, rather than tackling the deficiencies and excesses of the previous period, led to an over-bureaucratization of the decision-making processes and of the coordination efforts between administrative institutions. As a result, the resource-rich regions became sidelined from active participation in mineral resource management, and are currently being excluded from the distribution of rents from the extraction of hydrocarbon resources. If, for instance, in the 1990s the share of rents reached approximately 50–60 per cent of the budget of Khanty-Mansiysk autonomous okrug (KMAO, the largest oil-producing region in Russia), by 2008 this share decreased to 2–3 per cent and, by 2010, to zero.

The abolition of the 'two-keys' principle resulted in considerably reduced opportunities for the regions and, therefore, the population, to participate in policy formation regarding the use of natural resources and, thus, the overall socio-economic development of these territories.

Since 2004, the Russian federal legislation has completely altered the regulatory authority of the centre and the regions over subsoil use. A more democratic and transparent system of resources management in the 1990s was thus replaced by a highly centralized and bureaucratic system. In this respect, regional authority was limited only to fields of local significance (as opposed to those of federal or strategic significance) and which contained commonly occurring minerals. At the same time, regions began to play a 'static' role in implementing the federal guidelines for subsoil use. The federal administrative powers increased substantially, whereas the role of the regions, along with the municipalities and NGOs, was limited to the work of commissions charged with supervising whether the guidelines for subsoil use were adhered to. At the moment, these commissions do not have clear legislative status or authority. A given region's control over resource management depends on the bargaining power of its governor vis-à-vis the federal centre.

A further step in the bureaucratization of decision-making with regard to subsoil usage was taken in April 2008, when the definition of 'strategic' resources was introduced into Russian legislation. The exploration and extraction of natural resources from federal fields have gained strategic importance in the 'protection of the country and the government'. Fields bearing federal significance include those that:

- contain natural resources in excess of 70 million tonnes of oil; in excess of 50 billion cubic metres of gas; in excess of 50 tonnes of vein gold; in excess of 500,000 tons of copper;
- are located in the inland sea water, territorial sea water and the continental shelf of the Russian Federation.

Fields that fit these categories are transferred to state companies (or companies with governmental stakes) on a sole source basis. As a result of these measures introduced in 2008, the principle of bureaucratic admin-istration in dealing with issues of resource management became domi-nant.

8.2.2 Licensing policy in the oil and gas sector

Licensing policy is an important aspect of resource management: it can significantly reduce monopolistic tendencies within the mineral resources industry, and can also create conditions for the optimization of expenditures and the development of an effective institutional struc-ture (Kryukov *et al.*, 2002).

The difficult financial conditions of the 1990s led regional authorities to hold as many natural resource auctions and tenders as possible. When dealing with resources under joint jurisdiction, regions resorted to applying their exclusive ownership rights over local natural resources or employed the 'two-keys' principle. The main intention behind sales of licences (access rights) was not necessarily to provide solutions to the vast spectrum of socio-economic issues of the time, but rather to receive one-off payments (bonuses). In order to garner larger bonuses, regions auctioned off their best possessions, such as the Priobsk oil field (KMAO), the Yurobcheno-Takhomsk oil field (Evenkiisky autonomous okrug), the Talakan oil field (Yakutia) and the Kovyktinsk gas field (Irkutsk region). As a result of such practices, the regions lessened their opportunities to address future socio-economic issues within an improved resource management system, which could have come about from the use of access rights as strategic levers (Kryukov, 1998).

Despite the large number of successfully completed resource licensing auctions and tenders, many licences were not used by the companies that had won them. The number of unused licences, or licences with multiple violations, attests to the underdeveloped conditions that were present within the administrative institutions at differing levels of power. For example, the fundamental by-law, 'Resolution on licensing proce-dures' (1992), did not establish supervisory powers for Russian regions, implying that the norms set out in the federal law 'On Subsoil' were not developed. Regions did not have clear legislative authority over early termination, suspension or limitation of subsoil licences: the licensing procedures resolution states that subsoil licences can be terminated early, suspended and limited only by the Russian Ministry of Natural Resources or its respective regional branches. Therefore, the procedures for regional participation in this process were not clearly defined.

Throughout the 1990s and early 2000s, the federal centre and the regions held many resource licensing auctions in order to secure auction bonuses and subsequent tax payments to their respective budgets, which were vital for ensuring socio-economic stability. Whereas regional administrations were more interested in using these budgetary funds for solving pressing socio-economic problems, the federal centre was solely interested in securing tax payments from oil and gas production. Regions began to promote company–region licensing agreements, which contained additional company obligations in relation to urgent socio-economic projects in the region, soon after the regional rents share decreased in favour of the federal centre.

During the 2000s, the strengthening role of the state became the main impetus behind the changes to the Russian oil and gas sector's regulatory regime. As power became more concentrated at the federal level, improving the 'manageability' of subsoil usage became a governmental priority. The government hence obtained practically all rents from the oil and gas companies and gained direct control over key industry assets (such as Gazprom and Rosneft), in what can be considered the government's hard answer to the soft oil and gas sector business practices of the 1990s. Having thus restored relative control over the sector, the government's most important task at hand now became the fine-tuning of the resource management system, including the mobilization of investment into new projects and districts, along with strengthening the monitoring and oversight over field development.

Overall, the unfavourable conditions surrounding the licensing policy can be attributed to the following components:

- the fiscal orientation of national economic policy concerning the oil and gas sector;
- the ambiguity and contradictions of the principle of joint jurisdiction in practice;
- competition among different governmental institutions;
- underdeveloped and unclear regulatory measures concerning the role of licensing agreements in subsoil use, resulting in a weak legal basis for claims against oil companies;
- lack of recourse regulations, including the termination of licences due to violation of the agreement.

The main consequences of an ineffective licensing system for the use of hydrocarbon fields in Russia are:

- a significant number of unused licences (or licences that are being violated);
- lack of opportunity for efficient utilization of extracted hydrocarbon materials, as in the case of associated gas;

- lack of a stable and functioning financing system for general geological surveys of the territories.

8.2.3 The changing nature of mineral resource management in Russia

The increased role of the federal government through centralization has definitively shaped Russian legislation on subsoil use. Table 8.1 presents the most important changes made to the principal subsoil use legislation in Russia, and the state policy in the oil and gas sector.

As a result of the changes made to hydrocarbon regulations over time, the following significant developments took place in Russia as of 2001:

- a shift in the government's 'negotiating powers' vis-à-vis parties involved within the oil and gas sector, resulting in a strengthened

Table 8.1 Legislation on subsoil usage and government policy

Issues regarding subsoil use	First versions of the law on subsoil (since 1992)	Current legislation and policy on subsoil use passed after 2001
Subsoil ownership	State (federal–regional) ownership	State (federal) ownership
Oil and gas resource management	Joint jurisdiction between the Federation and the regions	Federal control
The role of oil- and gas-rich regions in the licensing	'Two-keys' principle	Regional approval with the federal centre adopting the main decision
Distribution of rents[1]	Regulated by the law on subsoil use	Regulated by the tax and budget legislation
Regional share of hydrocarbon rental incomes	60% of the royalty	0–5% of the oil production tax, 0% of the gas production tax
Monitoring and oversight of subsoil development	Weak federal control	Conditions implemented for the strengthening of the federal role
The role of local authorities in subsoil management	Weak role	Practically absent
Recourse/turnover for the subsoil use rights	No provision	No formal provision, but exists in practice
Access rights for subsoil use	Licensing through auctions and tenders	Licensing through auctions and tenders
Access to subsoil	Equal access principle	Limited access to subsoil for foreign companies

[1] In this case, rents imply royalty and/or production tax, excluding export duties and excise taxes.

role for the federal centre through administrative reforms and a consolidation of the 'power vertical';

- revenues from the oil and gas sector became the 'nuclei' of the country's entire financial system as a result of the rising oil prices and subsequent increase in the volume of rents. This, in turn, had a direct impact on the norms and regulations associated with rental tax collection and distribution.

8.3 How effective is the tax policy?

The basic characteristics of Russia's oil and gas taxation system include: flexibility of norms and regulations; tax optimization opportunities for companies; and an inclusive role for oil- and gas-producing regions in implementing tax policies. On the basis of these characteristics, one could divide the evolution of Russia's taxation system into the following stages.

Stage I. Formation of a fee-based system for subsoil usage (1992–2001):

- 1992–95 Creation of a new taxation system, based on the Russian law 'On Subsoil'; this period of political and economic transition was characterized by the widespread use of non-market mechanisms for the collection and distribution of rents, including price control measures;
- 1995–99 Resource-producing regions implement active tax policies combined with limited use of differentiated (flexible) taxation. Low oil prices in external markets are partially responsible for the active application of transfer pricing policies by oil and gas producers as well as tax optimization strategies aimed at maintaining minimum profitability in times of volatile economic conditions;
- 2000–01 Widespread use of tax optimization strategies by oil and gas producers; a gradual withdrawal of governmental policies on differentiated taxation also takes place.

Stage II. Development of a new taxation system:

- 2002–06 The role of regions in resource management is weakened; introduction of the mineral production tax becomes an effective solution to the problem of transfer pricing; absence of flexible approaches towards the collection of rental incomes;
- 2007–present Increased use of flexible taxation in oil production; a monitoring and oversight system for subsoil use is gradually developing.

As a result, distribution of oil rents in Russia changed drastically (see Figure 8.1).

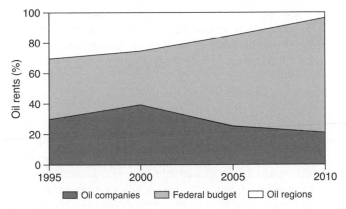

Figure 8.1 Distribution of oil rents in Russia

Improvement of the taxation system is a vital component of effective oil and gas resource management, along with an efficient regulation of hydrocarbon development and production, the licensing system and access to transport infrastructures. Such improvements are best made in stages and in sync with the reform of other elements within the resource management system.

8.3.1 Tax policy in the oil and gas sector from 1992 to 2001

The taxation of oil and gas production is of crucial importance to the Russian federal budget, as well as the budgets of oil- and gas-producing regions. The foundations for a new system of taxation in the oil and gas sector were established in 1992 when special taxes, designed to accumulate rents for the state budget, were introduced alongside regular taxes. The main mechanisms for the acquisition of rents from 1992 to 2001 included the mineral resource reproduction tax (MRRT), oil and gas excise taxes, royalties and export duties.

The MRRT comprised up to 10 per cent of marketable oil and gas production, and was absorbed by the federal and regional budgets. From 1992 to 2001, the primary purpose of the MRRT was to finance and support geological explorations, and it was justified as a measure of transitional economics. However, a significant portion of the MRRT was diverted to other areas which had no direct relation to oil and gas exploration.

From 1992 to 2001, the excise duties on oil served as one of the mechanisms for the acquisition of rents. This tax was forwarded to the federal budget in its entirety. From the perspective of the oil- and gas-producing regions, excise duties helped to shape the main regional tax bases. The increase in excise duty rates led to a reduction in the tax base, calculated on the basis of marketable production, including the redistribution of tax payments between the federal budget and the oil- and gas-producing regions.

A significant portion of oil and gas taxes, which went to the government prior to 2002, came from royalties. The share of royalties comprised 6–16 per cent of gross revenue/the value of marketable oil and gas production. The average royalty rate was 8 per cent for oil and 14 per cent for gas. The dependency of royalties on the market price of hydrocarbons resulted in considerable state transactional costs during the time of economic transformation, when domestic oil and companies adopted the practice of transfer pricing (Tokarev, 2000).

An important feature of royalties was their distribution between the different levels of the state hierarchy. The federal government received 40 per cent and the regions 60 per cent, of which half was set aside for the municipal government and half for the regional budget. As the greater part of royalty payments was sent to the regional budgets during the period 1992–2001, the federal government did not initially address the problem of transfer pricing in the oil and gas sector.

From 1995 to 2001, oil- and gas-producing regions placed additional conditions for the exemption of certain categories of fields from royalties. Such exemptions were particularly important for companies involved in the later stages of development of the oil- and gas-producing provinces and mature fields.

Hydrocarbon taxation policy has shown that, in order to build a rental-oriented taxation system which, from the government's point of view, is effective, it is necessary to have a number of pre-existing conditions, such as the:

- transparency of the hydrocarbon sector or government involvement (both regional and federal) within oil and gas company ownership;
- existence of a competitive environment at the regional level;
- development of a resource management system and also the presence of adequate monitoring and field development supervision systems;
- presence of a meaningful tax policy at the regional level.

During the 1990s, large-scale transformations occurred within the oil and gas sector in Russia. Vertically integrated oil companies responsible for the entire production process (from geological exploration and extraction to the marketing of processed products for consumers) were established during this time. Such companies had great influence on the effectiveness of the acquisition mechanisms for mineral rent.

The volume of payable hydrocarbon taxes (special and general taxes for all economic sectors) is mainly determined by the market price of oil and gas. Oil prices, used to determine the tax base, develop primarily within the framework of vertically integrated oil companies. In order to lower tax payments (especially royalties and the MRRT prior to 2001), companies broadly applied lowered transfer prices. Another important aspect of transfer pricing is that it allows the transfer of the tax base from producing regions to other regions and to optimize the general level of the tax burden.

The scale of transfer pricing can be demonstrated through a comparison of the share of tax payments by oil company Surgutneftegaz, which mostly did not use lowered pricing, with other oil companies (Table 8.2). Although responsible for only 25 per cent of oil production, Surgutneftegaz contributed about 50 per cent to all KMAO budget revenues in 1999–2001.

From 1998 to 2000, intercorporate pricing had a real negative effect on KMAO's budget – a territory that accounts for more than 55 per cent of Russian oil production. According to the Russian Accounts Chamber, the tax burden across different enterprises varied by a factor of two or three. As a result of the use of transfer pricing by oil companies, the KMAO budget sustained losses of $0.2 billion and $0.96 billion in 1999 and 2000 respectively.

Russian Institute for Financial Studies estimates reveal the scale of tax optimization in the oil sector (Vygon, 2002). In 2000, one of the most 'successful' years in terms of tax optimization in the hydrocarbon sector, tax evasion resulted in the loss of $4.9 billion. Throughout the period 2000–02, the consolidated Russian budget lost $3–5 billion annually (depending on price levels and volumes of production)

Table 8.2 Tax payments of the leading oil and gas companies (US$ per tonne)

Companies	1999	2000
LUKoil	26.1	42.3
Surguneftegas	43.6	72.4
Rosneft	38.4	60.2
Slavneft	21.9	34.8

Source: Report on the influence of oil and gas sector development on the formation of the Russian federal budget. Moscow, RF Accounts Chamber, 2001.

(Tokarev, 2003). Experts estimate that, at the same time, rents in the oil sector comprised around $25–30 billion in 2000–01.

The above-mentioned weaknesses in tax policy necessitated various modifications. This resulted in the development of a new system of taxation for the oil and gas sector starting in 2002.

8.3.2 Development of the special tax system in the 2000s

Significant changes occurred in the oil and gas taxation system when a production tax on mineral resources was introduced in 2002. The MRRT, excise duties and royalties were replaced by a production tax. A specific tax base rate (roubles per tonne) was introduced. The base rate is adjusted according to movements in global oil prices.

The creation of a specific *production tax* for hydrocarbons was an indication of the government's inability to establish norms and regulations that could have helped limit transfer pricing opportunities for oil and gas companies (Kryukov and Tokarev, 2006).

The key advantages of the production tax include the simplicity of its operation in terms of both the methods used for its calculation as well as the administrative costs involved. Another benefit of the production tax was its efficiency in counteracting transfer pricing practices previously employed by domestic oil companies. For example, the production tax (until 2007) applied a uniform rate for all hydrocarbon fields, regardless of their specific conditions, whereas the previously used royalties took into account the geological or economic diversity of different fields.

Under the new framework, 80 per cent of the production tax went to the federal budget, whereas the hydrocarbon-producing regions received 20 per cent. Subsequently, the regional share of the production tax for oil was reduced to 5 per cent, while the entire tax for gas production was retained by the federal budget. In September 2009, the government adopted new amendments to the Budgetary Code, which intends to abolish the regional oil tax share starting in 2010 when the federal centre will collect the 5 per cent share currently retained by the regions. As a result, the new taxation system has further lowered incomes for hydrocarbon-producing provinces.

The production tax immediately became the object of harsh criticism as it failed to take into account the diverse levels of development among hydrocarbon fields, because the degree of the field depletion determines the level of production expenditures. In view of this, in 2007, a more flexible and differentiated approach to the production tax was introduced, which focused on:

- the level of field depletion when estimating the production tax. For example, if depletion exceeds 80 per cent, it is possible to apply a reduction coefficient when calculating the production tax. 'Mature' oil- and gas-producing regions, such as Tatarstan and Bashkortostan, benefited especially from these new rules;
- the use of a zero tax rate for Eastern Siberian oil fields (applicable until production reaches 25 million tonnes in certain fields).

In addition to the production tax, *export duties on hydrocarbons* also play an important role in generating revenues for the federal budget. In 2002, Russian oil export duties began to be determined by a flexible scale system based on global oil prices.[5] Although this new approach significantly increased the tax burden for oil companies, it established clearer and more predictable rules for investors. If in the past the system of rates was regulated by governmental decrees, the new clearly defined system of export duties is based on a federal law. This new formula for collecting export duties is also more flexible in nature, helping to avoid the drastic fluctuations that tended to occur under the pre-2001 gradual scale system.

In the current context, the tax burden levied on oil companies has become considerably higher. This leads to lower geological exploration activities, slow development of new oil and gas areas and an increase in the number of abandoned wells in mature fields. For example, when oil prices soared above US$60 per barrel, the government used the taxation system to collect more than 80 per cent of companies' additional revenues (Figure 8.2). At the same time, oil companies faced a significant increase in oil extraction expenditures. For instance, 2006–07 witnessed a near 50 per cent rise in pipeline costs for the hydrocarbon sector. During this period, domestic oil companies also experienced rising costs as a result of the strengthening of the rouble in relation to the US dollar (used in Russian export contracts).

Since 2007, the government has been more responsive and efficient with regard to changes in oil industry taxation. For instance, it initiated a number of changes in the taxation system aimed at resolving specific problems, such as the reduction in the tax burden, stimulation of oil development in new areas and the modification of the preferential tax regime for developed 'old' fields (Table 8.3).

Another important challenge facing the hydrocarbon sector is improvement in the taxation system for the gas industry (Kryukov *et al.*, 2006). At the moment, there is a uniform production tax in place for all fields regardless of field depletion (maturity), an absence of mechanisms to stimulate the development of new gas areas, as well as a lack of any

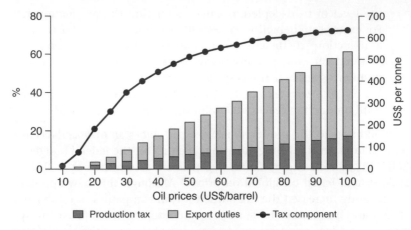

Figure 8.2 Production tax and export duties in relation to oil prices

Note: The tax component – the level of the production tax and export duties in the price of exported oil (%).

correlation between gas prices in external markets and gas export duties.

Overall, production tax and export duties currently remain the principal mechanisms for the collection of rents in the oil and gas sector (Figure 8.3).

8.3.3 Oil taxation and investments

If, in 2003, the share of taxes within the revenues of Russian oil companies comprised 35 per cent, by 2005, these companies were required to transfer nearly 60 per cent of their revenues to the budget. This sudden change resulted from tax reforms initiated by the government in the

Table 8.3 Tax policy in the Russian oil and gas sector

Taxation problems within the oil and gas sector	Solutions
High tax burden levels for oil production	Modifications to the production tax formula, resulting in lower tax levels
Inadequate taxation system for the development of new oil areas	Introduction of a preferential tax regime (tax benefits) for oil production in specific new areas
Lack of a preferential tax regime (tax benefits) for mature fields	Changes to the way hydrocarbon production is valued during mature stages of field development
Lack of flexible taxation for the gas sector	Discussions continue with no real decisions reached yet

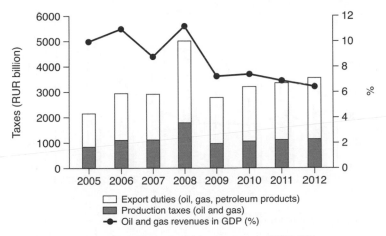

Figure 8.3 Russian federal budget oil and gas revenues, RUR billion

Source: Russian Ministry of Finance.

2000s, when the taxation of the oil and gas sector was substantially increased. Naturally, one would assume that companies, having paid their tax duties, would use a substantial portion of remaining revenues for investment into the sector, whereas the state would use the collected taxes as a means of ensuring socio-economic stability and for paying off any external debts.

However, in the Russian case, such assumptions are accurate only to a certain degree. The reality was that the largest part of oil revenues (and a smaller part of gas revenues) were transferred abroad. The remaining amount was used by Russian oil and gas companies for direct investments as well as for the acquisition of other domestic oil and gas companies.

In 2002, the Russian Accounts (Audit) Chamber highlighted that, prior to 2000, the investment situation in the oil and gas sector had been unsatisfactory and in a state of crisis. If, in 1990, investment levels in the Russian hydrocarbon sector reached 112 billion roubles, by 1999, they had decreased to 51.3 billion roubles. Equipment depreciation levels reached 50 per cent for oil production and 80 per cent for oil refining. More than half of the domestic oil trunk pipelines have been in operation for over 25 years, although their average working life is 30 years.

In the 2000s, investments in oil production increased (Figure 8.4). At the same time, the volume of direct investments into the industry never reached a level adequate for the maintenance of oil and gas

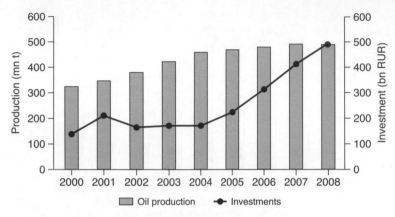

Figure 8.4 Russian oil production and investments

output and the development of new oil and gas fields and provinces (especially in Eastern Siberia).

It may be argued that a heavy tax burden levied upon the oil and gas sector by the government led to declining investment flows. Yet it is also important to note that, in 2000–05, Russian oil companies (such as Sibneft, YuKOS, TNK-BP and LUKoil) paid very high dividends to their shareholders, which often exceeded their corporate annual profits. Simultaneously, these companies transferred most of their financial assets abroad as part of a widespread capital flight. For example, according to the Central Bank of Russia estimates, by 2003, the Russian private sector had invested around $66 billion abroad. Even so, a number of experts assert that the real figure for Russian capital invested abroad reached over $300 billion (Bulatov, 2001). The Central Bank of Russia is unable to provide accurate figures on Russian capital flight because most of these funds were transferred abroad without the required registration procedure and without government permission.

There are several reasons for the lack of investment activities in the oil and gas sector:

- an unstable and unfriendly investment climate, including high tax burdens imposed on companies;
- the fragmented and inefficient nature of the state system of resource management in Russia;
- a pre-existing industrial infrastructure (developed in Soviet times) that has been advantageous for most Russian oil companies in the post-Soviet era. However, these same companies failed to re-invest

financial resources into the maintenance and refurbishment of the aged infrastructure, and to meet compliance with the technological rules and standards of the industry. Instead, some companies went so far as to use equipment and infrastructure depreciation payments as an additional source of revenue generation;

- a lack of financial resources, particularly for the implementation of key projects essential for further development of existing assets and resources, as well as for bringing new oil and gas fields on-stream.

8.4 To spend or to save? Issues confronting resource rents and special funds

Special financial funds (known as sovereign wealth funds or reserve funds) seek to facilitate sustainable socio-economic development in resource-rich countries by:

- promoting the accumulation of resource rents, which would otherwise be spent;
- prolonging the impact of lucrative resource-rich periods on the domestic economy and society for many generations to come;
- providing an additional source of income for the country and its regions;
- stimulating the diversification of the economy (Kryukov *et al.*, 1996; Warrack and Keddie, 1999; Fasano, 2000).

At the regional level, special financial funds are primarily intended to ensure sustainable development as hydrocarbon fields reach their production peak and maturity. At the national level, these funds also function as stabilizing mechanisms, ensuring the maintenance of a reasonable exchange rate, especially during periods of high oil prices. In this sense, the Russian Stabilization Fund was designed in 2004 along the same principles used in Norway and Chile, where special financial funds have played, and continue to play, such an important role.

In the Russian case, the level of investment functions of special funds is often seen as being linked to the level of inflation. However, direct investment into industrial fixed assets does not have a negative impact on inflation or the exchange balance. In fact, new real investments create new industrial assets, which promote reduced inflation levels (because of the growth of commodities relative to financial resources). These considerations led to the formation of the Russian Investment Fund, which aimed to boost Russia's economic development by promoting new investment projects. Practical realization of such projects through these special funds requires not only an adequate economic and industrial base, but also a developed civil society, political accountability and transparency of financial institutions.

8.4.1 Special financial funds in the 1990s: discussions at the federal level, real steps at the regional level

The development of natural resources has been widely perceived in modern Russian history as both a solution to pressing socio-economic problems, as well as a source for the formation of a modern economy that would ensure the stable, long-term development of the country. Russia is a resource-rich economy predominantly based upon the extraction, primary processing and sale of natural resources. Hence, Russia's economy faces problems similar to those of other resource-rich countries. Russia's biggest challenge is to transform its economy in order to make it less dependent on the raw materials sector. The successful development of high-tech and innovative (value-added) products and services could address these issues. A portion of rents from the extraction of raw materials can serve as a financial base for the diversification of the economy: discussions in Russia have focused on different ideas and approaches towards achieving such an 'appropriate' utilization of resource rents. Since the collapse of the USSR, the main discussions have revolved around the following topics:

* Should the rents from raw materials development be saved or spent?
* What roles should the federal centre and the resource-rich regions play in the utilization of resource rents?
* Should the resource rents go towards addressing urgent social issues or towards the modernization and diversification of the economy?
* What kind of legal frameworks and mechanisms should guide the use of funds drawn from resource rents?

There have been several approaches to the accumulation and utilization of resource rents in Russia, namely the formation of the Development Budget and special funds at the federal level and the creation of development funds (such as the Future Generations Funds) at the regional level.

The economic development of oil- and gas-producing regions is traditionally linked with key stages in the development of the local oil and gas sector. For instance, a newly discovered oil field and its subsequent development is likely to lead to intensive economic activity, including an influx of labour, rapid development of the relevant infrastructure and an emergence of new settlements for oil workers and personnel involved in support services. Conversely, with field depletion or unfavourable economic circumstances in external markets (such as low oil prices), there is bound to be a reduction in traditional economic activity. This leads to a number of socio-economic problems, such as growing unemployment and the lack of financial resources for the maintenance of vital local infrastructure. Therefore, the biggest challenge for oil- and gas-producing territories is how to establish and maintain stable conditions for their long-term socio-economic development (Kryukov, 2001a).

After the collapse of the USSR and during the subsequent economic transition in Russia, there were widespread attempts to form various development funds aimed at solving economic problems and facilitating economic and social stability specifically in resource-rich regions.

In the 1990s, the federal government did not have adequate financial resources to address vital socio-economic problems within the Russian regions, including the adequate maintenance of the social safety net, the healthcare and pension systems, and the vital regional infrastructure. As a result, the federal centre granted regional administrations considerable rights and responsibilities in relation to natural resource management and the formation of their own financial funds using a portion of the royalties. Thus, Moscow allowed the regions to form institutions that would facilitate the creation of conditions conducive to the stable, long-term socio-economic development of the periphery (Kryukov, 2001b).

For example, the KMAO Future Generations Fund was established in accordance with the local law on generation funds, in December 1994. It aimed to diversify the region's economy and to create supplementary budgetary sources once hydrocarbons became depleted. Until 2001, 15 per cent of regional royalties were transferred to the fund. From 2002, the KMAO Future Generations Fund received up to 15 per cent of the regional budget's share of the mineral production tax. In the 1990s and 2000s, around 15 per cent of regional rents (royalties and production tax) was saved in the main oil-rich regions.

The KMAO fund illustrates a balanced and well thought out approach to solving possible future problems in the resource-rich territories. The money is being invested not only into financial and fixed assets, but also into the development of human potential.[6]

Today, the fund allocates money for investment:

- in commercially efficient enterprises in the agro-industrial complex;

- into the creation of infrastructure for the forestry and wood-processing industries;
- into the creation of social infrastructures, including a winter sports centre, a children's physical education school, a state library and art gallery and a community centre 'Gostinny Dvor';
- in shareholdings in enterprises and banks;
- in property.

The Future Generations Fund aims to provide a material base for the region's socio-economic development. The Fund's assets comprise renewable fixed and financial resources, which supplement, and will eventually replace, tax payments from the production of oil and gas. The implementation of this approach should eliminate KMAO's one-sided dependency on oil development and should create guarantees for the provision of a high level of living standards and employment.

8.4.2 Changes at the federal level in the 2000s: from a stabilization fund to a system of funds

In 2000–03, the Russian government planned federal budgetary expenditures based on budget revenues generated under an oil price level of $20 per barrel. Although additional revenues accumulated during an era of higher oil prices (of more than $20 per barrel) were used to pay off Russia's external debt, no special financial institution (such as a stabilization fund) was established for this purpose. Since 2000, the federal government has primarily used oil and gas revenues to ensure the stability of its fiscal system. From 2000 to 2003, the Russian government focused on restoring macroeconomic stability, solving sovereign debt issues and protecting the budget and the entire economy from external price fluctuations. The ensuing fiscal policies proved relatively effective and prevented the economy from operating under a deficit.

Starting in 2004, the Russian government declared a transition to an 'active fiscal policy', directed at the creation of favourable conditions for economic development, resolution of the most urgent social problems and improvement in the efficiency of the public sector. As part of the tax reform measures addressed by these policies, rents from the production of mineral resources increased and were allocated to the federal budget, whereas the tax burden for other sectors of the economy was reduced.

Currently, one of the most contentious debates in Russian economic policy concerns the problems and implementation issues associated with the use of oil and gas government revenues. The Russian Ministry of Finance has taken a resilient stance on the necessity of creating state special funds. Its experts are aware of the fundamental issues, such as 'Dutch disease'.

Opponents of the concept of Russian special funds put forward the following concerns when arguing against the Russian Ministry of Finance's method of managing resource revenues: (Voronin, 2007):

- funds allocated from budget revenues, which are then invested into foreign stocks, can be considered a removal of resource rents from the country, thus benefiting foreign interests. As a result, the refinancing of the national economy is carried through foreign entities that receive Russian funds at nearly no cost. At the same time, these financial resources are later reintroduced through the private sector in the form of foreign bank loans, at higher interest rates;
- by collecting oil and gas revenues, the government impedes intersectoral capital flows and can hinder domestic economic activity, especially in the oil and gas sector;
- in contrast, investing oil and gas revenues into the national economy could benefit several issues, such as incurring high returns on currently 'frozen' governmental reserves, modernizing the economy through the development of high-technology sectors, helping to resolve issues regarding gross domestic product (GDP) growth, boosting living standards and lowering inflation.

However, according to the Russian Ministry of Finance, fiscal stability is most susceptible to a high budgetary dependence on oil and gas revenues. For instance, of particular concern are structural shifts resulting from the relatively slow growth of the oil and gas sector which, along with an increase in the real exchange rate of the rouble, have led to a decrease in the market share of this economic sector. In particular, when the tax burden for this sector considerably exceeds the tax burden in other sectors, a significant decrease in budgetary incomes could result. This can be exacerbated by any price fluctuations for hydrocarbons, as this would directly influence income from the oil and gas sector.

Therefore, the main features introduced by the federal government to improve the utilization of government resource revenues are:

- the accumulation of all rents into the federal budget;
- an emphasis on stabilizing the financial system, at the expense of infrastructure and production expenditures;
- the establishment of simple and transparent institutional arrangements to handle oil and gas revenues and improve resource management.

Nevertheless, during this period, the decision-making process becomes more bureaucratic, while simultaneously curtailing any participation from regional authorities and NGOs.

The significant exposure of the Russian economy and financial system to price fluctuations in the global oil markets was the core reason behind the formation of the Stabilization Fund. The Stabilization Fund was established in 2004, in accordance with the new Budget Code, with the intention of allocating revenues from hydrocarbon export duties and mineral resource production taxes into the Fund. The Stabilization Fund was designed to accumulate revenues from oil prices that exceeded the cut-off price set at $20 per barrel (increased to $27 per barrel in 2006) in order to balance the federal budget should oil prices fall below the cut-off level. In 2004–07, the Russian government used the Stabilization Fund to accumulate any additional hydrocarbon revenues. The Stabilization Fund secured around three-quarters of additional revenues due to high oil prices in external markets. The Fund's resources were then invested into foreign assets, converted into foreign currency or deposited into foreign banks.

Therefore, the Stabilization Fund was created to protect the national economy from negative consequences in the case of falling oil prices and to provide stabilization to the national currency in times of higher prices. The Stabilization Fund also played an important role as a mechanism to prevent inflation surges and to ensure currency stabilization during periods of trade surplus. By early 2008, the Russian national debt dropped to 7 per cent of its GDP as the result of a severe restriction on domestic borrowing, with almost a complete halt to external borrowing (in combination with preterm repayment of a considerable part of the national debt using Stabilization Fund resources). In effect, the Russian national debt, as a percentage of its GDP, became lower than its counterparts in other developed and transitional countries. Policy regarding early repayment of the national debt was a governmental reaction to the 1998 financial crisis, which sought to boost Russia's position within global financial markets and to relieve the national economy from a sizeable external debt accumulated in Soviet times and during the post-communist economic transition of the Yel'tsin era.

In January 2008, the Ministry of Finance split the Stabilization Fund into the Reserve Fund and the National Welfare Fund. The foreign currency reserves of each fund are denominated in US dollars (45 per cent), Euros (45 per cent) and GB pounds (10 per cent). As of 2008, oil and gas government revenues have been calculated separately from other federal budget revenues based upon: the production tax for oil

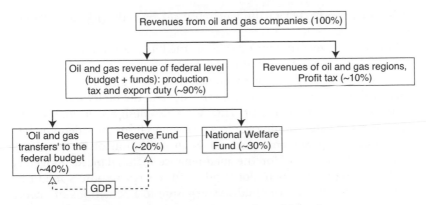

Figure 8.5 Oil and gas government revenues and special funds

Note: Estimated on the basis of Russian Ministry of Finance data for 2008.

and gas resources and export duties on oil; natural gas; and petroleum products.

A portion of oil and gas revenues defined as 'oil and gas transfers' are used annually to finance federal budget expenditures. The volume of oil and gas transfers is outlined in the law 'On the Federal Budget' for each upcoming fiscal year and planning period (Figure 8.5).

The proportion of 'oil and gas transfers' is determined according to the percentage of the predicted GDP amount for the year: 6.1 per cent in 2008; 5.5 per cent in 2009; 4.5 per cent in 2010; and 3.7 per cent in 2011. Once the amount of the oil and gas transfers is determined, the remainder of the hydrocarbon revenues is channelled into the Reserve Fund. The size of the Reserve Fund is defined by the 'Law on the Federal Budget' as a 10 per cent share of the predicted annual GDP. After the set limit for the Reserve Fund is reached, the remainder of the hydrocarbon revenues is collected into the National Welfare Fund (NWF).[7]

Revenues garnered from hydrocarbon development (in the framework of the state budget) are used for different purposes, such as the implementation of high-priority national projects and Federal Target Programmes, as well as contributing to the Russian Investment Fund. However, oil and gas revenues were only accumulated into the Stabilization Fund (until January 2008), and subsequently (from February 2008) shared between the Reserve Fund and the NWF.

The Reserve Fund is also used for making preterm repayments towards the external national debt. This reduces the federal budget tax burden, which may result from unplanned federal budget revenues, and also helps to preserve federal budget resources by reducing debt service expenditures.

The Russian government establishes the limits for authorized financial assets in the total volume of invested financial resources of the Reserve Fund. As mentioned earlier, Reserve Fund resources were intended to finance the oil and gas transfer and the preterm repayment of the external national debt. They were also designed to finance the oil and gas transfer should oil and gas revenues from the federal budget fall short in a given financial year. Such utilization of Reserve Fund resources would allow for the maintenance of a balanced budgetary policy during years when global prices for energy resources might be low, thereby reducing the budget's exposure to fluctuations in energy market prices.

The Reserve Fund is also utilized to make preterm repayments of the external national debt, hence reducing the federal budget tax burden, which may result from unplanned federal budget revenues, and also helping to preserve federal budget resources by reducing debt service expenditures.

The NWF, along with the Reserve Fund, was created from the splitting of the Stabilization Fund. It was designed primarily as a stabilizing mechanism for the long-term provision of pensions for Russian citizens. The Fund's main aims were: (1) to contribute to the voluntary pension savings for Russian citizens; and (2) to help balance the budget and resolve the deficit in the Russian Pension Fund.

The NWF is managed similarly to the Reserve Fund, with the long-term aim of ensuring security of the Fund's financial resources and maintaining a stable level of revenues from investments. The Russian government has also established that NWF funds can be invested into the same financial assets as those of the Reserve Fund. According to the Russian Budget Code, NWF resources can be converted into foreign currency or invested into financial assets denominated in foreign currencies, similar to the Reserve Fund.

The most crucial issue with regard to the formation and maintenance of these special funds is specification of the amount and volume of savings share. As illustrated in Figure 8.6, the savings share for 2004–09 has fluctuated. The 'proportion of revenues saved' is calculated as a ratio between the increment of the former Stabilization Fund, the Reserve Fund, the NWF and federal budget oil and gas revenues.

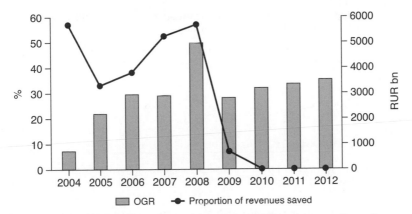

Figure 8.6 Federal budget oil and gas revenues (OGR) and 'proportion of revenues saved'

8.4.3 Oil and gas revenues and state investment: how efficient are they from a public perspective?

As oil and gas revenues accumulate within the federal budget (in the form of oil and gas transfers) they are used for various projects, including the implementation of Federal Target Programmes, high-priority national projects and the accumulation of funds into the Russian Investment Fund.

Improvement in the living standards of Russian citizens has become one of the main priorities of Russia's national policy. Russia's improved economic circumstances allowed it to more tangibly enhance general standards of living while maintaining microeconomic stability and suppressing inflation. The improved economic conditions thus created an environment conducive to the implementation of high-priority national projects focusing on healthcare, education, agriculture and housing. Such sectors determine the quality of life and social development, and are thus integral to the concept of 'human capital development'.[8] Therefore, the implementation of national projects is, in many ways, related to human capital investment.

And yet, from 2006 to 2008, direct investment into these 'human capital development' areas (not accounting for the federal budget social expenditures in other sectors) comprised only 6–9 per cent of the federal budget's share of oil and gas revenues (Table 8.4). In 2008, when financing for national projects exceeded Russian roubles (RUR) 330 billion (US$13.2 billion), this figure amounted to 6.7 per cent.

Table 8.4 High-priority national projects and oil and gas government revenues (OGR), RUR billion (US$ billion in parentheses)

National projects	2006	2007
Healthcare	91.2 (3.4)	131.3 (5.2)
Education	29.3 (1.1)	48.9 (1.9)
Affordable housing	33.8 (1.2)	50.9 (2.0)
Agriculture	21.9 (0.8)	25.4 (1.0)
Total	176.2 (6.5)	256.5 (10.1)
Total as share of OGR	6.0%	8.9%

Note: 2004–09: actual data; 2010–12: predicted. Estimated on the basis of Russian Ministry of Finance data.

The sufficiency of this amount for 'human capital development' is debatable, particularly considering the current lack of development within these areas (such as healthcare and housing) compared with world standards.

The Russian Investment Fund and Federal Target Programmes have become vitally important for the enactment of Russia's investment policies. The Federal Target Programmes are intended to help alleviate the most pressing socio-economic problems of the Russian economy, such as regional development and the development of various branches of the Russian economy in general. According to the Russian Ministry for Economic Development, 46 Federal Target Programmes and 36 auxiliary programmes are currently being implemented.

The Investment Fund's primary purpose is to provide governmental support for investment projects of federal significance. This can take the form of:

- co-financing based on specific investment project requirements;
- transfer of funds to authorized corporate bodies;
- provision of governmental guarantees for investment projects.

As demonstrated by 85 per cent of applications submitted to the Ministry for Economic Development requesting governmental support through the Investment Fund, co-financing is apparently the most popular option among investment project sponsors. This implies that the majority of investment projects use state funds to construct and upgrade federal infrastructure, thus attracting additional large-scale funding from the private sector.

As all federal budget natural resource payments have been centralized, major oil- and gas-producing regions have now become the recipients of the Investment Fund's monetary resources whereas, up to

2004, these same regions would have been independently financed or self-financed. For instance, in mid-2008, the Ministry for Regional Development allocated RUR80 billion (US$3.2 billion) for regional investment projects to resource-rich regions such as Yakutia, Bashkortostan, Krasnoyarsk and Tatarstan (Shpigel and Kaz'min, 2008).

A substantial problem related to the Investment Fund concerns the substantial length of time taken to consider and negotiate the projects – a process that normally takes a year to a year-and-a-half. This is probably caused by an overwhelming concentration of decision-making authority within the federal government and the relative exclusion of regions from this process.

According to the Federal State Statistics Service, the portion of budgetary funds within the fixed capital formation framework for the period 2000–07 was at a relatively high level (around 20 per cent). In 2007, the share of budgetary financing of fixed capital formation comprised 21.2 per cent. The share of the federal budget funds increased within the total volume of investments. The increase for this period comprised 2.4 percentage points (from 6.0 per cent in 2000 to 8.4 per cent in 2007).

However, the increased governmental efforts to promote and sustain economic growth through such projects simultaneously made apparent the lack of developed and effective institutions. For instance, during a June 2008 session of the Russian government Presidium, it was noted that, out of RUR218 billion (US$9.2 billion) allocated for high-priority national projects, nearly a fifth (17.7 per cent) remained unimplemented (Netreba, 2008). During an international investment forum in Sochi, the head of the Ministry of Regional Development at that time, Dmitry Kozak, acknowledged that the Investment Fund and other institutes for development were only using 10–15 per cent of their potential. Over-bureaucratization of the state apparatus has been responsible for such inefficiency, as well as the lack of clearly defined procedures for replenishing the Investment Fund. Previously, the size of the Investment Fund was directly correlated with the volume of the Stabilization Fund. However, following the split of the Stabilization Fund into the Reserve and National Welfare Funds, this link disappeared. Currently, there is an agreement with the Ministry of Finance that the Fund should receive RUR100 billion on an annual basis (Kukol, 2008).

8.4.4   Capital flight and government debts

Despite differing estimates, it is generally agreed that the Russian capital flight after the collapse of the Soviet Union was substantial. From 1992 to 1995, large disparities between domestic and global prices of oil, as well as other mineral, metal and chemical products, enabled Russian trading houses to accumulate tremendous profits. An absence of any state control over such trading activities, as well as high income taxes, also contributed to the capital flight.

The main reasons for Russian capital flight included:

- macroeconomic instability, linked to political instability, making investors nervous about future revenue prospects in Russia;
- the unstable and confiscatory nature of the domestic tax system which facilitated tax evasion and the transfer of funds abroad and away from Russian tax authorities;
- a lack of trust in the domestic banking system, boosting transfer of individual savings to foreign banks;
- institutional weakness of property protection measures and widespread corruption, discouraging companies and individuals from retaining their financial assets in Russia.

The main methods of capital flight are well known in Russia and include the following:

- submission of incorrect data regarding the volume of export revenues, especially in the fuel and energy sector (such as inaccurate export invoices; undeclared export volumes; the transfer of revenues to foreign corporate entities and accounts in foreign banks; sale of export volumes at low prices via offshore companies). So, for example, in 1995, the export prices in Russia lagged behind average global prices at the following rates: 7 per cent for crude oil; 29 per cent for petroleum products; 15 per cent for coal; 11 per cent for natural gas; 21 per cent for aluminium; and 13 per cent for copper. The weakness of customs and boundary controls in most states of the former USSR during the first years of reforms facilitated capital outflow through this channel. For instance, some Baltic countries became the re-export centres for goods illegally exported from Russia;
- larger than real payments for imported goods and services, including fictitious contracts on the imports of goods or services;
- fictitious advance payments for imported goods and services;
- Russian banks move funds via a network of their corresponding foreign banks in order to bypass the domestic jurisdiction.

Since 2003, the situation in relation to capital flight has changed: if, in the late 1990s, pure capital outflow was widespread, by 2008, it appeared to take on a new form. For example, the volume of resources used by Russian companies to acquire assets abroad increased threefold, from about $23 billion in 1999 up to $73.4 billion in 2005.

According to the Central Bank of Russia in 2008, the pure outflow of private capital from the country increased sharply reaching $130 billion, shared by the banking sector ($57.5 billion) and other sectors of the economy ($72.5 billion). According to the Central Bank, the largest share of capital outflow took place in the last quarter of 2008. Over the past few years, capital flight from Russia has reached new record levels. The previous record was reached in 2000 and was estimated at $24.8 billion per annum. In the first quarter of 2009, capital flight was estimated at $23.1 billion.

This dynamic of capital outflow has been directly connected to the government's policy on the taxation of the Russian oil and gas sector, as well as the aspiration of the state to accumulate the main tax revenues from the oil and gas industry into the Stabilization Fund. This policy coupled with the government's decision to pay off most of Russia's external debt and growing budgetary expenditures for social purposes has led to a significant increase in Russian internal public debt.

In 2006, Russia paid off its debt to the Paris Club, which included $1.27 billion in scheduled payments and $22.47 billion in early repayments. For this purpose, the Ministry of Finance used resources from the Stabilization Fund and saved Russia $7.7 billion as a result of early repayments. However, at the same time, the internal public debt has grown considerably through new debt obligations made from securing resources for the repayment of Russia's external debt. As a result, in 2002–06, the internal public debt went up from RUR545 billion (US$17.3 billion) to RUR1091.6 billion (US$40.2 billion) (Figure 8.7).

The most important developments in the changing character of Russia's consolidated (public and corporate) external and internal debts are:

- the transformation of Russia's external debt into Russian corporate debt to non-residents (foreign financial institutions and companies);
- the transformation of Russia's external debt into internal public debt: the external public debt is repaid on the basis of the government borrowing on the internal market;
- the departure of non-residents from the internal debt market: although the transactions with non-residents over state securities have been halted, the government has failed to find an alternative to non-residents;

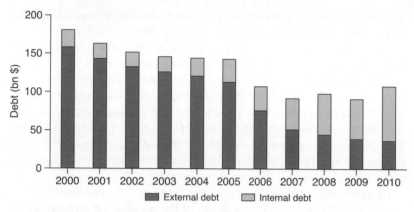

Figure 8.7 Russian external and internal debts

Note: Debts on 1 January.

Source: Russian Ministry of Finance.

- a sharp growth in the consolidated national debt, including the external and internal public debts: this occurred mostly as a result of growth in corporate debts.

8.4.5 Oil funds in crisis: the financial reserves have proven to be too small

The 2008–09 financial crisis has led to a new wave of capital flight from Russia. As a result, the entire banking system and the financial markets, as well as budgetary social payments, were brought under threat. In October 2008, the Russian government decided to change the way hydrocarbon revenues were utilized. In particular, the government aimed to use the resources of the Reserve Fund and the National Welfare Fund to stabilize Russian financial markets, to reduce the budget deficit and to provide financial aid to specific projects. In March–April 2009, the government used 1 trillion roubles (US$29.4 billion) from the Reserve Fund to finance budgetary expenditures.

At the same time, the government deposited the National Welfare Fund reserves (RUR625 billion or US$25.1 billion) into the state corporation 'Bank for Development and Foreign Economic Affairs' (Vnesheconombank). These resources were used to stabilize the financial markets and were also invested into portfolio shares in the sum of RUR168 billion (US$6.7 billion). In November–December 2008, the Vnesheconombank invested the deposited reserves of the National Welfare Fund into shares in key Russian corporate entities: LUKoil,

Rosneft, Gazprom, Russian Savings Bank, Norilsk Nickel and the Bank for Foreign Trade (VTB).

In November 2008, the total reserves of the National Welfare Fund were estimated at RUR1667.48 billion (US$61 billion), reaching RUR2863.08 billion (US$90 billion) on 1 September 2009, whereas the reserves of the Reserve Fund declined from RUR3572.78 billion (US$130.7 billion) on 1 November 2008 to RUR2238.6 billion (US$77 billion) on 1 December 2009.

In 2009, all hydrocarbon revenues, instead of being sent to the Reserve Fund and the National Welfare Fund, were directly incorporated into the budgetary revenues to cover the day-to-day expenditures of the federal budget.

In 2011–2012, the deficit in the Russian budget is supposed to remain at around 3.1–3.5 per cent of GDP. At the same time, however, budgetary expenditures are not being reduced but, on the contrary, could increase due to the government's modernization scenario. The government assumes that a reduction in social and investment expenditures could undermine the future potential of the Russian economy.

There has not been a drastic decline in world oil prices in comparison to the 2003–04 period (when the Russian Stabilization Fund was formed). Although external market conditions have not changed, the domestic budgetary situation has changed dramatically: instead of a budget surplus, the government now has limited financial resources at its disposal. The current situation with the Russian budget evolved from the 2004–09 period when the government expanded the scope of budgetary expenditures.

It was initially assumed that the Stabilization Fund's primary objective was to stabilize the financial situation in the country: that is by withdrawing parts of the hydrocarbon revenues from the domestic market, inflation could be curtailed. However, this governmental objective was achieved only once (just before the formation of the Stabilization Fund) when inflation remained at the planned annual level of 12 per cent. However, before the current crisis period, the government failed to keep inflation at bay when it increased to over 13 per cent per annum.

Capital flight, decline in oil and gas prices and an increase in budgetary expenditures have forced the government to change the way the Russian budget is formed. In September 2009, the Russian State Duma passed amendments to the Budget Code, allowing the government to increase budgetary expenditures in 2010 and up to 2012. The amended legislation promotes centralization of the following payments, which are allocated into the Federal Budget:

- revenues from the mineral resource production tax (for oil and gas condensate). At the moment, 5 per cent of this tax goes to the producing regions. This means that Tyumen oblast, in particular, being the main source of Russia's hydrocarbon outputs, will lose a large share of its regional budgetary revenues.
- all revenues of the Reserve Fund and the National Welfare Fund. This implies that such revenues will remain in the Federal Budget without being transferred to the regional level.
- additionally, in 2010–12, profits payable by the Central Bank of Russia to the Federal Budget will increase from 50 per cent to 75 per cent.

Between February 2009 and February 2011, the Reserve Fund declined from US$137.34 billion to US$25.96 billion whereas the National Welfare Fund increased from US$84.47 billion to US$90.15 billion. In 2009–2010 official estimates based on $65 per barrel of oil forecasted that growing budgetary expenditures would lead to a situation whereby Russia would use accumulated hydrocarbon revenues faster than previously envisaged (Figure 8.8). In 2010 the government was planning to cover the Russian budgetary deficit by tapping into the Reserve Fund (US$60.5 billion), the National Welfare Fund (US$13.6 billion) and borrowing US$14.2 billion in external markets and US$8.6 billion in internal markets.

Although the Reserve Fund was expected to disappear almost completely by 2011, the rise of oil prices to $100 per barrel changed the situation and the government expects the Fund assets to double in size reaching US$49 billion by the end of 2011. If the government decides

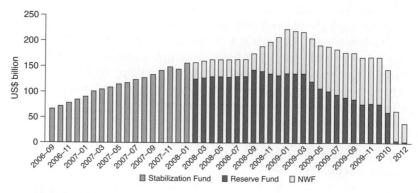

Figure 8.8 Dynamics of special oil funds in Russia (US$ billion)
Source: Russian Ministry of Finance.

to use these extra revenues to stabilize the budget, Russia could bring its budget deficit to nil by 2015. However, some official figures suggest that the economic modernization could involve extra spending on education, health and science with an annual budget deficit of 2% of GDP (at $100 oil prices) with a public debt reaching 30% by 2030.

8.4.6 Economic diversification plans: never implemented

During the period 1992–2009, Russia failed to create an effective model of resource management – in terms of both exploration and development of oil and gas resources and adequate use of oil and gas revenues for the diversification of the national economy in order to curtail its 'resource curse' symptoms (Figure 8.9).

Russia has failed to develop adequate methods and procedures for the effective accumulation of oil and gas revenues for purposes of economic diversification. An example of such a failure can be illustrated by the government's decision, in 2007, to set up state corporations with the intended aim of promoting economic diversification. The seven established state corporations – including Rostechnologia (Russian Technologies), Rosatom (Russian Atomic Industries), Olimpstroi (Olympic Games Construction), RosNano (Russian Nano Technologies) and ZhKKH Development Fund (Fund for the Development of Housing Support Services) – were granted special rights and authorities, similar to those of state bodies, while retaining many features and capabilities of large commercial entities. The government also transferred RUR2

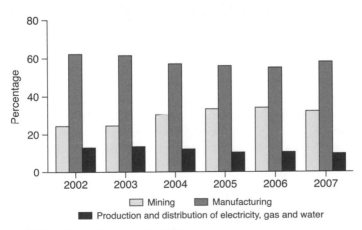

Figure 8.9 Structure of value added (%)

trillion (US$78.4 billion) worth of assets to these companies in addition to the RUR640 billion (US$25 billion) derived from the state budget (which constitutes nearly 20 per cent of the annual budgetary expenditures). Owing to their official status as non-commercial entities, the main agenda of these corporations was to deal with specific state goals, and not to generate profit. However, once state assets and financial resources have been transferred to the control of these corporations, the state ceased to be their owner. Hence, in 2009, questions were raised about the legality of such utilization of state finances.

The influx of oil and gas revenues, associated with high oil prices in external markets, was used by the government to solve pressing social problems mainly by increasing the levels of pension payments and basic salaries. In 2000–06, the per capita income of Russian citizens increased fourfold from $80 to $370, whereas the standard pension level tripled from $25 to $90. Astoundingly, over the past 8 years, gross revenues of oil companies surpassed $1 trillion, whereas their net income reached $150 billion, of which $50–70 billion were invested. During this period, the state received over $700 billion in oil and gas taxes and duties. However, these large oil and gas revenues did not increase the workforce in the Russian economy: if, in 2006, the Russian workforce was estimated at 51 million, by 2008, this figure had fallen to 48 million.

In the 2000s, the dependence of the Russian economy and society on the domestic oil and gas sector increased dramatically. This could explain why, in the second half of 2008 through to the first half of 2009, Russia surprisingly showed the biggest decline in GDP and industrial production among all the countries of the former Soviet Union.

In the future, the situation could be very complex, because of the:

- absence of an effective model of oil and gas resource management coupled with increasingly challenging conditions for the exploration and development of new fields located in difficult to reach territories with severe climates and complex geology;
- lack of incentives for private investors (both foreign and domestic) to develop new fields under the existing legal framework and in a sector dominated by state-controlled companies (which determine whether a given independent company gains access to vital infrastructure and key export routes);
- substantial tax burden recently imposed on the oil and gas sector, coupled with the dominance of state-controlled oil and gas companies, which impedes the facilitation of exploration and the development of new oil and gas fields. Various tax exemptions and

privileges granted by the government in 2008–09 to companies operating in new fields could not compensate for the high expenditures incurred during their industrial development;

- growing economic dependence upon the resource sector over the past 8 years with a very limited role for the hi-tech and other modern industrial sectors in facilitating economic growth and budgetary revenues;
- successful transformation of the Russian economy from resource dependent into hi-tech and innovative areas, which depend on successful promotion of incentives for investors and greater opportunities for entrepreneurs, not only in the oil and gas sector but also in other sectors of the economy. In the 2000s, the growing tax burden forced Russian companies to compensate for their diminishing revenues by borrowing in external markets. This resulted in an accelerated economic decline in Russia during the crisis period.

In September 2009, Russian President Dmitry Medvedev highlighted that the latest financial crisis was particularly acute in Russia because of continued economic dependence upon the hydrocarbon sector (Medvedev, 2009). In accordance, President Medvedev seeks to boost Russian economic diversification through the promotion of world-leading innovation. The Russian Ministry of Economy predicts a substantial increase in the share of the technological innovation sector by 2020 (Figure 8.10). The next few years will reveal whether these Russian government plans can be implemented.

8.5 Conclusion

The evolution of the Russian resource management system reveals a complex picture in terms of already adopted decisions and future strategies in relation to resource development and revenue utilization. At the same time, it is essential to take into account the overall socio-economic and political problems of the post-Soviet transition in Russia when assessing the factors behind certain key decisions that have shaped the development of the oil and gas sector.

1. During the 1990s, the post-Soviet centre–periphery bargaining game in Russia and ambiguous legal reforms pertaining to subsoil utilization resulted in a spontaneous system guiding field usage at the regional and local (municipal) levels. The weakness of the federal government in view of mounting socio-economic problems in the resource-rich regions resulted in provincial administrations

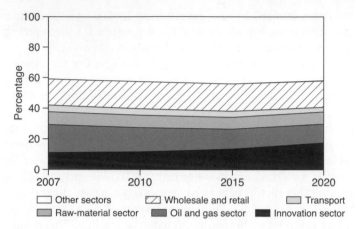

Figure 8.10 Structure of value added by major sectors of the economy (in 2007 prices)

Source: Concept of long-term socio-economic development of the Russian Federation until 2020.

expanding their authority over subsoil use and actively seeking to resolve problems associated with the exploration and production of hydrocarbons within their domains.

At the same time, during this period, the decision-making system was mostly democratic with a well-functioning 'two-keys' approach, whereby regions took a very active role in resource management. The involvement of NGOs (such as local associations of indigenous peoples) in the decision-making processes at the regional level was a very positive trend In the resource management system that existed in Russia in the 1990s. Unfortunately, this period was also characterized by a tendency to view the resource licensing process primarily as an ultimate solution to the pressing socio-economic problems of resource-rich regions.

2. In the 2000s, a new trend developed in Russia whereby the federal centre concentrated most of the authority over mineral resource management into its hands. As a result, the role of the bureaucratic administration over issues of subsoil use increased at the expense of regions and NGOs.

   This reduced regional and societal role in resource management has led to a situation whereby oil and gas companies no longer see it as their priority to promote stable socio-economic development in the specific resource-rich regions within which they operate. Hence, active regional participation in resource management is an important precondition for sustainable development as:

- environmental and social benefits and costs are primarily felt at the regional level;
- unlike the federal centre, regional administrations and NGOs are closer to the actual locations of hydrocarbon production and, therefore, could be more effective in adopting more appropriate administrative mechanisms;
- the impact of the oil and gas sector on Russian society is increasing especially in regions with mature and depleting hydrocarbon fields;
- effective monitoring and oversight of subsoil development by the federal centre is difficult to manage without active regional participation, due to the large areas to be monitored.

3. Starting in 2001, the government began using revenues from the development of mineral resources to stabilize the budget. The following steps were thus taken:

- all oil and gas revenues were accumulated into the federal budget and special funds;
- emphasis was placed on the stability of the financial system, at the expense of implementing new infrastructure and re-investment projects;
- focus was placed on designing simple and transparent procedures for mineral resources management, as well as resource revenues;
- the federal bureaucratic administration was strengthened at the expense of the regions and NGOs in addressing all the above-mentioned issues.

4. During the period 1992–2009, Russia failed to create an effective model of hydrocarbon resource management in terms of both the exploration and development of oil and gas resources and the adequate use of oil and gas revenues for the diversification of the national economy in order to curtail its 'resource curse' symptoms.

Notes

1 See Section 8.4.3.
2 This section is partially based on Shamil Yenikeyeff's forthcoming book, *The Battle for Russian Oil: Corporations, Regions and the State*, Oxford University Press, 2011.

302   *Kryukov* et al.

3 Konstutitsiia Respubliki Tatarstan, Konstututsiia Respubliki Bashkortostan, *Zakon o Nefti i Gaze Respubliki Tatarstan, ot 12 iiunia 1997 goda*, No. 1211, Kazan': Izdanie Apparata Prezidenta Respibliki Tatarstan, 1997.
4 Paragraph 3 of Article III, *Federativnyi Dogovor ot 31 marta 1992 goda*, Moskva: Izdanie Verkhovnogo Soveta Rossiiskoii Federatsii, 1992.
5 The tax was not levied if prices fell below $109.5 per tonne.
6 http://www.fphmao.ru, 2009.
7 Russian Ministry of Finance, official website: www.minfin.ru, 2009.
8 Prioritetnye natsional'nye proekty [High-priority national projects]. Official website: www.rost.ru.

References

Bulatov, A. (2001) 'Kapitaloobrazovanie v Rossii' [Capital accumulation in Russia], *Voprosy ekonomiki*, No. 3.
Fasano, U. (2000) *Review of the Experience with Oil Stabilization and Savings Funds in Selected Countries*. International Monetary Fund, IMF Working Paper, No. 12, p. 20.
Kryukov, V. (1998) *Instituttsional'naya struktura neftegazovogo sektora: problemy i napravleniya transformatsii* [Institutional structure of the oil and gas sector: problems and transformations]. Novosibirsk: Institute of Economics, p. 280.
Kryukov, V. (2001a) 'Strategiia ustoichivogo razvitiia' [Strategy of sustainable development of resource-rich regions], *Neftegazovaya vertikal'*, 3, 92–5.
Kryukov, V. (2001b) 'Zhadnost' 'bogov': komu idut na pol'zu 'fondy razvitiia' – obshestvu ili otdel'nym grazhdanam?' [Problems of special oil fund use], *EKO*, 9, 23–51.
Kryukov, V. and A. Tokarev (2005) *Uchet interesov korennykh malochislennykh narodov pri prinyatii reshenii v sphere nedropolzovaniia* [Indigenous peoples' interests and decision-making process in the field of subsoil use: Russian case study]. Moscow: Tsentr sodeistviia korennykh narodov Severa, p. 172.
Kryukov, V. and A. Tokarev (2006) *Investitsionnyi klimat v neftegazovom sektore Rossii* [Investment climate in the Russian oil and gas sector]. Seriia: Sotsial'no-ekonomicheskie nauki, Vol. 6, pp. 84–97. Novosibirsk: Vestnik NGU.
Kryukov, V. and A. Tokarev (2007) *Oil-and-gas Resources in a Transitional Economy: Comparing Realized and Potential Social Value of Mineral Wealth (Theory, Practice, Analysis, and Estimates)*. Novosibirsk: Science-Centre, p. 588.
Kryukov, V., A. Sevastyanova and V. Shmat (1996) *Utopicheskaya ideya ili real'naya nadezhda? Otsenka vozmozhnostei sozdaniya i deyatel'nosti spetsial'nykh finansovykh fondov syr'evykh territorii v Rossii i analiz zarubezhnogo opyta* [Special financial funds in resource-rich regions and analysis of foreign experience]. Novosibirsk: Assotsiatsiya Banki Sibiri.
Kryukov, V., A. Sevastyanova, A. Tokarev and V. Shmat (2002) *Evolutsionnyi podkhod k formirovaniiu sistemy gosudarstvennogo regulirovaniia neftegazovogo sektora ekonomiki* [Evolutionary approach to the formation of the oil and gas resource management system]. Novosibirsk: Institute of Economics, p. 168.
Kryukov, V., V. Seliverstov and A. Tokarev (2004) 'Federalism and Regional Policy in Russia: Problems of Socio-Economic Development of Resource Territories and Subsoil Use' in P.H. Solomon (ed.). *The Dynamics of 'Real Federalism': Law, Economic Development, and Indigenous Communities in Russia and Canada*.

Toronto: Centre for Russian and East European Studies, University of Toronto, pp. 96–127.

Kryukov, V., V. Silkin, V. Shmat and A. Tokarev (2006) *Podkhody k differentsiatsii nalogooblozheniia v gazovoi promyshlennosti* [Approaches to flexible taxation in the gas sector]. Novosibirsk: Institute of Economics, Sova, p. 169.

Kukol, E. (2008) 'Den'gi iz 'odnogo okna'. Minregion razrabotal novye pravila dlya Investfonda' [Money from 'one window'. Ministry for Regional Development has come up with new rules for the Investment Fund], *Rossiiskaiia gazeta*, 24 September.

Medvedev, D. (2009) 'Go Russia!'. http://eng.kremlin.ru/speeches/2009/09/10/1534_type104017_221527.shtml.

Netreba, P. (2008) 'Dlya uspekha natsproektov ne nuzhny den'gi' [No money is required for the success of the national projects], *Kommersant*, 10 June.

Shafranik, Yu and V. Kryukov (2000) *Zapadno-Sibirskii phenomen. Tyumen na styke vekov: mezhdu legendarnym proshlym i neyasnym budushim?* [Western Siberian phenomenon. Tyumen at the turn of the centuries: between a legendary production and an unclear future]. Moscow: Polteks, p. 240.

Shpigel, M. and D. Kaz'min (2008) 'Raspredilili den'gi' [The funds have been divided], *Vedomosti*, 21 July.

Tokarev, A. (2000) *Nalogovoe regulirovaniie neftegazovogo sektora: regional'nye aspekty* [Tax policy in the oil sector: regional aspects]. Novosibirsk: Institute of Economics, p. 256.

Tokarev, A. (2003) 'Analyz struktury dokhodov rentnogo kharaktera v neftyanom sektore Rossii: uchet interesov syr'evykh regionov' [Analysis of Russian oil rents: taking into account the interests of resource-rich regions] in V. Kryukov and A. Sevastyanova (eds) *Neftegazovyi sector Rossii v teorii i na prak tike* [Russian oil and gas sector: theory and practice]. Novosibirsk: Institute of Economics, pp. 73–105.

Voronin, Yu (2007) 'Neneftegazovyi budzhet: dovody i kontrdovody' [Non-oil budget: pro and contra], *Ekonomist*, 8, 62–9.

Vygon, G. (2002) *Otsenka nalogovoi nagruzki na rossiiskie neftyanye kompanii v 2000 godu* [Evaluation of the tax burden on Russian oil companies in 2000]. Moscow: Institute for Financial Studies, p. 29.

Warrack, A. and R. Keddie (1999) *Alberta Heritage Funds vs Alaska Permanent Fund: A Comparative Analysis*. Faculty of Business, University of Alberta, Edmonton, p. 19.

Yenikeyeff, S. (2011) *The Battle for Russian Oil: Corporations, Regions and the State*. Oxford: Oxford University Press.

9
Copper Mining in Zambia
From collapse to recovery

Christopher Adam and Anthony M. Simpasa

9.1 Overview

This chapter examines the macroeconomic management of Zambia's natural resource endowment over the past century. We describe how the state has adopted different strategies to secure a share of the rents from copper mining, how these strategies have affected incentives for exploration and production and how the associated macroeconomic policy regimes have shaped the value and distribution of the natural resource rents. We focus principally on the shift from public back to private ownership and control of the sector that took place at the end of the 1990s, and on how the terms of the privatization of the mining industry affected the impact of the commodity price boom of 2003–08 on the domestic economy. We suggest that, although the state and people of Zambia captured a nugatory share of the rents accruing from this boom, high levels of investment in the sector, combined with recent reforms to the mining taxation regime and in the conduct of macroeconomic policy, have left Zambia better placed to benefit from future growth in the copper sector.

9.2 Introduction

The history and economics of modern Zambia are intimately entwined with that of the copper industry. It is a history in three acts, beginning with the successful exploitation and development of remote, and initially unpromising, ore reserves in the late 1800s, which eventually led to Zambia, a country of less than two million people, becoming one of the 'big five' global copper producers in the first half of the twentieth century (Davis, 1933). The second act traces the period from the late

1950s through to the end of the twentieth century. This period witnessed the apotheosis of the copper industry, with high and rising prices from the 1950s to the early 1970s setting the stage for the emergence of the vast nationalized mining conglomerate, Zambia Consolidated Copper Mines (ZCCM), as a 'state within a state'. By the mid-1980s,'Zambia was ZCCM and ZCCM was Zambia'.

But this exalted status was short-lived: the final quarter of the twentieth century saw a persistent decline in prices, production and profitability, which brought about the near collapse of the copper industry in Zambia and bankruptcy to the economy. By the mid-1990s, and despite political opposition from many quarters, the losses of ZCCM posed such a severe threat to public finances that its privatization became inevitable. The privatization of the mines, the subsequent recovery of the sector – against the background of the 2003–08 global commodity price boom – and the contest over the shape of the regime for mining taxation constitute the (unfinished) third act of the story.

We emphasize three themes in this chapter. The first concerns the nature of property rights over mineral resources, how the state has adopted different strategies through time to secure a share of the rents from copper mining and how these strategies have affected incentives for both exploration and production. The second theme concerns macroeconomic management of copper price movements. Copper mining in Zambia is an enclave activity, both technically and spatially. Over time, as mining has moved deeper underground, it has become increasingly capital and import intensive and, although the mines have been the largest employer in the formal economy after the government, forward and backward market linkages with the domestic economy beyond the local environs have been weak: fiscal and quasi-fiscal transfers have therefore been the key link between the mining sector and the rest of the economy. The manner in which fiscal and other macroeconomic policy instruments were deployed in the 1970s and 1980s, however, had disastrous consequences for the economy so that the potential benefits of the boom of the early 1970s failed to be exploited, whereas the adverse effects of the subsequent 20-year slide in world copper prices were hugely magnified through the application of increasingly distortionary macroeconomic policy measures. As Hill and McPherson (2004) note, since the beginning of Zambia's economic difficulties, successive governments have consistently failed to implement reforms with sufficient vigour to return the economy to a sustainable growth path. We argue that, in contrast, the 2003–08 mineral price boom appears to have been managed rather more effectively. In particular, choices made over the exchange rate and monetary regime have improved the capacity of the authorities to respond flexibly to the volatility in copper prices, thereby avoiding the excessive real exchange rate misalignment that characterized the macroeconomy in the 1970s and 1980s, whereas fiscal reforms offer the prospect of significantly increased efficiency in the public investment of windfall incomes.

This leads directly to our third theme, namely the shifting perspectives on the capacity of the Zambian state to manage external volatility. The state-ownership model adopted in the immediate post-Independence decades ultimately proved poorly suited to efficiently manage the inherent volatility of the global copper market. A direct consequence of this failure was that the shift away from state ownership was both rapid and comprehensive: the sale of ZCCM decisively improved the efficiency of mining operations and the long-term prospects for the sector, but it also effectively handed entitlement to an overwhelming share of the future rents from the sector to foreign owners. The copper price boom of 2003–08 revealed the magnitude of this transfer which, against a background of rising political opposition, prompted the government into a renegotiation of the resource contract in an attempt to gain control over a larger share of the rents from the sector.

We argue that this has been partially successful, and attempts to shift this balance further in favour of the state are likely to play an important role in the political economy of Zambia in the coming years. In particular, how the government responds to persistent calls for reinstatement of the windfall tax after the rebound in metal prices will decisively determine the outcome of the change in the mining sector landscape.

The remainder of this chapter is structured as follows. Section 9.3 provides a brief overview of the history of copper mining in Zambia from the development of the industry in the late nineteenth century to the nationalization of the mines in the early 1970s. Section 9.4 then offers a brief normative perspective on macroeconomic management given the structure of mining in Zambia. This sets the scene for Sections 9.5 and 9.6, which describe the disastrous macroeconomics of the 1970s and 1980s and the reorientation of economic management in the 1990s under the Movement for Multiparty Democracy (MMD) government. Section 9.7 describes the privatization of ZCCM in the late 1990s, and Section 9.8 discusses the management of the copper price boom of 2003–08. Section 9.9 concludes.

9.3 Copper mining in Zambia: history, geography and politics

9.3.1 History

Copper mining in Zambia has its origins in British colonial interests in southern Africa at the end of the nineteenth century. The existence of rich copper deposits lying close to the surface in the crescent of land stretching 500 km from Luanshya in modern-day Zambia to Katanga in the modern-day Democratic Republic of Congo had been known for centuries, but systematic prospecting in the area dates from the height of the European 'scramble for Africa' when a wave of small-scale prospectors licensed by Cecil Rhodes's British South Africa Company (BSAC) converged on the area. Prospecting rights were secured in the system of mutual recognition established at the Congress of Berlin in 1884, which defined the limits of the BSAC's concession to the north (thereby ceding rights over the immensely rich surface deposits around Katanga to the Congo Free State, later the Belgian Congo). In doing so, it conferred authority to the BSAC for prospecting over the territory of modern-day Zambia. These rights were secured through a treaty with the Paramount Chief of Barotseland, whose chieftaincy covered the entire modern Copperbelt area; in exchange for providing security to the Chief, the BSAC acquired in perpetuity monopoly rights to the prospecting and mining of copper within the territory.

Initially, mining developed through numerous small concessions resulting in an artisanal industry. Although this model thrived in the geology of Katanga, it was less successful on the Northern Rhodesian concessions and, until the 1920s, few of the mines on the Copperbelt were economic. The reason was essentially geological: although the ore body around Katanga was predominantly above ground and consisted of extremely high-grade copper oxide ores (the copper content was as high as 15 per cent compared with a global average of 1–2 per cent), the ores on the Zambian side were comparatively low grade (3–5 per cent) and were predominantly underground. At these grades, and given the remoteness of the deposits, incentives for mining were limited.

Prospects changed radically in the decade following the end of the First World War. Continued industrialization of the global economy, and especially the industrialization of war, underpinned a sustained growth in global demand for copper, but Zambia's participation in the global copper market was driven more by geological happenstance and enlightened public policy. The former was the discovery that the thin oxidized layer of ore body mined in the early part of the century in fact overlaid vastly richer sulphide seams below the surface. This simple discovery massively increased the potential commercial value of the ore body.[1]

This potential was exploited thanks to two critical decisions by the BSAC. First, in 1922, the policy of allocating prospecting and mining rights to small concessionaires was abandoned in favour of granting rights to larger commercial operations, most notably Ernest Oppenheimer's Anglo American Corporation (AAC). The second was the decision to extend Rhodes' 'Cape to Cairo' railway from Victoria Falls to the Copperbelt (with a coaling stop halfway along at what is modern-day Lusaka). The consolidation of rights and the provision of infrastructure created the conditions in which large-scale private capital investment allowed the mining industry to incur the fixed costs necessary to exploit the economies of scale in deep-mined copper production.[2] Two foreign mining houses, Anglo American Corporation of South Africa and the Rhodesian (later Roan) Selection Trust, owned by the American Metal Climax Inc., quickly consolidated their grip on the industry and between them established Northern Rhodesia as one of the 'big five' producers (the others being the USA, Russia, Chile and Congo/Zaire). Within a decade, Northern Rhodesia had emerged as a major supplier of copper to the world economy, accounting for 10 per cent of world production in the 1930s and 1940s, and reaching its maximum share of almost 15 per cent in 1959[3] (see Figure 9.1).

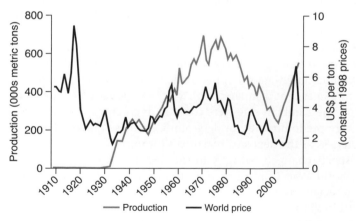

Figure 9.1 A century of copper production

Sources: Coleman (1971); Bank of Zambia.

With this basic ownership structure in place, the industry rode the long post-Second World War boom, with production responding hand-in-hand with rising world demand and prices. At Independence in 1964, Zambia could boast the highest per capita income in sub-Saharan Africa (albeit one that was very poorly distributed).

9.3.2 Geography, linkages and state ownership

In 1969, copper production peaked at 700,000 tons. In the same year, the government of Zambia took its first steps towards state ownership of the mining sector. The case for state ownership, first articulated in President Kenneth Kaunda's Mulungushi Declaration in 1968, rested fundamentally on the basic notion of economic nationalism – Zambia's national identity was defined by copper but control remained in foreign hands – but was reinforced by an intellectual climate at the time that championed the state's capacity to absorb and manage economic risk. In the case of Zambia, the feasibility of this model of economic management was further reinforced by the apparent success of the mining industry itself (even though the state long contended that the private mine owners had underinvested in the sector since Independence). The region of the Copperbelt is large and, before the emergence of large-scale industry, was very sparsely populated, principally by subsistence farmers. To create and sustain an effective supply of skilled labour to the mines, the mining houses had, since the early 1930s, made substantial investments in the training, health and social welfare of their labour forces (see, for example, Robinson, 1933; Coleman, 1971). By the early 1970s, the Copperbelt was, in effect, a collection of well-run and prosperous company towns populated by a relatively well-educated, well-paid and heavily urbanized labour force enjoying high-quality cradle-to-grave welfare provision, courtesy of the mining houses, and constituting an important source of aggregate demand.

The Mulungushi Declaration can be seen, in part, as an attempt to recast this 'company town' model on a national scale. The fundamental problem, however, was that the expanded model relied on exactly the same resource base which, unknown to the government at the time, was at its zenith. State ownership on its own did little to strengthen backward linkages (although large state-owned, import-substituting industrial conglomerates such as the Zambia Industrial and Mining Corporation (ZIMCO) were created to supply the copper industry); it could and did strengthen forward linkages, principally through the widening remit of the state-owned copper industry and through fiscal means. As was soon to become clear, however, this strategy was fundamentally unsustainable, particularly when world copper prices declined.

The Matero Declaration of August 1969 implemented the Mulungushi Declaration in the mining sector. The government acquired a 51 per cent controlling stake in the Roan Selection Trust and Anglo American's operations in Zambia, creating Roan Consolidated Mines (RCM) and Nchanga Consolidated Copper Mines (NCCM) and, in 1982, RCM and NCCM were merged to create ZCCM. At that point, the government of Zambia held 60 per cent of the equity, AAC 27 per cent and the remainder was held by a range of private investors.

9.4 A growth strategy for Zambia: normative considerations

9.4.1 The macroeconomic framework

Ever since the discovery of extensive copper reserves in the 1920s, the country has faced the same fundamental challenge: how to convert this natural wealth into an equitably distributed and sustainable flow of resources to the citizens of the country in a manner that supports employment and growth in the non-mineral economy but does so without destroying the incentives for mining exploration and production.[4] This is a difficult challenge on a number of grounds. First, the Zambian mining houses have never been large enough players in the global market to exert market power: they have always been price takers in a market where prices are highly volatile and subject to occasional short sharp spikes and long troughs.

Historically, the demand for copper has been driven by war and investment booms, particularly property booms: prices for copper are therefore driven more by 'accelerator' effects than by income effects, arguably exacerbating their volatility. Outside the long armaments-driven boom from the 1930s to the 1960s, price spikes have tended to be relatively short-lived. Cashin and McDermott (2002), for example, estimate the half-life of mineral booms to be less than 4 years. Volatility emanating from global demand-side effects has, however, been exacerbated by supply-side factors. Copper mining in Zambia is capital intensive, and uncertainty about future prices and the cost of production is heightened by a complex local geology and substantial sunk costs associated with exploration activities, environmental legacies and geographical isolation. Investors typically face a high option value of waiting to invest. (This option value is further enhanced when, as in Zambia, property rights are secure and the threat of expropriation is low.) Moreover, the 'bad news principle' prevails in such environments, generating excess sensitivity to adverse changes in expected prices or taxes, thereby further raising investment hurdles and contributing to an uneven and strongly pro-cyclical pattern of investment at both local and global levels.[5]

Second, the intrinsic geology of Zambia makes it a high-cost producer dependent on an import- and capital-intensive technology. This has meant that not only does the sector have weak market links to the rest of the economy, but the potentially taxable economic rents from the sector – the flow of value that could potentially be consumed or re-invested elsewhere in the economy – are limited on average. Only in particularly good times does the sector generate potentially transforma-tive rents, but then policy-makers are confronted with the well-known range of challenges associated with managing large resource inflows to ensure that periodic resource booms do not inflict long-term damage on the non-resource economy.

Third, outside the enclave mining sector and its immediate local economy, Zambia suffers from many of the disadvantages of the *resource-scarce*, landlocked economies of Africa: distance to markets, low population densities and an unpromising neighbourhood (Collier and O'Connell, 2007). The priorities for development, then, are twofold. The first is in the penetration of regional exports where possible, and the second the development of activities that are either not distance critical (such as e-commerce) or can exploit other natural advantages (such as horticulture and tourism and, increasingly, time zones for back-office processing for corporate clients to the west and the east). The common theme is that all the elements in this strategy require the provision of complementary inputs, in the form of physical infrastruc-ture in transport, power and communication networks, in terms of a flexible and well-trained skilled labour force and in terms of a strongly export-oriented trade policy.

9.4.2 A dual strategy: smooth mining output and strong fiscal response

Given these conditions, mining production would optimally be strongly pro-cyclical with producers choosing to leave resources in the ground when prices are below their long-run trend, mothballing mines as required, and vice versa when prices are high. This is exactly what happened in Zambia in the 1930s when most mines were small and were still on, or close to, the surface (Coleman, 1971). Over time, how-ever, fixed costs in Zambian mining have risen sharply, partly as a result of the geology (mines went deeper underground and Zambia now has a number of very wet deep mines that require constant pumping) and geography (Zambia is a long way from markets), but also from rising fixed costs of employment (exacerbated by low investment) and, through the 1970s and 1980s, sharply rising non-mining costs as the remit of the state-owned ZCCM widened beyond its core mining business. As a result, the scale of production became less able to respond to changes in price.

These characteristics shift the macroeconomic burden on to trade and fiscal policy and, at the same time, they put pressure on monetary policy to minimize the adverse transmission of short-run price volatility in the mining sector to the rest of the economy through excess volatility in the exchange rate and/or inflation.

Fiscal policy in this setting must succeed in two areas. The first is to generate high public saving from periodic temporary price booms. Given the ownership structure in the sector, this has direct implications for the design of the tax regime. The second is to ensure flexibility in public expenditure, so that the authorities can credibly commit to adjust expenditure downwards as mining revenues first peak and then decline. The required degree of expenditure flexibility depends on broader fiscal flexibility (for example, whether the government can efficiently substitute non-resource taxation for mineral-based taxes in the downturn) and the country's capacity to smooth out revenue instability, through either external borrowing or accessing (deep) domestic debt markets. As the following sections suggest, both these features were conspicuous by their absence during the period from the early 1970s to the late 1990s. The preliminary evidence from the macroeconomic response to the 2003–08 boom suggests that progress has been made towards establishing a more responsive mining sector and a more flexible macroeconomic framework.

9.5 Macroeconomic management I: the 1970s and 1980s

The three decades from nationalization were a disaster for the mining industry in Zambia and for the economy as a whole. Bad luck played a major part: almost as soon as the government had acquired majority control of the industry, world copper prices started their long decline, the geological conditions in mining became more challenging and the geopolitical environment of southern Africa severely disadvantaged landlocked Zambia's engagement with the world economy.[6] But bad luck was compounded by poor management. What really destroyed the sector was the sharp rise in the unit costs of production throughout the period. Only a small proportion of this increase can be attributed to the worsening geological conditions: as Figure 9.2 shows, production costs fell sharply from the mid-1990s, long before substantial new investment occurred in the sector and when geological conditions were, if anything, continuing to deteriorate. Rather, the rising cost base reflected the lack of checks and balances to control the enormous expansion in unprofitable non-core activities and outright rent-seeking activities that accompanied the progressive dissolution of the boundaries between the state, the United National Independence Party (UNIP) and ZCCM (see Bates and Collier, 1993). By the early 1990s, when the one-party state of the Second Republic was successfully challenged, ZCCM had been drawn so far into the indirect financing of state and party activities that rents in the mining sector in Zambia had been all but eliminated.

The macroeconomic mismanagement of the 1970s and 1980s in Zambia has been extensively documented (for example, Gulhati, 1989; Aron and Elbadawi, 1992; Bates and Collier, 1993; Adam and Musonda, 1999; Bigsten and Kayizzi-Mugerwa, 2000; Mwanawina and Mulungushi, 2008). Problems emerged early when, following a sharp doubling between 1972 and 1974, world copper prices fell sharply and steadily. Treating the temporary positive shock as if it were permanent and the negative shock as if it were temporary, the authorities failed to

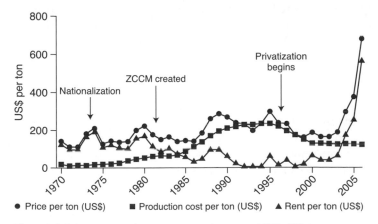

Figure 9.2 Price, cost and rent per ton of copper, 1970–2006

Source: World Bank Metals and Minerals database.

save during the boom and sought to sustain absorption during the long slump through extensive external borrowing. During the late 1970s, borrowing to smooth domestic expenditure appeared appropriate (and indeed the strategy was initially supported and financed by the World Bank and other donors) as Zambia's credit rating was good and most observers expected a rapid upturn in the price of copper. As the decade continued, however, the Bank and others revised their price expectations downwards. The government of Zambia did not. Its continued strategy of high borrowing and high absorption pushed the current account further into deficit. Delays in adjustment proved very costly, and the subsequent crisis of the 1980s thus stemmed in large measure from the combination of a failure to save when copper prices were temporarily high and a failure to adjust when they were persistently low.

With absorption consistently exceeding gross domestic product (GDP) through the late 1970s and 1980s and with output growth declining, debt grew rapidly and the country's access to all but the most expensive credit dried up. When adjustment came, consumption was sustained mainly through a severe squeeze on investment in general, but also in the mining sector.

Gross fixed capital formation as a share of GDP decreased from an average of over 30 per cent of GDP per annum from 1965 to 1974 to 23 per cent per annum in the decade from 1974 and to around 15 per cent per annum at the end of the 1980s and early 1990s, barely sufficient to maintain, let alone increase, the capital–labour ratio. Mining investment, in particular, plummeted. Gross public investment through ZCCM barely covered the depreciation of the capital stock in mining, whereas Anglo American's investment effectively dried up. The depletion of non-renewable natural resources during the 1980s (at low world prices) thus financed public and private consumption and was used to service external debt. For most of the last 40 years, Zambia's investment rate has fallen well short of satisfying the Hartwick (1977) rule;[7] as a consequence, total wealth was severely depleted (see Figure 9.3).

Low investment and adverse external conditions saw total output stagnate in both the mineral and the non-mineral sectors. As a result, per capita incomes contracted sharply in the 1970s and 1980s (and continued to do so through much of the 1990s), so that per capita income in 2000 was more than a third lower than in 1970, while standard development indicators worsened dramatically. For example, despite the absence of war, sanctions or catastrophic crop failure, infant mortality rose sharply during the 1980s: by 2006, the infant mortality rate was no lower than it had been in 1970.

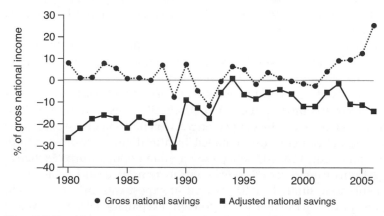

Figure 9.3 Zambia gross and adjusted national savings (% gross national income), 1980–2006

Source: World Bank Metals and Minerals database.

As the 1980s proceeded, the macroeconomic control regime became increasingly distorted as the authorities repeatedly delayed adjustment and thwarted reforms. With access to credit becoming more difficult and a reluctance to actively use the exchange rate to effect adjustment, the external balance was increasingly enforced by the application of strict exchange controls, quantity rationing on imports and domestic price controls. This highly distorted structure of relative prices served to favour (privileged) urban consumers – through undervalued imports and domestic food – but did so by creating a severe anti-rural and anti-export bias (Adam and Musonda, 1999). At the same time, capacity utilization in the highly import-intensive domestic economy collapsed dramatically as the external balance worsened.[8]

9.5.1 Reform initiatives

From the late 1970s, it was increasingly clear that a substantial economic adjustment was required. Adjustment programmes were negotiated in 1978 and again in 1983 but with limited success. The 1983 reforms did, however, put pressure on the government to liberalize the exchange rate regime to eliminate the severe real exchange rate overvaluation, but this was thwarted by a weak external position and an incompatible fiscal stance. The effect was that price decontrols and the removal of subsidies on basic foodstuffs were accompanied by a rapid nominal exchange rate depreciation, which hit the previously protected but politically powerful urban population on the Copperbelt hard.

Food riots ensued in 1986, prompting the suspension of reform efforts (Bates and Collier, 1993).

The denouement of the failed adjustment efforts of the 1980s, and indeed of President Kaunda's Second Republic, began in May 1987 when the government broke off relations with the International Monetary Fund (IMF) and adopted its *Growth from Own Resources* economic recovery programme (ERP). Ironically, this period coincided with a brief recovery in copper prices which, arguably, would have eased the adjustment costs entailed by the donor-supported reform programme. But, instead, policy took a more populist turn. Exchange rate reforms were reversed, price controls reinstated and debt service payments were limited to 10 per cent of export earnings. As a result, relative prices, particularly for foreign exchange, became severely distorted, the anti-export bias increased and investment expenditure collapsed. Open and disguised unemployment rose dramatically. With the rents from the mining sector exhausted, any remaining political support for the programme and for President Kaunda dissolved. The ERP collapsed in 1989, and a new reform package was agreed with the IMF. The details of the 1989 programme are relatively unimportant: much more important was that re-engagement with the IMF – which included the humiliating appointment of an IMF-approved expatriate governor of the central bank[9] – was a critical nail in the coffin of the economic and political model of the Second Republic. Within a year, President Kaunda had acceded to pressures to hold competitive multiparty elections and, in October 1991, he suffered a landslide defeat at the hands of the Movement for Multiparty Democracy (MMD) candidate, Frederick Chiluba, while UNIP ceded 125 of the 150 parliamentary seats to the MMD. Kaunda's dignified departure from the presidency of Zambia was, however, a decisive political landmark for the continent: he was the first of the generation of African Independence leaders to peacefully leave the political stage through electoral defeat.

Although the election of 1991 was not fought on the issue of ZCCM and the copper industry, the change in regime ushered in a shift in thinking about the role of the state in economic management and in the management of natural resources. The realization that the state-driven model had come close to driving the mining sector to extinction saw discussion over the nature of ownership of the mining sector, including the possibility of privatization to foreign investors, emerge into mainstream political debate.

9.6 Economic management in the 1990s: stabilization, liberalization and privatization

On taking office, the MMD government immediately embarked on an aggressive programme of macroeconomic stabilization and reform, transforming Zambia from one of the most *dirigiste* economic regimes in the 1980s to one of the most liberal. Trade restrictions were relaxed, controls on domestic financial markets removed, the exchange rate regime was liberalized (Zambia was one of the first African countries to remove all controls on capital account transactions) and the government embarked on an ambitious programme of privatization. By mid-decade, the state had divested itself of the vast majority of the roughly 400 state-owned non-mining enterprises that had been built up over the preceding 30 years, including iconic organizations such as Zambia Airways.

The MMD government was broadly successful in achieving the short-term stabilization objectives, thanks in large measure to strong donor support and a protracted period of tight fiscal and monetary regime. As a result, inflation was rapidly brought under control, falling from 250 per cent per annum in mid-1994 to less than 10 per cent per annum by the end of 1994 (Adam, 1995), while the extreme overvaluation of the real exchange rate that had built up during the late 1980s was eliminated.

Macroeconomic stabilization in the early part of the 1990s required steely commitment by the government, but it proved difficult to sustain. Weaknesses in governance and mounting political tension within the MMD saw the reformist zeal of their early years in government rapidly dissipate as the political rivalries that had been successfully subordinated to the common objective of overturning Kaunda's and UNIP's hegemony broke the surface, causing the associated goodwill of donors to dissolve (Cheeseman and Hinfelaar, 2009). Even without these problems, stabilization would have been hard to sustain as the economy was hit by a sequence of poor harvests and as copper prices continued to decline, further exposing the parlous state of the mining sector. With official reserves already at the minimum level required to satisfy the IMF and no access to external capital other than through aid flows (including debt rescheduling), adjustment to the deteriorating external conditions was overwhelmingly through continued expenditure reduction, both public and private. With public consumption already severely squeezed by the cash budget, the burden of adjustment fell on aggregate investment, and once again growth stagnated, with the consequence that external indebtedness continued to grow as a share of GDP, social indicators remained poor and stocks of both public and private capital continued to deteriorate (Dinh *et al.*, 2002). The tight fiscal control exerted in the early part of the decade could not be sustained and, with quasi-fiscal losses at ZCCM escalating, many of the macroeconomic gains posted in the early part of the 1990s were lost.

It was against this background that the privatization of ZCCM was launched. There was none of the fanfare or evangelism of the non-mining privatization programme. Instead, an air of inevitability that the end-game had arrived prevailed.

9.7 Privatization

To this point, progress with the non-mining privatization programme was unexpectedly rapid, although many of the sales essentially entailed closure of state-owned enterprises that had only survived thanks to high but now rapidly diminishing tariff barriers. Initially, the mining sector fell outside the purview of the Zambian Privatization Agency (ZPA), not even being considered suitable for privatization.

However, by the mid-1990s, the steady decline in world prices, worsening geology and continued rent-seeking saw the fortunes of ZCCM collapse precipitously. Capital expenditure had fallen to less than a quarter of its value in the early 1970s, production was prematurely halted at a number of mines and no resources were being devoted to prospecting (World Bank, 2002). Between 1997 and 1998, ZCCM's reported pre-tax losses totalled approximately $650 million – almost US$1 million per day – equivalent to over 20 per cent of total turnover (Craig, 2001). By the time the first components of the ZCCM conglomerate were privatized in 1998, mining output was 42 per cent of its level at Independence in 1964 and only one-third of its 1969 peak production, and decidedly not as the outcome of an optimal response to below-trend world copper prices.

9.7.1 The privatization process

In large measure, the steady deterioration in the financial condition of ZCCM dictated the pace and the options for privatization. Recognizing that no investor was prepared to absorb the whole of ZCCM, the conglomerate was sold in a set of separate packages with the state retaining a range of contingent liabilities including those arising from pension and environmental obligations. Moreover, given the heterogeneity and complexity of each unit – and the rapidly changing financial environment – it was deemed impossible to conduct the sale by auction.

Component parts were sold one by one through often opaque bilateral negotiations with preselected preferred bidders.

The process was initially run by ZPA and ZCCM itself, but the agency was quickly supplanted by a presidentially appointed agency to lead the negotiations under the chairmanship of Francis Kaunda, former Chairman and Chief Executive Officer of ZCCM. Mr Kaunda brought in his own team, which included former senior managers from ZCCM, raising concerns that the task force was fundamentally opposed to the privatization programme and would seek to frustrate the sale process (World Bank, 2002). Tenders for the sale of the ten asset packages were issued in March 1997. Bids were reviewed by the negotiating team, and recommendations on preferred bidders were made to a Committee of Ministers and the ZCCM board, after which negotiations for sale commenced. Each agreement was defined in a legally binding development agreement (DA), which remained closed to scrutiny by either parliament or other stakeholders, including those in the mining sector. The process took over 3 years, with the last (and, in terms of mining potential, the largest) block of assets – Konkola Copper Mines – finally being sold to the Anglo American Corporation in March 2000.

Although the government retained the services of top-flight advisers (the merchant bank N.M. Rothschild and lawyers Clifford Chance), bargaining power lay overwhelmingly in the hands of the eventual purchasers. World prices remained depressed through most of the negotiation period and losses mounted across ZCCM, while a combination of brinkmanship by potential purchasers – frequently based on 'revelations' from the execution of due diligence investigation into the financial accounts of ZCCM – and relentless pressure from the donor community to conclude the process saw both strike prices and the general terms of sale move sharply against the vendor. Given the pessimistic outlook for the world market at the time, it was seen as a success to have sold most of the components of ZCCM as going concerns for a positive cash price: the potential problems of negotiating away such generous fiscal terms were heavily discounted. It was only when market conditions recovered that the full consequences of the sale conditions became apparent.

Not all packages were equally sized or of similar quality. A number were sold quickly and with little controversy, although two had to be resold almost immediately when the original buyer encountered financial difficulties. These units eventually found new private owners. The real complexity in the privatization process occurred with the sale of the core mining activities, the Nkana, Nchanga, Konkola, Konkola Deep and Mufulira divisions, which together were responsible for over two-thirds of total production. Despite the size and potential of this package, only one bid was received at the initial tender stage from the Kafue Consortium, a group of investors comprising Anglovaal Mining of South Africa, Noranda Mining and Exploration Inc. of Canada, Phelps Dodge of the USA and the Commonwealth Development Corporation (CDC) of the UK.

Suspecting collusion, the government team rejected the Consortium's initial bid as too low. As the copper price continued to fall, however, the Consortium demanded increasingly more generous terms and in each case the government team rejected the offer. Following a failure to agree terms in June 1998, the Consortium was dissolved and negotiations terminated.

The delays and apparent unwillingness of the government team to finalize the sale of the core assets created substantial uncertainty, particularly in the eyes of the World Bank, the IMF and other donors.[10] The IMF withheld balance of payments support, as did other donors, effectively forcing the government back to the negotiating table. Hence, in August 1998, Anglo American Corporation was invited to bid for the core assets. A further protracted negotiation ensued with Anglo finally acquiring a controlling interest in the Nchanga, Konkola and Konkola Deep mining divisions in March 2000 (renamed Konkola Copper Mines, KCM), with a Swiss–Canadian consortium of First Quantum and Glencore AG acquiring a similar controlling interest in the Mulfulira and Nkana divisions.[11] When it came, the final settlement was substantially less favourable to the government than the rejected offer from the Kafue Consortium 2 years earlier.

In each of the sales, the government retained an indirect minority equity share in the mining sector through its ownership of ZCCM Investment Holdings (ZCCM-IH), an investment company charged with the management of legacies arising from former ZCCM operations including debt consolidation, pension fund obligations and the environmental legacies. These operations were to be funded through dividend income arising from minority equity participation and 'price participation' (see Table A.9.1).[12] In practice, throughout most of the period since privatization, income from dividends and price support was minimal. In view of this, ZCCM-IH was, and remains, technically insolvent, although it continues to operate.

9.7.2 The exit of Anglo American Corporation

In January 2002, less than 2 years after acquiring a controlling interest in KCM, and citing the inability given the low level of copper prices to secure capital to invest in the Konkola Deep Mining Project, Anglo American withdrew completely from the mining industry in Zambia, after almost 80 years as the dominant player in the sector. Anglo American, along with the International Finance Corporation (IFC) and CDC, relinquished its equity holding in Zambia Copper Investments (ZCI), passing it free of charge to a newly created independent foundation, the Copperbelt Development Foundation, established as a not-for-profit organization to invest in projects aimed to mitigate the consequences of KCM's eventual closure and support diversification initiatives.

As a result of Anglo's withdrawal, the government's equity ownership, through ZCCM-IH, rose back to 42 per cent but, in November 2004, Vedanta Resources plc, an Indian mining company listed in London, acquired a controlling stake in KCM. Vedanta owned 51 per cent of equity in KCM, with 20.6 per cent held by ZCCM-IH and 28.4 per cent by ZCI. In April 2008, Vedanta exercised a call option over the ZCI equity, raising its holding in KCM to 79.4 per cent financed from the company's cash resources.

In retrospect, given the subsequent copper price boom, Anglo's decision to withdraw from Zambia may appear to have been spectacularly mistimed. But in reality, it reflected the changing nature of Anglo American at the time. In 1999, it had moved its corporate headquarters to London and was expanding its global operations away from southern Africa. The ties of history and the close historical links it had forged with Zambia, especially during the era of the Second Republic, had been broken.

9.7.3 Development agreements and the tax regime

Although the sale of each component of ZCCM was negotiated on a bilateral basis and embodied a range of specific conditions, each of the contracts contained broadly similar tax arrangements. By the conclusion of the privatization process, the *de facto* tax code for mining was as follows:

- corporate income tax was levied at 25 per cent on taxable profits (compared with 35 per cent for the non-mining sector);
- the effective royalty rate was 0.6 per cent of gross proceeds (and capped at a maximum of 3 per cent);
- recurrent and capital input were exempted from import duties;
- interest costs and repatriated dividend income were fully deductible;
- capital expenditure was fully expensed in the year in which it was incurred;
- loss carry-forward provisions extended for up to 15–20 years.

In addition, new mining companies were relieved from assuming financial liabilities and environmental legacies originally incurred by ZCCM, which were transferred to ZCCM-IH Ltd. Finally, each DA established a 'stability period' of between 15 and 20 years during which the agreed terms and conditions were guaranteed.

9.7.4 Tax design

By international standards, the tax structure embedded in the DAs was liberal, generous and biased towards the taxation of rents which, at the time of negotiation, were historically low. The effective royalty rate of 0.6 per cent of gross proceeds was particularly low and well below the global average of between 2 and 5 per cent (PricewaterhouseCoopers, 2008) and the IMF estimate of between 5 and 10 per cent for developing countries (Table 9.1).

The negotiated tax regime incorporated aspects of the so-called 'R-based cash flow tax regime' which, in the absence of other taxes,

Table 9.1 Comparative mining taxation, *2008*

Country	Profit tax rate (%)	Expensing of capital expenditure	Loss carry forwards	Royalty rate
Australia	36		Indefinite	5% gross sales
Argentina	33		5 years	3% gross sales
Bolivia	25		Indefinite	NA
Botswana	25		Indefinite	15% net sales
Brazil	33		Indefinite	3% gross
Canada	29	Yes	10 years	20% on profits
Chile	15		Indefinite	NA
Guyana	35		Indefinite	5% gross sales
Indonesia	30	Yes	8 years	Variable $/kg
Mexico	34		10 years	NA
Peru	30		4 years	Variable $/kg
South Africa	43	Yes	Indefinite	NA
Suriname	35		10 years	2% gross sales
USA	35		20 years	2.25% gross sales
Venezuela	30		3 years	3% gross sales
Zimbabwe	38		Indefinite	0.875% gross sales
Zambia (DAs)	25	Yes	10–20 years	0.6% gross sales
Zambia (post-2008)	30%	Plus variable profits tax	10–20 years	3% gross sales+ windfall tax

NA, not available.

Source: PricewaterhouseCoopers (2008).

approximates a pure (neutral) tax on rents (Boadway and Keen, 2008). Under an R-based regime, capital expenditures are expensed and profits and losses treated symmetrically, with the former taxed at the marginal rate and the latter attracting a tax credit at the same rate. An equivalent treatment of losses entails a perpetual carry-forward provision with an appropriate rate of interest. With these provisions in place, an R-based regime provides no additional offsets for interest costs or the return on equity. The regime negotiated under the DAs had elements of the pure R-based scheme – the expensing of capital expenditure and a partial loss carry-forward provision – but also allowed for the deductibility of both interest costs and a return on equity. As a pure R-based regime allows for *either* capital expenditure to be expensed *or* financing costs – interest and the return on equity – to be deductible but not both, the DA regime was arguably more favourable than the R-based benchmark (although in the latter, neutrality would require no royalty levied on production).

9.7.5 Summary

The privatization of ZCCM sought to achieve two financial goals. The first was to stem the operating losses that were borne by the public budget and crowding out already low public expenditure, and the second was to reverse the 30-year trend of underinvestment in exploration and production, which in large measure was responsible for the losses. It was anticipated that, with sufficient investment, the mines would return to profitability and remain viable at expected long-run prices, generating public revenue, directly through mineral taxation and indirectly through the local multiplier.

Although the government had limited instruments to enforce the investment commitments made under the DAs, capital inflows to the sector have been substantial since privatization and have exceeded the commitments originally anticipated (whether the investment commitments would have been honoured if prices had remained low is a moot point). The bulk of this investment was initially for rehabilitation of existing mining and smelting operations, but was followed by new investment, most notably at KCM in the context of the Konkola Deep Mining Project, and with the opening of the Lumwana mine by the Australian–Canadian consortium Equinox. The new mine, opened at the end of 2008, is projected to be the largest copper mine in Africa. Initial mining projections anticipate a steady-state output of around 125,000 tons per year, equivalent to 20 per cent of current total Zambia copper output, over a 40-year horizon.

9.8 Macroeconomic management II: the 2002–08 boom

In terms of world market conditions, the privatization of ZCCM could not have occurred at a worse time. Between the issue of tenders in March 1997 and the decision by Anglo American to relinquish its equity in KCM in January 2002, world copper prices, in constant US dollars, fell by almost 40 per cent reaching an all-time low. The average price in 2002 was US$1514 per ton compared with a previous low of US$1520 in 1932 and a long-run average for the twentieth century of around US$3560. It was these consistently falling prices that forced repeated renegotiation downwards of the final sale price.

In retrospect, the Anglo American withdrawal from KCM occurred at the very bottom of the market. The handback to government coincided with the turnaround in the copper market, which heralded the start of a dramatic but relatively short-lived boom in copper prices, fuelled in the main by the global investment boom led principally by China and other emerging economies and speculative trading by highly leveraged hedge funds. Between 2002 and the top of the market in April 2008, copper prices rose six-fold, from around US$1500 per ton to over US$9000 per ton, in current prices. Between April and December 2008, however, prices fell by about 70 per cent to just under US$3000 per ton before stabilizing. By mid-2009, prices had returned to approximately US$6000 per ton. This price boom dwarfed anything seen since Independence (measured in constant prices, world copper prices at their peak in 2008 were 20 per cent higher than their peak value in 1974) and double the average price since the end of the First World War. The only time in the last century when copper prices were higher was when the combatants on the Western Front were hurling millions of copper-tipped shells at each other in 1916 and 1917 (see Figure 9.1).

The combination of above-trend prices and the substantial investment in the sector by new foreign owners has led to a substantial increase in productive capacity. Between 1991 and 1999, mining output contracted by 32 per cent and, by 2000, annual output was less than 250,000 tons. By 2004, this had increased to 400,000 tons and to well over 600,000 tons in 2008. The bulk of the increase came from output at KCM and Mopani Copper Mines (MCM), the sector's two largest producers. Production still remains below the levels attained in the early 1970s but, with the commencement of production at the new Lumwana mine in December 2008, capacity is expected to reach and exceed these levels. This increase in production also saw Zambia's market share rise from less than 2 per cent of the world market in 2000 to 3.5 per cent in 2008.

The privatization of the mines and the increased investment in rehabilitation and new mines have been accompanied by a substantial expansion in prospecting activity, leading to a sharp upward revision in the prospective economic life of the industry. In 1974, for example, it was estimated that copper mines would be exhausted by around 2020: current estimates extend this to at least the final decades of the twenty-first century. A portion of this increase reflects the application of new mining technology. For example, recent technological developments in extracting copper from the accumulated waste materials from the past century of mining (the tailings dumps) have effectively presented the mining houses with new pre-crushed surface ore bodies that can be 're-mined' for copper. But most of the revision reflects an intensification of exploration and prospecting. The Mines and Minerals Act 1995 ensured that the privatization of ZCCM was accompanied by a generally permissive environment for prospecting. As a result, there has been an expansion in prospecting not just in remote unmapped areas but often on the fringes of existing ZCCM concessions.

9.8.1 The boom: savings, investment and public finance

Between the mid-1990s and the early 2000s, Zambia witnessed a radical change in the framework for economic management. The state relinquished ownership and control in the mining sector and elsewhere, withdrawing from the intensive micro-management of the 1980s, while liberalization measures eliminated a wide range of macroeconomic policy levers including price and exchange rate controls, directed credit allocation and a wide range of trade policy instruments. The authorities thus confronted the commodity price boom with a much reduced set of policy instruments at their disposal. In this section, we examine how this altered the macroeconomic management of the boom.

Between 2002 and mid-2008, copper prices rose from US$1600 per metric ton in January 2003 to US$8840 per ton in April 2008, a rise of 450 per cent in nominal dollar terms. Cobalt prices rose by a similar amount. With this increase and rising production, export earnings from the mineral sector rose from US$670 million in 2002 to US$4 billion in 2008, an increase of almost 500 per cent. To put this into perspective, we can compare copper revenues with aid flows. In 2002, earnings from copper were around twice as large as net overseas development assistance; in 2008, the ratio was approximately 6.6.

In what follows, we calculate the overall scale of the windfall accruing to Zambia from the copper and cobalt price booms before examining the private and public sector responses. In order to compute a coherent counterfactual for the boom, we make the following assumptions. First, prices for copper (and cobalt) began to rise above trend in 2003.[13] Between 2002 and 2008, average copper prices rose from US$1500 to US$6300 per ton, and average cobalt prices rose from US$13,600 to US$68,600 per ton. We treat this increase as unanticipated (as witnessed, for example, by Anglo American's decision to withdraw from copper mining in Zambia in 2002).

World prices in 2002 therefore define the counterfactual. A key issue is how we define counterfactual production levels. One possibility would be to take 2003 levels as the baseline and treat all excess production as an endogenous response to rising prices. This would be appropriate if we assumed that production was already at its optimal long-run level and that the industry could adjust its output in the short run, so that variations reflected an optimal response to current prices. As we have noted above, however, the constraining factor on output in Zambia throughout the 1990s (and possibly earlier) was the lack of investment. The privatization of ZCCM committed purchasers to substantial investment designed to increase mining capacity. Evidence suggests that, even before prices started rising in 2002, capacity and output were already rising. Hence, a reasonable alternative is to assume that the increase in production reflects investment decisions prior to the price boom. These two alternatives define the limiting bases for the counterfactual. In what follows, we adopt the latter as our baseline, but make note of how results vary under the alternative assumption.

The boom peaked in the first half of 2008 and, by the end of the year, prices had returned to around their 2003 level. We therefore take the end of 2008 as marking the termination of the boom (see Figure 9.4).

9.8.2 The scale of the windfall

Table 9.2 calculates the scale of this windfall gain in net export earnings in terms of initial GDP and as a contribution to permanent income. Full details of the calculations are reported in Adam and Simpasa (2009, Table A.2). Reflecting their different prices, we treat copper and cobalt separately before aggregating the two. The year 2002 is taken as the baseline. Columns [1] and [2] report actual prices and export volumes. Given our assumption about prices and production in the absence of the boom, the counterfactual value of exports is reported in column [4], and the current price windfall in column [5]. Over the period 2002–08,

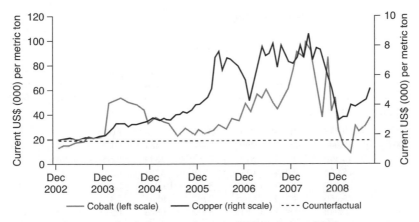

Figure 9.4 Copper and cobalt prices, January 2003 to August 2009

Source: Bank of Zambia and text.

however, the cost of imports has also risen, reflecting rising world prices for oil, food and other goods. We therefore adjust the nominal windfall for the change in the world price of imports. The relevant index is reported in column [6] and the windfall in purchasing power terms in column [7]. Finally, column [8] reports the windfall as a share of constant price non-boom GDP.

Combining the results for copper and cobalt, these calculations suggest that the total net windfall income accruing from 2002 to 2008 was K14.8 trillion, equivalent to around 66 per cent of base year GDP. The vast bulk of this accrued from the copper price boom; the boom in cobalt contributed only around 8 per cent of initial GDP.

This is a substantial positive terms of trade shock. But the boom has been short-lived. It is useful to express the magnitude in terms of its contribution to permanent income by computing the annuity value of the addition to national wealth. Using a discount rate of 8 per cent suggests that the boom has increased permanent income by around 5.3 per cent of pre-boom GDP. A lower discount rate of 5 per cent *raises* the present value of the windfall to 74 per cent of 2002 GDP, but lowers the increment to permanent income to 3.7 per cent of baseline GDP.

These variations in discount rates do not substantially change the central point: the recent mineral boom generated a very substantial windfall, of the order of 66–80 per cent of pre-boom GDP. But the boom was relatively short-lived, consistent with the international evidence on the duration of resource booms (Cashin and McDermott, 2002), so

Table 9.2 The 2003–08 mineral boom

Year	Price per ton K000s	Quantity (000 tons)	Value of exports (kbn)	Counter-factual value of exports (kbn)	Windfall in current kbn	Import price index	Windfall in constant prices	Windfall as % of GDP
1. Copper								
2002	6715	367.4	2467	2467	–	1.00	0	0.0
2003	8046	361.5	2909	2428	481	1.17	344	2.1
2004	12,498	414.1	5175	2781	2394	1.28	1293	8.0
2005	15,068	449.6	6775	3019	3755	1.34	1637	9.5
2006	27,149	491.7	13,350	3302	10,048	1.45	3555	21.6
2007	26,680	490.9	13,098	3297	9801	1.37	3359	18.9
2008	30,348	587.1	17,818	3943	13,875	1.93	3042	15.7
2. Cobalt								
2002	59,237	7.4	440	440	–	1.00	0	0.0
2003	84,351	10.5	884	621	263	1.17	188	1.1
2004	222,737	6.2	1380	367	1013	1.28	547	3.4
2005	129,988	5.7	738	336	402	1.34	175	1.0
2006	137,520	4.9	669	288	381	1.45	135	0.8
2007	208,830	4.8	1004	285	719	1.37	247	1.4
2008	331,751	4.6	1529	273	1256	1.93	275	1.4

3. Cumulative windfall	Constant price (kbn)	As a % of non-boom 2002 GDP
Copper	13,230	58.7
Cobalt	1567	7.5
Total	14,797	66.2
Change in permanent income as a % of 2002 GDP		5.3

that the contribution to permanent income was modest but not trivial, estimated at between 4 and 6 per cent. The next step in the analysis is therefore to consider how the public and private sectors responded to this increase.

9.8.3 Saving and investment

Table 9.3 examines the savings and investment responses to the windfall, exploiting the identity that domestic gross fixed capital formation (including any change in inventories) plus net foreign asset accumulation (the sum of capital account outflows plus the accumulation of official reserves) is equal to domestic savings. As we have no independent accurate data on consumption and savings, we work from the investment side of the identity, using IMF data on investment and the balance of payments.[14] As before, the detailed calculations are reported in Adam and Simpasa (2009, Table A.3). The top panel of Table 9.3 examines gross fixed capital formation and the accumulation of foreign net claims. The lower panel identifies the shares of gross investment and foreign asset accumulation attributable to the mining sector.

Following the methods used in Table 9.2, we compute windfall gross investment as the difference between actual and counterfactual gross investment. We assume that the counterfactual gross investment rate is simply the average investment rate over 2002–08 and apply this average to a counterfactual real income, which is defined as constant price GDP *less* that amount representing the return on windfall investment. The calculation of foreign savings out of the windfall proceeds in exactly the same way, applying the counterfactual foreign savings rate

Table 9.3 Saving, investment and financial flows: the distribution of mining revenues

	Gross fixed capital formation			Capital outflows[1]		
Year	Actual	Counterfactual	Windfall	Actual	Counterfactual	Windfall
1. Asset accumulation out of windfall						
2002	3252	3252	0	–2374	–2374	0
2003	4512	4017	495	–2618	–2137	–481
2004	4827	4236	591	–1560	–2253	693
2005	4673	4445	227	–2022	–2365	343
2006	5384	4710	673	389	–2506	2894
2007	6023	5001	1022	–2124	–2660	536
2008	5901	5292	609	–2645	–2815	170
Net present value of windfall asset accumulation as a share of windfall income						6548 (59.9%)

2. *Distribution of asset accumulation*

		Attributable to mining sector[2]
Gross fixed capital formation	46.5%	62.4%
Foreign capital outflows	53.5%	73.9%

See Adam and Simpasa (2009, Table A.3) for details.

[1] Capital outflows defined as sum of official net foreign asset accumulation plus private capital outflows.
[2] Mining sector share of foreign outflows consists of dividend payments to foreign shareholders; remainder principally official reserve accumulation.

to the counterfactual income series to generate counterfactual foreign savings and hence windfall foreign savings. Here, we assume that the counterfactual foreign savings rate is –12.5 per cent of income, corresponding to the current account deficit before aid prevailing prior to the boom. Approximately half this deficit is financed by official aid flows, and the rest by remittances and net private capital flows. Given the authorities' reasonably strong commitment to a floating exchange rate, official reserve depletion represented a very minor source of foreign saving. The calculation of windfall foreign savings is, however, overstated by the successful conclusion of the Multilateral Debt Relief Initiative (MDRI) for Zambia in 2006. The MDRI transaction, which reduced the net present value of public sector external debt from around 80 per cent to 12 per cent of average export earnings, generated approximately US$500 million (or 5.1 per cent of GDP) of additional net foreign savings in 2006 (and a flow saving on external debt service of around 0.25 per cent of GDP (IMF, 2008). The calculations in Table 9.3 adjust for this inflow, treating the debt relief as essentially orthogonal to the copper price boom.

Summing over these two uses, we arrive at an estimate of the net present value of total windfall savings to have been approximately K6.5 trillion at 2002 prices out of windfall income, computed on the same basis, of K10.9 trillion, which implies a savings propensity of 60 per cent.[15] Of this, approximately 47 per cent of total saving was represented by domestic gross fixed capital formation, with the remaining third represented by change in the net asset position of the economy.

Superficially, this represents a remarkably high overall savings propensity and certainly out of all recognition from the boom of the early 1970s, whereas the disposition of savings would appear to be consistent with an efficient expenditure response to a temporary resource boom in which savings accumulate initially in the form of foreign assets and then are drawn down to finance domestic capital formation as the limits of the domestic supply capacity dictate. But this simple picture is significantly incomplete as a substantial share of the windfall income accrued to the foreign owners of the mines in Zambia so that, given the tax regime, a substantial proportion of the measured foreign asset accumulation is, in fact, the repatriation through the balance of payments of profits and payment of dividends by Zambia-based mining houses to their foreign shareholders. The lower half of Table 9.3 computes the mining sector share of gross capital formation and foreign savings, suggesting that almost 60 per cent of the fixed investment can be *directly* attributable to (foreign) investment in the mining sector, whereas almost three-quarters of all the net capital outflows can be attributed to profit and dividend remittances by the mining houses.

9.8.4 Public finance and public investment

Although there is clearly a powerful local multiplier effect from the mining sector to the economy of the Copperbelt, these figures underline the enclave nature of the sector. Indeed, the bulk of the non-mining investment response to the boom represents substantial construction activity in the Copperbelt and Solwezi, deriving directly from the growth in direct investment in the mining sector (including the development of the Lumwana mine). Nonetheless, the income from the windfall has accrued overwhelmingly in the form of rents to the mine owners, which, net of investment, have in turn been almost entirely remitted offshore in the form of profits.

Given this structure, the burden of transferring some of these rents to the domestic economy lies with the tax system. In practice, this did not occur and, arguably, it was the failure of the government to be seen to capture any amount of the rents accruing during the boom that fuelled the sharp rise in support for opposition parties in the presidential and parliamentary elections of 2006, most notably the Patriotic Front (PF) led by Michael Sata. Cheeseman and Hinfelaar (2009), for example, argue that the MMD government's decision to revise the mining tax code in 2008 was a direct response to the growing political support for Sata's populist anti-foreign investment platform and his intention to revisit the tax regime if elected.

The extent to which the tax regime embodied in the DAs failed to generate fiscal revenue from the boom is illustrated in Table 9.4, which shows the complete absence of any fiscal response to the mineral boom prior to tax reform. Total tax revenue as a share of GDP remained more or less constant at just under 18 per cent over the boom period, with virtually no revenue accruing directly from the mining sector. The revenue yield attributable to specific tax measures levied on the sector in 2007, prior to reform of the tax system, totalled only 0.2 per cent of GDP, virtually all of which was earned through the royalty on production.[16] Conventional profit taxes in the mining sector yielded precisely zero revenue to the government, reflecting the twin effects of large loss carry-forward provisions afforded to the mining houses and the provision for full expensing of investment expenditure. Together, these reduced the mining tax liability to zero.

Some share of the rents did accrue to the government indirectly through its residual equity participation in the sector via the holding

Table 9.4 Central government revenue, 2001–08 (% GDP)

	2001	2002	2003	2004	2005	2006	2007	2008
Total revenue and grants	24.9	26.2	24.9	23.8	23.7	21.6	22.9	22.0
Tax revenue	19.1	17.9	18.0	18.3	17.2	17.2	18.4	18.2
Tax on incomes and profits	7.2	7.6	7.2	7.8	7.4	7.5	8.1	7.8
Individuals	5.7	5.9	5.6	6.5	6.0	5.7	5.5	5.4
Corporations	1.5	1.7	1.6	1.3	1.4	1.8	2.6	2.4
–of which mining company tax	0.00	0.00	0.00	0.00	0.00	0.00	0.00	0.23
Taxes on goods and services	4.9	4.7	4.3	4.1	4.2	3.6	2.7	1.8
–of which mining licence	0.00	0.00	0.00	0.00	0.00	0.00	0.01	0.01
Mineral royalty	0.05	0.02	0.04	0.02	0.12	0.11	0.17	0.39
Taxes on international trade	6.5	5.2	5.1	5.6	5.1	5.1	6.7	7.5
Other revenue	0.5	0.3	1.4	0.8	0.4	0.9	0.7	0.7
Grants	5.7	8.3	7.0	5.5	6.4	4.4	4.5	3.7
Direct taxation on mining								
Mining taxes (US$ m)		0.69	1.86	1.15	8.90	10.19	20.84	69.01
As share of total revenue	0.27	0.10	0.24	0.12	0.71	0.67	0.95	3.41
As a share of GDP	0.05	0.02	0.04	0.02	0.12	0.11	0.18	0.62
Memo: IMF estimates (US$ million)							166.28	155.60

company ZCCM-IH. Although dividends and 'price participation fees' were paid to ZCCM-IH, this income was used entirely to meet operating costs: ZCCM-IH has not declared a dividend to its shareholders.[17]

Thus, by 2007, the copper price boom had yielded virtually no revenue to the government. IMF and government projections, following the budget reforms in 2008 – which we discuss in the next section – anticipated sharply rising revenues. The IMF estimates made in June 2008 suggested that mining taxes would account for 3.2 per cent of GDP in 2008 and almost 5 per cent in 2009, compared with 0.6 per cent of GDP in 2006 (IMF, 2008). There appeared, therefore, to be scope for a significant increase in public expenditure (or, equivalently, scope for a reduction in dependence on aid).

Given the precipitous decline in copper prices in the second half of 2008, these short-run projections were clearly over-optimistic, and by a large margin. Taxation from the mining sector did rise sharply following the implementation of the 2008 budget measures. Revenues tripled to US$70 million, accounting for over 3 per cent of total revenue and 0.6 per cent of GDP. Moreover, given that Zambia is a relatively high-cost producer, rents in the mining sector are likely to remain modest so that, barring a major expansion in (low-cost) production from opencast mines, revenue flows will also be limited. Nonetheless, the capacity of the mining sector to generate between 2 and 4 per cent of GDP per annum in revenue – estimates towards the lower end of the IMF's medium-term projections made in 2008 – would represent a very substantial improvement in fiscal conditions compared with the late 1990s when ZCCM's losses were approaching 10 per cent of GDP per annum. Thus, although the recovery in revenue is never likely to be transformative for Zambia, it will allow the government to pursue a public investment programme commensurate with its level of development without excess debt accumulation.[18]

The projected revenue consequences from the 2008 tax reforms were not included in the 2008 budget. Given the lack of a budgetary mandate, it was decided that identifiable mining revenues would be saved, initially by the government increasing its claims on the central bank, which would, in turn, accumulate foreign assets.

At the same time, the Ministry of Finance engaged in extensive consultation aimed at developing an appropriate institutional structure for spending. Recognizing that the scale of revenues is likely to be modest and volatile, and that current investment needs are substantial, there was no strong case for the creation of an offshore 'future generations' fund along the lines of Norway. Rather, attention was focused on developing a coherent public expenditure strategy in which additional resources are devoted to investment in public infrastructure projects identified as priorities in the 2006–10 Fifth National Development Plan and *Vision 2030* (both published in December 2006). These strategy documents placed heavy emphasis on diversification away from mining and into the growth of regional and non-traditional exports, and identified as major constraints deficiencies in the domestic and regional transport system, communications and information technology provision, capacity constraints in power generation as well as long-established weaknesses in skills and training. It was expected that the windfall-financed public expenditure programme, to be included in the 2009 Budget, would reflect these priorities.

Thus far, the government's policy announcements surrounding the proposed public savings and investment response to the current windfall have been exemplary. But the rhetoric went untested. The boom passed (although prices began to recover sharply again in 2010), but the huge political pressures to demonstrate that the 2008 tax reforms will deliver some share of the mining sector's recent prosperity to the people of Zambia means that the government is likely to face spending pressures that may prove difficult to resist, drawing government into increased consumption spending or, indeed, excessively quick investment spending when absorptive capacity is limited.

9.8.5 The renegotiation of the tax regime

The apparent failure of the state to extract any substantial revenue from the copper boom increased the pressure on the government to redefine its relationship with the mining industry. As noted, populist opposition to the mining privatization, or more particularly to foreign ownership and control in the sector, has been on the increase, spearheaded since the turn of the century by Michael Sata's Patriotic Front. Sata won only 3 per cent of the popular vote in 2001, but this rose to almost 30 per cent in the 2006 presidential elections after campaigning on a platform portraying the ZCCM privatization as a sell-out to foreign investors.[19]

In early 2007, the government embarked on a delicate process of seeking to renegotiate the development agreements with the mining houses, but without halting the burgeoning investment in exploration and exploitation in the mining sector that followed the ZCCM privatization. As the DAs had initially been negotiated on a sale-by-sale basis and most included clauses securing the terms for periods of not less than 10 years, the government initially sought to establish a revised code for new mining investment by renegotiating the existing agreements one by one. But even with the support of the donor community (including public support from the IMF)[20] and an unexpected and substantial element of goodwill from the industry itself, a coordinated transparent renegotiation of all 11 DAs proved difficult. The government of Zambia reverted to a more direct legislative strategy, announced in the 2008 Budget, which cancelled the pre-existing DAs and established a new fiscal regime for the sector.

The new tax code introduced in the 2008 Budget consisted of two main elements. The first was to shift the tax code decisively in favour of generating a larger revenue flow to the government, principally through an adjustment to the royalty rate. The central elements in this were:

- an increase in the corporate income tax rate to 30 per cent from 25 per cent previously applied (at the same time, the corporate tax rate in the non-mining sector was reduced from 35 per cent to 30 per cent);

- an increase in the mineral royalty rate on base metals from 0.6 per cent to 3 per cent of gross revenue (the royalty rate for other precious metals was raised from 2 per cent to 3 per cent);
- the reintroduction of withholding tax on interest, royalties, management fees and payments to affiliates or subcontractors for all mining companies at a standard rate of 15 per cent;
- reduction in capital allowances from 100 per cent expensing to a conventional 25 per cent per annum straight-line allowance (and deductible only in the year in which production commences rather than in the year in which the expense is incurred).

The second key element was the introduction of a degree of progressivity into the tax code through two channels:

- a variable profit tax rate under which the marginal tax rate would rise from 30 per cent to 45 per cent when taxable profits exceed 8 per cent of gross revenue;
- a graduated windfall (royalty) tax levied at a rate of 25 per cent on gross proceeds when the copper price exceeds US$2.50/pound (US$5600 per ton); at a rate of 50 per cent when the copper price exceeds US$3.00/pound (US$6720 per ton); and 75 per cent in excess of $3.50/pound (US$7840 per ton).

Finally, an export levy (of 15 per cent on value) was introduced on the export of copper concentrates, ostensibly as an incentive to produce finished copper products (bars, ingots, cathodes).

9.8.6 Dispute, revision and assessment

The result of the reforms was to significantly increase the notional effective tax rate on mining. Assessment by the IMF suggested that, at prevailing 2008 copper prices and aggregating over all instruments, the average effective tax rate on mining in Zambia rose from around 31 per cent to 47 per cent, taking Zambia from being one of the lowest to one of the highest tax regimes among developing countries, although much of this increase resulted from high prevailing prices and the strong progressivity of the graduated windfall tax. As noted below, the steepness of the graduated windfall tax was subsequently scaled back and eventually abandoned. Given the current level of investment and the accumulated losses still being carried forward, the actual tax yield was somewhat lower. At prevailing prices, the 2008 Budget measures were estimated to raise revenue from mining from the US$20 million raised in 2007 to approximately US$400 million in 2008, equivalent to a tax yield of 10 per cent of gross mining proceeds.[21]

Nonetheless, the 2008 measures immediately drew sharp criticism from the mining houses and their representatives and from the international donor community, including the IMF. In part, this reflected the sense that the government had reneged on its commitment to sequential negotiation. This was true although, from the perspective of the government, direct negotiation left it exposed to potentially collusive behaviour on the part of the mining houses and to a range of other hold-up problems. The legislative route, on the other hand, had the advantage of being transparent – redressing one of the key criticisms of the DAs – and arguably shifted the burden of coordination costs on the mining houses by facing them with a take-it-or-leave-it option. But the main force of the criticism levied at the government was the genuine concern that the new regime radically increased both the marginal burden of tax and the degree of price distortion it entailed. There were three principal elements to this. First, at the prices prevailing at the time of the budget debate, mining houses were initially liable to the graduated windfall tax at the top marginal rate of 75 per cent but, being non-deductible (unlike the basic royalty rate), it was claimed that this would result in extremely high marginal rates (potentially exceeding 100 per cent). The second concern was that, given the highly variable geology of Zambian mining – combining the Konkola Deep Mine and the new Lumwana open-cast pit – which creates very different unit costs, the shift towards royalty-based taxation entailed by the reforms created significant spatial variation in effective tax rates. Third, it was suggested that the export duty proposal was unnecessary and failed to recognize current realities in the sector. The explicit objective of the export duty was to encourage domestic value-added through smelting. However, given current constraints on capacity and the highly import-intensive nature of smelting, the contribution to value-added was felt to be limited. (An alternative, but more politically controversial, interpretation of the duty is that it was introduced to limit transfer pricing and smuggling by the mining houses.)

The government reacted rapidly in response to some of these concerns, clarifying that, when the graduated windfall tax was operative, the variable profit tax would not be effective, and vice versa. In addition, it removed the top two bands of the graduate tax in July 2008 leaving only the single-step rate, in order to cushion the mining companies from the effects of the global financial meltdown. Taken together, these two adjustments substantially reduced the maximum marginal rates generated by the revised tax structure. The government announced the complete removal of the windfall tax in the 2009 Budget, a measure arguably aimed at ensuring continued long-term investment in the mining industry. Given the collapse in world copper prices, the windfall tax was, in fact, not generating any revenue at this time, and was not projected to do so in 2009. This adjustment removed the most distortionary and most contentious element of the 2008 fiscal reforms. The government did not, however, cede ground on the basic royalty rate or on any of the other elements of the 2008 package.

The 2008 reforms highlight many of the difficulties in implementing mining tax regimes that are capable of generating revenue for the government but also limit disincentive effects on mining companies. The pragmatic shift towards royalty-based taxation and the reintroduction of withholding taxes on cross-border payments has served to secure a current revenue stream as well as obviate administrative difficulties (and delay) in administering a pure rent-based tax, including the risk that taxable profits can be shifted out of the jurisdiction, but at the cost of moving further from a first-best non-distortionary taxation of pure rent. This shift was far from smooth, and the government was challenged at each turn, with mining houses threatening legal action against the government's negation of the stability clauses in the DAs and, *in extremis*, disinvestment. However, the sensible retreat by the government to cede the more egregious distortions created by the graduated windfall tax appears to have defused much of the tension. The likelihood is that the 3 per cent royalty and the variable profit tax regime will remain central to the tax code and, assuming the sector remains profitable and that high front-loading of investment expenditure tapers off, loss carry-forward and investment offsets against taxable profits will decline, ensuring that the conventional profit tax will begin to yield revenue to the government while guaranteeing more investment in the sector.

This episode reveals much about the politics of the economic management of mineral resources and how, even in the relatively unified and peaceful environment present in Zambia, negotiations over both the privatization of ZCCM and the renegotiation of the tax regime were suffused with suspicion. Although there has been no call for re-nationalization of the sector, the parliamentary and popular opposition did coalesce around the charge that, at least viewed from the middle of the copper price boom, foreign mine-owners had received too favourable terms during privatization and that, as a consequence, the government's primary objective was to redress the imbalance.

9.8.7 The copper boom and non-traditional exports

In Section 9.4, we discussed the elements of an optimal growth strategy for Zambia and stressed the importance of ensuring that periodic copper price booms do not severely undermine the growth prospects of the non-mining sector of the economy. As the discussion in Sections 9.5 and 9.6 made clear, ill-conceived choices in the 1970s and 1980s imparted a profound anti-export bias to economic policy towards the non-mining sector. The most damaging biases were slowly unwound with the stabilization and liberalization measures of the 1990s, albeit against a background of low growth and low investment. In this final section, we briefly consider how this shift in policy has supported the growth in the non-mining economy. We pay particular attention to the conduct of monetary policy during the recent boom and the extent to which it has supported diversification away from mining.

Since around 2001, the authorities in Zambia have adopted an increasingly conventional monetary programme, often referred to as 'inflation targeting – lite', which has been built around a set of monetary targets and a commitment to a floating exchange rate. Monetary policy has been increasingly focused on inflation control as the authorities have sought to bring inflation consistently below 10 per cent per annum. The most recent Poverty Reduction and Growth Facility (PRGF) programme establishes an explicit target for inflation of 7 per cent per annum in 2008 and 5 per cent in 2009.

Inevitably, however, given the positive terms of trade effect, the period of the copper boom was associated with a strong appreciation of the nominal and real exchange rate, even though the appreciation was muted by the high import content of the investment boom. Nonetheless, the real exchange rate appreciated by around 30 per cent against the US dollar between January 2003 and the height of the boom in mid-2008.

Although the appreciating currency helped the Bank of Zambia to hit its inflation target, the monetary authorities found themselves drawn into making a first-order monetary policy error in 2005, which temporarily severely exacerbated the exchange rate appreciation and imposed extremely heavy costs on the export- and import-competing sectors of the economy. This error was not directly attributable to the management of the boom in copper prices, but arose from problems with managing debt relief. Nonetheless, it highlights a well-known problem associated with strict adherence to reserve money programmes in the face of the positive shocks to domestic money demand that can occur during a period of surging export earnings or capital inflows.

After an extended qualification period, Zambia eventually qualified for official debt relief under the heavily indebted poor countries (HIPC)/MDRI initiative in 2005. From a monetary management perspective, this had two self-reinforcing effects. The first was a direct fiscal benefit: debt relief reduced the pressure on domestic deficit financing requirements, *ceteris paribus* reducing the supply of domestic money. But at the same time, successful completion of the debt relief exercise had a powerful effect on private sector demand for the Kwacha. With expectations of credibly lower inflation and higher growth, there was a sharp portfolio shift towards the Zambian Kwacha by the domestic private sector. Under pressure to hit the monetary targets agreed with the IMF, the authorities did not accommodate this powerful demand shift, but rather sought to stick to the now too tight monetary targets. In such circumstances, money market equilibrium could only be achieved through a sharp overshooting of the exchange rate appreciation (see Figure 9.5), severely undercutting the competitiveness of the non-copper economy and putting a severe squeeze on the non-tradable and import-competing sectors of the economy.

The authorities' attempts to stick to their money targets drew them into bond sterilization, which exacerbated the problem as foreign investors, taking full advantage of the liberalized capital account, entered the government debt market to profit from high domestic interest rates, thereby further appreciating the exchange rate.

The policy error in this episode stemmed directly from the vulnerability of a strict money-anchored programme in the face of portfolio shifts. In such circumstances, the appropriate monetary policy response

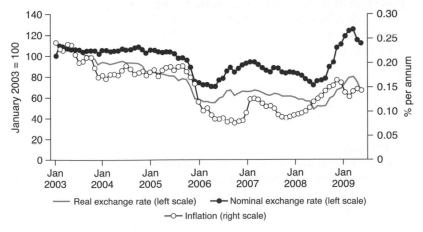

Figure 9.5 Bilateral exchange rate indexes and inflation

Source: Bank of Zambia.

would have been to accommodate the shift in money demand, most readily through unsterilized foreign exchange rate intervention. Unsterilized intervention increases the money supply but, in these circumstances, this is exactly what is required to meet the increased demand for the Kwacha at the prevailing exchange rate.

The response to the events of 2005 and 2006 therefore represented a major monetary policy error. But what is more important is that the authorities moved very quickly to re-establish a coherent (and apparently credible) monetary framework. Thus, from mid-2006, the stance of monetary policy was relaxed, and the excess appreciation of the exchange rate had been eliminated (the real exchange rate returned to its (appreciating) trend by early 2007). Despite correcting the monetary policy error and increasing the degree of intervention, the continued copper boom ensured that the real exchange rate continued to appreciate. This appreciation has inevitably raised fresh concerns about the risks of Dutch disease effects adversely affecting the non-mining export sector, and has increased calls for the authorities to lean more heavily against the trend appreciation so as to benefit the non-mining sector (see Calì and Velde, 2007; Weeks, 2008).

From a macroeconomic perspective, it is not obvious that the Zambian authorities should have sought to engineer a more depreciated real exchange rate during this period or, indeed, whether the instruments were available to do so. Fundamentally, engineering a depreciation in the real exchange rate requires a reduction in domestic absorption (that is, a net increase in foreign asset accumulation). As noted above, however, the income flow to the public sector from the copper boom has overwhelmingly accrued to the foreign private sector and not to the government. A reduction in domestic absorption would therefore require a reduction in private spending (which, as noted, is overwhelmingly investment expenditure in the mining sector) or a tightening of the fiscal stance. The former is not obviously desirable at present, and nor is the latter. The cost of using fiscal policy to engineer a real exchange rate appreciation is the return on forgone public expenditure.

Given the parlous state of the public infrastructure in Zambia and the clear evidence that the binding constraints to the export sector are deficient complementary inputs (see below), the case for a fiscal tightening at present is weak at best.

In any case, the pessimism expressed by Weeks (2008) and others about Dutch disease effects on non-traditional exports does not appear to be borne out in the data. More precisely, concerns about poor growth in this sector have much more to do with structural policies and weaknesses on the supply side than they do with real exchange rate misalignment. During the 1970s and 1980s, the non-traditional export sector was tiny and accounted for only a few thousand employees. In the first decade of the MMD government, the sector grew only very modestly although, as copper exports declined, the non-traditional share of exports rose from around 10 per cent to 12 per cent. The real take-off has occurred since 2002 so that, despite the strong appreciation of the Kwacha and the growth in copper exports, the share of non-traditional exports in total exports has risen sharply, accounting for almost 24 per cent by value of total exports between 2002 and 2007.

Although real exchange rate movements impact at the margin – non-traditional export growth dipped sharply in 2006 in the face of the sharp appreciation – survey evidence and interviews suggest that the binding constraints to further export diversification are on the supply side rather than resulting from movements in the real exchange rate or, critically, from an incoherent macroeconomic stance. The macroeconomic reforms of the 1990s, combined with the broadly successful conduct of monetary and fiscal policy in the current decade, have removed the extreme overvaluation of the real exchange rate and consequent anti-export bias that plagued Zambia in the 1970s and 1980s. The key constraints now are overwhelmingly structural. The lack of reliable and competitively priced infrastructure dominates in all surveys of constraints to exporting. The World Bank *Doing Business Survey* (World Bank, 2009) ranks Zambia 100th out of 181 (compared with, for example, Kenya (82nd), Ghana (87th), Nigeria (118th), Cameroon (164th) and Chile (40th)). The most serious constraints identified by the *Doing Business Survey* reflect inflexibility in labour markets (Zambia ranks 135th out of 181); administrative costs in the construction sector, particularly in the cost and provision of utilities (146th); and the costs of cross-border trade (153rd), where the transport and related costs per standardized container facing exporters are estimated at US$2700 compared with an Organization for Economic Co-operation and Development (OECD) average of US$1000 and a regional average of US$1800. In all cases, these high costs can be traced to the same underlying constraints: decades of underinvestment that have left transport and energy provision expensive and unreliable; telecommunications and information and communications technology (ICT) services that are still too expensive and underpowered for Zambia-based firms to compete effectively in areas such as e-services; and long-run weaknesses in education and training that drive up real wages for skilled labour relative to key competitors and reduce the flexibility of labour markets.

9.9 Conclusions

It has often been said that it was Zambia's good fortune to be 'born with a copper spoon in its mouth' although, for much of the 45 years since Independence in 1964, natural resource dependence has been more of a curse than a blessing. The central economic challenge facing Zambia at the time of Independence and the central challenge now and in the future is to find the right model for the efficient exploitation of its natural resource endowment and the equitable distribution of the rents arising from this exploitation.

Since Independence, we have seen a radical shift in the way in which the state has sought to exploit this endowment. In the first decade following Independence, the prevailing view was that state ownership of the industry offered the best means of capturing and distributing the rents to the people of Zambia. The subsequent dramatic, indeed traumatic, 25-year failure of the state to efficiently manage the volatility in the copper market and its fundamental inability to avoid the dysfunctional rent-seeking that flourished in the state-dominated economy meant that, when the pendulum eventually swung away from state ownership and control, it did so decisively. Thus, although the sale of ZCCM proved successful in re-invigorating the mining industry and staunching the state-owned company's mounting losses, it did so by not only divesting the state of direct responsibility for managing the industry but on terms that more or less completely eliminated its capacity to share in the future rents from the sector, at least over the medium term.

The 2003–08 copper price boom, which was described in the popular press and by opposition politicians in Zambia as a 'cashless boom' – one in which the unfavourable terms of the privatization meant that the people of Zambia saw few of the benefits from the boom, in terms of either employment or other transfers, but bore the costs associated with the appreciation of the exchange rate – starkly illustrated how much the previous decades of mismanagement had forced the government's hand during the privatization process.

But the boom also allowed for two vitally important and positive developments for the mining industry and the economy as a whole. The first is that the favourable price conditions meant that the investment commitments made by the new mine-owners at the time of privatization were not just realized but substantially exceeded. Mining industry investment is powerfully pro-cyclical and, for once in its history, conditions in the sector combined with reasonable macroeconomic stability and a broadly credible economic policy regime to allow a substantial and efficient mining investment boom to occur. Existing mines and supporting plant were rehabilitated, new activities, most notably the Lumwana mine, were brought on line, while the intensification of exploration activity identified substantial new economic reserves of copper and other minerals on the fringes of the Copperbelt. Barring a catastrophic collapse in the long-run price of copper, the boom allowed the mining industry in Zambia to be reset. Although Zambia will remain a relatively high-cost mining location, the investment boom has served to stabilize and lower unit mining costs and has left the industry better placed to generate profits in the medium term and to confront any possible short-run decline in world prices as happened during the global economic crisis.

The second major effect of the boom was the renegotiation of the tax code. The boom starkly exposed the imbalance in the distribution of gains from positive price developments. The renegotiation of the mining code was far from straightforward, but represented a crucially important milestone in economic policy-making in Zambia, both to the extent that the government was able to put in place a new code which, broadly speaking, appears to have successfully balanced the revenue imperative with the requirements of a competitive tax regime and to the extent that it was able to modify and fine-tune the code in response to criticism and reactions from stakeholders. Moreover, it would appear that the revision of the structure of mining taxation did not undermine investors' perceptions that the government remains committed to maintaining a competitive and non-opportunistic tax and regulatory regime in the non-mining economy.

Huge challenges still remain in Zambia. There are enormous challenges in overcoming the legacy of the past mismanagement of the economy, including deep poverty, substantial inequality and a badly depleted public infrastructure. And there is the challenge of managing expectations about future public spending capacity when needs are so high but the rents from mining are likely to remain modest. But the past decade has witnessed a number of encouraging developments including the rehabilitation of the mining sector and a clear articulation of a coherent strategy for growth and development of the non-mining sector. Realizing this strategy will be a formidable challenge, but there is little doubt that Zambia has entered a new phase in mining in a stronger position than it did with previous copper price booms.

Acknowledgements

This chapter was written as part of a project funded by the Revenue Watch Institute, which acknowledges the support of the Bill and Melinda Gates Foundation. We are grateful to participants at the Revenue Watch seminar in December 2008, participants at the Global Development Network 10th Annual Conference in Kuwait in January 2009 and to the project coordinators, Paul Collier and Tony Venables, for comments on our earlier presentations and paper. All errors and opinions are our own.

Notes

1 The production of copper from sulphides involves four steps. First, copper-bearing ore is crushed and passed through a concentrator where it is combined with water and chemicals to separate fine mineral particles from waste materials (tailings). Second, the concentrated material is then smelted to produce a copper matte which, in the third step, is passed through a converter where the copper sulphides in the matte are oxidized to produce molten metallic copper, known at blister copper. Finally, blister copper is refined through electrolysis. Pure copper is exported either as cathodes or as wire, bars or ingots. The extraction of pure copper from copper oxide ore, as found around Katanga, requires an additional (and expensive) leaching process using sulphuric acid before smelting can occur.

2 Collier and Venables (2008) note how the same consolidation of rights allowed De Beers to develop the Kimberley diamond mines in South Africa.

3 In the first half of the nineteenth century, the UK accounted for almost 40 per cent of world copper production. By the end of the First World War, UK production was almost negligible whereas the US accounted for almost 60 per cent of global output, with Latin American mines, principally those in Chile, accounting for much of the remainder. Although the US remained a major producer, the twentieth century saw the dramatic rise of production in Africa, Russia and, in particular, South America (Chile and Peru) (US Geological Survey, 2008).

4 This challenge was clearly articulated by Austin Robinson as early as 1993 when he contributed to the London Missionary Society's enquiry into the impact of the 'modern industry' of mining on the livelihoods and (spiritual) well-being of the people of the Copperbelt region. Robinson's analysis, although stripped of contemporary language, differs very little from modern analyses of the challenges to managing natural resource endowments (Robinson, 1933).

5 The 'bad news principle' reflects the asymmetric effect of positive and negative shocks on the option to wait: as the option value is the ability to avoid bad outcomes, 'good news' (positive shocks) does not change the value of the option, whereas 'bad news' (negative shocks) increases the option value, further delaying investment (Dixit and Pindyck, 1994).

6 Regional political crises cut off transport routes through (the then) Southern Rhodesia, Angola, Mozambique and South Africa, while the economic crisis in Tanzania at the time severely reduced throughput at the port of Dar es Salaam. At times during the late 1970s and early 1980s, ZCCM considered shipping copper by air (Rotberg, 2002).

7 The Hartwick rule defines the level of capital accumulation required to exactly offset the depletion of non-renewable resources and leave the society's net wealth (inclusive of natural resources) unchanged.

8 The import and capital intensity of domestic production was itself a consequence of the economic strategy of the period. The combination of paternalistic state ownership in the mining sector, high protection, an overvalued real exchange rate and widespread financial repression meant real wages were 'too high' relative to some long-run equilibrium and capital 'too cheap' (Gulhati, 1989). The high wage–rental ratio led to production structures that were inconsistent with the economy's factor endowment valued at world prices.

9 Jacques Bussière, from the Bank of Canada, was appointed governor of the Bank of Zambia from 1990 to 1992 before being replaced by the first MMD-appointed governor, Dominic Mulaisho.

10 Francis Kaunda's (2002) personal memoir of the privatization process offers a conflicting version of events surrounding the (non)-sale of the core assets to the Kafue Consortium, casting it not simply as a commercial cartel but as a thinly disguised front for pursuing donor interests.

11 The Anglo American ownership of KCM was indirect and was one element in a complex ownership structure. KCM was owned 65 per cent by ZCI (in which Anglo American held a 51 per cent share), 7.5 per cent by the International Finance Corporation of the World Bank, 7.5 per cent by the Commonwealth Development Corporation and 20 per cent by ZCCM-IH, the residual investment holding company 87 per cent owned by the government of Zambia. Anglo American held the management contract for KCM.

12 The price participation scheme was a revenue-sharing mechanism operating independently of the mining houses' dividend policy, which diverted a fixed proportion of rents earned above a predefined trigger price to ZCCM-IH.

13 In Zambia, cobalt is mined exclusively as a by-product of copper.

14 We obtained investment data from IMF (2008) and balance of payments data from the IMF Balance of Payments online statistics database.

15 Total windfall savings are computed as the net present value (NPV) of total investment in gross fixed capital formation plus the NPV of foreign asset accumulation *less* the NPV of imputed saving out of the permanent income arising from the boom.

16 In 2007, for example, royalty payments of approximately US$20 million were raised from proceeds of US$3.4 billion, a yield of precisely 0.6 per cent, as established in the development agreements (DAs).

17 ZCCM-IH is a public listed company. The government of Zambia holds 87.6 per cent of the equity, with the remaining 12.4 per cent spread widely across some 2500 shareholders in Zambia and the rest of the world. It is anticipated that the government will dispose of its shareholding through a public offering in due course. In 2005 (the last year for which financial statements are available), ZCCM-IH dividend income was approximately US$5 million

and price participation US$33 million, approximately 2 per cent of the total export proceeds of the sector (ZCCM-IH Report of the Directors and Financial Statements for the year to 30 June 2005).

18   To put this in perspective, official aid flows to central government, excluding debt relief, average between 5 per cent and 7 per cent of GDP per annum (IMF, 2008).

19   Popular discontent increased sharply following a decline in safety standards in the sector, which saw fatalities rise sharply from less than 10 per year between 1997 and 2002 to over 70 per year in 2004. Fatalities hit a new high in 2005 following a deadly explosion at the Chinese-owned explosives factory at Chambisi Mine in which 50 Zambian workers were killed. Discontent was further stoked by the owners' delay in making compensation payments to victims' families and the low level of the compensation awarded.

20   'The IMF mission supports the authorities' attempts to obtain greater revenue from the mining sector through the renegotiation of the fiscal terms of existing development agreements' (press release, IMF Mission, September 2007).

21   The tax measures also eliminated the price participation schemes. Although this had no revenue implications for the central government budget, it stands to erode the income base of ZCCM-IH, which drew the bulk of its income from these schemes, thereby possibly drawing the government into either recapitalization of the company or the provision of an increased current subvention.

References

Adam, C. (1995) 'Fiscal Adjustment, Financial Liberalization and the Dynamics of Inflation: Some Evidence from Zambia', *World Development*, 23, 735–50.

Adam, C. and F. Musonda (1999) 'Trade liberalization in Zambia 1970–1995' in A. Oyejide, J.W. Gunning and B. Ndulu (eds). *Regional Integration and Trade Liberalization in Sub-Saharan Africa: Volume 2 (Case Studies)*. London: Palgrave-Macmillan.

Adam, C. and A.M. Simpasa (2009) 'Harnessing Resource Revenues for Prosperity in Zambia', University of Oxford, OxCarre Research Paper 30.

Aron, J. and I. Elbadawi (1992) *Parallel Markets, the Foreign Exchange Auction and Exchange Rate Unification in Zambia*. Research policy working paper (WPS) no. 909. World Bank.

Bank of Zambia (various years) *Annual Report*. Lusaka: Bank of Zambia.

Bates, R. and P. Collier (1993) 'The Politics and Economics of Policy Reform in Zambia', *Journal of African Economies*, 4, 115–43.

Bigsten, A. and S. Kayizzi-Mugerwa (2000) *The Political Economy of Policy Failure in Zambia*. Working Papers in Economics, no. 23. Department of Economics, Göteborg University.

Boadway, R. and M. Keen (2008) *Theoretical Perspectives on Resource Tax Design*. Mimeo, IMF.

Calì, M. and D.W. Velde (2007) *Is Zambia contracting Dutch Disease?* Working paper 279. Overseas Development Institute.

Cashin, P. and J.C. McDermott (2002) 'The Long Run Behaviour of Commodity Prices; Small Trends and Big Volatility', *IMF Staff Papers*, 49, 175–99.

Cheeseman, N. and M. Hinfelaar (2009) *Parties, Platforms and Political*

Mobilization: The Zambian Presidential Elections of 2008. Mimeo, Department of Politics and International Relations, University of Oxford.

Coleman, F. (1971) *The Northern Rhodesia Copperbelt 1899–1962*. Manchester: The University Press.

Collier, P. and S. O'Connell (2007) 'Opportunities and Choices' in B. Ndulu, S. O'Connell, J.-P. Azam, R.H. Bates, A.K. Fosu, J.-W. Gunning and D. Njinkeu (eds). *The Political Economy of Economic Growth in Africa 1960–2000*. Cambridge: Cambridge University Press.

Collier, P. and A. Venables (2008) 'Managing the Exploitation of Natural Resources: Lessons for Low Income Countries'. University of Oxford, Oxcarre discussion paper 2008-11.

Craig, J. (2001) 'Putting Privatisation into Practice: the case of Zambia Consolidated Copper Mines', *Journal of Modern African Studies*, 39, 389–410.

Davis, J.M. (ed.) (1933) *Modern Industry and the* African. London: Macmillan.

Dinh, H., A. Adugna and B. Myers (2002) *The Impact of Cash Budgets on Poverty Reduction in Zambia: A Case Study of the Conflict between Well-intentioned Macroeconomic Policy and Service Delivery to the Poor*. World Bank Policy Research Working Paper 2914. World Bank.

Dixit, A. and R. Pindyck (1994) *Investment under Uncertainty*. Princeton: Princeton University Press.

Gulhati, R. (1989) *Impasse in Zambia: the Economics and Politics of Reform*. World Bank Economic Development Institute Development Policy Case Studies no. 2.

Hartwick, J. (1977) 'Intergenerational Equity and the Investment of Rents from Exhaustible Resources', *American Economic Review*, 67, 972–4.

Hill, C. and M. McPherson (eds) (2004) *Promoting and Sustaining Economic Reform in Zambia*. Cambridge, MA: John F. Kennedy School of Government, Harvard University.

IMF (2008) *Zambia: Request for Three-year Agreement under PRGF: Staff Assessment*. IMF Country Report 08/187. Washington, DC: IMF.

Kaunda, F. (2002) *Selling the Family Silver: The Zambian Copper Mines Story*. Kwa-Zulu Natal: Interpak Books.

Mining Journal (various issues). London: Mining Communications Ltd.

Mwanawina, I. and J. Mulungushi (2008) 'Zambia' in B. Ndulu, S. O'Connell, J.-P. Azam, R.H. Bates, A.K. Fosu, J.-W. Gunning and D. Njinkeu (eds). *The Political Economy of Economic Growth in Africa 1960–*2000. Cambridge: Cambridge University Press.

PricewaterhouseCoopers (2008) *Comparative Mining Tax Regimes – A Summary of Objectives, Types and Best Practices*. PricewaterhouseCoopers.

Robinson, E.A.G. (1933) 'The Economic Problem' in J.M. Davis (ed.). *Modern Industry and the* African. London: Macmillan.

Rotberg, R.I. (2002) *Ending Autocracy, Enabling Democracy: the Tribulations of Southern Africa 1960–2000*. Washington, DC: Brookings Institution.

Weeks, J. (2008) *Is a 'Resource Curse' inevitable in Resource-rich Countries? Comparing Policies in Azerbaijan and Zambia*. Development Viewpoint no. 13. Centre for Development Policy Research, School of Oriental and African Studies (SOAS), London.

World Bank (2002) *Zambia: Privatization Review, Facts, Assessment and Lessons*. Report prepared at the request of the Minister of Finance and National Planning.

World Bank (2009) *Doing Business Survey 2009*. Washington, DC: World Bank.

Further Reading

Fraser Institute (2008) *Fraser Institute Annual: Survey of Mining Companies (2007/2008)*. Vancouver: Fraser Institute.

US Geological Survey (2008) *Historical Statistics for Mineral and Material Commodities*. http://minerals.usgs.gov/ds/2005/140/.

World Bank (2008) *Metals and Mineral Rents Database*. http://siteresources.world bank.org/EXTEEI/Resources/Metals_and_Minerals.xls.

Appendix

Table A.9.1 Major unbundled units for initial privatization phase of ZCCM

Package	Unit	Sold to	Date of sale	New mine name	ZCCM-IH equity retention (%)	Terms of transaction				Stability period (years)
A	Nchanga, KDMP,	Anglc American Corporation (UK/South Africa),	Mar-00	Konkola Copper Mines (KCM) plc	21	US$30.0 m	US$60.0 m	US$125.0 m	US$208.0 m for existing mines	
	Chingola Refractory Ores and	IFC (World Bank) and CDC (UK)							US$523.0 m for KDMP	
	Nampundwe Pyrite									
A1	Chibuluma (originally part of A)	Meteox (South Africa)	Oct-97	Chibuluma Mines plc	15	US$17.5 m	–	US$7.6 m	US$34.0 m	15
B	Luanshya division	Binani Industries (India) [1]	Jun-97	Roan Antelope Mining Company (RAMCOZ) plc	15	US$35.0 m	–	–	US$69.0 m	15
C	Mufulira division and Nkana	Glencore and First Quantum (Canada)	Mar-00	Mopani Copper Mines	10	US$20.0 m	US$23.0 m	US$422.0 m	US$159.0 m	

Table A.9.1 (cont.)

C	Mufulira division and Nkana	Glencore and First Quantum (Canada)	Mar-00	10	US$20.0 m	US$23.0 m	US$422.0 m	US$159.0 m	
D	Chambishi copper mine	China Non-Ferrous Metal Industries (China)	Jun-98	15	US$20.0 m			US$70.0 m	
E	Kansanshi copper mine	Cyprus Amax Minerals (US)	Jan-97	15	US$3.0 m			US$30.0 m	15
G	Chambishi cobalt and acid plant	Avmin Ltd (South Africa)	Sep-98	10	US$50.0 m		US$45.0 m	US$70.0 m	15
H	Ndola precious metals plant	Binani Industries (India)[1]	Jun-97	15	US$0.35 m			US$1.4 m	15
I	Konkola North (special package)	Avmin Ltd (South Africa)[2]	Sep-98	20	US$8.5 m			US$12 m	
J	Power division	Midland Power and National Grid (UK)	Nov-97	20	US$50.0 m	US$73.0 m in debt	US$7.5 m	US$25.5 m	

C	Mopani Copper Mines			
D	NFC Africa Mining plc			
E	Cyprus Amax Kansanshi plc			
G	Chambishi Metals plc			
H	Minerva			
I				
J	Copperbelt Energy Company (CEC)			

[1] RAMCOZ and Minerva experienced severe financial and operational problems in its first year of operation and was put into receivership in 1997. The company was sold to J&W Investments of Switzerland in 1998 for US$8 m and an investment commitment of US$28 m. The mine was renamed Luanshya Copper Mines plc.

[2] The Konkola North mine has been closed (and flooded) since 1956. This was an exploration concession. As of 2008, a major investment by Teal of Canada is under consideration.

Sources: Mining Journal (2000); Craig (2001).

Index